Indian Cities or Suburbs?

Indian Cities or Suburbs?

Trends and Causes of Suburbanization

KALA SEETHARAM SRIDHAR

OXFORD
UNIVERSITY PRESS

OXFORD
UNIVERSITY PRESS

Great Clarendon Street, Oxford, OX2 6DP,
United Kingdom

Oxford University Press is a department of the University of Oxford.
It furthers the University's objective of excellence in research, scholarship,
and education by publishing worldwide. Oxford is a registered trade mark of
Oxford University Press in the UK and in certain other countries

Published in the United States of America by Oxford University Press
198 Madison Avenue, New York, NY 10016, United States of America

British Library Cataloguing in Publication Data
Data available

Library of Congress Control Number: 2024950724

ISBN 9780198958116

DOI: 10.1093/9780198958147.001.0001

Pod

The manufacturer's authorized representative in the EU for product safety is
Oxford University Press España S.A., Parque Empresarial San Fernando de Henares,
Avenida de Castilla, 2 – 28830 Madrid (www.oup.es/en).

*Dedicated to the memory of my beloved father,
who inspired me with his excellent memory
and rapidity of work.*

Acknowledgements

This book is the outcome of my Fulbright fellowship, which was based at the University of California, Los Angeles (UCLA), Luskin School of Public Affairs, Department of Urban Planning. First, I thank the United States-India Educational Foundation (USIEF) for funding this significant research in the form of awarding me the prestigious Fulbright-Nehru Academic and Professional Excellence Fellowship. Thanks are very much due to USIEF's Adam Grotsky, Sudarsan Dash, and especially Vijee Ninan who was involved in every step of the fellowship, ranging from my selection for the fellowship, to travel, my stay in the US, and my return.

Taking up the Fulbright fellowship itself would not have been possible without the support and encouragement from my home institution, the Institute for Social and Economic Change (ISEC). The Director then of ISEC, Prof. M. G. Chandrakanth, was very supportive of my Fulbright application and highly appreciative when I was selected for the same through a competitive process. I thank him very much for his motivation for this fellowship. Thanks are due to Prof. D. Rajasekhar who, as Director of ISEC, facilitated my travel to UCLA for the fellowship in both years of the grant, by granting me the entitled study leave.

The Fulbright fellowship at UCLA was made possible because of UCLA Professor Paavo Monkkonen's kind support in hosting me. Paavo was the one who suggested the use of the Global Human Settlements Layer (GHSL) for understanding the sprawl of India's cities, until which time I was depending on Census data at the ward level. The GHSL data are at a much more minute, grid level of the cities. Many thanks are due to him for his friendly collaboration, which resulted in a paper which is now published in the Elsevier journal, *Cities*. The first leg of my visit and stay in Los Angeles, in 2021, was at the peak of Covid, so I did not have an office, but Paavo met with me frequently over Zoom and we had productive discussions. During my second visit in 2022, Covid was on the decline, so I got an office at UCLA and met with Paavo regularly. He facilitated a seminar during each year of my visit—in 2021 (online, publicized) and in person in 2022 (which was publicized). He was generous enough to put me in touch with other faculty in the Department and Luskin School. I wholeheartedly thank Paavo for the collaboration. I also thank all the participants of the seminars who attended my talks at UCLA in 2021 and 2022 for their comments and suggestions.

Yale University's School of the Environment's Urban Learning Community, the South Asia Studies Council, and Inclusion Economics hosted a talk on this in April 2022. My wholehearted thanks to Prof. Karen Seto at Yale School of the Environment who made this possible, to Dr Charity Moore who coordinated the talk, and to the seminar participants for their comments. I thank Richard Green at the University of Southern California for organizing a seminar on this, and Matt Holian at San Jose State University who organized a talk on this in June 2021. I appreciate the comments of the participants at these seminars.

The book would not have come to fruition without the time afforded to me by my visit to George Mason University's Global South Hub in June–July 2023, which ISEC's Director Prof. Rajasekhar facilitated by granting the entitled study leave. I particularly thank Dr Manjusha Nair at George Mason University for the invitation and facilitating my visit as I wrote significant parts of the book during my stay in Baltimore in 2023.

I thank my affiliation with Stanford University's Center for South Asia during May–August 2024 when I also spent a significant amount of time writing the book. My sincere thanks are due to Dr Michael Kahan who referred me to Stanford's Center for South Asia. My very special thanks and gratitude are due to Dr Lalita du Perron, Associate Director of Stanford University's Center for South Asia, who welcomed me to Stanford with her full enthusiasm and friendship during both the years—2024 and 2025. ISEC's Director Prof. Rajasekhar facilitated the affiliation with Stanford greatly by granting me the study leave (in 2024) and subsequently the sabbatical leave (in 2025) for which I am eligible, so I thank him sincerely.

I thank Anjali Mahendra at the World Resources Institute (WRI) who put me in touch with Raj Bhagat at the WRI who in turn connected me with Babin T Praise who eventually gave his excellent assistance with the GHSL data. I thank Raj Bhagat for connecting me to Babin who made the GHSL data amenable for running regressions for the 112 cities in both

1975 and 2015. Without Babin's assistance, this project would not have been possible, so I remain grateful to him.

I thank Tusi Das who helped me with the concentric circles for each of the cities. Tusi also helped with the formatting of the book, the table of contents, the list of abbreviations, and the references, for which I am very thankful. I thank Shivakumar Nayka for his assistance with GIS maps of cities in Karnataka, as also with the shape files of 19 cities across all India which are used in the employment suburbanization analysis.

I am extremely thankful to Alain Bertaud for giving permission to reproduce graphs from his earlier work co-authored with Steve Malpezzi, and very quickly and delightfully too. I appreciate my co-authors—Matthew Holian, Priya Narayanan, and S. Manasi—for their collaboration on previous works, parts of which have served as the basis for some research reported in this book. I thank Elsevier for giving me permission to draw from an earlier paper I published in *Regional Science and Urban Economics* when preparing a modified version for this book. I thank Matthew Freedman at the University of California Irvine, co-editor at *Regional Science and Urban Economics*, for facilitating Elsevier's response for the same.

This project would not have resulted in this published work out of Oxford University Press without the positive views and energies of Dhiraj Pandey, Commissioning Editor, who was very supportive of the project which has understandably had a long gestation period. I thank Dhiraj very much for his interest and enthusiasm in the project from the beginning and for facilitating a quick review of the manuscript. I am grateful to Amrita Brahmo, Senior Project Editor, for her very helpful suggestions and patience in answering my numerous questions, during the first round of copyediting. No need to say that I thank the anonymous reviewers of the manuscript for their constructive suggestions and positive feedback which have made this book a valuable resource.

Taking up the fellowship during the peak of a pandemic would not have been possible without support from my family: most importantly, my husband, who secured himself a visiting scholar position at the University of Southern California during both legs of my grant. He endured Covid himself upon our arrival in Los Angeles for the first leg of the grant. Fortunately, he recovered and there were no major adverse health impacts. I remain indebted to him. My daughter, who was pursuing Medicine then in Manipal, India, was very sick and hospitalized when I was at UCLA during the first year of the grant, with the result that she had to depend on friends for her care. I thank her friends a lot for taking care of her during my absence. I owe a ton of thanks to my daughter for putting up with my fellowship.

All errors remain mine.

Contents

Figures

Tables

Abbreviations

AMRUT	Atal Mission for Rejuvenation and Urban Transformation
BBMP	Bruhat Bengaluru Mahanagara Palike
BEST	Brihanmumbai Electricity Supply and Transport
BHEL	Bharat Heavy Electricals Limited
BIMARUO	Bihar, Madhya Pradesh, Rajasthan, Uttar Pradesh, Odisha
BT	British Telecom
BWSSB	Bangalore Water Supply and Sewerage Board
CBD	Central Business District
CMC	City Municipal Council
CRCs	Citizen Report Cards
DC	District of Columbia
FAR	Floor Area Ratio
FGDs	Focus Group Discussions
FSI	Floor Space Index
GDP	Gross Domestic Product
GHSL	Global Human Settlements Layer
HH	Household
IBM	International Business Machines
ISEC	Institute for Social and Economic Change
JNNURM	Jawaharlal Nehru National Urban Renewal Mission
Km	Kilometre(s)
KMDS	Karnataka Municipal Data Society
KSRTC	Karnataka State Road Transport Corporation
KSRTC	Kerala State Transport Corporation
LPA	Local Planning Authority
LPCD	Litres per Capita Daily
M	Metre(s)
MC	Municipal Corporation
MCGM	Municipal Corporation of Greater Mumbai
MG Road	Mahatma Gandhi Road
MoHUA	Ministry of Housing and Urban Affairs
N	Number
NASA	National Aeronautics and Space Administration
NBER	National Bureau of Economic Research
NCAER	National Council of Applied Economic Research
NPP	Nagar Palika Parishad

OLS	Ordinary Least Squares
OTA	Office of Technology Assessment
PAC	Public Affairs Centre
PCA	Primary Census Abstract
PHCs	Primary Health Centres
PM	Particulate Matter
PwC	PricewaterhouseCoopers
RSPM	Respirate Suspended Particulate Matter
SNDI	Sprawl Network Disconnectedness Index
Std. Dev.	Standard Deviation
Std. Err.	Standard Error
SWM	Solid Waste Management
TCPO	Town and Country Planning Organization
TDRs	Transfer of Development Rights
UA	Urban Agglomeration
UDAs	Urban Development Authorities
UIDSSMT	Urban Infrastructure Development Scheme for Small and Medium Towns
ULB	Urban Local Body
ULCRA	Urban Land Ceiling and Regulation Act
USA	United States of America
VIIRS	Visible Infrared Imaging Radiometer Suite
WRI	World Resources Institute

Note: The terms below have been used interchangeably in this book:

Suburbanization and sprawl
Suburbs, peripheries, and fringes
Centre and core
Cities and urban areas
City core and primary city
Proximity and distance
Urbanized and metropolitanized
Absolute value and modulus
Negative and inverse
Radius and compass

1
Introduction and Existing Studies

Most countries of the world become high income only at higher levels of urbanization. At only 31% urbanization as of 2011, and an estimated 34% urbanization as of 2020, India has more than 7,000 cities and towns which contribute nearly 70% of the nation's GDP. As urbanization and growth are moving together, there are significant increases in land and property values in India's cities. Further, sharp disparities are now observed in land valuations and housing values between Indian central cities and their suburbs (Sridhar, 2004), which has presumably led to their sprawl. Nonetheless, these explanations are just speculative.

There is limited research that documents the suburbanization of cities in India (Sridhar, 2007; Sridhar & Narayanan, 2016; Holian & Sridhar, 2017; Dowall & Monkkonen, 2008). The suburbanization of cities is significant to understand for predicting their future growth and planning for their land use, transportation, and delivery of public services. Literature on Indian cities' sprawl is growing but continues to be sparse, given the inadequate data on intra-city population and employment distribution for Indian cities. In this book, my objective is to understand the distribution of primarily population, and households and employment to a limited extent, in Indian cities, being a pioneering endeavour to understand the extent of their suburbanization and sprawl, using diverse measures, based on standard urban models and study their causes and consequences.

Is there an optimal level of this spatial growth, and a point at which it may be understood as sprawl? The Government of India, in its Smart Cities Mission concept note, recognizes that unplanned development of India's urban areas has resulted in their sprawl. The programme recognizes that, 'It is . . . essential that while planning for the smart cities, emphasis is given to planned development and decongestion of the

Indian Cities or Suburbs? Kala Seetharam Sridhar, Oxford University Press. © Kala Seetharam Sridhar 2025.
DOI: 10.1093/9780198958147.003.0001

CBD' (Central Business District) (MoHUA (2021)). While the goal of all Indian urban policies is simplified to 'the naive principle of reducing central city congestion', as pointed out by Bertaud (2002), if we cannot understand or document urban sprawl, it is not practical to merely 'de-congest' the CBD. In one of the first attempts to understand the suburbanization and sprawl of India's cities, I apply standard urban models in this exciting research.

It is important and intriguing to study the urban sprawl of Indian cities, as they throw light on the intra-city location of people and jobs. They also help us to understand if cities are monocentric or polycentric. Such research is highly policy relevant, especially so in developing countries like India, aspiring to become developed at some point sooner or later, which is only 31% urban as of 2011, but could be significantly more urban, if India's definition of urbanization were to be a little more relaxed (Sridhar, 2020). Sridhar (2020) finds that if the Census of India's criteria for an area to be considered urban were to be based only on population density, as of 2011 the country would have been 69% urban. This finding is similar to what the Government of India found in the midterm Economic Survey published in August 2017, based on nighttime satellite data. This report declared that in 2015, India was 63% 'urban', compared with the 31% urbanization rate documented as of 2011 by the Census of India. This was arrived at by the Economic Survey by simulating the population threshold for urbanization at 2,500 persons (down from the current 5,000 persons) and making the minimum qualifying population density to be 800 persons per sq. km (the current density definition relies on 450 persons per sq. km) in that report.

The rest of this chapter summarizes the existing research on suburbanization in the United States (USA) first, followed by that in the rest of the world and then discusses that on India. In this, the review covers both volumes and papers. As one may imagine, the volumes are more exploratory, descriptive, and provide the big picture of the extent of suburbanization in various countries. As expected, individual papers are more analytical and sharper in their focus in terms of their geographical area of study, the models used, and their policy conclusions. I also summarize in this chapter the vast literature on the factors explaining the suburbanization of cities in the world.

1.1 Suburbanization in the Rest of the World: USA

Until now, suburbanization has been viewed as a developed-country phenomenon, related to high income, because it is believed that it is dependent on the urbanization level of countries. It is common knowledge that the richer and more urbanized countries are also more suburbanized and vice versa. The less developed countries and those which recently urbanized such as those in Asia were viewed to be largely agricultural, also due to the definitional problem discussed earlier. Naturally, therefore, these countries were not viewed as important enough to be studied for their urbanization, let alone their suburbanization. This possibly explains the limited research on suburbanization of emerging economies like India. But there is a huge volume of literature on the suburbanization of the developed world, the Americas and Europe, which I first summarize before getting to studies on the developing world. There is also a body of theoretical literature on the subject, which I attempt to touch upon here.

At a theoretical level, Walker (2018) developed a structure for understanding suburbanization in the USA as a geographic process characterized by three features: spatial differentiation, decentralization, and identification of the waves of the municipal landscape in the aftermath of 1945. He pointed out that spatial differentiation is a universal feature of urbanization in capitalist societies, although its extent and specific characteristics depend on the context of different societies. According to him, decentralization implies 'functional decongestion'. In the discussion of the identification of waves of the urban landscape, he elaborated on the temporal dimension of asset accumulation in suburbanization, attributing it to economic, political, and cultural factors; institutions; mode of behaviour; and type of industry. Also at the theoretical level, Alperovich and Deutsch (1992) warned about the problems with interpreting a declining density gradient as indicative of suburbanization. They showed, using an example, that misspecification of the central part of a city can lead to an underestimation of the density gradient. Further, they also warned that a decline in the density gradient could be due to other factors, of which suburbanization is only one.

As Sridhar and Monkkonen (2024) point out, the standard urban model demonstrates the density gradient as the outcome of locality selections by businesses and families within a city. As emphasized by Anas et al. (1998), the selection of neighbourhoods within cities by businesses and people is the outcome of the recognition by them of the access advantages of central locations, and disadvantages of their higher land costs, with transport costs restoring the equilibrium between commute and space. White (1976) presented a model of a firm which has the option of exporting via a CBD or a suburban terminal. She explained why suburbanization makes sense in this context since freight costs may be lower, and wages also may be lower than in the central city, but labour may be scarce in the suburbs. Under conditions of labour scarcity, households' utility levels may increase if they locate in the suburbs, given wages are bid up amid labour scarcity. Thus, the size of the city increases overall, and the price of land increases indeterminately.

Richardson (1976) tried to demonstrate how the population density gradient can be revised to reflect growth in population and income. Making assumptions about the willingness to pay for space as and when income changes, they reflected on the relative contribution of population and income growth, taking four cities in the USA—Baltimore, Milwaukee, Philadelphia, and Rochester. They found in these cities that population rather than income growth has been more important to explain their density gradients since 1930.

An early study is by Berry et al. (1963) who studied the theoretical rationale underlying the population density function initiated by Clark (1951) and investigated why the density gradient declined over time in cities of the West (indicating suburbanization), while they remained constant in other cities, and what factors influenced changes in the density gradient over time. For cities in the USA, Berry et al. (1963) reported a positive association of density gradients and central city densities. This essentially meant that cities that were more suburbanized were less dense at the central city and vice versa, quite in contrast to Indian cities as reported recently by Sridhar and Monkkonen (2024). The case of Chicago was interesting as summarized by Berry et al. (1963); the city experienced steadily increasing central city density during 1860–1910, but this steadily decreased during 1910–1950. Thus, Chicago saw a continuous decline in its density gradient all the way from 1860 to 1950. Explaining the density gradient, Berry et al. (1963) postulated that it depends on the magnitude of the city's population, the degree of its shape distortion, and the share of manufacturing outside the central city, and found only city size to be significant in explaining the density gradient. Berry et al. (1963) also postulated regarding the location of the rich and the impoverished in urban areas of the West, where the central city is dominated by the poor, and the rich move to the periphery where they consume more land and housing. They argued that by contrast, in the non-Western cities, the reverse was true, since the poor who were relatively less mobile were confined to the periphery.

Thurston and Yezer (1994) documented that population suburbanization in the USA closely followed higher wages, and the sprawl of employment in transport, commerce, and retail services. This research found interesting interactions between the suburbanization of certain industrial sectors and decentralization of others.

Macauley (1985) 'corrected' the bias created by Mills (1972) and updated the population and employment density gradients which were originally estimated by Mills (1972) for 18 metropolitan areas in the USA from 1948 to 1963. In the decades of the 1960s and 1970s, suburbanization at a rapid pace was documented to have occurred in Columbus and Toledo in Ohio, and Sacramento and San Diego in California. Macauley (1985) noted that suburbanization increased in these cities anywhere between 32% and 67%, although this was associated with an expansion in suburban land in Columbus and Toledo. It is instructive to note that large cities sprawl mainly to take advantage of cheaper land costs in the suburbs and periphery, compared with the high cost of land in the centre.

Guest (1975) found huge decongestion in the central parts of metropolitan areas of the USA during 1940–70, along with large-scale deconcentration of suburbs. He reported that the US population was starting to congregate randomly near the central city, pointing to a nonlinear relationship between population concentration and increasing distance to the city centre.

Edmonston and Davies (1976) documented the population deconcentration of cities in the USA during 1900–70, attributing this primarily to rising incomes and technological improvements. Their findings indicated the necessity for urban planning for at least 50 years in the future. Edmonston and Guterbock (1984) used parameters of the standard population density function and computed urban densities for 1950, 1960, 1970, and 1975 for 200 US metropolitan areas, showing their associations with city scale, geographical location, length of life of the core city, and epoch. They found that population suburbanization was closely determined by the distribution of employment, transport costs, and increasing incomes which determined the population's ability to afford to travel longer distances.

Mills and Price (1984) attempted to empirically understand the impacts of central city socio-economic conditions on urban sprawl of the USA. They found that the existence of minorities in the central city was the only factor triggering suburbanization there. Similarly, Massey and Denton (1988) studied the residential location of blacks, Hispanics, and Asians during 1970 and 1980, taking the case of 59 US metropolitan areas. They found that blacks continued to locate in the city core, and were more segregated there than in the suburbs, with Hispanics and Asians significantly more suburbanized than blacks.

Sridhar and Sridhar's (2003) primary goal was to understand the effect of work from home on suburbanization in the pre-Covid period, as they hypothesized that work from home would make the cities much more suburbanized by enabling households to stay farther away from their workplace. They found, based on the average calculated population gradient for all US cities, the continued suburbanization of cities in the USA,[1] and an inverse association of the population density gradient with city size, indicating that large cities suburbanize. The most important finding of this paper was that technology and telecommuting did not have the expected effect on suburbanization. Rather, the existence of mixed workers (whom they used to denote those who worked from home, in addition to working from office) was found to have a positive relationship with suburbanization, as work from home (implied by telecommuting) presumably called for greater organizational monitoring, necessitating that these workers locate closer to their workplace (assumed to be in the city centre).

Stanback (2019) views suburbanization as a challenge to the central city by examining the sectoral composition of industry, and how it has changed between the central city and suburbs since 1970. Given the significant

[1] They found that the most centralized cities were Eugene-Springfield in Oregon and Reading in Pennsylvania, and the most suburbanized was Atlanta, Georgia, which was also the largest city in the sample.

proportion of population suburban in the USA (46%, compared with only 31% located centrally), 14 major cities in the USA are examined for their shift from manufacturing to services, and across gender and racial groups. This book finds that city residents' options for suburban employment are greatly restricted by housing and the transport/commute choices available. The ratio of earnings of workers by industry (manufacturing, trade, transport, communications, government employment, and so on) suggested that the suburban workforce earn more compared with their central city counterparts. Undoubtedly they found the city depends on the peripheral labour force for their education and skills, as the central city is inhabited by African Americans who do not possess the required skills. Hence, the book foresees a competition between the central city and suburbs for both economic opportunities and skills. Comparing population and employment ratios across the central city and suburbs, the book finds undoubtedly that greater employability follows from higher education in both the city and the suburbs. Nonetheless, this book brings to the fore one interesting finding, which is the importance of agglomeration in the suburbs, which hitherto was thought to be confined to the central city. The location of services—most importantly of retail, finance, insurance, and real estate—leads to their agglomeration in suburbs. However, employers in suburban labour markets have the challenge of recruiting a workforce willing to accept a lower wage and part-time jobs especially in retailing. So, the central policy problem seemed to be to help the poor central city workforce to find jobs in the suburbs, and both central city and suburban low-skilled workers to find jobs without having to commute for long or changing their household location.

Jordan, Ross, and Usowski (1998) examined if they could find disparities in sprawl across US cities during the decade of the 1980s. They reported three findings which were of interest: the first was that the US metropolitan areas' suburbanization rate remained on average the same during the 1980s and the 1970s; their second finding of interest was that the conventional framework was a sound explanation of the location of persons for fewer cities; and third, both indicators representing the market-based theory (such as income or transport costs) affecting the entire city and those that represented differences across the centre and its peripheral parts, with regard to various attributes, were found to be significant in explaining suburbanization.

Margo (1992) found empirical evidence from the USA for a natural evolution-based explanation of suburbanization. He found that household income has a positive effect on suburbanization, showing that nearly half of the suburbanization which occurred in US cities during 1950–80 was due to increasing family incomes. However, Kneebone and Garr (2010) documented that the poor in suburban areas of the largest cities of the USA grew by 25% during 2000–08, when compared with the five times by which it increased in the primary cities.

Franco (2020) studied how parking charges and the supply of these spaces affected choice of commuting modes and the city's urban form; she also examined how proposed changes regarding parking could accomplish certain policy targets of Los Angeles in California, USA. This paper elaborated on how parking spaces provided by the employer to employees, to satisfy the city's requirements, along with other factors, affected consumption of land, automobile possession, and its utilization. She reported that a higher level of suburbanization due to an increase in the parking subsidy led to a decline in urban welfare and a higher level of auto usage. Brueckner and Franco (2018) found that an increase in employer-provided parking led to an inefficient increase in suburbanization as well. They found that when the responsibility of parking shifted from road users to central city businesses, it inefficiently increased usage of the roads, given the parking subsidy, and encouraged investment in roads, while leading to an inefficient increase in suburbanization.

Lin (2014) analysed how different suburbanization is between the USA and China. He clarified an important difference between sprawl in the two countries: with suburbanization, the usefulness of the core in Chinese cities remained unaffected, much different from how it made central cities quite dull beyond working hours in the USA.

Kahn (2000) explored the environmental sustainability of suburbanization in the USA and reported that suburban households drove 31% more than their urban counterparts. He found that air quality had not deteriorated despite the increasing vehicular usage, partly due to the existence of emissions controls. He concluded on an optimistic note that with the increasing use of technology and innovation, it was possible to mitigate the negative environmental effects of suburbanization. Jones and Kammen (2014) more recently investigated the environmental implications of suburbanization by examining which cities in the USA contributed to carbon emissions, given the war against climate change is successful or vanquished in cities. They formulated an analytical framework of demand for energy, food, and transport and derived average household carbon footprints, which they found were higher in the suburban areas than in central cities. They found that suburbs alone accounted for greater than 50% of the total carbon footprint of all households in the USA, which should make such a pattern of urban growth concerning, what with increasing warnings about climate change and greenhouse gas emissions. Thus, we should now be pessimistic about the environmental sustainability of suburbanization.

1.2 Suburbanization in Europe and the Rest of the World

What Broitman and Koomen (2020) find with respect to 15 large and historic cities (with more than 150,000 inhabitants) in the Netherlands during 2000–17 is quite a contrast to what is found with cities in the USA. They found that while both population and dwelling unit densities followed the standard exponential density function, the population and dwelling density gradients increased in absolute value during the period and became steeper over time during the study period, indicating centralization of those cities. They attributed the centralization to the existence of heritage and related services in the city centre. They also pointed to the significance of density for the deployment of fundamental infrastructure like transport.

The focus of the edited volume by Phelps and Wu (2011) is on post-suburban developments, and how occurrences in various countries could be considered that way. It concentrates on post-suburbia in the Americas, along with that in compact Europe including south-east England, East Asia (Seoul and Tokyo), and Russia (Moscow). Teaford (2011), a chapter in this volume, provides an interesting hypothesis that suburbia in Britain was possibly created because of the corrupt central core, with businesses wanting to free themselves of the bureaucracy of the central core—hence office, retail, and research facilities located along the fringe of cities. The edited volume by Phelps and Wu (2011) also contains chapters from Latin America—Santiago in Chile and a suburb of Buenos Aires, Argentina—which explore if there is anything unique about Latin American suburbanization. It may be noted that Central America is also a highly urbanized part of the world. The story from a suburb of Buenos Aires, Argentina—Pilar—studied by Roitman and Phelps (2011), is that it is distinct from the suburbanization of the USA. Roitman (2010) points out that Latin American suburbs are quite heterogeneous, characterized by the existence of both poor neighbourhoods and gated communities. Heinrichs et al. (2011), who discuss the case of Santiago, Chile, found that it is only recently that the social, economic, and ecological processes of suburbanization there have attracted the attention of urban analysts, after the USA and Europe. They attributed the suburbanization of Santiago, Chile to several factors: the return to democracy in 1990; and economic liberalization in 1970 which changed the face of urbanization in that country. Further, the government initiated social programmes to provide residences in the fringes of cities, mega private projects at the urban fringe, and facilitated the development of transport infrastructure. Thus, the differences between suburbanization of the USA and that in Latin America are the recent return to democracy in the latter, and the social housing and mega private projects at their urban fringes.

Bontje and Burdack (2011) take the case of continental Europe, where suburbanization occurred in the 1980s, and speculate that the suburbs there are much more interrelated with the core cities. Stanilov and Sýkora (2014) focus on the suburban explosion in Eastern and Central Europe after the financial crisis of 2008, and this is especially relevant given the compact urban forms of cities there, with high densities and extensive public transit. This book focuses on suburbanization in several cities there including Moscow, Tallinn, Sofia, and Warsaw, among others, and understands its causes and management. One interesting feature of this edited volume is that the case studies of all cities are based on a common methodology. The introductory chapter argues that the process of dismantling of government investments, decentralization of jobs and other activities, and public services have led to suburbanization in that part of Europe. Case studies of cities within Central and Eastern Europe are presented in the volume. A review of this book by Szabó (2014) indicates that Ljubljana's suburbanization was viewed to be less negative by Pichler-Milanović (2014) because the dispersed pattern of settlements led to energy-efficient construction and improvement in public services such as sewerage. However, the perspective from Prague is quite different, where the authors make a case that suburbanization led to negative consequences, primarily due to the lack of metropolitan governance concerning the environment, even though road connectivity and transport improved greatly.

Garcia-Lopez (2012) extended the work of earlier studies on the impact of transportation upgradation on Barcelona's sprawl, using two different measures—highways measured with their ramps and railroads via their stations—with both causing suburbanization. This study used information at a disaggregated census level, which may be considered big in terms of its geographic area, hence the sprawl as documented by Garcia-Lopez (2012) in Barcelona is not conducted at a minute level, as done here.

Gnat and Bas (2013) studied Szczecin in Poland, simply analysing the mobility of that city's population to contiguous cities in Poland. Taking the general definition of suburbanization, which is a rise in the population of a city in its peripheral areas, while keeping the urbanized area inhabitants the same, they concluded that sprawl was happening in Szczecin, entirely devoid of the theoretical framework typically used for understanding it.

Leetma et al. (2014) examined the sprawl of Tallinn in Estonia, and highlighted the challenges of interpretation, documenting suburbanization (which they referred to broadly as urban decentralization) during the 1990s and the period 2000–08. They attributed the early phase of suburbanization to a rise in the costs of habitation in the city core, although they also pointed to other factors such as housing demand, macroeconomic conditions, and historical factors.

Reckien and Luedeke (2014) discussed suburbanization by explaining the interaction among groups in suburbs of two cities in the United Kingdom (UK) and Germany. They documented social interactions and dynamics leading to suburbanization in the two study regions, although the social interaction was stronger in Wirral/Liverpool (than in the suburb of Leipzig, Germany). The suburbanization was triggered by the preference to live closer to family and friends, in greener surroundings and affordable housing. Their analysis showed that suburbs morph into standalone areas themselves, as they found that most relocations happened from one suburb to another, or into them from externally, rather than from the urban centre.

Salvati (2014) analysed built-up areas in Rome, Italy, with high-resolution maps over more than five decades, during 1949–2008. The analyses showed the structure of Rome developing in three phases (which were characterized as 'compact growth', 'medium-density growth', and 'low-density growth') with the city's morphology changing fast. The study concluded by suggesting that reforms to guide suburbanization must target a concise urban form which saves land, with the use of frameworks that acknowledge such a structure's characteristics and sustainability benefits. Annunziata and Cossu (2010) pointed out how Roman suburbs neglected the delivery of infrastructure, other urban spaces, and good-quality construction to enable mobility.

The focus of Hanlon and Vicino (2018) is on providing a historical overview of suburbanization in the Global South and North. It is international in its investigation and interdisciplinary in its approach. It focuses on the 'discontent' of suburbs in the world, laying emphasis on variations in the suburbs of Europe, Latin America, Australia, and Asia (in which India is included, along with Jakarta and Seoul), taking a historical approach. It also focuses on poverty and inequality in suburbs of the world, taking examples from Sweden, the USA, Rio de Janeiro, and Cairo. It then summarizes a series of chapters on policy implications for and governance of suburbs, taking the cases of Paris, Turkey, and the USA.

Clapson and Hutchison (2010) take essentially a sociological approach to suburbanization. This volume is an edited collection of papers on suburbanization in the Global North (USA, Paris, Rome) and cities of the Global South (Sydney, Rio de Janeiro, Latin America, Singapore, and cities of China and India). The particular focus in this volume across the cities in the above set of developed and developing countries is on social and cultural change, not really an economic perspective as I take in this book.

Petersen (2010), taking the case of Johannesburg, pointed out how South African suburbanization is similar to suburbanization in the USA. On the other hand, Pinnegar et al. (2010) described the process of 'incremental suburban renewal' taking the case of Sydney, Australia, where such suburbanization was accompanied by knockdown and rebuilding of individual housing stock on a large scale. Very similarly in Brazil's Rio de Janeiro, Veloso (2010) pointed out how the poorer workers have to deprive themselves of the cultural attractions of the central city which the elite have access to, because the suburbs offer a much cheaper option for them to live in.

Kahimbaara (1986) investigated the density gradient of Nairobi, Kenya, hypothesizing that it is sectoral; different socio-racial groups have different gradients relating to different geographical centres; and finally, that the boundary changes of the city influenced its density gradient. The study confirms these hypotheses but qualifies matters carefully in that the standard urban model applies to Nairobi not because of the traditional factors, but owing to political and economic features. The study also showed that the extent of suburbanization depends on city scale.

Alperovich (1980) estimated density gradients, using a panel dataset for Tel Aviv (in Israel), and found that during 1961–76 the slope of the city's population density function steadily declined. This paper also found lower transportation costs, higher income, and larger metropolitan area population explained the suburbanization of Tel Aviv to a large extent.

Asabere and Owusu-Banahene (1983) examined the suburbanization of cities in Ghana during 1960–70 and found declining values of the density gradients from 0.59 (in 1960) to 0.55 in 1970. They recognized that their estimates were much higher than for cities in the USA, UK, and South America, but lower than for Indian cities and those in Korea.

1.3 Suburbanization in Asia

Moving to Asia, Firman (2011) in his chapter on the suburbanization of Jakarta, Indonesia, viewed the suburbanization phenomenon as part of Jakarta's larger extended metropolitan region, a trend towards which all Asian urbanization is moving. Lee and Shin (2012) demonstrated, through their case study of Pangyo (a town outside of the Seoul metropolitan area), how it exemplified a new form of governance arrangement, characterized by tensions between the central, provincial, and municipal governments, and the pro-growth coalition and environmental conservation groups. The case from Pangyo illustrated that suburbanization in South Korea mostly has taken the form of polycentric regions instead of the suburbanization of lower-income strata frequently observed in South-East Asia, and suburbanization primarily led by the private sector as in the USA and UK. Wu and Phelps (2011) pointed out that 'post-suburbia' is not independence from sprawl, but merely refers to cities which have suburbanized.

Trân et al. (2012) documented that the peripheral parts of the largest urban agglomerations in South-East Asia are becoming increasingly important because of their residential, commercial, and industrial functions. Analysing social and occupational changes in the southern cities of Vietnam, they provided recommendations for sustainable peri-urbanization and claimed that this was the new perspective their volume brought to the body of knowledge on suburbanization. Even though there were significant differences in lifestyle, culture, employment, and investment opportunities across rural and urban areas, they argued that it was artificial to separate them, hence a more integrated approach to a study of both is necessary. As part of this treatment, they pointed to the reality which accompanies suburbanization: the problems that have occurred at the urban fringes of Vietnam and South-East Asia. Although suburbanization must be planned first, in Vietnam, the planning for public services, construction, and land use happens after the actual sprawl has taken place, very similar to what one finds in India. The volume therefore expressed its concerns about the environmental impacts of suburban sprawl where pollution is ignored, and where conflicts of interest exist as they relate to land, along with employment and cultural aspects. Hence, suburban sprawl must be regulated with a holistic approach, not only with an urban lens.

Padawangi (2010) pointed out in the case of Singapore, how the ideas of Ebenezer Howard, who highlighted planned new spaces, found a place in the city state's new towns, which emphasize greenery rather than the holistic 'garden city' concept Howard advocated. China's suburbanization is similar to that observed in India, as pointed out by Ren (2010), who documented the case of a Wangjing suburb outside of Beijing, where migrant workers lived, being unable to bear the costs of central city living. Wang et al. (2010) studied Shanghai in China and Kolkata in India for their suburbanization processes. In Shanghai, the authors took the cases of Shanghai International Automobile City and Songjiang New City. In Kolkata, the chapter took the examples of Kolkata West International

City and Rajarhat New Town. The authors demonstrated how in the case of each of the two suburbs both in Shanghai and in Kolkata, the suburbanization was itself the result of planned development of new towns, quite in contrast to the haphazard growth that suburbanization implies. Nonetheless, based on the research, the authors pointed to the fact that the planned suburbanization met with a great deal of resistance against land acquisition for the provision of infrastructure in Kolkata, but was marked by its conspicuous absence in Shanghai. The research viewed suburbanization essentially as something that benefits the rich at the cost of the poorer sections of society.[2] Planned suburbanization may have some of these characteristics, but the form of suburbanization that is considered in this book does not suffer from those inequities: it is based on democracy, market-based decisions, and the free, unrestricted location of migrants and households wherever they can afford the same, even if that is the outcome of planned projects. This, it should be acknowledged, is part of a worldview based on the market and democracy which is a key perspective today, challenged by non-democratic and autocratic urban regimes (China among them).

For Asian cities, Berry et al. (1963) summarized a steep negative association between city size and the density gradient, implying that the largest Asian cities were characterized by extreme sprawl, while the smallest Asian cities were compact. Yudhistira et al. (2019) examined the suburbanization of Jakarta (Indonesia), by investigating census data and nighttime satellite data. They found that improved transport access as manifested in highway and rail networks had important influences on suburbanization of the metropolis.

While Sun et al. (2012) provided a nonparametric analysis of suburbanization in the Beijing metropolitan area, Zhou and Ma (2000) examined the suburbanization of four major cities in China—Beijing, Dalian, Shanghai, and Shenyang. They found that with economic restructuring, the central city of these four metropolises experienced net population loss during 1982–90 while the inner suburbs experienced gains in their population. They attributed this trend to the by-products of economic restructuring—commercialization of land, the movement to tertiary uses

[2] However, what is not clear is how, if the 'poor' had ownership of land in the periphery, they could be considered the 'poor'.

of land, significant improvements in transport, and construction of new houses in their suburbs, among other factors. Differentiating this from the US type of suburbanization, they attributed the suburbanization in China to the significant role of the state, whereas the US suburbanization is more market driven.

Uduporuwa and Manawadu (2015) discussed the decentralization of Kandy in Sri Lanka. They documented that the concentric areas were characterized by high density and located in close proximity to the centre of that city. They estimated the population density function, which they found to be a negative exponential form, as shown in the standard framework, and found flattening of the city's slope during 1957–2001.

Khatun et al. (2015) found the negative exponential population density function to be an appropriate explanation of the urban form of Dhaka as well. They further found that the density gradient of this city flattened over time, indicating suburbanization, which they attributed to improvements in transportation, and to disparities in land prices across the core and suburban parts of the city, much as Sridhar (2004) documented with respect to Indian cities.

I note most volumes in this emerging area are edited, not authored like this one. Apart from the aforementioned volumes, I have not been successful in locating even one authored book on suburbanization in India. There are several aspects in which this proposed volume builds on the existing body of literature on suburbanization. This chapter next summarizes the limited existing literature on suburbanization in India.

1.4 Studies on the Suburbanization of India

For India, Berry et al. (1963) is one of the earliest studies, which found the density gradient for Hyderabad to be −1.41 (this was possibly for 1951 although a date is not mentioned for the same), representing a negative exponential function. Interestingly, for the then Calcutta, the density gradient of −0.41 that they found was constant during 1921–51, indicating that it was much more suburbanized than Hyderabad. Despite the suburbanization, it was found that central city density in Calcutta increased steadily (just as Sridhar and Monkkonen (2024) find in general with respect to Indian cities).

Shaw (2018), who focuses on India in a volume by Hanlon and Vicino (2018), highlights the unique characteristics of suburbanization in India. Quite opposed to the concept of planned suburbanization pursued by Wang et al. (2010), Shaw points to the mix of planned suburbanization and unplanned developments in several of India's new towns. She points to the fact that there were two policy trends in place to manage India's urbanization. In the aftermath of independence, India's large cities had to accommodate refugees for whom housing had to be built in the peripheries, which led to 'planned suburbanization'. In later years, however, the need to decongest large cities was envisaged, and factories/firms were explicitly encouraged to locate in the outskirts of cities.

The role played by the unduly restrictive floor area ratios (FARs) in the horizontal sprawl of India's cities were recognized by Sridhar (2010), Bertaud and Brueckner (2005), and Brueckner and Sridhar (2012). The Government of India started to relax the FAR in 2012, as pointed out by Shaw (2018). Nonetheless, Shaw (2018) points to the by-products of suburbanization: class conflicts between various income groups settled in the peripheries, because of the heterogeneous mix of high-income and low-income habitation there. As problems of suburbanization, Shaw (2018) also alludes to the natural environmental fallout of using resources lavishly and land use distortions when land is converted from agricultural to non-agricultural uses, as part of which the poor may be inadvertently adversely impacted, just as Wang et al. (2010) highlighted. The edited volume by Hanlon and Vicino (2018) therefore is pessimistic in the sense that it predicts the end of suburbanization globally, even though I find in this book that suburbanization has become more important than urbanization itself in India.

Sridhar (2007) examined the population and employment suburbanization of Bengaluru at the ward level, based on regressions, besides *computing* two-point gradient estimates for all Indian urban agglomerations, using Mills' two-point gradient technique; Sridhar (2007, 2010), based on data from the Census of India, computed job, household, and population density gradient estimates for more than 100 Indian cities, focusing on the significant part of policies governing land use. Sridhar and Narayanan (2016) documented the population and employment suburbanization of Kalaburagi, during 2001–11. Dowall and Monkkonen (2008) *estimated* the population density function of Chennai during

1971–2001 and found high densities near the city centre which rapidly declined towards the edge, which was characterized by low-density expansion. Holian and Sridhar (2017) *computed* gradients for India's urban agglomerations, using Mills' two-point estimates, and based on data from the 2001 Census of India. Holian and Sridhar (2017) found that the population density gradient (at an absolute value of 0.62) for India's cities in 2001 had increased from its 1991 value of 0.55.[3] However, these numbers must be read with caution; it should be noted that during the study period, many urban agglomerations in India were merged with the neighbouring urban local governments, with the result that the central city became more centralized for better consolidated metropolitan governance. As evidence of this, Denis and Marius-Gnanou (2011) found that during 1991–2001, merged cities in the country became greater in number, rising from 103 to 221. Therefore, the centralization of cities Holian and Sridhar (2017) observed could be an arithmetical twist rather than illustrating a genuine change in suburbanization. However, they found that, ignoring the coefficient sign, the least population density gradient decreased during 1991–2001, while the maximum declined during 1991–2001, showing sprawl during the decade.

Sridhar et al. (2018) reported the suburbanization of Bengaluru by regressing the number of persons per square kilometre of land, on distance from the city centre, as in the standard model, assuming various centres, using 2011 Census data for the city, finding centralization since the earlier decade. Using simple descriptive statistics, Munshi et al. (2018) found 28 secondary job hubs in Ahmedabad, documenting that the centrality of the CBD in jobs continuously decreased. While employment in the then existing job centres of the western Indian city constituted 83% in 1980, this declined to only 69% in 2010, with employment moving to suburban areas, much as Sridhar (2007) reported for Bengaluru.

Morya and Ram (2020) studied the suburbanization of Delhi. Much as the metropolis is a magnet, they found the powerful influence of Delhi

[3] Sridhar (2007) found the average absolute values of density gradients for India's cities to be 0.49 for 1981 and 0.47 for 1991, indicating suburbanization of the typical city. Holian and Sridhar (2017) found different gradient values for 1991, attributable possibly to using different characterizations of urban agglomerations, and a different composition of the cities included in the dataset.

on towns 50 km away. While Delhi is experiencing a decline in its population growth, distant towns in the periphery continue to get influenced by the growth of Delhi, serving as its rural hinterland. Jain et al. (2013) claimed that Delhi has constantly been sprawling from 1981 onwards over several decades, with the outward expansion coupled with a lack of adequate infrastructure.

As may be clear, the limited studies on Indian suburbanization span either individual cities (using estimation or descriptive statistics) or all cities in India, using *calculated density gradients*. No study has used the *estimation technique* at a small geographic level, like I do here, to understand the sub-city distribution of population and employment (to a limited degree) for major Indian cities in a single volume.

1.5 Contribution of This Book

Very important as urbanization is, the suburbanization of India has received less attention. This volume is the first comprehensive one on suburbanization in India. This chapter makes an attempt to position this research within the framework of the existing body of work on this important aspect of urbanization. There are several aspects in which this proposed volume builds on the published work on suburbanization thus far.

First, suburbanization in the context of the developing world needs a different and unique treatment. We cannot combine suburbanization in India with that in Asia, let alone Europe or North America. In Paris for example, richer households live centrally, while the poorer ones settle in the suburbs; this is quite the opposite in the USA. India is closer to the European and Asian models where the richer households locate in the centre, and poorer households settle in the periphery,[4] thus a unique treatment is necessary.

[4] It should be mentioned that there is no definitive evidence regarding this, and we are still not able to provide this evidence in this book based on our review of various nighttime satellite datasets.

Second, the approach of the research thus far on suburbanization has been primarily qualitative, with the conspicuous absence of standard urban models being applied to understand this phenomenon, which I do here.

Third, this volume uses unique data from the Global Human Settlements Layer (GHSL), Census of India, and state-specific (for Karnataka) datasets, and standard indicators to measure and understand the population and jobs sprawl of India's cities at a very granular level.

1.6 Overview of This Book

This book is organized as follows. This chapter has focused on the motivation and background for studying suburbanization in the Indian context, and has summarized existing international literature on the subject, pointed out gaps, and positioned this research amidst the existing published research on the subject. Chapter 2 provides a summary of the theoretical frameworks, methodology, and datasets of the research. Chapter 3 begins to describe the findings of the research starting with the suburbanization of population and households. In this it dwells both on estimated and on calculated population density gradients along with estimated household density gradients for different periods of time. In the findings from estimated density gradients, Chapter 3 dwells separately on the ward-level (from the Census) and grid-level data for cities. Chapter 3 also presents a detailed analysis of the concentric circles drawn for each of 100 cities in India and engages with an analysis of sprawl in each of them. Chapter 4 concentrates on regional variations in population suburbanization. It classifies states in many ways—the northern and southern; the urbanized and less urbanized; the progressive and lagging states—and distinguishes between the suburbanization of cities in each of the categories of states indicated. Chapter 5 focuses on the jobs sprawl of India's cities, although this is limited to a smaller city dataset and estimated at the Census ward rather than at the grid level. Even though the dataset for understanding the suburbanization of jobs is smaller, a section in this chapter focuses on regional variations in the suburbanization of jobs, using the same classifications as in Chapter 4. It focuses on the employment suburbanization of individual cities (Bengaluru and

Kalaburagi in Karnataka). Chapter 6 tries to explain the sprawl using the regression approach highlighted in Chapter 2; this chapter also provides a detailed discussion of the literature on the explanation of suburbanization. Chapter 7 dwells on qualitative views of several experts in India representing academics, policy makers, and real estate developers regarding suburbanization, its causes, and its consequences, and provides policy suggestions, analogous to the quantitative research presented in earlier chapters. Chapter 8, the final chapter, deals with the consequences of urban sprawl, and presents findings with respect to the delivery of basic services such as water supply, and accessibility of healthcare in Bengaluru, understanding if there is a difference between the central and peripheral parts. Chapter 8 also examines the environmental effects of suburbanization, using evidence on air quality from the cities studied. Chapter 8 further attempts to make policy suggestions for suburban development in India, and concludes, by indicating the caveats of the work and areas of future research.

2
Research Questions, Theoretical Framework, and Methods

The literature review in Chapter 1 indicated that the suburbanization of India has not gained the recognition that it ought to in research on urbanization, especially so in the framework of the accepted theoretical model for understanding the phenomenon. This chapter summarizes the research questions, the theoretical framework, the methodology, and the data sources used for research in this book.

Considering the survey of the existing body of work presented in Chapter 1, the gaps identified, and the limited research on the suburbanization of India's urban agglomerations, this book tries to investigate the following research questions:

1. Do population and households in India's urban areas sprawl? Did they sprawl during 1975–2015?
2. Are jobs of urban India suburbanized? Is the job sprawl to the same extent as that of population or households?
3. Are there regional variations in the sprawl of persons or jobs in India's urban areas?
4. Is the suburbanization pattern of population, households, and employment alike in the southern, more urban, slow-growing, and northern states?
5. What are the factors that associate with sprawl in India's urban areas?
6. What are some consequences of suburbanization and the associated policy suggestions?

Considering the past work on suburbanization in Chapter 1, it is not clear if Indian cities have suburbanized, and if so, to what extent (although Sridhar (2007) and Holian and Sridhar (2017) provide some answers

Indian Cities or Suburbs? Kala Seetharam Sridhar, Oxford University Press. © Kala Seetharam Sridhar 2025.
DOI: 10.1093/9780198958147.003.0002

based on the two-point gradient technique). It is significant to note the suburbanization of population, families, and jobs to plan cities, and associated infrastructure. This chapter lays out the framework for examining suburbanization, then describes the underlying theory, the methodology adopted along with caveats, and data sources for the research.

2.1 Theoretical Framework

The standard theory for understanding suburbanization and urban sprawl is fairly well established. In general, suburbanization is known to occur when there is an expansion of the city's population in the fringes, holding the population of the metropolitan area constant. In delineating this process I exclude the phenomenon of migrants settling in the periphery of a metropolitan area being termed as suburbanization.

In a specific sense termed b-suburbanization (see Sridhar, 2007), suburbanization is an activity best defined by the smoothening of a city's population (or employment) density curve in relation to distance from the city centre (termed the gradient). This is typically a downward-sloping function. The ascent/descent of the population density function understandably differs across cities, with sharper slopes showing compact cities, and smoother slopes presenting more sprawling cities, with the associated caveats from the existing literature discussed in Chapter 1. Hence, rightly, b-suburbanization occurs when there is a decrease in the slope of the population density function, an activity by which a city becomes 'flatter'.

The theory for this work is standard, being represented by the conventional population density function, which is empirically estimated to obtain a slope, which we understand as the gradient, b, represented in equation (2.1).

$$D(r) = D_0 e^{-br}. \qquad [2.1]$$

In equation (2.1), D (r) refers to number of people per square kilometre of land area, at r km from the core of the city. Equation (2.1) is frequently transformed into logs for purposes of empirical estimation, as shown in equation (2.2). Transformed in this way, equation (2.2) represents the well-known double log equation, showing the percentage change in population density as one goes a kilometre away from the city core, with b representing the gradient (population, household, or employment density, as the case may be).

$$\text{Ln } D(r) = \text{Ln } D_0 - br. \quad [2.2]$$

Equation (2.2) is estimable, but is very demanding of data, because it requires information on persons, area of land, identification of the city core, and the proximity of various areas in the city to the identified core, all at the sub-city level. Such data are quite rare, but these are the strengths of this book, as is clear from the next section on data.

Given such disaggregated data within the city are hard to get in cities of emerging countries, to overcome the challenge, Mills (1970) developed a two-point method to *calculate the gradient, rather than estimate it using the procedure above* in equations (2.1) and (2.2). The two-point technique which Mills (1970) developed requires data on just four points in a city—inhabitants of the city centre (L_C), residents of the entire city (L), area (radius) of the city core (R_C), and area (radius) of the full city (R)—rather than the data for many points in the city that are required by the estimation method. Given the four data points for every city, the two-point technique is a fairly straightforward method which uses the population density function shown in equation (2.1).

Using the individual population density function shown in equation (2.1), one integrates L_C across the circumference of a city, which is 2Πr, to yield the population of the central city, as shown below and also demonstrated by Sridhar (2007):

$$L_C = \int_0^{R_C} 2\pi r D(r)\,dr = \int_0^{Rc} 2\pi r D_0 e^{-br} = \frac{2\pi D_0}{b^2}[1 - e^{-bRc} - bRc^{e-bRc}] \quad [2.3]$$

As Mills (1970) suggested, one follows the same procedure as above for obtaining the metropolitan area population (which I call L), yielding the equation below, as shown by Sridhar (2007):

$$L = \int_0^{R} 2\pi r D(r)\,dr = \int_0^{R} 2\pi r D_0 e^{-bR} = \frac{2\pi D_0}{b^2}[1 - e^{-bR} - bRe^{-bR}]. \quad [2.4]$$

Then, taking the ratio of L_C in equation (2.3) to L in equation (2.4), as Mills (1970) suggested, gives us

$$\frac{L_C}{L} = \frac{1-e^{-bRc} - bR_C e - bR_C}{1-e^{-bR} - bRe^{-bR}}. \qquad [2.5]$$

The mathematically astute reader will recognize that equation (2.5) is solvable for b, the population density gradient, given it is a single equation and has a single unknown.[1] Thus, Mills (1970) showed that with information on merely four areas in a city (as opposed to the several data points the estimation procedure involves), it was possible to *calculate* rather than *estimate* the population density gradient.

However, equation (2.5) does not yield a unique value for the density gradient b, which means that multiple values of b satisfy this equation. Further, the b *calculated* this way has no range within which it could statistically lie, or level of statistical significance, to enable us to understand its importance for any given city. Besides, it should be borne in mind that estimates arrived at using the 'short-cut' technique are likely to be biased upwards for smaller cities, as McDonald (1989) points out. This is because the functional form for a city with a small spatial area pulls down its population density, swiftly resulting in high densities in the city core.

The interpretation of b, irrespective of whether it is calculated or estimated, is standard: flattening of the gradient (lower value of the gradient) implies greater suburbanization. Therefore, any reduction in the gradient value means suburbanization, and any increases in its value demonstrate centralization. To show some anecdotal examples from the existing literature of cities with flatter and steeper density gradients, I depend on Bertaud and Malpezzi (2003).

Figures 2.1 and 2.2 estimated from Bertaud and Malpezzi (2003) show the density gradients for Los Angeles (LA) in the USA and Brasilia in Brazil: −0.026 and 0.037, respectively. Whereas LA's density function is a negative exponential, Brasilia's is a positive exponential form. This implies that whereas in LA, the density was decreasing as one moved away

[1] The density gradient value b may be solved for using a moderately sophisticated hand calculator, the 'solve' function in Excel, or programming software such as Visual Basic. Sridhar (2007) employed this *calculation* approach using Visual Basic and *calculated* population, employment, and household density gradients for all Indian cities.

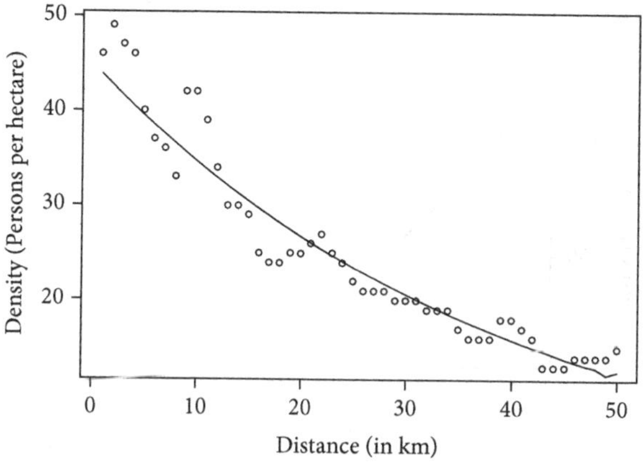

Figure 2.1 Population Density Function, Los Angeles
Source: Reproduced with permission from Bertaud and Malpezzi (2003).

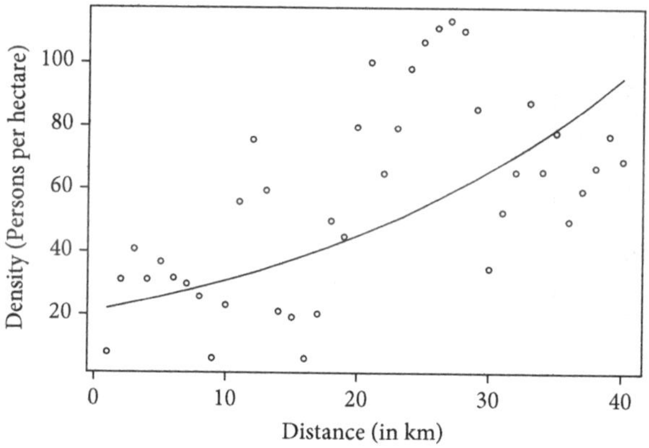

Figure 2.2 Population Distribution, Brasilia
Source: Reproduced with permission from Bertaud and Malpezzi (2003).

from the city core, in Brasilia, it was increasing from the identified city centre towards the city edge. Having said that, Brasilia's population is also more centralized than that of LA, judging from the exponential functions shown in Figures 2.1 and 2.2 and absolute values of their density gradients (0.04 for Brasilia versus 0.03 for LA).

A couple more examples are provided here from Bertaud and Malpezzi (2003) to understand flat and steep density gradients from other continents: Toulouse (France), which had a gradient of −0.377

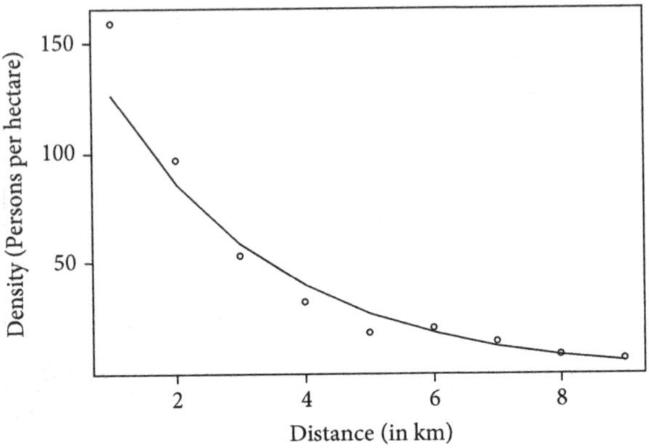

Figure 2.3 Population Density Gradient, Toulouse, France
Source: Reproduced with permission from Bertaud and Malpezzi (2003).

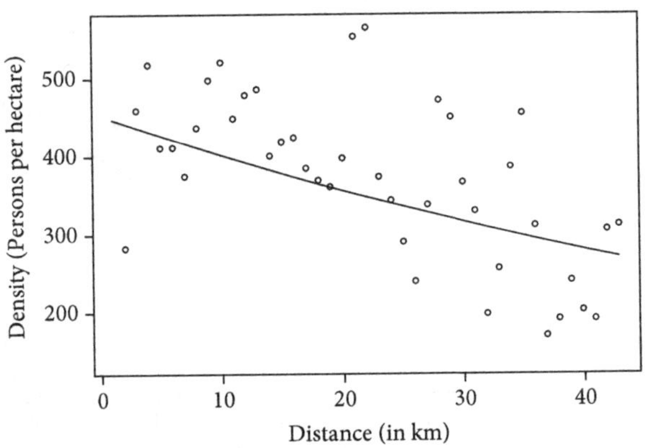

Figure 2.4 Population Distribution, Bombay/Mumbai, India
Source: Reproduced with permission from Bertaud and Malpezzi (2003).

(see Figure 2.3), and Mumbai (India) (see Figure 2.4), whose population density gradient was only –0.012, which indicated that Mumbai was a lot more suburbanized than was Toulouse, although both cities exhibited the negative exponential functional form at the time of their research, in the early 2000s.

In this research, which I believe is the first comprehensive study on the spread of population at the sub-city level in Indian urban areas, I apply the standard urban model and *estimate* population, household, and job density functions using detailed data at the sub-city Census ward levels for more than 100 Indian cities. By estimating 324 regressions for more than 100 cities each in 2015 and 1975, as well as employment and household functions for 62 cities in 2011, I explore the sprawl of cities in Indian states and regions. As is clear, I review the extent of 'b-suburbanization' of Indian cities over time, in this research, even as one may define suburbanization as an increase in the proportion of suburban inhabitants, keeping the urban area's population the same, to rule out the effect of migrants locating in peripheral areas.

2.2 Methods and Data

The methods of the research are primarily quantitative, relying on the conventional framework. To test the standard model, I use data from Florczyk et al. (2019) at the sub-city (sub-kilometre grids) level for more than 100 Indian cities, each in 1975 and 2015, and at the Census ward level on households, employment, land area, and proximity from the core of the city to each ward for 62 cities. The GHSL is granular, open, and freely downloadable data, and based on satellite imagery.

I perform regressions to arrive at the population, job, and household density functions for a large number of Indian cities, running more than 324 regressions for the cities, with their population, household, and employment density regressed on distances from an identified city centre. The coefficient in such a regression is the slope of the density function, which is interpreted such that the lower its absolute value, the more suburbanized or sprawling a city is. This is natural to understand as this coefficient refers to the density gradient. The lower its absolute value, the flatter is the curve and vice versa, along with the associated caveats stated earlier.

There is a minute distinction in this research even for *estimated* density gradients, as I had data for some cities at the level of the Census ward, and some at the more granular grid level. The grid data are available for population alone from the GHSL for the same cities for both 1975 and 2015 (Florczyk et al., 2019). For all cities, the 1975 regressions and estimates of the gradient are based on the *grid level* only. However, for 2015, I had the choice of using either the ward level (for 62 cities for which I obtained shape files from the Internet freely), or the grid level from the

GHSL (for all the 100-plus cities). The ward-level data are for only 62 cities for which I was able to get shape files from the Internet. I obtained shape files for 44 of Karnataka's cities from the Karnataka Municipal Data Society (KMDS). The remaining cities are those for which I was able to download shape files from the Internet as described before. This discrepancy exists because the Census of India stopped publishing data on cities' spatial area at the sub-city level in 1991, hence even two-point estimates for the gradients, like what Sridhar (2007) did, are now not possible.

As is clear, the methodology of this research is primarily quantitative, relying on information at the grid and sub-kilometre levels for 100 major cities of India, extracted from open and free data (Florczyk et al., 2019) for population. The list includes all 53 prominent Indian cities which had a million-plus population as of 2011. In addition, included are those cities for which I obtained data from the GHSL. I downloaded the applicable datasets[2] for two years four decades apart, to examine the sprawl for these same cities over the time period, assuming the *same city centre*. Thus, it should be clear that for 1975 and 2015, the files for all cities are from the GHSL (Florczyk et al., 2019).

Given the caveats associated with *calculated* gradients, I compare the *estimated* density gradients for this study with *calculated* gradients for Indian cities from other secondary sources for 1991 and 2001, and understand the relationship between them in the form of correlations.

I choose the period 1975–2015 for this research due to the reasons listed below:

1. These two years are the earliest and latest for which the GHSL information exists. Although we are in the post-pandemic period, 2015 is the last year for which the GHSL published data on population, built area, and economic activity for many cities in India, hence I did not have any more recent years of data to depend upon for this research, at the time this book was completed.
2. The year 1975 represents the pre-liberalization period in India and 2015 represents the post-liberalization period. It should be remembered that the post-independence period in India saw the setting

[2] The datasets were downloaded from https://human-settlement.emergency.copernicus.eu/datasets.php.

up of several steel plants at Bokaro, Durgapur, and Rourkela, which marked the beginning of industrialization and urbanization in the country as towns were built around these factories. However, the overall emphasis of policy in the post-independence period was on food security and building self-sustainability in agriculture. The pre-liberalization (1991) period was also characterized by the focus on rural development and poverty reduction for what was a largely agrarian country then. Hence, 1975 may be considered as the baseline urbanization for India. As is now well known, India launched on a path of economic liberalization from the late 1980s onwards, culminating in the 1991 economic reforms. The emphasis of liberalization was on privatization. With free trade in agriculture too, naturally farmers could expect to get remunerative prices for their crops and produce everywhere, but that also meant uncompetitive farmers would go out of business. This resulted in increasing levels of urbanization, with many farmers moving to cities in search of alternative employment. Tripathi (2019) reported that selected aspects of the 1991 economic reforms had a positive effect on the country's urbanization, although it was found that economic reforms influenced urbanization only slowly. Thus, by choosing 1975 and 2015, I have constructed a controlled experiment to examine the effect of the 1991 liberalization on city sprawl.

As described earlier, I obtained shape files for 44 of Karnataka's biggest cities from the KMDS, as well as some 18 cities across all India, for which I downloaded shape files that were freely available from the Internet. This is to be understood with the caveat that different results might have been obtained had I used satellite data for understanding household and employment suburbanization. For purposes of understanding and measuring the extent of household and employment suburbanization, given the unavailability of employment or household data at the grid level in the GHSL, I obtained data disaggregated to the municipal ward level, on households, jobs, land area, and their proximity to the city centre, from the Census of India 2011, for which I also managed to get shape files, as described above.

Based on the GHSL satellite data, I econometrically *estimate* (not *calculate* gradients as earlier studies have done) population density functions for all cities in the country for which the information exists for both 1975 and 2015. Based on Census data and city-level shape files which were available for free download for several other cities, I was able to calculate distances of every ward to the city centre in all Indian cities for which I obtained such data. Then I employed simple regressions to *estimate* job and household density functions for 62 cities.

In the case of most cities, I chose transport hubs such as the railroad terminus or the city's main bus stop, the state government headquarters, or the city government office as the core of the city, excepting those cases where the aforementioned points were located beyond the municipal boundaries. Appendix 2A.1 lists the centres chosen in the case of each of the 143 cities (100 cities from the GHSL (including Bengaluru) and 43 cities from Karnataka for which I had shape files from the KMDS (excluding Bengaluru); the remaining 18 cities for which I obtained shape files from the Internet are included in the 100 cities). Nonetheless, in Chapter 4, where I present the regional variations in suburbanization, the sprawl of only selected cities (not all the 43) from Karnataka is presented.

For cities for which I obtained the data from the GHSL, and selected 12 cities from Karnataka, I drew concentric circles around the identified core of the city, using a minute distance like a 0.1-km, 0.2-km, or 0.3-km radius to arrive at a minimum of 30 observations for every city for the estimation for each of 1975 and 2015. Chapter 3 presents the analysis of the concentric circles and boundaries for the 100 cities, with the concentric circles for each city shown in the Appendix.

Having done this for every city, I estimated how the natural log of the number of persons per square kilometre was associated with proximity to the identified city core for each of the 100-plus cities, in both 1975 and 2015, as shown in equation (2.2).

The constraint in estimating employment and household density regressions for all cities was the lack of data on employment or households at the grid level, which are not available in the GHSL. Therefore, I obtained ward-level data on employment and households from the 2011 Census, which, however, does not publish information on land area disaggregated at the level of the ward.[3] Hence, I am unable to estimate

[3] The Census of India used to publish land area at the ward level until the 1991 Census, following which it was stopped. Given that ward delimitations are continuously being redone, the earlier ward land areas will not be valid for researchers to use.

the density of employment or households at the ward level, except where I had shape files for the cities. I also do not have data to estimate household and employment density gradients for more than a year, given the same problem with comparability of Census wards over decades.

I estimated 100-plus population density gradient regressions for 2015, in addition to the population density gradient regressions for 1975 for the same cities. Additionally, I estimated 62 employment and 62 household density gradient regressions for 2011, each at the ward level, for cities for which the relevant city shape files were available.

2.3 Qualitative Methods

In addition to the quantitative tools and techniques highlighted above, qualitative methods such as focus group discussions (FGDs) were used for authenticating the quantitative analyses of suburbanization. To supplement the quantitative methods, a panel discussion was organized on suburbanization in India, to solicit the views of real estate developers, academics, and policy makers in November 2021 at the Institute for Social and Economic Change. The purpose of this webinar was to solicit views from various stakeholders regarding the suburbanization of India, and its possible causes. Below are the questions which were formulated, to which speakers responded in this discussion:

- What is the extent to which India's cities are suburbanized?
- Are there geographic differences in the sprawl of India's cities? If yes, which regions are characterized by sprawl? Which regions of the country have cities that are more compact?
- What are the causes of sprawl in India's urban areas?
- Have land use regulations such as the FAR (which guide building height restrictions) in the country's cities led or not led to sprawl? If yes, why? If no, why?
- Have zoning regulations in the country's urban areas affected their suburbanization?
- Are there investments by these developers in real estate and housing projects in other countries? If yes, which ones?

- What explains urban sprawl in those countries? Is this different from the sprawl observed in India's cities? Why or why not?

The above questions and discussion were meant to supplement the quantitative analyses with qualitative views regarding the reasons for suburbanization, which are elaborated in Chapter 7.

The next Chapter 3 summarizes in detail the findings on the sprawl of population, households, and jobs, using quantitative methods, and the general and specific terms elucidated in this chapter.

Appendix 2A.1

Number	State	Urban agglomeration/ city	City centre chosen
1	Kerala	Kochi UA	Ernakulam Junction Railway Station
2	Kerala	Kozhikode UA	Kozhikode Main (Calicut) Railway Station
3	Kerala	Thrissur UA	Thrissur Railway Station
4	Kerala	Malappuram UA	Malappuram KSRTC Bus Terminal
5	Kerala	Thiruvananthapuram UA	Thiruvananthapuram Central Station
6	Kerala	Kannur UA	Kannur Railway Station
7	Kerala	Kollam UA	Kollam Junction
8	Tamil Nadu	Tiruppur UA	Railway Station
9	Tamil Nadu	Salem UA	Railway Station
10	Tamil Nadu	Erode UA	Railway Station
11	Tamil Nadu	Tirunelveli UA	Tirunelveli Junction
12	Tamil Nadu	Vellore UA	Vellore Old Bus Stand
13	Andhra Pradesh	Greater Visakhapatnam (MC)	Visakhapatnam Railway Station
14	Telangana	Warangal UA	Warangal Railway Station
15	Andhra Pradesh	Guntur UA	Guntur Railway Station
16	Andhra Pradesh	Nellore UA	Nellore Railway Station
17	Andhra Pradesh	Rajahmundry UA	Rajahmundry Railway Station
18	Puducherry	Puducherry UA	Puducherry Bus Stand
19	Rajasthan	Jodhpur UA	Jodhpur Junction

Appendix 2A.1 Continued

Number	State	Urban agglomeration/ city	City centre chosen
20	Rajasthan	Kota (MC)	Kota Junction Station
21	Rajasthan	Bikaner (MC)	Bikaner Junction
22	Rajasthan	Ajmer UA	Ajmer Junction Station
23	Odisha	Cuttack UA	Cuttack Junction Station
24	Odisha	Rourkela UA	Rourkela Junction
25	Assam	Guwahati UA	Guwahati Railway Station
26	Gujarat	Ahmedabad UA	Ahmedabad Junction
27	Gujarat	Surat UA	Surat Railway Station
28	Gujarat	Vadodara UA	Vadodara Railway Station
29	Gujarat	Rajkot UA	Rajkot Junction Station
30	Gujarat	Bhavnagar UA	Bhavnagar Terminus
31	Gujarat	Jamnagar UA	Jamnagar Railway Station
32	Chhattisgarh	Raipur UA	Raipur Junction
33	Chhattisgarh	Durg-Bhilainagar UA	Durg Junction
34	Jammu & Kashmir	Jammu UA	Jammu Tawi Railway Station
35	Jammu & Kashmir	Srinagar UA	Srinagar Railway Station
36	Jharkhand	Jamshedpur UA	Tata Nagar Junction
37	Jharkhand	Dhanbad UA	Dhanbad Junction
38	Jharkhand	Ranchi UA	Ranchi Junction
39	Jharkhand	Bokaro Steel City UA	Bokaro Bus Stand
40	Punjab	Ludhiana (MC)	Ludhiana Junction
41	Punjab	Amritsar UA	Amritsar Junction
42	Punjab	Jalandhar UA	Jalandhar Junction
43	Madhya Pradesh	Indore UA	Indore Junction
44	Madhya Pradesh	Jabalpur UA	Jabalpur Junction
45	Madhya Pradesh	Gwalior UA	Gwalior Junction
46	Madhya Pradesh	Ujjain (MC)	Ujjain Junction
47	West Bengal	Siliguri UA	Siliguri Junction
48	West Bengal	Durgapur UA	Durgapur Junction
49	Haryana	Gurgaon UA	Gurgaon Bus Stand
50	Uttar Pradesh	Kanpur UA	Kanpur Central
51	Uttar Pradesh	Ghaziabad UA	Ghaziabad Junction
52	Uttar Pradesh	Agra UA	Agra Railway Station

(*continued*)

Appendix 2A.1 Continued

Number	State	Urban agglomeration/ city	City centre chosen
53	Uttar Pradesh	Varanasi UA	Varanasi Junction Railway
54	Uttar Pradesh	Meerut UA	Meerut City Junction
55	Uttar Pradesh	Allahabad UA	Prayagraj Junction
56	Uttar Pradesh	Bareilly UA	Bareilly College Bareilly
57	Uttar Pradesh	Aligarh UA	Aligarh Junction
58	Uttar Pradesh	Moradabad (MC)	Moradabad Junction
59	Uttar Pradesh	Saharanpur (MC)	Saharanpur Railway Station
60	Uttar Pradesh	Gorakhpur (MC)	Gorakhpur Junction
61	Uttar Pradesh	Firozabad (NPP)	Firozabad Bus Stand
62	Uttar Pradesh	Jhansi UA	Jhansi Junction
63	Uttar Pradesh	Muzaffarnagar UA	Muzaffarnagar Railway Station
64	Maharashtra	Greater Mumbai UA	Shivaji Terminus
65	Maharashtra	Pune UA	Pune Junction Station
66	Maharashtra	Nagpur UA	Nagpur Junction
67	Maharashtra	Nashik UA	Nehru Garden, Nashik
68	Maharashtra	Vasai-Virar City (MC)	Vasai Road, Vasai-Virar
69	Maharashtra	Aurangabad UA	Siddarth Garden and zoo, Aurangabad
70	Maharashtra	Solapur (MC)	Solapur Railway Station
71	Maharashtra	Bhiwandi UA	Bhiwandi Bus Depot
72	Maharashtra	Amravati (MC)	Amravati Railway Station
73	Maharashtra	Malegaon UA	Malegaon Bus Stand
74	Maharashtra	Kolhapur UA	Kolhapur Bus Stand
75	Maharashtra	Nanded-Waghala (MC)	Hazur sahib Nanded Station
76	Maharashtra	Sangli UA	Sangli Railway Station
77	Bihar	Patna UA	Patna Junction
78	Uttarakhand	Dehradun UA	Dehradun Railway Station
79	West Bengal	Asansol UA	Asansol Railway Station
80	Madhya Pradesh	Bhopal	33 Madan Mohan Malaviya; State Assembly (Government organisations located in the ward)
81	Odisha	Bhubaneswar	36 Vidhan Soudha
82	Haryana	Chandigarh	Ward 17
83	Tamil Nadu	Chennai	60 Vidhan Sabha, Parry's Corner

Appendix 2A.1 Continued

Number	State	Urban agglomeration/ city	City centre chosen
84	Tamil Nadu	Coimbatore	28 Central Bus Stand
85	Delhi	Delhi	NDMC CHARGE 4, Sansad Bhavan
86	Haryana	Faridabad	Ward no. 30; Municipal corporation
87	Telangana	Hyderabad	Ward 91 Khairatabad; state secretariat
88	Rajasthan	Jaipur	Ward no. 44 Malaviya Nagar; State assembly
89	Bihar	Katihar	Ward no. 31; Nagar Nigam
90	Bihar	Bodh Gaya	Ward no. 18
91	Rajasthan	Kishangarh	Ward no. 15; Madangang-Kishangarh railway station
92	West Bengal	Kolkata	Ward no. 45; Vidhan Sabha Bhavan
93	Uttar Pradesh	Lucknow	Ward no. 48 Mahatma Gandhi; Vidhan Sabha
94	Bihar	Purnia	Ward no. 9; Municipal corporation
95	Tamil Nadu	Tiruchirappalli	Ward no. 44; Municipal corporation
96	Andhra Pradesh	Vijayawada	Ward no. 13; Municipal corporation
97	Tamil Nadu	Madurai	Ward no. 10
98	Karnataka	Gangavathi	Central Bus Stand and Municipal office
99	Karnataka	Mandya	Central Bus Stand, Railway Station, and Municipal office
100	Karnataka	Chamarajanagara	KSRTC Bus Stop
101	Karnataka	Hubballi-Dharwad (MC)	KSRTC Bus Stop
102	Karnataka	Karwar	Karwar Municipal Council
103	Karnataka	Bagalkot	New Circuit House-IB
104	Karnataka	Belagavi	KSRTC Bus Stop
105	Karnataka	Bellary	City Bus Stop
106	Karnataka	Bengaluru	Vidhana Soudha
107	Karnataka	Bhadravathi	KSRTC Bus Stop

(continued)

Appendix 2A.1 Continued

Number	State	Urban agglomeration/ city	City centre chosen
108	Karnataka	Vijayapura	Vijayapura Mahanagar Palike—Government office
109	Karnataka	Chickballapur	City Municipal Council Chickballapur—Government office
110	Karnataka	Chinthamani	KSRTC Bus Stop
111	Karnataka	Chitradurga	Chitradurga City Municipal Council—Government office
112	Karnataka	Doddaballapur	Town Hall
113	Karnataka	Gokak	City Municipal Council Gokak—City government office
114	Karnataka	Kalaburagi	City Corporation Kalaburagi—Government office
115	Karnataka	Harihar	Harihar Railway Station
116	Karnataka	Hassan	Hassan New Modern Bus Stand
117	Karnataka	Hospet	KSRTC Bus Stop
118	Karnataka	Kolar	KSRTC Bus Stop
119	Karnataka	Kollegal	KSRTC Bus Station
120	Karnataka	Koppal	Koppal Municipal office
121	Karnataka	Mangaluru	City Corporation Mangaluru—Government office
122	Karnataka	Mysuru	Mysore Railway Station
123	Karnataka	Nippani	Chatrapati Shivaji Maharaj Sanskrutik Bhavan—City or town hall
124	Karnataka	Rabkavi Banahatti	KSRTC Bus Stop
125	Karnataka	Raichur	Zilla Panchayat Office—Local government office
126	Karnataka	Ranibennur	KSRTC Bus Stop
127	Karnataka	Shivamogga	KSRTC Bus Stand, Shivamogga
128	Karnataka	Sirsi	Sirsi Market Sub Post Office
129	Karnataka	Tumakuru	Zilla Panchayat Office Tumakuru

Appendix 2A.1 Continued

Number	State	Urban agglomeration/ city	City centre chosen
130	Karnataka	Gadag-Betageri	Gadag City Municipal Council—Government office
131	Karnataka	Davanagere	City Railway Station and City Municipal office
132	Karnataka	Bidar	Bidar Railway Station
133	Karnataka	Dandeli	CMC Dandeli—Municipal office
134	Karnataka	Channapatna	KSRTC Bus Stand
135	Karnataka	Ramanagaram	KSRTC Bus Stand
136	Karnataka	Udupi	Udupi Municipal office
137	Karnataka	Sindhanoor	Sindhanur Bus Station
138	Karnataka	Yadgir	City Municipal Council—Government office Yadgir
139	Karnataka	Jamakhandi	KSRTC Jamkhandi Bus Stand
140	Karnataka	Ilkal	KSRTC Ilkal Bus Stand
141	Karnataka	Kollegal	KSRTC Bus Stand Kollegala
142	Karnataka	Sira	Sira New Municipal office
143	Karnataka	Tiptur	Town Hall Tiptur—City government office Tiptur

Source: Author's compilation.

3
Have India's Population and Households Suburbanized?

This chapter dwells on answering the first research question raised at the beginning of the book: the degree of suburbanization of India's population and households. If one were to consider the general definition of suburbanization (which is the proportion of residents living in the non-central areas of the city), using grid-level data, on average, only 64% of the population in Indian cities was suburban in 1975, whereas in 2015, 82% was suburban.[1]

For the intervening period, Sridhar (2007) throws light on the extent of population and household suburbanization during 1981–91. Using the two-point technique described in Chapter 2, Sridhar (2007) found that the extent of population suburbanization was 20.67% in 1981, and 21.33% in 1991, demonstrating augmentation of sprawl. India's households were also suburbanized to a greater extent (22%) than was the population in 1991. The next section analyses the sprawl of India's cities during 1975–2015 using concentric circles as described in Chapter 2.

3.1 Analysis of City-Wide Concentric Circles

As explained in Chapter 2, I drew concentric circles for each of the 100-plus cities to understand how their boundaries changed between 1975 and 2015. In terms of the actual radii of the 112 cities, I present the concentric

[1] The way in which we computed the proportion of suburban population in each of the cities, for 1975 and 2015, using the sub-city-level data was as follows: The central city was defined as the area within 1 or 2 km of the identified city centre, with all residents beyond the aforementioned radius being defined as suburban. For smaller cities a 1-km radius was used, whereas for most of the other cities, a 2-km radius was used to define the central city.

Indian Cities or Suburbs? Kala Seetharam Sridhar, Oxford University Press. © Kala Seetharam Sridhar 2025.
DOI: 10.1093/9780198958147.003.0003

circles separately for each city. The boundaries (in radius) for each of the 112 cities are depicted using a sub-kilometre distance of concentric circles from the city centre identified and are presented in the Appendix.

The concentric circles for each of the cities in the Appendix in dark black represent the city's boundaries in 1975, and the grey boundaries represent the expanded city boundary in 2015. Ward boundaries are indicated where we had access to the shape files of the cities. The circles for Delhi indicate that the metropolitan area's expansion was more than twofold during 1975–2015, increasing from only a 10-km radius in 1975 to more than a 20-km radius in 2015. Mumbai sprawled over the period as well, as may be seen from the fact that its boundary increased from an 18-km radius in 1975 to a 30-km radius in 2015. Kolkata's sprawl was modest, from a 14.5-km radius in 1975 to a 23.5-km radius in 2015. The capital city of the country's most urbanized state (Tamil Nadu), Chennai, sprawled from an 18-km radius in 1975 to a 30-km radius in 2015.

In Andhra Pradesh, Guntur's radius doubled from 3 km in 1975 to 6 km in 2015. Nellore's boundaries increased a lot more rapidly, from only a 2.1-km radius in 1975 to 7 km in 2015. In Visakhapatnam too, the extent of increase was larger, from 7.2 km in 1975 to nearly 18 km in 2015. However, for Rajahmundry, the extent of increase was smaller, from 3.7 km in 1975 to 7 km in 2015. Vijayawada's as well increased only from 6 km in 1975 to 7.4 km in 2015. So in smaller cities, the extent of increase in expansion was much smaller.

The extent of increase in the boundaries, based on the concentric circles I drew for every kilometre (as explained in Chapter 2), varied across cities in various states. Guwahati (Assam), which Barrington-Leigh and Millard-Ball (2020) observed had a high street disconnectedness index, sprawled greatly based on the concentric circles.[2] The picture for Guwahati in the Appendix shows that its boundaries increased from 5.1 km in 1975 to 15 km in 2015, nearly threefold.

[2] The street disconnectedness index measures the degree to which streets are straight or disconnected. The index includes indicators measuring proportion of circuity, dead ends, etc., and whether the streets are poorly connected with cul-de-sacs and loops. The higher the extent of street disconnectedness the more difficult it is to move around, and the city sprawls. Barrington-Leigh and Millard-Ball (2020) reported that the index was highly correlated with vehicular use, energy consumption, and carbon emissions. They reported that during 1975–2013, about 90% of the 134 most populous countries in the world had their streets grow in a less connected way and therefore they sprawled, making it difficult for them to be serviced by transit.

On the other hand, cities in the less urbanized states did not grow much at all. For instance, Purnia in Bihar did not see any increases in its boundaries (at a 3.5-km radius) during the decades from 1975 to 2015; the case was similar with Bokaro (in Jharkhand) whose area remained constant at a 7-km radius during the four decades. Katihar (Bihar)'s boundary increased from a 2.1-km radius in 1975 to only a 3-km radius in 2015. Dhanbad's (Jharkhand) boundaries expanded from a 7.8-km radius in 1975 to a 10.2-km radius in 2015. Ranchi (Jharkhand) expanded its boundary from a 6-km radius to a 9-km radius over the four decades. Jamshedpur's boundary expanded from a 6-km radius in 1975 to a 9.9-km radius in 2015. However, the least urbanized state Bihar's capital Patna's boundaries doubled from a 6-km radius in 1975 to a 12-km radius in 2015, clearly showing sprawl.

In Madhya Pradesh, a slowly urbanizing state, cities' sprawl was limited. Its capital Bhopal grew its boundary from a 6.3-km radius in 1975 to a 12-km radius in 2015. Gwalior grew only from a 7-km radius to a 9.9-km radius over the period. Indore's growth was greater, where its boundary grew from a 4.5-km to a 12-km radius during the four decades. Jabalpur's growth was similar as it grew from a 4.5-km radius in 1975 to a 9.9-km radius in 2015. Ujjain's as well was modest, from a 4.8-km radius in 1975 to a 7-km radius in 2015.

Chhattisgarh is another less urbanized state, which was carved out of Madhya Pradesh in 2000. Its capital Raipur grew at a scorching pace from only a 3.6-km boundary in 1975 to a nearly 12-km radius in 2015. However, the boundaries of Durg-Bhilai, a twin city in Chhattisgarh, increased from only a 7.3-km radius in 1975 to a 12-km radius in 2015. In the mountainous state of Jammu & Kashmir, Jammu's boundary increased from a 4.4-km radius to a 7-km radius over the period. Srinagar (Jammu and Kashmir)'s boundary expansion was a lot more drastic, from an 8.1-km radius in 1975 to a 15-km radius in 2015, indicating sprawl, even though it was the most compact in 2015 (with the highest population density gradient value).

Odisha is one of the slower-growing and less urbanized states. However, Bhubaneswar, its capital, sprawled, increasing its boundary from a 4.5-km radius in 1975 to an 11.7-km radius in 2015. Even Cuttack's boundaries increased from a modest 6-km radius in 1975 to a 9-km radius in 2015. Rourkela's radius remained constant at 6.2 km during the four decades.

Rajasthan is deemed as another slow-growing state. Nonetheless, Ajmer's boundaries doubled from a 4-km radius in 1975 to an 8-km radius in 2015. Bikaner's boundary radius increased from 4.4 to 9 km over the period. However, the boundary of Jaipur, the capital, expanded only modestly from a 9.3-km to a 12-km radius. Jodhpur expanded from an 8.1-km radius in 1975 to a 12-km radius in 2015. But Kishangarh, a smaller city of 3.6 lakh population, sprawled from a 1.6-km radius to a 7.2-km radius over the period. Kota the coaching town's boundary doubled from an 8.1-km radius in 1975 to a 15-km radius in 2015.

In Uttar Pradesh, the most populous state, which is also one of the least urbanized, cities did not grow very rapidly, limiting their sprawl. Agra increased its boundary from a 5.1-km radius in 1975 to a 9.9-km radius in 2015. Jhansi's boundary expanded from a 4.2-km radius in 1975 to a 6-km radius in 2015. Kanpur's growth was moderate, from a 10.2-km radius in 1975 to a 15-km radius in 2015. Meerut also increased its sprawl moderately, from a 4-km radius in 1975 to a 7-km radius in 2015. Moradabad as well was in the same league, increasing its boundary from a 3.2-km radius in 1975 to a 7-km radius in 2015. Gorakhpur's growth was compact, from a 3.2-km radius in 1975 to a 6-km radius in 2015. Allahabad (now Prayagraj) expanded from a 5-km radius in 1975 to a 7-km radius in 2015. The growth of Bareilly as well was modest, exhibiting a less than twofold increase in its boundary from a 3.6-km radius to a 7-km radius over the four decades. Saharanpur exactly doubled its boundary from a 3-km radius in 1975 to a 6-km radius in 2015. Varanasi, the most suburbanized city as of 2015 based on the density gradient analysis, moderately increased its boundary from a 5-km radius in 1975 to only a 7-km radius in 2015.

Nonetheless, Uttar Pradesh's capital Lucknow more than doubled its boundary size, from a 6.3-km radius in 1975 to a 13.8-km radius in 2015. Aligarh more than doubled its boundary as well, from a 3-km radius in 1975 to a 7-km radius in 2015. Firozabad was one city which increased its boundaries fourfold, from a mere 1.5-km radius in 1975 to a 6-km radius in 2015. Muzaffarnagar tripled its boundaries from a 2-km radius in 1975 to a 6-km radius in 2015. Interestingly, Muzaffarnagar was one of the country's most centralized cities in 1975, based on the density gradient analysis reported next, but sprawled in the next four decades. Ghaziabad in the National Capital Region (of Delhi) sprawled at a scorching pace from a 3.3-km radius in 1975 to a 14.1-km radius in 2015.

Uttarakhand was carved out of populous Uttar Pradesh in 2000. Cities in this hilly state grew moderately. Dehradun, its capital, saw an increase in its boundaries from a 5.1-km radius in 1975 to a 7-km radius in 2015. That is the only city for which I had data in this hilly state.

Nonetheless, some richer cities did not sprawl during the four decades, as we would expect. Chandigarh's boundaries increased from a 4.8-km radius in 1975 to a 6.8-km radius in 2015. Similarly Bhavnagar (in Gujarat, an urbanized state) increased its boundaries from a 5.3-km radius in 1975 to a 7-km radius in 2015. Amravati in urbanized Maharashtra expanded only modestly its boundaries from a 4-km radius in 1975 to a 6-km radius in 2015. The same was the case with Kolhapur, which grew in a compact way from a 4.7-km radius in 1975 to a 6-km radius in 2015, and Sangli, whose boundary increased from a 4.5-km to a 6-km radius over the period. Aurangabad's boundary increased to a greater extent, from a 3.8-km radius to a 9-km radius over the four decades. Solapur moderately sprawled from a 3.2-km radius to an 8-km one during the four decades. Nashik's boundary increased from a 6.3-km radius in 1975 to a 12-km radius in 2015.

However, Bhiwandi in Maharashtra sprawled over the four decades, increasing its boundary from only a 1.95-km radius in 1975 to a whopping 10.8-km radius in 2015. Nagpur's boundary expanded from a mere 6-km radius in 1975 to a 16-km radius in 2015. Pune's sprawl during the four-decade period was also remarkable, its boundary increasing from a 10.2-km radius to a 24-km radius. Nanded-Waghala's boundary expanded threefold, increasing from a mere 1.9-km radius in 1975 to a 6-km radius in 2015. Vasai-Virar sprawled more than fourfold, from a mere 2.15-km radius in 1975 to a 10.2-km radius in 2015. Malegaon's boundary increased threefold, from a 2-km radius in 1975 to a 6-km radius in 2015.

Cities in other urbanized states sprawled a lot as well. In Gujarat, for instance, Ahmedabad's boundaries grew from a 6-km radius in 1975 to a 15-km radius in 2015. Jamnagar's boundaries increased from a 3-km radius in 1975 to a 7-km radius in 2015. Rajkot's boundaries increased from a 4-km radius to a 9-km radius. Similarly, Surat's boundaries grew from a 4.2-km radius in 1975 to a nearly 15.3-km radius in 2015, a whopping more than threefold increase. Vadodara's boundaries expanded from a 5.1-km radius in 1975 to a 12-km radius in 2015, which was more than a twofold increase.

Cities in another urbanized state, Haryana, also sprawled a lot during the study period of four decades. Faridabad's expansion was probably the steepest as its area grew from a radius of only 1.5 km in 1975 to a 15-km radius in 2015. Similar was the case with Gurgaon (now Gurugram) whose area grew from only a 2.1-km radius in 1975 to a 9-km radius in 2015.

In urbanized Punjab, Amritsar's boundary doubled from a 6-km radius in 1975 to a 12-km radius in 2015. Jalandhar's sprawl was less dramatic with an expansion in its boundary from a 4.2-km radius in 1975 to an 8-km radius in 2015. Ludhiana's boundary sprawled from a 3.6-km radius to a 12-km radius over the four decades, representing a more than 3.5-fold increase.

Cities in urbanized West Bengal sprawled. Beyond Kolkata, Asansol's boundary tripled from a 4-km radius in 1975 to a 12-km radius in 2015. Durgapur's growth was moderate, from an 8.4-km radius in 1975 to a 14.1-km radius in 2015. Siliguri, the border town of West Bengal, sprawled at an unprecedented pace, growing from a 2.1-km radius in 1975 to a 13.8-km radius in 2015.

Kerala was one of the most urbanized states as of 2011. Kannur's boundaries sprawled at a spectacular rate from a mere 3.3-km radius in 1975 to a whopping 24-km radius in 2015. So did Kollam's boundaries, from a 3.6-km radius in 1975 to an 18.9-km radius in 2015. Kozhikode's boundary increased from a 7.8-km radius in 1975 to a 24-km radius in 2015, also huge. Thrissur's boundary growth sprawled a lot during the four-decade period, from only a 3-km radius in 1975 to a 23.1-km radius in 2015. However, some cities in the state sprawled less. Modest was the sprawl in Kochi's growth from a 7.2-km radius to a 20.1-km radius over the four decades. Malappuram's boundary grew from a 3.6-km radius in 1975 to a 14.1-km radius in 2015. Unsurprisingly it was one of the most sprawling cities based on the density gradient analysis. Thiruvananthapuram's spatial growth was a lot more modest, from a 6-km radius to a 14.7-km radius over the four decades. It will be seen from the forthcoming density gradient analysis that Thiruvananthapuram's urban form changed from a positive exponential to a negative exponential density function during the four decades, but the city centralized during the period.

Undoubtedly Bengaluru in urbanized Karnataka sprawled, increasing its boundary from only a 7.5-km radius in 1975 to a 16-km radius in 2015, consistent with what was reported by Sridhar (2007). The coastal city Mangaluru's spatial growth was rapid, increasing from a 5.5-km radius in 1975 to a 15-km radius in 2015. However, Hubballi-Dharwad's expansion was modest, from a 6-km radius in 1975 to a 9-km radius in 2015. The same was the case with Mysuru, whose boundary increased from a 3.4-km radius to a 7.2-km radius over the four decades. In Karnataka, of course, Bengaluru is the primate city, accounting for 33% of the state's urbanized population, and it was 10.17 times the size of the next biggest city, Mysuru, in 2019. There is no doubt that Bengaluru's spatial growth was the highest over the four decades. But given Bengaluru's primacy, Mangaluru is set to be the next fastest growing city in the state, based on their spatial growth.

Primate Hyderabad in newly carved Telangana increased its boundaries from an 8-km radius in 1975 to a 14-km radius in 2015; I also note here that Hyderabad was one of the most suburbanized cities in the country as of 1975, based on the forthcoming density gradient analysis. The second biggest city in Telangana, Warangal, tripled its boundaries from a 4-km radius in 1975 to a 12-km radius in 2015.

Puducherry's boundary sprawled from a 3.8-km radius in 1975 to a 7-km radius in 2015. The most urbanized state, Tamil Nadu, saw its cities sprawl in interesting patterns. Coimbatore, the second-biggest city in Tamil Nadu, sprawled from a 9-km radius to a 16-km radius over the four decades. Tiruppur, the textile town, sprawled its boundaries from a 4.7-km radius in 1975 to a 15-km radius in 2015. Vellore saw a more than doubling of its boundary from a 3-km radius in 1975 to a 7-km radius in 2015. Erode exactly doubled its boundary over the four-decade period, from a 4-km radius to an 8-km radius. However, not all cities in the most urbanized state sprawled. For instance, Madurai's boundary increased only from a 6-km radius in 1975 to a 7-km radius in 2015. Similar was the case with Tiruchirappalli, which saw an increase in its boundaries from a 5-km radius in 1975 to a 7-km radius in 2015. Salem's boundary expanded from a 5-km radius to a 12-km radius over the period, recording a more than twofold growth. Tirunelveli as well recorded an increase in its boundary but by less than twofold, from a 4.8-km radius in 1975 to a 9-km radius in 2015. Thus, not all cities in the country's most urbanized state sprawled during the four-decade period, while cities in the lagging states were compact and stable.

The forthcoming section elaborates on the empirical findings from the density gradient analysis, which corroborate those from the concentric circle analysis.

3.2 Analysis of Population Suburbanization

Table 3.1 summarizes the parameter estimates of the population distribution functions (which I interpret for understanding the relative sprawl of a city) for the 100 Indian cities studied (at the grid level) during 1975–2015. The table shows that, even based on the density gradient approach, on average, the typical Indian city sprawled during the four decades of study. This is the case even though the average Indian city's central city population density in 2015 (at 29,893 persons) was higher than that in 1975 (which was at 24,869 persons per sq. km of land area). In 1975, there was a 45% decline in the number of persons per square kilometre of land area with increasing distance from the city centre, whereas in 2015, there was an analogous decrease of only 31% in the typical Indian city, using grid-level data. Hence, the average city's density was declining more gradually and its population density function flattened in 2015. I found 62% of our cities sprawled during the study period, based on grid-level data. It is instructive to note that Sridhar (2007), basing its findings on two-point estimates of the population density gradient, reported as well that Indian cities sprawled during 1981–91. Based on the GHSL data, the maximum population gradient decreased from 0.59 in 1975 to 0.05 in 2015, indicating sprawl, and the (absolute value of the) minimum decreased from 1.69 to 1.25.

However, some cities became more centralized (compact) during the study period (Table 3.1).

Nonetheless, it should be clear that we are concerned only about the cities and towns that are sprawling, not so much about those that are centralized. The condensed cities (those with higher values of the density gradient) are usually the smaller ones.

It is instructive to note that, in 1975, Muzaffarnagar in populous Uttar Pradesh was the most centralized. This is interesting, given its 'disconnected' street network and its street disconnectedness value of 3.41, which encourages cities to sprawl (see Figure 3.1 for Muzaffarnagar's population

Table 3.1 Description of Population Gradients (Grid Level), Indian Cities, 1975–2015

	1975		2015	
Average estimated population density gradient	0.50 (−0.45)*		0.31 (−0.31)*	
Maximum estimated population density gradient	1.69	Muzaffarnagar, Uttar Pradesh	1.25	Katihar, Bihar
Minimum estimated population density gradient	0.00	Guwahati, Assam	0.01	Varanasi, Uttar Pradesh, and Kolhapur, Maharashtra

Sources: Florczyk et al. (2019) and author's analyses.

*This table presents the modulus of the density gradients estimated. In parentheses are the average values for the cities which had negative gradients. In 2015 only 1 city exhibited a positive gradient value; in 1975, 11 cities presented with positive gradient values, out of which 7 cities' gradients were statistically insignificant.

density function). Figure 3.1 shows that the peak of Muzaffarnagar's population density occurred within less than 0.5 km from the city centre (identified as its railroad terminus). Quite in contrast, Guwahati in Assam was the most suburbanized based on the modulus of the gradient (see Figure 3.2 for its population density function). Here, in contrast, the population density in 1975 peaked at a little after 3 km from its centre (railway station).

In 2015, the most sprawling city was Varanasi (Figure 3.3). This is unsurprising and easy to believe, given that it was Prime Minister Modi's electoral constituency in 2014, and it received a lot of infrastructural development, which presumably led to its suburbanization. This finding is consistent with earlier studies that have noted better infrastructure leading to or co-existing with sprawl in various cities across the world. At the end of the study period, Kolhapur (Maharashtra) was the other most sprawling city (Table 3.1 and Figure 3.4), for which one may hold responsible the poor infrastructure in its primary city. This is supported by Chimanna and Kulkarni (2020) who highlighted the sore needs for basic services such as water supply, roads, and municipal transport in central Kolhapur.

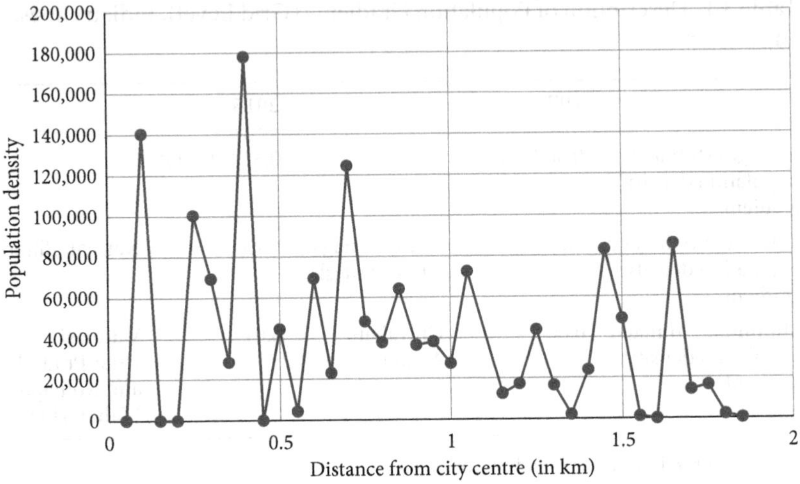

Figure 3.1 Population Density Function, Muzaffarnagar, 1975
Source: Author's analysis based on Florczyk et al. (2019).

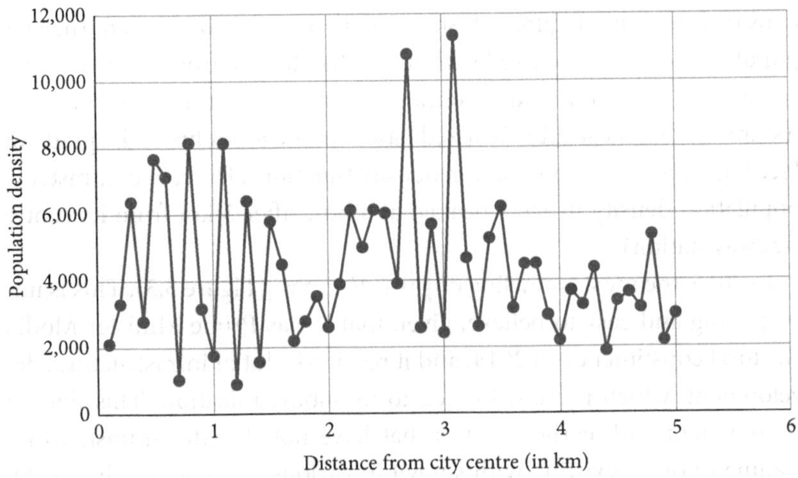

Figure 3.2 Population Density Function, Guwahati, 1975
Source: Author's analysis based on Florczyk et al. (2019).

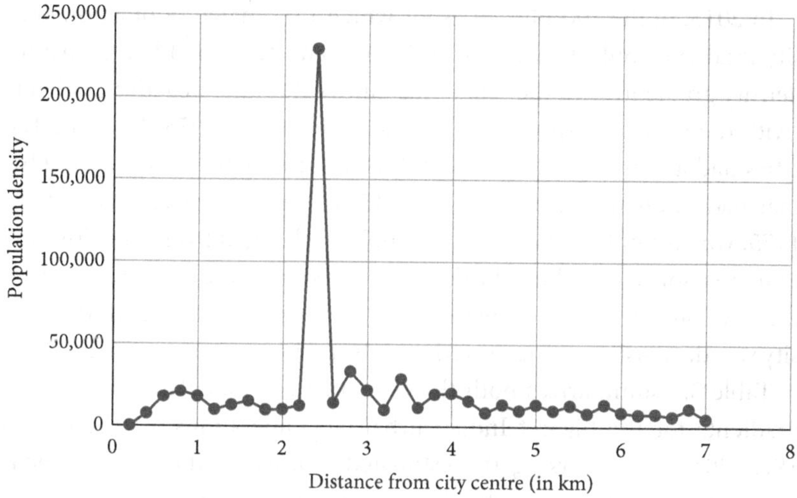

Figure 3.3 Population Density Function, Varanasi, 2015
Source: Author's analysis based on Florczyk et al. (2019).

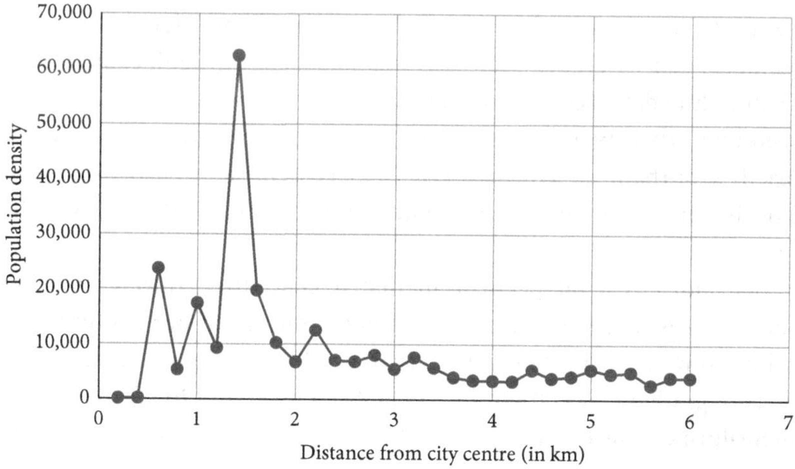

Figure 3.4 Population Density Function, Kolhapur, 2015
Source: Author's analysis based on Florczyk et al. (2019).

In 2015, of the 100-plus cities for which I estimated population density gradients, only 1 (Srinagar in Jammu and Kashmir) had a positive density gradient, with the remaining cities exhibiting negative gradients (with the negative exponential functional form). In 1975, 11 of the 100 cities had a non-negative gradient. It is interesting that a few cities (10) that had gradients below zero in 2015 had non-negative gradients in 1975, which implies that their morphology changed from a positive exponential form—in which the density was rising as one moved away from the city core—in 1975, to a negative exponential one—in which the density was decreasing as one moved away from the city centre—in 2015.[3]

Table 3.2 summarizes both the estimated and calculated population gradients for the biggest Indian urban agglomerations for the period 1975–2015, interspersing the estimated density gradients and calculated ones for 1981 and 1991. Understanding the caveats of *calculated* versus *estimated* density gradients, we see that Delhi has continuously suburbanized since 1981. For 1975 and 2015, I note that Delhi's estimated density gradient was statistically insignificant. The same was the case with Mumbai, Chennai, and Kolkata too: they sprawled over the period 1991–2015, as observed in their decreasing gradient values (Table 3.2). Kolkata's density gradient for 1975 was statistically insignificant, like for Delhi. Ahmedabad centralized during the decade of the 2000s, as may be seen by its density gradients during the period, excepting 2001 when it briefly suburbanized. During 1991–2015, Hyderabad suburbanized with a decline in the modulus of its gradient from −0.30 in 1991 to only −0.06 in 2015.

Bengaluru is a bit peculiar in that it centralized during 1975–81 (based on its *estimated* density gradients), but thereafter continuously suburbanized during 1981–2001. Sridhar (2007) estimated Bengaluru's density gradient in 2001 to be −0.05. Sridhar et al. (2018) found that Bengaluru's density gradient in 2011 ranged from −0.08 to −0.10,

[3] The cities which had a positive gradient in 1975 and a negative gradient in 2015 were Visakhapatnam (in present-day Andhra Pradesh), Rajamahendravaram or Rajahmundry (in present-day Andhra Pradesh), Hyderabad (in newly carved out Telangana), Delhi, Ghaziabad and Meerut (both in Uttar Pradesh), Jalandhar (in Punjab), Surat (in Gujarat), Trivandrum (now Thiruvananthapuram in Kerala), and the erstwhile Calcutta (now Kolkata) (in West Bengal). Srinagar (in Jammu and Kashmir) was the only one which had a non-negative population gradient in both the time periods of study—1975 and 2015.

Table 3.2 Estimated and Calculated Population Gradients, Largest Indian Cities, 1975–2015

City	Estimated population gradient, 1975	Calculated population gradient, 1981	Calculated population gradient, 1991	Calculated population gradient, 2001	Estimated population gradient, 2015
Delhi	0.01Ω	−0.21	−0.17	−0.01	−0.03Ω
Mumbai	−0.07	NA	−0.19	−0.11	−0.08 (−0.01)*
Chennai	−0.16	−0.35	−0.30	−0.28	−0.11
Kolkata	0.02Ω	−0.19	−0.12	−0.11	−0.13
Bengaluru	−0.06Ω	−0.36	0.10 (estimated)◊	−0.05 (estimated)◊	−0.20 (−0.13)*
Ahmedabad	−0.15	NA	−0.29	−0.18	−0.36 (−0.12)*
Hyderabad	0.01Ω	NA	−0.30	−0.26	−0.06 (−0.11)*

Source: Florczyk et al. (2019), Holian and Sridhar (2017), Sridhar (2007), Sridhar et al. (2018), Bertaud and Malpezzi (2003), and author's analyses.

* In brackets are the estimates of population gradients for the respective cities, reported by Bertaud and Malpezzi (2003).

Ω Of no statistical significance in the population density function.

◊ Estimated by Sridhar (2007).

NA: Not available.

depending on the city centre used. Thus, during 2001–11, Bengaluru centralized. It further remained stable or centralized during 2011–15, with a population density gradient of −0.08.

Table 3.2 shows that Chennai and Mumbai were similar in terms of the extent of suburbanization in 2015. In each of these large cities (Chennai and Mumbai), there is an 8% decrease in density per kilometre that one shifts away from the city centre. The smallest of the cities in Table 3.2, Ahmedabad, with a population of 5,600,000 in 2011, is the most compact of all, with a rapid decline of 36% in its density for each kilometre of shift from its centre. The foregoing figures demonstrate the decline in population density in each of these seven largest cities of the country, during 1975–2015.

Figures 3.5 and 3.6 present the population density functions of Mumbai for 1975 and 2015, with density gradients of −0.07 and −0.08, respectively, demonstrating insignificant centralization during the period; however, the curve flattened in 2015. It should be noted that both the

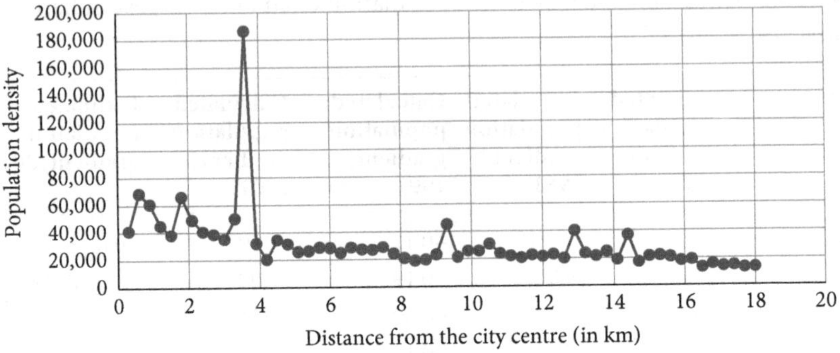

Figure 3.5 Mumbai's Population Density Function, 1975
Source: Author's analysis based on Florczyk et al. (2019).

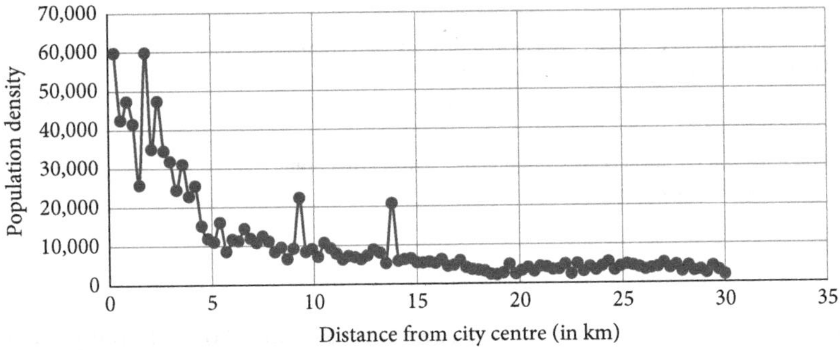

Figure 3.6 Mumbai's Population Density Function, 2015
Source: Author's analysis based on Florczyk et al. (2019).

population density functions for Mumbai for 1975 and 2015 are based on the GHSL (Florczyk et al., 2019).

Figures 3.7 and 3.8 present the density functions for Delhi for 1975 and 2015, respectively, with statistically insignificant gradients of 0.01 (positive) in 1975 and −0.03 in 2015, when estimated at the grid level. This indicates that Delhi had a density function with a positive slope in 1975 and a negative slope in 2015, when estimated at the grid level, implying that its density was growing with proximity to the city edge (centre taken at Sansad Bhavan, the Parliament) in 1975 but declining in 2015; nonetheless, the values are insignificant. Surprisingly, during both years, the R-squared was quite low, with the coefficient being statistically

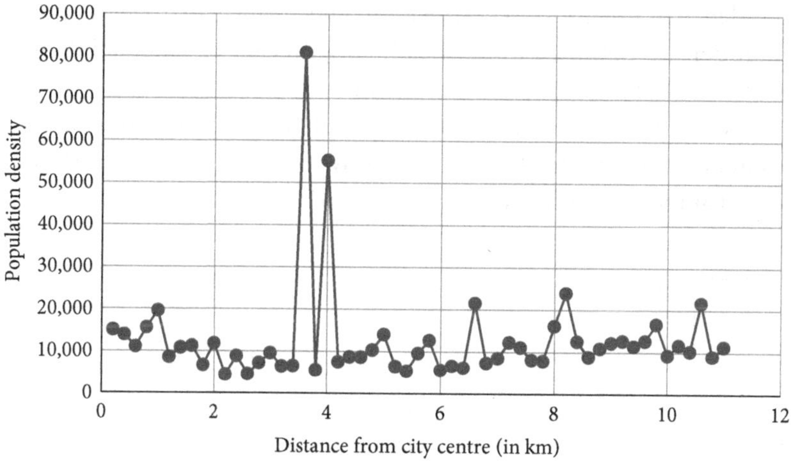

Figure 3.7 Delhi's Population Density Function, Grid-Level, 1975
Source: Author's analysis based on Florczyk et al. (2019).

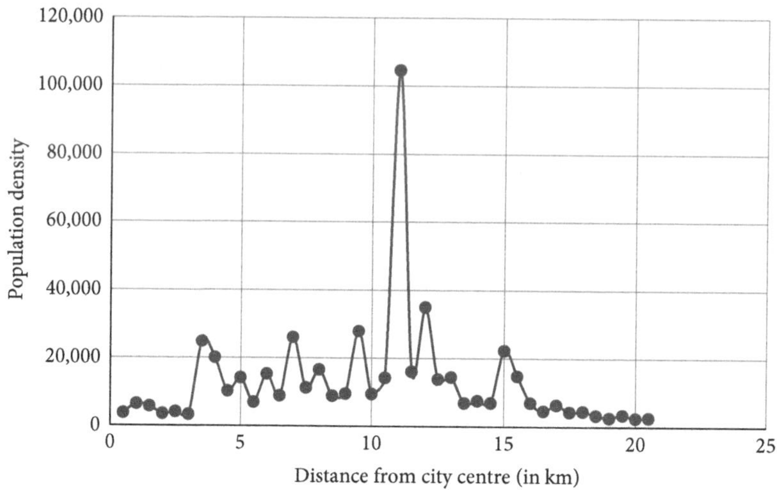

Figure 3.8 Delhi's Population Density Function, Grid-Level, 2015
Source: Author's analysis based on Florczyk et al. (2019).

insignificant. But when estimated at the ward level, Delhi's population density was declining with a 9% reduction as one moved away by 1 km from Sansad Bhavan (in 2011). Given the grid level is more minute and recent (from 2015) than the ward-level data from 2011, I place a lot more confidence in the grid-level estimation, and surmise that Delhi's population density exhibited a statistically insignificant exponential density function in both the time periods of study.

Figures 3.9 and 3.10 present the population density functions for Chennai for 1975 and 2015, respectively, with St. George's Fort considered as the city centre in both time periods.

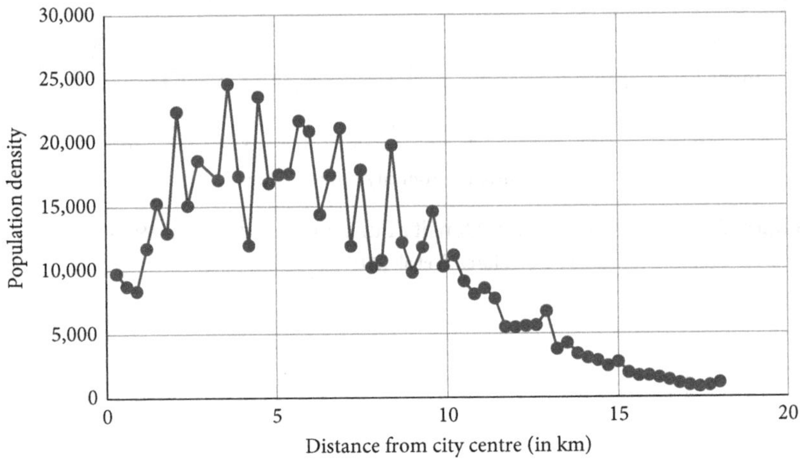

Figure 3.9 Chennai's Population Density Function, 1975
Source: Author's analysis based on Florczyk et al. (2019).

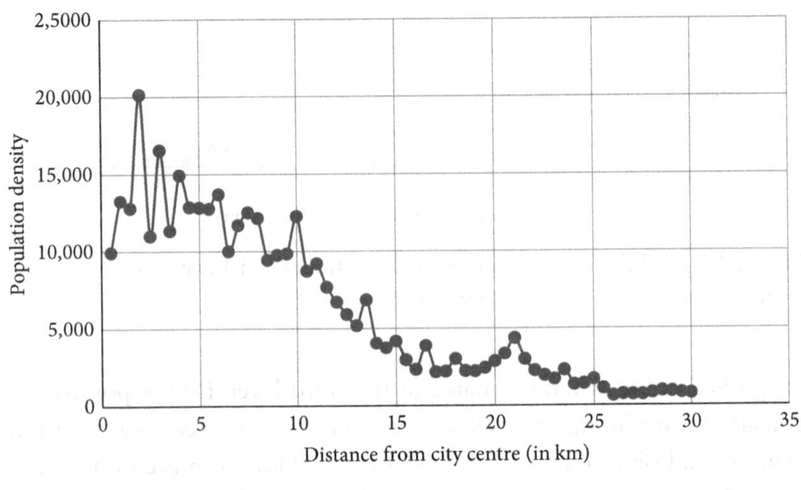

Figure 3.10 Chennai's Population Density Function, 2015
Source: Author's analysis based on Florczyk et al. (2019).

Chennai's population density function clearly flattened during the four decades, as observed in its gradient which declined from −0.16 in 1975 to −0.11 in 2015. This implies that its population density declined only at 11% in 2015, compared with 16% in 1975, per kilometre from the centre.

Figures 3.11 and 3.12 compare the population density functions of another metropolitan city, Kolkata, during 1975–2015.

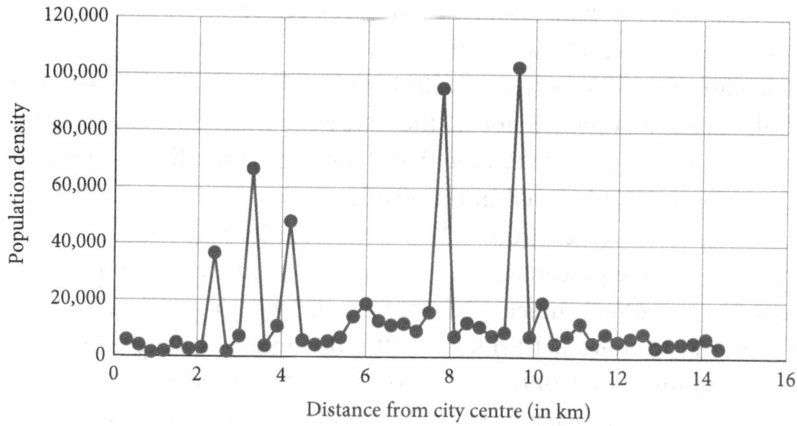

Figure 3.11 Population Density Function, Kolkata, 1975
Source: Author's analysis based on Florczyk et al. (2019).

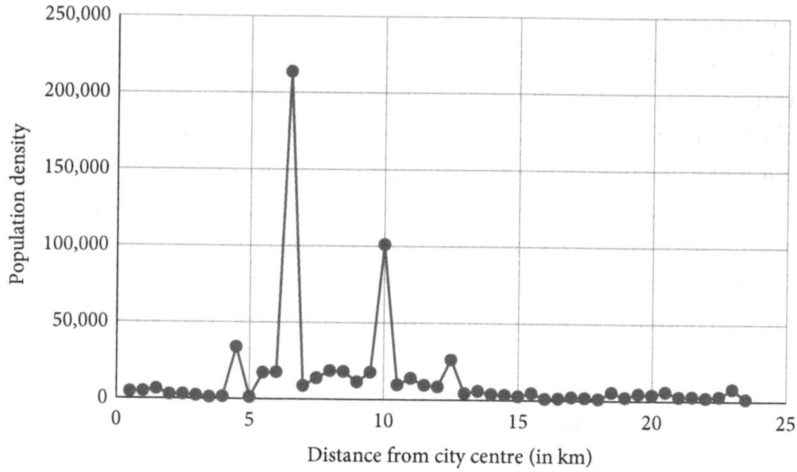

Figure 3.12 Population Density Function, Kolkata, 2015
Source: Author's analysis based on Florczyk et al. (2019).

Kolkata's population density function was positive exponential with a gradient value of 0.02 in 1975 (which was, however, statistically insignificant), indicating a flat density function, implying an increase of population density as one shifted each kilometre from its city core (taken as Bidhan Sabha) (Table 3.2).

In 2015, Kolkata's density function had become negative exponential, although somewhat more centralized, with a density gradient value of −0.05. This means that in 2015, its population density had started to decline more rapidly with distance from its city centre.

Figures 3.13–3.17 show the population density functions for Bengaluru for 1975, 1991, 2001, 2011, and 2015, respectively,[4] assuming Vidhana Soudha (which houses the state government headquarters) as its core. It is instructive to note that Bengaluru centralized during the four decades, as observed in the absolute value of its population gradient which increased from 0.06 in 1975 to 0.20 in 2015. This is true even though the percentage of its suburban population (using a 2-km central city radius) increased from 89% in 1975 to 95% in 2015. It is instructive to note that Sridhar (2007) documented Bengaluru's suburbanization during 1991–2001, estimating its population density gradient, using ward-level data. Further, Sridhar et al. (2018) found that Bengaluru centralized during 2001–11 (with the slope of the density function increasing in modulus from 0.05 to 0.08 during the period), using ward-level data again. Thus, what I find here is consistent with the existing evidence.

Figures 3.18 and 3.19 depict the population density functions of Ahmedabad, for 1975 and 2015, respectively. Ahmedabad is another city which centralized over the four decades, as may be seen in its density gradient value of 0.15 in 1975 having increased in absolute value to 0.36 in 2015. Nonetheless, its suburban population rose from 88% in 1975 to 90% in 2015, using a 2-km radius for the central city.

I compare these gradient values with corresponding ones for global cities, reported by Bertaud and Malpezzi (2003). The study of some

[4] It should be remembered that whereas the 1975 and 2015 density functions for Bengaluru are estimated based on grid-level data from the GHSL, the 1991, 2001, and 2011 density functions for the city are estimated based on ward-level data from the Census.

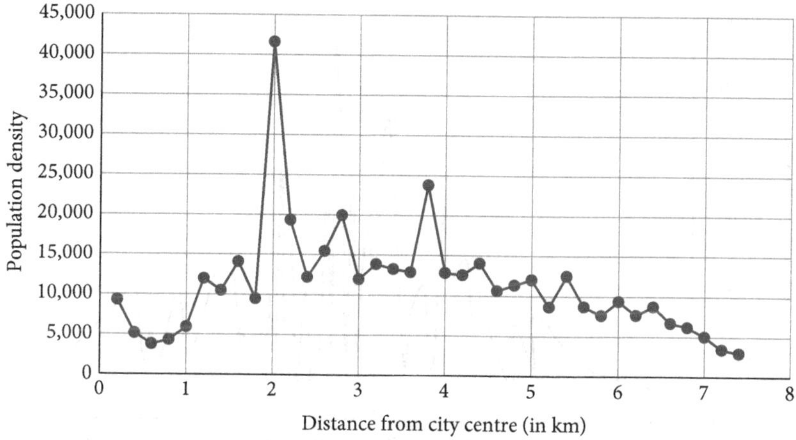

Figure 3.13 Population Density Function, Bengaluru, 1975
Source: Author's analysis based on Florczyk et al. (2019).

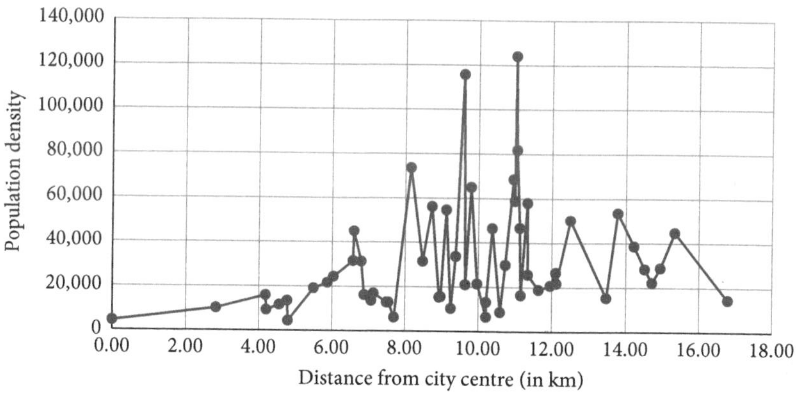

Figure 3.14 Population Density Function, Bengaluru, 1991
Source: Author's analysis based on Census of India (2001).

50 cities in the world by Bertaud and Malpezzi (2003) reported a gradient estimate of only −0.03 for LA in the US, which in absolute value terms is much lower than our gradient estimates for Indian cities. Bertaud and Malpezzi (2003) found a positive slope (0.03) of the population density function for Brasilia, Brazil, also a lot lower in absolute value than the estimates I find here for Indian cities. So, the gradients reported by

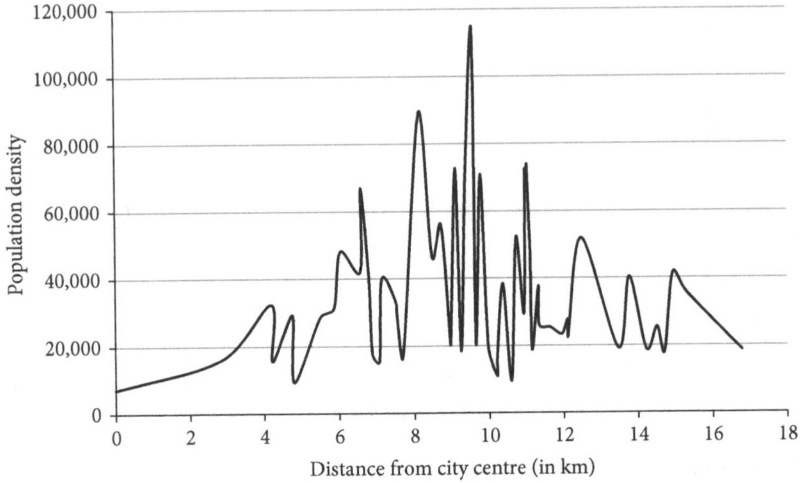

Figure 3.15 Population Density Function, Bengaluru, 2001
Source: Created by the author using data from Sridhar (2007).

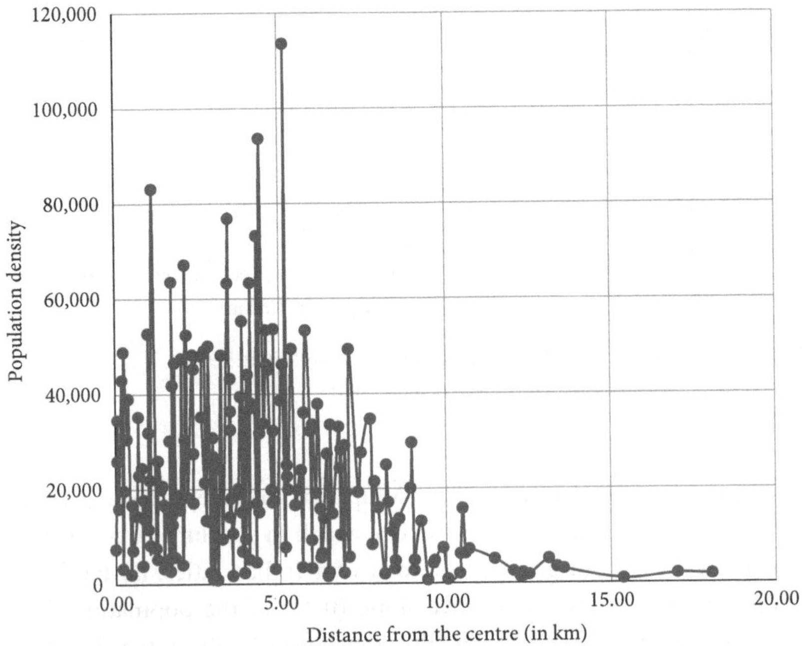

Figure 3.16 Population Density Function, Bengaluru, 2011
Source: Created by the author based on data from BBMP.

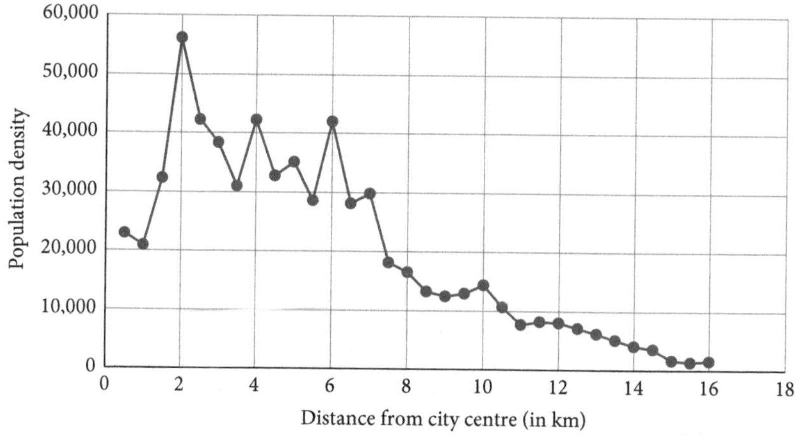

Figure 3.17 Population Density Function, Bengaluru, 2015
Source: Author's analysis based on Florczyk et al. (2019).

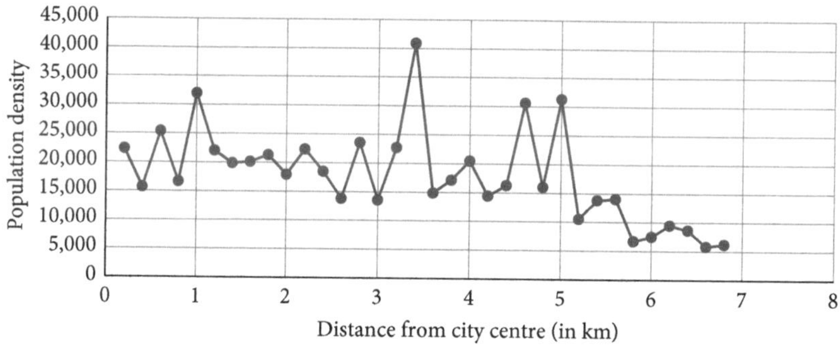

Figure 3.18 Population Density Function, Ahmedabad, 1975
Source: Author's analysis based on Florczyk et al. (2019).

Bertaud and Malpezzi (2003) are much lower than ours for Mumbai, and Ahmedabad, which may have centralized during the time period from 2000 to 2015. Bertaud and Malpezzi's (2003) gradient estimates were higher for Bengaluru and Hyderabad, which have suburbanized significantly recently (Table 3.2).

Hyderabad also suburbanized during 1975–2015, as may be seen in the fact that 93% of its population was already suburban in 1975, which further increased to 97% in 2015, using the same 2-km central city radius

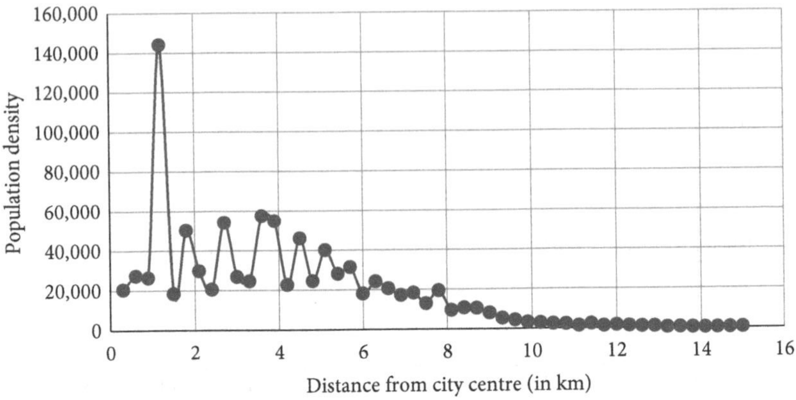

Figure 3.19 Population Density Function, Ahmedabad, 2015
Source: Author's analysis based on Florczyk et al. (2019).

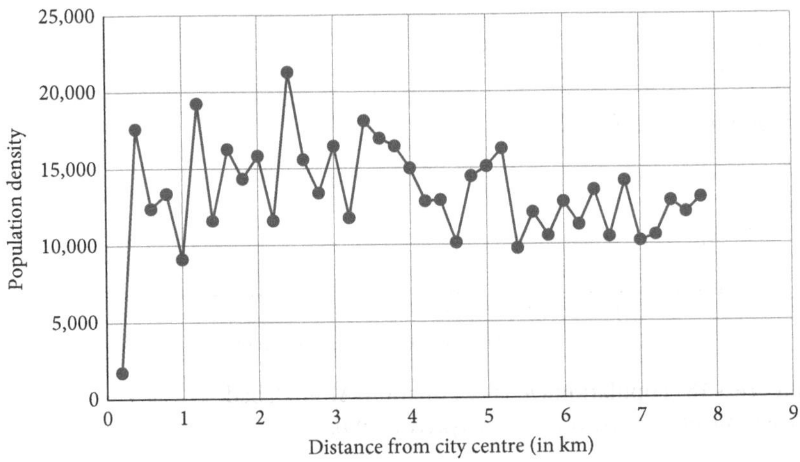

Figure 3.20 Population Density Function, Hyderabad, 1975
Source: Author's analysis based on Florczyk et al. (2019).

in both the years of reference. One interesting observation I note about Hyderabad's population density gradient in 1975 is that it was very flat and positive, meaning that density was then advancing with proximity to the city edge (Figure 3.20). However, in 2015, the city became significantly centralized and had a negative exponential density gradient of −0.33 (Figure 3.21).

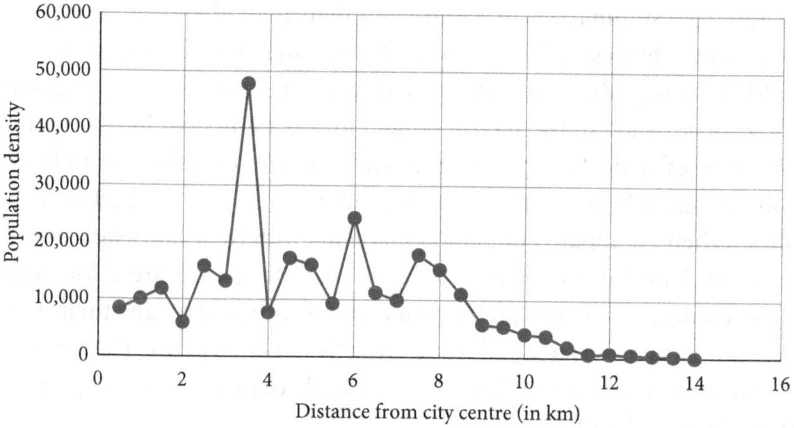

Figure 3.21 Population Density Function, Hyderabad, 2015
Source: Author's analysis based on Florczyk et al. (2019).

3.3 Suburbanization of India's Households

The location decisions of residents in a city are a lot more about families (households) than about individual persons (population). Whereas population refers to the location of individuals across the city, the location of households refers to the location decisions of families. Given I find the population has clearly suburbanized, I seek to understand if India's households have suburbanized too.

As discussed in Chapter 2 on methodology, I have much more limited data available on households as the Census of India did not publish data on land area after 1991, so I depend on cities for which I was able to download shape files from the Internet (https://github.com/HindustanTimesLabs/shapefiles/tree/master/city, accessed 30 April 2020); there were 18 of these, plus some 44 cities in Karnataka (including Bengaluru) for which I obtained shape files from the Karnataka Municipal Data Society (KMDS). Thus, I estimated household density gradients for the 62 cities for which the data were available (see Chapter 2 on methodology for why I was able to estimate household density gradients for only these cities). Nonetheless, using information from Sridhar (2007), I can compare the household density gradients estimated for 1991 with the ones estimated for 2011 for selected cities.

Table 3.3 summarizes the household density gradients during 1991–2011 for the biggest of India's cities, although the caveat is that the household density gradient for 1991 is calculated and the corresponding one for 2011 for each of the metropolitan cities is estimated. Judged by the criterion of a decline in the gradient's (absolute) value, households suburbanized in each of the metropolitan cities during the two decades. When I compare population gradients with their household counterparts, I find households in Kolkata and Bengaluru are a lot more suburbanized than their population counterparts, expressing their preference to use more land and move away from the city core. However, in Delhi, households are a lot more centralized compared with the population (Tables 3.2 and 3.3).

One finds that based on ward-level data on households and their density, Hyderabad was the most suburbanized of all with a negative household density gradient of −0.06 (Table 3.3). The most centralized in terms of households in 2011 were Delhi and Kolkata with an estimated household density gradient of −0.10 each (Table 3.3, Figure 3.22 (Delhi) and Figure 3.23 (Kolkata)).

Figure 3.24 displays the 2011 *household* density function for Hyderabad. It is instructive to observe that the ward-based *population* density function, when estimated, also yields the same value of the density gradient, i.e. −0.06, for the city.

Table 3.3 Suburbanization of India's Households, 1991 and 2011

City	Calculated household density gradient, 1991	Estimated household density gradient, 2011
Delhi	−0.17	−0.10
Mumbai	−0.18	NA
Chennai	−0.29	−0.08
Kolkata	−0.12	−0.10
Bengaluru	−0.37	−0.07
Ahmedabad	−0.28	NA
Hyderabad	−0.27	−0.06

Sources: Census of India 1991, Census of India 2011, https://github.com/HindustanTimesLabs/shapefiles/tree/master/city (accessed 30 April 2020), and author's analyses.

NA: Not available.

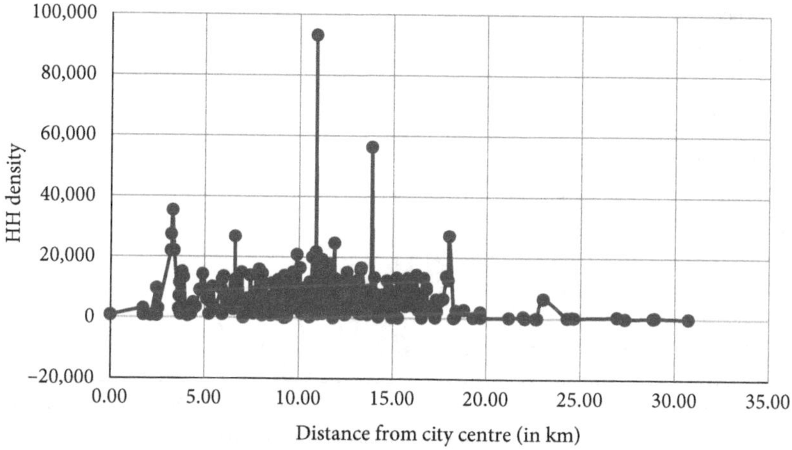

Figure 3.22 Household Density Function, Delhi

Source: Author's analysis based on Census of India (2011) and https://github.com/HindustanTimesLabs/shapefiles/tree/master/city (accessed 30 April 2020).

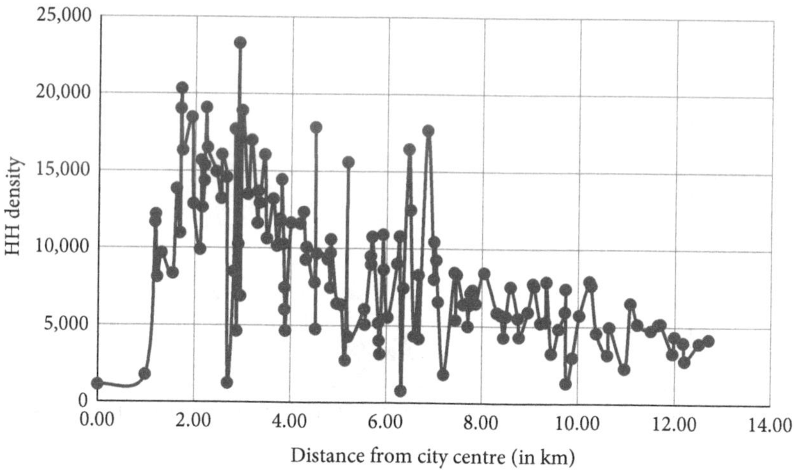

Figure 3.23 Household Density Function, Kolkata

Source: Author's analysis based on Census of India (2011).

Chennai and Bengaluru are in between (Figures 3.25 and 3.26, respectively) with their household density gradient values of −0.08 and −0.07, respectively.

Appendix 3A.1 summarizes and presents the ward-level population density gradient estimates for 2015 and the ones for comparable cities for

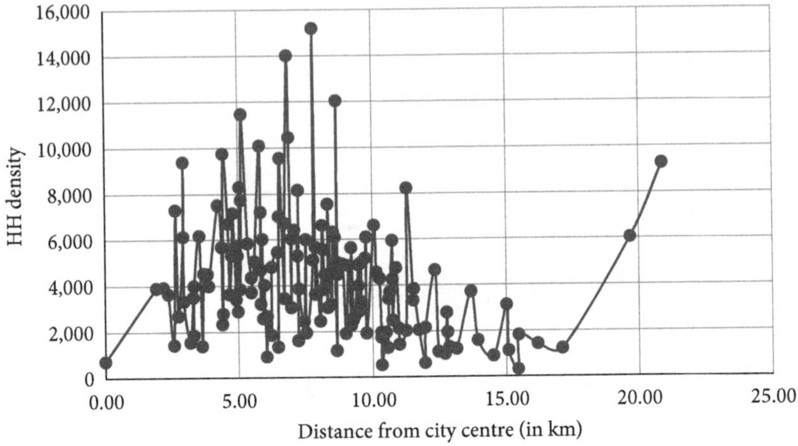

Figure 3.24 Household Density Function, Hyderabad

Source: Author's analysis based on Census of India (2011) and https://github.com/HindustanTimesLabs/shapefiles/tree/master/city (accessed 30 April 2020).

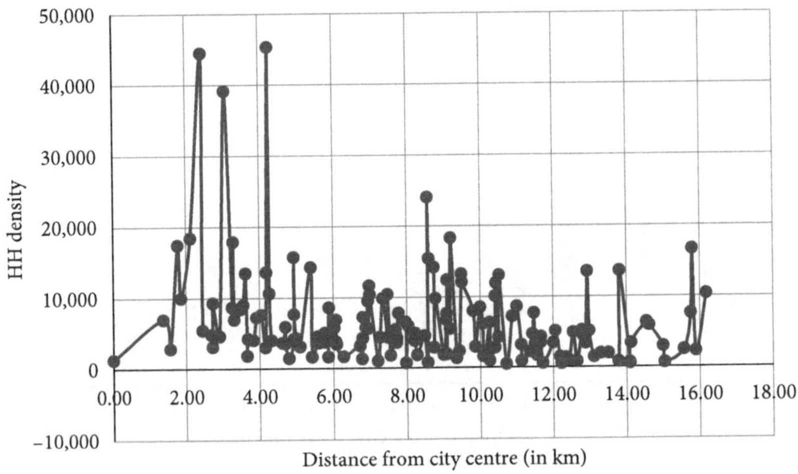

Figure 3.25 Household Density Function, Chennai

Source: Author's analysis based on Census of India (2011).

1991 and 2001 which are calculated using Mills' two-point gradient technique. It should be noted that the 1991 calculated density gradients are from Sridhar (2007) and those from 2001 are from Holian and Sridhar (2017).

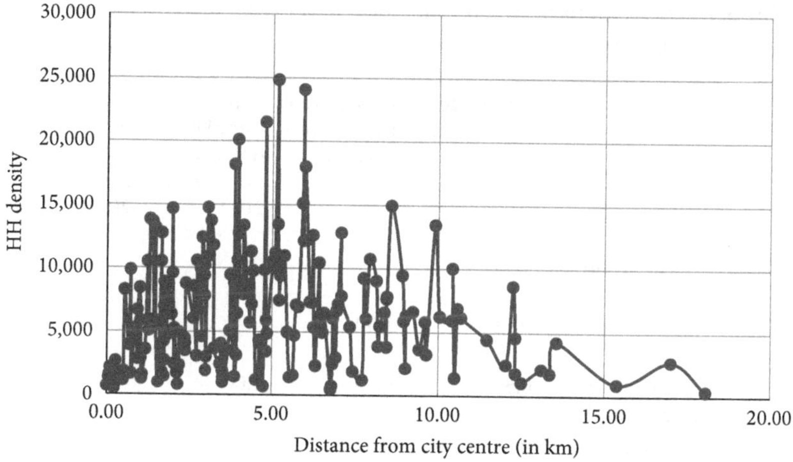

Figure 3.26 Household Density Function, Bengaluru
Source: Author's analysis based on Census of India (2011).

3.4 Are Population and Household Density Gradients Related?

I wanted to understand the extent to which the estimated and calculated population density gradients and household density gradients are related. I computed simple correlations between the calculated population density gradients for 1991 and 2001, along with the ward-level estimated population density gradients (using shape files) and household density gradients for 2011.

Table 3.4 summarizes the correlations. What I find is that the calculated 1991 and 2001 gradients are quite highly correlated as we would expect. This shows the two-point gradient technique works consistently across the same cities for both years. Nonetheless, there is a positive, strong association as well of the 2011 *estimated* population density gradient with the *calculated* (using Mills' two-point technique) density gradient for that year. This shows that even though the two-point technique yields no statistical range for the real value, or statistical significance of the gradient, it correlates quite well with the estimated gradient. It is to be expected that the calculated population density gradient for 2001 correlates a lot better with the 2011 estimated gradient. This shows that the

Table 3.4 Correlations between Calculated and Estimated Population and Household Density Gradients, 1991–2011

	Calculated population gradient, 1991	Calculated population gradient, 2001	Estimated population density gradient, 2011	Estimated household density gradient, 2011
Calculated population gradient, 1991	1.00			
Calculated population gradient, 2001	0.72	1.00		
Estimated population density gradient, 2011	0.53	0.65	1.00	
Estimated household density gradient, 2011	0.53	0.67	1.00	1.00

Sources: Sridhar (2007), Holian and Sridhar (2017), and author's analysis.

urban forms of the cities continuously evolved and in 2001 they were a lot closer to the ones in 2011, even though the gradient in 2001 was calculated and the coefficient in 2011 was estimated.

In fact, the estimated population and household density gradients at the ward level both correlate exactly with a correlation coefficient of 1. This is quite interesting because the urban model is about household location decisions, and it is quite intriguing to note that both population and household location decisions are quite closely related to each other within the city.

This gives us confidence that the calculated and estimated population and household density gradients are consistent, hence they reflect the changing morphology of the cities during 1991–2011.

Sridhar (2007) reported population density gradients for categories of cities, with various combinations of central city vis-à-vis suburban densities. Table 3.5 is an excerpt from Sridhar (2007) which shows that cities characterized by higher central city relative to suburban densities are also the ones which are less suburbanized (using 1991 data). For instance, for cities which had their core density more than 10 times higher than that in the fringes, the density gradient was 0.81. These were highly centralized, compared with cities characterized by their central city

Table 3.5 Population and Household Density Gradients for India's Cities, by Ratio of Central City to Suburban Population Density

	Gradients for UAs with central city's population density:			
	Less than that in fringes	**1–5 times more than that in fringes**	**5–10 times more than that in fringes**	**>10 times that in fringes**
Population gradient, 1991	NA (NA)	0.44 (0.26)	0.64 (0.25)	0.81 (0.09)
Household gradient, 1991	0.02 (0.02)	0.44 (0.25)	0.60 (0.24)	0.80 (0.07)
Population gradient, 1981	0.36 (0.36)	0.48 (0.25)	0.70 (0.24)	0.56 (0.04)

Source: Created by author based on data in Sridhar (2007).
Values in the table are shown as average (standard deviation). NA: Not available.

density being only between 1 and 5 times their suburban density, with an average population density gradient of only 0.44 and much more suburban. The story is similar with the household density gradients. This strongly implies that high central city densities are associated with compact cities. Alternatively, cities having low central city densities are those which are excessively suburbanized. For instance, cities characterized by their core density being lower than that in their peripheries had on average a density gradient of their households at only 0.02. This strongly suggests that if we want to encourage compact cities, then high central densities in terms of both population and employment (Table 3.6) should be incentivized.

Sun et al. (2022) found that constructing robust city centres is a superior mechanism to advance growth in the smaller cities in their nascent phases of progress. In this context, I note that most central cities in the US are active during the workday but fall dead once the workday is over. This led to a movement backing a move back to the central city (Voith, 1992). Lin (2014) clarified that suburbanization did not weaken the core in Chinese cities in the manner it rendered the US city centres ineffective, because city centres gained greater autonomy in the Asian giant when sprawl was happening. Further, the city core in the Asian country persisted to provide a good quality of living and employment chances, even

Table 3.6 Population and Household Density Gradients for India's Cities, by Ratio of Central City to Suburban Employment Density

	Gradients for cities with core city job density			
	Less than that in fringes	**1–5 times more than that in fringes**	**5–10 times more than that in fringes**	**>10 times that in fringes**
Population gradient, 1991	0.10 (0.13)	0.45 (0.26)	0.65 (0.26)	0.79 (0.09)
Household gradient, 1991	0.19 (0.36)	0.44 (0.25)	0.62 (0.26)	0.78 (0.07)
Population gradient, 1981	0.37 (0.35)	0.49 (0.26)	0.69 (0.26)	0.56 (0.04)

Source: Created by author based on data in Sridhar (2007).
Values in the table are shown as average (standard deviation).

with suburbanization. However, worldwide, the Covid pandemic of 2020 accelerated the move towards de-densification of cities and encouraged workers to move away from central cities, towards suburbs and smaller cities (see Peiser and Hugel (2022); Ramani and Bloom (2021) for the effect of Covid-19 on cities in the US). Sridhar and Monkkonen (2024) find that Indian cities suburbanized but at the same densified their city centres during the 1975–2015 period. But in general, all Indian urban policy boils down to the simple rule of decreasing 'central city congestion' as Bertaud (2018) points out. I comment more on this in Chapter 6 which focuses on the explanation for suburbanization.

3.5 Summary and Conclusions

This chapter has tried to address the research question of whether India's population and households have suburbanized. The answer, based on concentric rings, analysis of population, and household density gradients, is a resounding yes. Indian cities have sprawled in terms of their boundaries predicted based on concentric circles I have drawn around an identified city centre. Further, population and households have also decentralized towards the suburbs. Furthermore, population and household suburbanization are also highly and positively correlated. Although the earlier evidence was that compact cities are those which are characterized by higher central city densities, recent evidence shows that Indian cities are increasing their central city density and suburbanizing at the same time, just as Sridhar and Monkkonen (2024) find. One way to encourage compact growth is to further increase central city densities by improving central city infrastructure. I have more to say on this in Chapter 7 where I elaborate on regulations governing land use and land cover in the country's urban areas.

Appendix 3A.1 Summary of Calculated and Estimated Population and Household Density Gradients, Selected Indian Cities

Number	State	Urban agglomeration/ city	Calculated population gradient, 1991	Calculated population gradient, 2001	Estimated population density gradient, 2015	Estimated population gradient, 1975	HH density gradient, 2011
1	Andhra Pradesh	Guntur UA	NA	NA	−0.57	−0.57	NA
2	Andhra Pradesh	Greater Visakhapatnam (MC)	−0.46	−0.23	−0.13	0.03	NA
3	Andhra Pradesh	Nellore UA	NA	NA	−0.44	−0.98	NA
4	Andhra Pradesh	Rajahmundry UA	−0.35	−0.10	−0.32	0.03	NA
5	Andhra Pradesh	Vijayawada	−0.55	−0.60	−0.42	−0.52	−0.11
6	Assam	Guwahati UA	NA	NA	−0.27	−0.0049	NA
7	Bihar	Patna UA	−0.13	−0.12	−0.30	−0.33	NA
8	Bihar	Katihar	NA	NA	−1.25	−1.48	−0.60
9	Bihar	Purnia	−0.36	−0.49	−0.32	−0.37	−0.05
10	Bihar	Bodh Gaya	NA	NA	−0.38	NA	−0.38
11	Chhattisgarh	Durg-Bhilai UA	−0.12	−0.17	−0.19	−0.27	NA
12	Chhattisgarh	Raipur UA	−0.60	−0.18	−0.36	−0.31	NA
13	Delhi	Delhi	−0.17	−0.01	−0.03	0.01	−0.10
14	Gujarat	Ahmedabad UA	−0.29	−0.18	−0.36	−0.15	NA
15	Gujarat	Bhavnagar UA	−0.14	NA	−0.35	−0.19	NA
16	Gujarat	Jamnagar UA	−0.95	−0.77	−0.38	−0.30	NA
17	Gujarat	Rajkot UA	−0.87	NA	−0.33	−0.30	NA
18	Gujarat	Surat UA	NA	−0.29	−0.16	0.55	NA

19	Gujarat	Vadodara UA	−0.70	−0.58	−0.32	−0.08	NA
20	Haryana	Gurgaon UA	NA	−0.74	−0.11	−1.14	NA
21	Haryana	Faridabad	NA	NA	−0.35	−1.11	−0.02
22	Haryana	Chandigarh	NA	NA	−0.07	−0.03	0.19
23	Jammu and Kashmir	Jammu UA	NA	−0.33	−0.27	−0.37	NA
24	Jammu and Kashmir	Srinagar UA	NA	−0.28	0.05	0.59	NA
25	Jharkhand	Bokaro Steel City UA	NA	NA	−0.34	−0.37	NA
26	Jharkhand	Dhanbad UA	−0.14	NA	−0.31	−0.37	NA
27	Jharkhand	Jamshedpur UA	−0.27	NA	−0.39	−0.27	NA
28	Jharkhand	Ranchi UA	−0.03	NA	−0.38	−0.39	NA
29	Karnataka	Bengaluru	−0.38	−0.26	−0.20	−0.06	−0.07
30	Karnataka	Mangaluru	−0.25	−0.07	−0.12	−0.22	0.12
31	Karnataka	Hubballi-Dharwad (MC)	NA	NA	−0.60	−0.95	−0.06
32	Karnataka	Mysuru	−0.44	−0.69	−0.21	−0.47	−0.56
33	Karnataka	Karwar	NA	NA	−0.06	−1.16	−0.06
34	Karnataka	Ilkal	NA	NA	−2.14	−2.53	−2.16
35	Karnataka	Ramanagaram	NA	NA	−1.08	−3.96	−1.08
36	Karnataka	Belagavi	NA	NA	0.09	−1.29	0.10
37	Karnataka	Davanagere	NA	NA	−0.96	−1.69	−0.95
38	Karnataka	Bellary	NA	NA	−0.87	−0.50	−0.88
39	Karnataka	Vijayapura	NA	NA	−0.52	0.36	−0.52

(continued)

Appendix 3A.1 Continued

Number	State	Urban agglomeration/ city	Calculated population gradient, 1991	Calculated population gradient, 2001	Estimated population density gradient, 2015	Estimated population gradient, 1975	HH density gradient, 2011
40	Karnataka	Shivamogga	NA	NA	−0.81	−0.41	−0.81
41	Karnataka	Tumakuru	NA	NA	−0.42	−2.92	−0.41
42	Karnataka	Bidar	NA	NA	−0.61	−1.35	−0.57
43	Karnataka	Raichur	NA	NA	−1.06	−1.18	−1.01
44	Karnataka	Kalaburagi	NA	NA	−0.51	−0.69	−0.53
45	Kerala	Kannur UA	−0.20	−0.09	−0.09	−0.15	NA
46	Kerala	Kochi UA	−0.20	−0.15	−0.12	−0.08	NA
47	Kerala	Kollam UA	NA	NA	−0.18	−0.06	NA
48	Kerala	Kozhikode UA	−0.18	0.01	−0.13	−0.18	NA
49	Kerala	Malappuram UA	NA	0.02	−0.04	−0.44	NA
50	Kerala	Thiruvananthapuram UA	−0.13	NA	−0.19	0.15	NA
51	Kerala	Thrissur UA	−0.20	0.31	−0.09	−0.19	NA
52	Madhya Pradesh	Gwalior UA	−0.05	−0.19	−0.54	−0.83	NA
53	Madhya Pradesh	Indore UA	−0.80	−0.45	−0.32	−0.42	NA
54	Madhya Pradesh	Jabalpur UA	−0.30	−0.37	−0.42	−0.29	NA
55	Madhya Pradesh	Ujjain (MC)	−0.45	NA	−0.51	−1.18	NA
56	Madhya Pradesh	Bhopal	NA	NA	−0.28	−0.24	−0.26

57	Maharashtra	Amravati (MC)	NA	NA	−0.43	−0.71	NA
58	Maharashtra	Aurangabad UA	−0.27	−0.40	−0.33	−0.08	NA
59	Maharashtra	Bhiwandi UA	−0.58	−0.51	−0.16	−0.95	NA
60	Maharashtra	Greater Mumbai UA	−0.19	−0.11	−0.08	−0.07	NA
61	Maharashtra	Kolhapur UA	NA	1.50	−0.01	−0.52	NA
62	Maharashtra	Malegaon UA	NA	NA	−1.09	−1.24	NA
63	Maharashtra	Nagpur UA	−0.24	−0.11	−0.25	−0.28	NA
64	Maharashtra	Nanded-Waghala (MC)	NA	NA	−0.61	−1.47	NA
65	Maharashtra	Nashik UA	−0.21	−0.29	−0.34	−0.44	NA
66	Maharashtra	Pune UA	−0.23	−0.03	−0.20	−0.19	NA
67	Maharashtra	Sangli UA	−0.26	0.07	−0.52	−0.98	NA
68	Maharashtra	Solapur (MC)	NA	NA	−0.50	−0.07	NA
69	Maharashtra	Vasai-Virar City (MC)	−0.36	−0.26	−0.16	−1.16	NA
70	Odisha	Cuttack UA	−0.36	−0.35	−0.35	−0.50	NA
71	Odisha	Rourkela UA	NA	NA	−0.31	−0.48	NA
72	Odisha	Bhubaneswar	NA	NA	−0.32	−0.50	−0.15
73	Puducherry	Puducherry UA	−0.46	−0.33	−0.51	−0.48	NA
74	Punjab	Amritsar UA	NA	NA	−0.23	−0.15	NA
75	Punjab	Jalandhar UA	NA	NA	−0.25	0.01	NA
76	Punjab	Ludhiana (MC)	NA	NA	−0.24	−0.18	NA
77	Rajasthan	Ajmer UA	NA	−0.27	−0.42	−1.53	NA
78	Rajasthan	Bikaner (MC)	NA	NA	−0.48	−0.66	NA

(*continued*)

Appendix 3A.1 Continued

Number	State	Urban agglomeration/ city	Calculated population gradient, 1991	Calculated population gradient, 2001	Estimated population density gradient, 2015	Estimated population gradient, 1975	HH density gradient, 2011
79	Rajasthan	Jodhpur UA	NA	NA	−0.35	−0.57	NA
80	Rajasthan	Kota (MC)	NA	−0.15	−0.20	−0.05	NA
81	Rajasthan	Jaipur	−0.24	NA	−0.13	−0.34	−0.20
82	Rajasthan	Kishangarh	NA	NA	−0.51	−1.48	−0.71
83	Tamil Nadu	Erode UA	−0.90	−0.78	−0.29	−0.82	NA
84	Tamil Nadu	Salem UA	−0.78	−0.47	−0.28	−0.07	NA
85	Tamil Nadu	Tirunelveli UA	−0.43	−0.54	−0.35	−1.19	NA
86	Tamil Nadu	Tiruppur UA	−0.56	−0.68	−0.30	−0.74	NA
87	Tamil Nadu	Vellore UA	−0.89	−0.82	−0.35	−0.87	NA
88	Tamil Nadu	Chennai	−0.30	−0.28	−0.11	−0.16	−0.08
89	Tamil Nadu	Coimbatore	−0.40	−0.32	−0.16	−0.15	−0.16
90	Tamil Nadu	Madurai	−0.84	−0.61	−0.39	−0.73	−0.24
91	Tamil Nadu	Tiruchirappalli	−0.64	−0.25	−0.39	−0.31	−0.24
92	Telangana	Warangal UA	NA	NA	−0.27	−1.01	NA
93	Telangana	Hyderabad	−0.30	−0.26	−0.33	0.01	−0.06
94	Uttar Pradesh	Agra UA	−0.36	−0.47	−0.18	−0.12	NA
95	Uttar Pradesh	Aligarh UA	NA	NA	−0.59	−0.64	NA
96	Uttar Pradesh	Allahabad UA	−0.79	−1.03	−0.19	−0.38	NA

97	Uttar Pradesh	Bareilly UA	−0.48	−0.52	−0.32	−0.83	NA
98	Uttar Pradesh	Firozabad (NPP)	NA	−0.56	−0.55	−1.13	NA
99	Uttar Pradesh	Ghaziabad UA	−0.16	NA	−0.15	0.56	NA
100	Uttar Pradesh	Gorakhpur UA	NA	NA	−0.32	−0.14	NA
101	Uttar Pradesh	Jhansi UA	−0.65	−0.91	−0.32	−0.27	NA
102	Uttar Pradesh	Kanpur UA	−0.11	−0.18	−0.25	−0.35	NA
103	Uttar Pradesh	Meerut UA	−0.23	−0.34	−0.11	0.13	NA
104	Uttar Pradesh	Moradabad (MC)	−0.36	NA	−0.54	−1.21	NA
105	Uttar Pradesh	Muzaffarnagar UA	NA	NA	−0.61	−1.69	NA
106	Uttar Pradesh	Saharanpur (MC)	NA	NA	−0.59	−1.23	NA
107	Uttar Pradesh	Varanasi UA	−0.39	−0.32	−0.01	−0.24	NA
108	Uttar Pradesh	Lucknow	−0.25	−0.27	−0.22	−0.29	−0.13
109	Uttarakhand	Dehradun UA	−0.58	−0.57	−0.35	−1.05	NA
110	West Bengal	Asansol UA	−0.37	−0.07	−0.27	−0.26	NA
111	West Bengal	Durgapur UA	NA	NA	−0.15	−0.21	NA
112	West Bengal	Siliguri UA	NA	NA	−0.32	−0.67	NA
113	West Bengal	Kolkata	−0.12	−0.11	−0.05	0.02	−0.10
		Average	**−0.39**	**−0.30**	**−0.31**	**−0.45**	**−0.17**
		Max	**−0.03**	**1.50**	**0.05**	**0.59**	**0.19**
		Min	**−0.95**	**−1.03**	**−1.25**	**−1.69**	**−0.71**
		Number of observations	**62**	**61**	**100**	**100**	**21**

Sources: Author's analysis based on Sridhar (2007), Holian and Sridhar (2017), Census of India (2001), and Florczyk et al. (2019).

NA: Not available.

4

Regional Variations in Population Suburbanization

4.1 National Variations in Suburbanization across Regions

India is a very diverse country and there are substantial differences in income, level of public services, and access to assets across various regions of the country. Paul and Sridhar (2015) demonstrated these differences between the south and north Indian states over several decades, concluded that there was a dramatic transformation and turnaround in the economic growth of the south Indian states, and attempted to explain the same. In fact, Drèze and Sen (1997) pointed out that if the same rates of economic growth continued in the Indian states, there would be a situation when certain northern states would become similar to Sub-Saharan Africa, and the fast-growing states would become like the East Asian tigers—Singapore and Taiwan. This, they cautioned, would lead to an eventual fault line between the divergent set of states in the country. Paul and Sridhar (2015) further demonstrated the dramatic transformation of the south Indian states when compared with their northern counterparts over their study period of several decades and probed the factors leading to the economic disparities between them.

There are reasons to believe that the population density gradients and urban form may also follow a similar pattern, and be different in states located in different parts of the country when these are classified by income and their urbanization status, as various studies have demonstrated. As per the classification used by existing studies (e.g. Paul & Sridhar, 2015), the south of India (Andhra Pradesh, Kerala, Karnataka, Tamil Nadu, and Telangana) started growing much faster during the decade of the 1990s

Indian Cities or Suburbs? Kala Seetharam Sridhar, Oxford University Press. © Kala Seetharam Sridhar 2025.
DOI: 10.1093/9780198958147.003.0004

Table 4.1 Summary Statistics, Estimated Population Gradients, Grid Level, 1975–2015, South Indian Cities

	1975		2015	
Average	−0.40		−0.22	
Maximum	0.15	Thiruvananthapuram, Kerala	−0.19	Thiruvananthapuram, Kerala
Minimum	−1.19	Tirunelveli, Tamil Nadu	−0.60	Hubballi-Dharwad, Karnataka

Sources: Florczyk et al. (2019) and author's analyses.

when compared with their northern counterparts[1] which have been termed as lagging. Because of this, I examined population gradients for metropolitan areas in the southern states (Table 4.1) and those in the lagging regions (Table 4.2).

Table 4.1 shows that like their all-India counterparts (presented in Table 3.1, Chapter 3), the south Indian cities suburbanized, with their average population gradient (modulus) reducing significantly during the four decades from 0.40 to only 0.22. Not only this, I also note that the south Indian cities are much more sprawling, when benchmarked against all Indian cities during both years, as may be seen in the lower value of the population density gradient in both decades of the study period. The (absolute) value of the population density gradient was 0.50 for all India when compared with only 0.40 for cities in the south in 1975, and 0.31 for cities in the entire country, as opposed to only 0.22 for south Indian cities, in 2015.

When I consider the modulus of the population gradients, the most sprawling city in the south was Hyderabad in 1975 (with an absolute value of 0.01 for its density gradient), in the former Andhra Pradesh. Haynes (2020) describes the continuous increase in Hyderabad's urban built-up area from only 35 sq. km in 1930 to 51 sq. km in 1975, indicating its sprawl. Quite in contrast, in 2015, Malappuram (in the most urbanized state, Kerala), which had an absolute value of 0.04 for its density

[1] These are Bihar, Chhattisgarh, Jharkhand, Madhya Pradesh, Odisha, Rajasthan, Uttar Pradesh, and Uttarakhand.

Table 4.2 Description of Estimated Population Density Gradients, 1975–2015, Cities of Lagging States

	1975		2015	
Average	−0.57		−0.37	
Maximum	0.56	Ghaziabad, Uttar Pradesh	−0.01	Varanasi, Uttar Pradesh
Minimum	−1.69	Muzaffarnagar, Uttar Pradesh	−1.25	Katihar, Bihar

Source: Florczyk et al. (2019) and author's analyses.

gradient, was the most suburbanized of all the cities considered. This is consistent with the evidence from its concentric circles analysis reported in Chapter 3, where I documented that this city's radius increased from a mere 3.6-km radius in 1975 to a 14.1-km radius in 2015. As per a survey published by the Economist Intelligence Unit in 2020, Malappuram, with its urban growth at 44% between 2015 and 2020, was the fastest-growing city in the world, hence its sprawl is to be expected.

Certain cities in the south became centralized during the study period, as made evident by the rise in the maximum gradient (absolute) value (for Thiruvananthapuram, from 0.15 in 1975 to 0.19 in 2015, see Table 4.1). Nonetheless, the lowest value of the gradient somewhat rose over the period (from −1.19 for Tirunelveli in Tamil Nadu in 1975, to −0.60 for Hubballi-Dharwad in Karnataka in 2015), showing compactness in cities of the south. However, the modulus of the minimum density gradient for the south Indian cities during the four-decade period decreased from 1.19 to 0.60, showing sprawl and decentralization.

Conversely, what is the situation with the lagging states (see Paul & Sridhar, 2015),[2] termed BIMARUO here? Table 4.2 summarizes this for the states of Bihar, Chhattisgarh, Jharkhand, Madhya Pradesh, Odisha, Rajasthan, Uttar Pradesh, and Uttarakhand whose per capita incomes have been increasing more slowly than that of the all-India average.

[2] It should be mentioned that Paul and Sridhar (2015) did not include Odisha in the list of lagging regions; here it is included as its indicators such as per capita income strongly suggest this.

The expectations are right. As summarized by Table 4.2, cities in the lagging regions of the country are characterized by compactness when compared with the all-India average, as may be seen in their average density gradient which as early as 1975 was −0.57 as opposed to −0.45 for all cities. Even for the most recent year, 2015, cities in the slow-growing parts of the country had a higher gradient (in absolute value terms) of 0.37 as opposed to the corresponding value (0.31) for all cities. Not only this, but during 1975–2015, the highest gradients for urban areas in the slow-growing states also declined to a mere −0.01 (for Varanasi in Uttar Pradesh) from a high of 0.56 (for Ghaziabad in the same state in 1975), and the minimum declined from −1.69 to only −1.25, making the BIMARUO states in both 1975 and 2015 those with the most suburbanized and centralized cities in the country. So, I note that even the cities in the lagging regions suburbanized during the four decades as observed in the modulus of their population gradient decreasing from 0.57 in 1975 to 0.37 in 2015.

Why do we observe compact urbanization in the lagging regions compared with their more urbanized counterparts? One reason is that these are low-urbanization states, hence the centre of their large cities is well developed, thus they are compact. Another reason could be that these low-income states are not particularly effective with their public service delivery in peripheral areas, hence they remain less developed. So, population density also is confined to the city core.

Our expectation was that cities in the urbanized states would be more efficient in managing their sprawl, hence such states would have higher values of the population density gradient and more compact cities. This expectation is however not correct, as summarized in Table 4.3. First, urban areas in the developed states sprawled too, like the other cities, as observed in their decreasing population gradient during 1975–2015 on average. Next, benchmarked against all Indian cities, their counterparts in the more developed regions continue to be sprawling and decentralized (with a gradient estimate of −0.26 compared with −0.30 for all Indian cities in 2015, and −0.40 as opposed to an estimate of −0.45 for all cities in the country in 1975). This is plausible as the biggest metropolitan areas of the country—Mumbai, Kolkata, Delhi, and Bengaluru—are in urbanized states. Large cities sprawl by definition as I explain in Chapter 7.

Table 4.3 Estimated Population Gradients, 1975 and 2015, Cities of Urbanized States

	1975		2015	
Average	−0.40		−0.26	
Maximum	0.55	Surat, Gujarat	−0.19	Thiruvananthapuram, Kerala
Minimum	−1.47	Nanded-Waghala, Maharashtra	−1.09	Malegaon, Maharashtra

Sources: Florczyk et al. (2019) and author's analyses.

4.2 Suburbanization of Karnataka's Cities

In this section, I first summarize, in the aggregate, the suburbanization of all cities in Karnataka (excluding Bengaluru). This is followed by a detailed description and analysis of the suburbanization of Bengaluru. Bengaluru is the capital city of Karnataka, its primate city, and has grown by leaps and bounds, hence its study undoubtedly deserves attention. I then elaborate on the suburbanization of the biggest 11 cities in Karnataka, many of which are based on ward-level information provided by the Karnataka Municipal Data Society (KMDS) for 2011. In addition, I also rely on the GHSL 1975 dataset for these cities. Following this, I focus on the suburbanization of Kalaburagi in Karnataka, documented by Sridhar and Narayanan (2016). While the importance of Kalaburagi in northern Karnataka is explained in detail later, I highlight that this is a part of what is called Kalyana Karnataka, which is one of the state's backward regions, adjoining the Hyderabad-Karnataka region, hence its study deserves special importance.

Table 4.4 first summarizes in the aggregate these estimates of population and household gradients for cities in Karnataka excluding those for Bengaluru, given Bengaluru is the primate city, whose population is disproportionately large when compared with that of the next largest city, Mysuru, as already explained in Chapter 3. So, Bengaluru is a large city, and we cannot combine its spatial growth with that of smaller cities in the state. Its analysis deserves special treatment, which follows after the aggregate analysis, as explained earlier.

Table 4.4 Description of Population and Household Suburbanization, Cities in Karnataka

	Population, 2011	Est. 1975 population gradient (grid level)	Est. 2015 population gradient (grid level)	Est. 2011 HH gradient (ward level)
Average	198,108	−1.78	−0.84	−0.85
Max	943,788 (Hubballi-Dharwad)	0.38 (Nippani)	0.34 (Bagalkot)	0.31 (Bagalkot)
Min	52,069 (Dandeli)	−3.96 (Ramanagaram)	−2.14 (Ilkal)	−2.16 (Ilkal)
Count	43	43	43	43

Sources: KMDS and author's analyses.

The most suburbanized cities in Karnataka as of the 2011 Census (based on ward-level data) were Hubballi-Dharwad in the northern part of the state and Karwar in the north-western part of the state, both with the same slope of their population density function of −0.06 (based on the modulus of the population density gradient; it should be noted Table 4.4 summarizes the actual values of the estimated slope based on grid-level data). Hubballi-Dharwad's population is about a million now, as it is a twin city, due to which it understandably sprawls, across a geographic area of 213 sq. km. However, Karwar is a town of only 63,755 as of the Census 2011, with a spatial area of only 10.9 sq. km (see Figures 4.1 and 4.2 for the population distribution functions of Hubballi-Dharwad and Karwar, respectively). While the most centralized city is Ilkal, a small town of 60,000 (see Figure 4.3) with an area of 13.16 sq. km in 2011, famous for its handloom sarees, the most compact city in 1975 was Ramanagaram with a population density gradient of −3.96 (see Figure 4.4).

Hubballi-Dharwad is yet another big city which is slated to become one with a million-plus population. This twin city had several peaks of population density in 1975, to be expected, as Hubballi is known as a commercial centre, whereas Dharwad is known for its educational institutions. Its peaking population density in 1975 came only at 2.4 km from its identified centre then (the Hubballi railway station). In 2011, the twin city's population density function almost approximated the negative

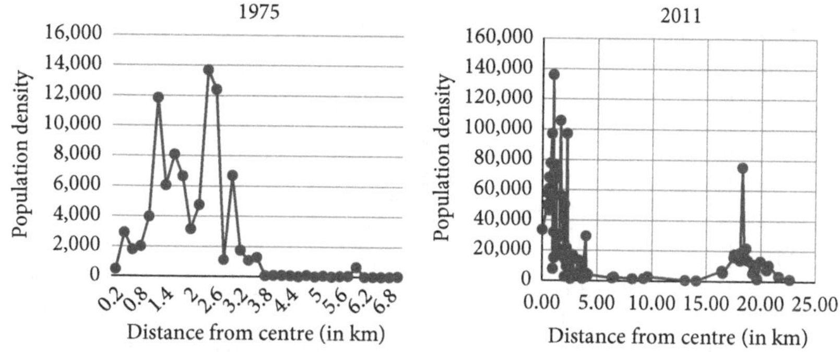

Figure 4.1 Population Density Function, Hubballi-Dharwad, 1975 and 2011

Sources: Florczyk et al. (2019), Karnataka Municipal Data Society, Census PCA (2011), and author's analyses.

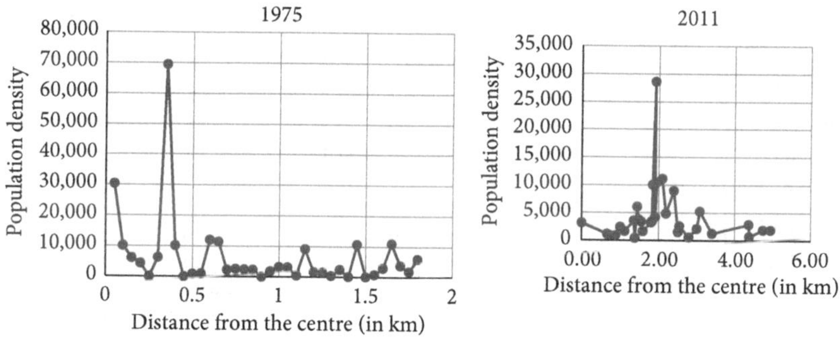

Figure 4.2 Population Density Function, Karwar, 1975 and 2011

Sources: Florczyk et al. (2019), Karnataka Municipal Data Society, Census PCA (2011), and author's analyses.

exponential form, save for a small peak (which was primarily a quite diverse residential area), when its bus stand was used as the centre, nearly identical to its employment density function, as will be seen in Chapter 5.

Karwar too sprawled, as may be seen in Figure 4.2, from a radius of less than 2 km in 1975 to nearly 5 km in 2011. Consistently enough, the peak of population density in this coastal town also moved from less than 1 km from the centre in 1975 (its bus stand) to what we observe in 2011: nearly 2 km from its centre (its municipal office).

Figure 4.3 summarizes the population density function of the most centralized city in the state, Ilkal, based on grid-level data (Table 4.4). The

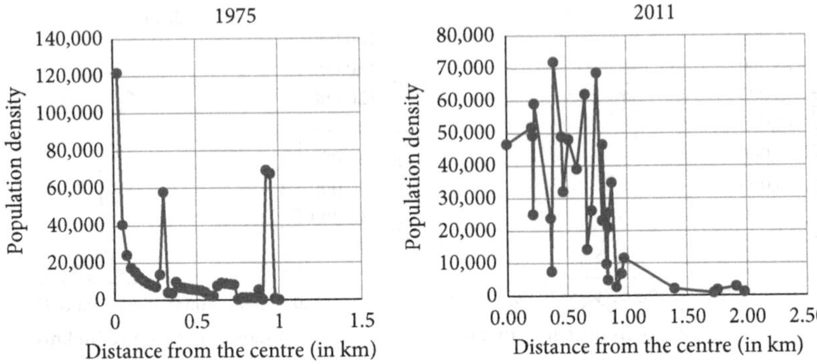

Figure 4.3 Population Density Function, Ilkal, 1975 and 2011

Sources: Florczyk et al. (2019), Karnataka Municipal Data Society, Census PCA (2011), and author's analyses.

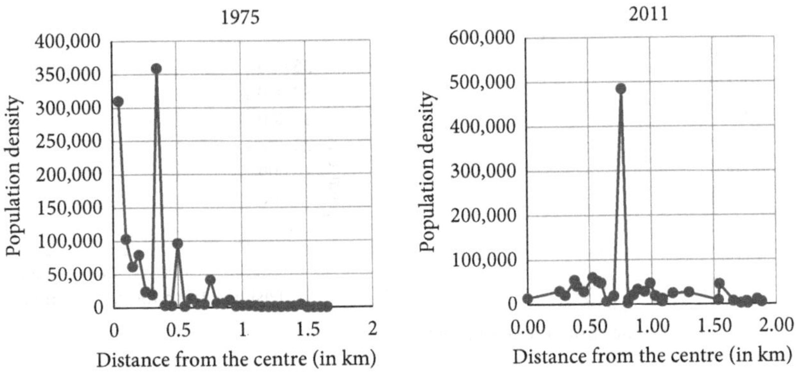

Figure 4.4 Population Distribution of Ramanagaram, 1975 and 2011

Sources: Florczyk et al. (2019), Karnataka Municipal Data Society, Census PCA (2011), and author's analyses.

small town is polycentric in both the time periods considered, although its population structure had the negative exponential form in 1975, but not so in 2011, with its bus stand considered as the centre in both years.

Figure 4.4 summarizes the distribution of the most centralized city in Karnataka in 1975, Ramanagaram, known as the silk city (where silk is produced for use in the famous Mysore silk; the town has a silk cocoon market among the largest in Asia), whose spatial growth was moderate during 1975–2011. Even then, its peak of population density shifted outward from 0.35 km in 1975 (when the town's railway station was considered its centre) to a distance of 0.77 km from its considered centre in 2011 (its bus stand).

As demonstrated in Chapter 3, population and household density gradients move closely together. So, in 2011, Hubballi-Dharwad and Karwar were also the most suburbanized as far as households are concerned. This finding is quite noteworthy because the household-level density gradients were estimated for 2011, using *ward-level* data, whereas the population density gradients were estimated at the *grid level*, for 2015, using the GHSL. It is quite interesting to note the same regarding Ilkal being the most suburbanized in terms of households too, for 2011, just like it is in 2015 for population, using grid-level data. Thus, these results and analyses are robust.

4.2.1 Suburbanization of Bengaluru

As elaborated in Chapter 2 on methodology, for 1991–2011, the population density function (shown in equation (2.2)) for Bengaluru was estimated using ward-level data. This is documented in Sridhar (2007) for 1991 and 2001 and in Sridhar et al. (2018) for 2011.[3] The log linear function was estimated by ordinary least squares (OLS) by using the natural logarithm of population density as shown in equation (2.2). Table 4.5 presents two population density gradient estimates for Bengaluru a decade apart—at the beginning of reforms, 1991, and a decade later, 2001, initially taking the city centre as Sampangiramanagar (the municipal ward in which the state government headquarters (termed Vidhana Soudha) functions). Table 4.5 also summarizes other population density function estimates for Bengaluru, taking other places in the city as plausible centres. These estimates show that Bengaluru's urban form had a positive exponential distribution in 1991 (pre-economic reforms), which not only became a negative exponential function a decade later in 2001, but also declined in absolute value.

[3] In 1991, Bengaluru had only 57 municipal wards, which by 2001 had increased to 97. Since the data on geographic area were accessible for the original 57 wards, which were the same across the two decades, it was conjectured by Sridhar (2007) that the geographic area of the original wards was constant during the two decades. Because of this, 57 observations were used for the 1991 estimation, while 97 wards were used for the estimation of Bengaluru's population density function in the 2001 regression in Sridhar (2007).

Table 4.5 Estimates of Population Density Functions for Bengaluru, 1991 and 2001

Response variable: log of population density, 1991			
	Coefficient	**Std. Err.**	**t value**
Constant	9.17***	0.28	33.21
Parameter estimate (with Vidhana Soudha as the centre)	0.10***	0.03	3.49
R^2	0.18		
Response variable: log of population density, 2001			
	Coefficient	**Std. Err.**	**t value**
Intercept	10.75***	0.18	59.92
Parameter estimate (with Vidhana Soudha as the centre)	−0.05***	0.01	3.64
R^2	0.12		
Response variable: log of population density, 1991			
	Coefficient	**Std. Err.**	**t-ratio**
Constant	10.77***	0.20	54.68
Parameter estimate (with highest density ward 20 as centre)	−0.06***	0.02	−3.94
R^2	0.22		
Response variable: log of population density, 2001			
	Coefficient	**Std. Err.**	**t-ratio**
Constant	10.79***	0.11	97.82
Parameter estimate (with highest density ward 32 as centre)	−0.05***	0.01	−6.83
R^2	0.33		

Source: Created by author based on data in Sridhar (2007).

N = 57 for 1991 estimations; 97 for 2001 regressions.

***Statistically significant at the 1% level.

Certain observations are in order here.

First, when I considered the municipal ward containing Vidhana Soudha as the city's central point, Bengaluru's population function was sloping upwards in 1991, but sloping downwards exponentially in 2001. This demonstrates that Bengaluru in 1991 was characterized by increasing density with increasing distance from the identified centre. By the next decade, this tendency had changed, with declining density as distance from the centre increased.

Second, between 1991 and 2001, 'b-suburbanization' of population happened in Bengaluru, as was seen by Sridhar (2007) in the (modulus of the) declining gradient.[4] When I considered Vidhana Soudha as the city centre, there were a few new peaks of population density in 1991. Interestingly, these multiple peaks gave way to a single climax in 2001, as was found by Sridhar (2007). Indeed, Sridhar (2007) documented that the density of the tallest point in 1991 decreased by 44% from about 120,000 persons per square kilometre to only about 69,000 persons per square kilometre in 2001.

Sridhar (2007) re-estimated the gradients for Bengaluru in the two decades of study by treating the city's maximum density points as the new centres and found that population density became a negative exponential function, declining towards the suburbs during 1991–2001. These regressions from Sridhar (2007) are presented in Table 4.5.

The use of various city centres naturally leads to an enquiry regarding the actual centre of the city. If one were to adopt Alperovich's (1982) criterion, and as also indicated by Small and Song (1994), the actual centre of the city is indicated by the regression which has the maximum R^2, given it is a measure of goodness of fit.

When this benchmark was used, Sridhar (2007) found that the actual centre of Bengaluru was ward 32 (with an R-squared of 0.33) (see Table 4.5). This area is mainly zoned for residential uses, mostly housing for economically lower sections of society, certain retail and artisan activities, and small industry.[5]

For the Bengaluru of 2011, Sridhar et al. (2018) performed regressions associating the metropolitan area's density of population with proximity

[4] Interestingly enough, Sridhar (2007) reran the OLS estimation (considering the matching wards in the two decades) by transforming logarithms on both distance (independent variable) and population density (the dependent variable). It was found that density increased by 79% in 1991 with increasing distance from the city centre, but by only a little over half of that, at 36% per square kilometre, in the following decade.

[5] As pointed out by Sridhar (2007), as per Bengaluru's Master Plan 2015, the city was projected to expand in concentric circles until 2025. The Master Plan of 2015 categorized the city into five concentric belts, predicating this on the current and proposed land uses. The five belts were construed to be the city's older areas, city rehabilitation zones, domestic areas, manufacturing pockets, with the pastoral zones representing the farthest circle.

Table 4.6 Population Density Gradients for Bengaluru, Assuming Various Points as City Centre, 2011

	Distance to Majestic (ward 95)[a]	Distance to ward with highest population density (ward 135)[b]	Distance to ward of state government headquarters (ward 110)	R-squared	Model F value
Model 1	−0.10 (−7.32)[c]***	NA	NA	0.21	53.57
Model 2	NA	−0.09 (7.40)***	NA	0.22	54.70
Model 3	NA	NA	−0.08 (−4.92)***	0.11	24.26

Source: Created by author from data in Sridhar et al. (2018) for 198 wards in the city.

N = 198 in all models. NA: Not available.

***Statistically significant at the 1% level.

Notes:

a. The outcome variable in all estimations is the log of population density.

b. Constants are unreported.

c. In parentheses are the t values of the respective coefficients.

to its centre, as per the conventional framework, to understand its spatial distribution. The various regression specifications assumed three city centres—Sampangiramanagar, the ward containing the state government headquarters, the Vidhana Soudha, as done by Sridhar (2007); Subashnagar, the ward containing Majestic, which has the city bus stand and is generally considered to be the central point; and Padarayanapura, with peaking density as of the 2011 Census (Table 4.6).

All the estimations presented in Table 4.6 from Sridhar et al. (2018) confirm that population density in the city decreased towards the suburbs, regardless of whichever ward is perceived as the centre. As reported by Sridhar et al. (2018), the gradient (which is the coefficient in the regressions presented in Table 4.6) is the lowest in modulus terms when the state government headquarters is considered the centre, hence Bengaluru was deemed the flattest when this was considered. The coefficient was the maximum in modulus terms when the city's central bus stand (Majestic) was taken as the centre, hence the metropolitan area was the most compact with this consideration.

With the ward containing the state government headquarters as centre of the city, the coefficient estimates obtained in Sridhar (2007) for Bengaluru were 0.10 and 0.05 (in absolute value terms) for 1991 and 2001, respectively. As reported by Sridhar et al. (2018), the gradient estimate for the same city centre of Bengaluru for 2011 is 0.08 (as may be seen from model 3, Table 4.6), indicating the sprawl of the metropolitan area since 1991, but compactness since 2001, possibly because of the annexation of the surrounding local bodies into the fold of the primary city, leading to the emergence of the Bruhat Bengaluru Mahanagara Palike (BBMP) in 2007. Another reason for the centralization I find could be the fact that the density of the central city is constantly increasing, as documented recently by Sridhar and Monkkonen (2024).

All the estimated population density gradients summarized in Table 4.6 are negative, showing the decreasing density as one moves away from the city centre, irrespective of whichever centre is considered. As discussed earlier, Sridhar (2007) documented that the highest population density (Sadashivanagar ward) declined by 44%, from about 120,000 persons per square kilometre in 1991 to a low of 69,000 persons per square kilometre in 2001. Sridhar et al. (2018) further reported the density of the most dense ward (Padarayanapura) rose to the city's 1991 level, to 124,478 persons per square kilometre in 2011, a rise of nearly 80% based on ward level data. On average, the city's density continuously decreased from 20,000 to 19,000 per square kilometre, to a further low of 11,000 per square kilometre during 1991–2011, which could be due to the expansion in the city's boundaries to about 740 sq. km in 2006 when the surrounding urban local bodies were annexed into the city's primary municipal body.

Since decisions to locate within a certain part of the city are much more relevant for a family than for an individual, Sridhar et al. (2018) reported results from regressions of the natural log of the household density as associated with proximity to the centre, considering the same city centres discussed earlier (shown in Table 4.6). The findings are not very different from that observed for population density. As Sridhar et al. (2018) documented, the gradient for households is negative as well, irrespective of the centre. This shows the decreasing density of families when one moves away from the centre to the suburbs. Second, families in Bengaluru are the most sprawling when the state government headquarters is taken as the centre (Table 4.7).

Given the consideration of multiple possible city centres, the findings again lead to enquiry regarding the actual city centre. As discussed

Table 4.7 Household Density Gradients for Bengaluru, Assuming Various Points as City Centre, 2011

	Distance from Majestic (ward 95)	**Distance from ward with highest household density (ward 122)**	**Distance from ward of state government headquarters (ward 110)**	**R-squared**	**Model F value**
Model 1	−0.10 (−7.01)***	NA	NA	0.20	49.07
Model 2	NA	−0.09 (7.47)***	NA	0.22	55.77
Model 3	NA	NA	−0.07 (−4.40)***	0.09	24.26

Source: Created by author based on data in Sridhar et al. (2018).

N = 198 for all models. NA: Not available.

***Statistically significant at the 1% level.

In parentheses are the t values of the respective coefficients.

earlier, taking into account the criterion given by Alperovich (1982) and Small and Song (1994), Sridhar et al. (2018) reported the real centre of Bengaluru to be Padarayanapura, if one were interested in population density, and Kempapura Agrahara, if considering household density, both of which lead to the maximum R^2 in their respective models (see Tables 4.6 and 4.7), much as Sridhar (2007) had found.

4.2.2 Have the Smaller Cities in Karnataka Suburbanized?

The list of cities in Karnataka which are studied in this chapter is given in Appendix 4A.1, along with their estimated population gradients in 1975 and 2011 (or 2015, for some from the GHSL) and household density gradients (also estimated) using 2011 data. In this section, I present the population distribution functions of the biggest 15 cities in Karnataka (apart from Bengaluru).[6]

Figure 4.5 summarizes the population distribution function of Mysuru, the next city after Bengaluru in terms of population, which is historically

[6] These cities are: Hubballi-Dharwad, Mysuru, Ilkal, Karwar, Ramanagaram, Belagavi, Mangaluru, Davanagere, Bellary, Vijayapura, Shivamogga, Tumakuru, Raichur, Bidar and Kalaburagi.

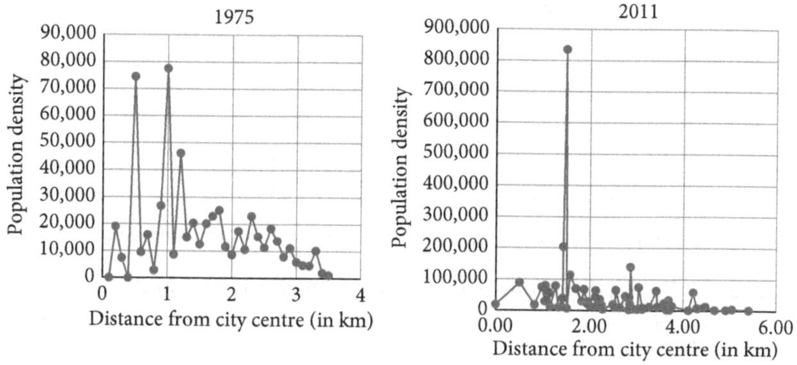

Figure 4.5 Population Density Function, Mysuru, 1975 and 2011

Sources: Florczyk et al. (2019), Karnataka Municipal Data Society, Census PCA (2011), and author's analyses.

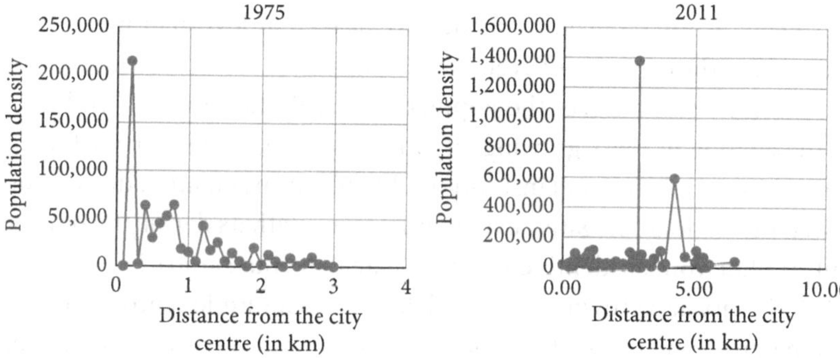

Figure 4.6 Population Density Function, Belagavi, 1975 and 2011

Sources: Florczyk et al. (2019), Karnataka Municipal Data Society, Census PCA (2011), and author's analyses.

known for its palaces, royal family, and cultural heritage. In 1975, Mysuru was polycentric as there were a couple of centres which experienced peaking population density, within less than 1 km of the identified city centre (its railway station). In 2011, the city had become monocentric with a single peak of population density, using the same city centre as earlier, but which occurred a bit later, at about 1.5 km from the centre, showing the city's gradual flattening over the period, also seen in its radius' steady growth from only 3.5 km in 1975 to nearly 5.4 km in 2011.

Figure 4.6 presents the population distribution function of another important city in the state, Belagavi, where the state assembly holds its winter

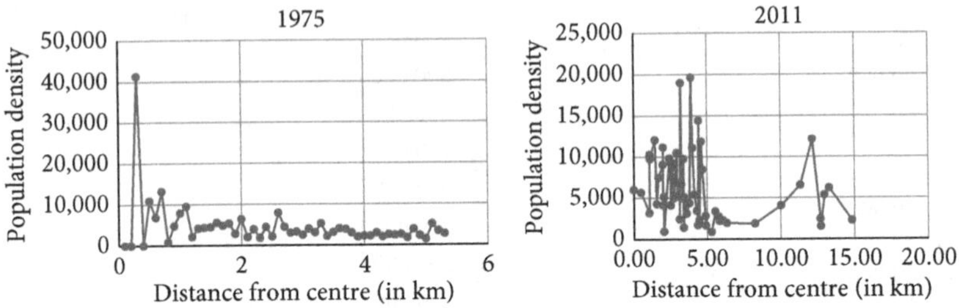

Figure 4.7 Population Density Function, Mangaluru, 1975 and 2011
Sources: Florczyk et al. (2019), Karnataka Municipal Data Society, Census PCA (2011), and author's analyses.

session every year, for both 1975 and 2011. Belagavi is monocentric as its population density peaks at about 2.8 km from the assumed city centre (the KSRTC bus stop in 2011). In 1975, when the city's head post office was taken as the city centre, its density peaked at less than half a kilometre from the centre, and even then Belagavi was monocentric.

Figure 4.7 summarizes the population distribution in 1975 and 2011 of the coastal and fast-growing city in Karnataka, Mangaluru, which is known for its educational institutions. In 1975 its population density followed the standard negative exponential form, with its density peaking at only 0.3 km from its identified centre (State Bank bus stand). However, by 2011, the city had grown rapidly and developed multiple centres of population density (with its city corporation office as the centre). It should be noted that the city's population density peaked at nearly 4 km from its centre in 2011, when its radius also increased to nearly 15 km, from only about 5 km in 1975, during the four decades.

Figure 4.8 displays the population distribution of Davanagere in both 1975 and 2011. The growth of the city has been quite dramatic, as it was a small municipality in 1975 with a radius of 1.6 km, but became a city corporation in 2011 with a sprawling radius of 4.6 km, an increase of nearly three times. While the city had a couple of peaks of population density in 1975 (using its old bus stand as the centre), these collapsed to a single peak in 2011, at 1.5 km from the city centre (its railway station and its municipal office). I also note that in the earlier decade, the peak of population density was reached well within 1 km of the city centre, whereas in 2011, it was reached much later.

Figure 4.9 shows the population distribution of yet another small town in Karnataka, Bellary, in 1975 and 2011. In this town, in 2011 the

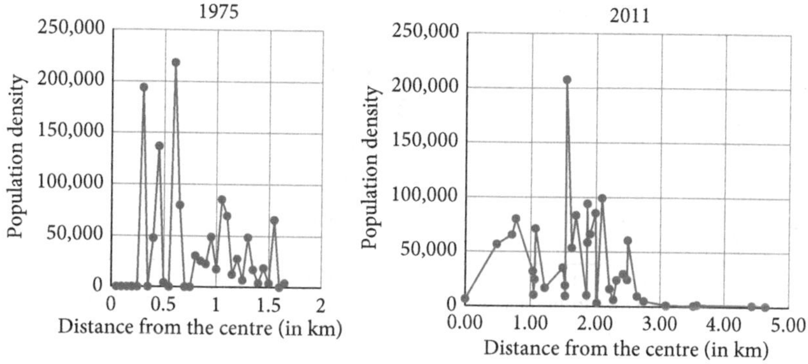

Figure 4.8 Davanagere's Population Distribution, 1975 and 2011

Sources: Florczyk et al. (2019), Karnataka Municipal Data Society, Census PCA (2011), and author's analyses.

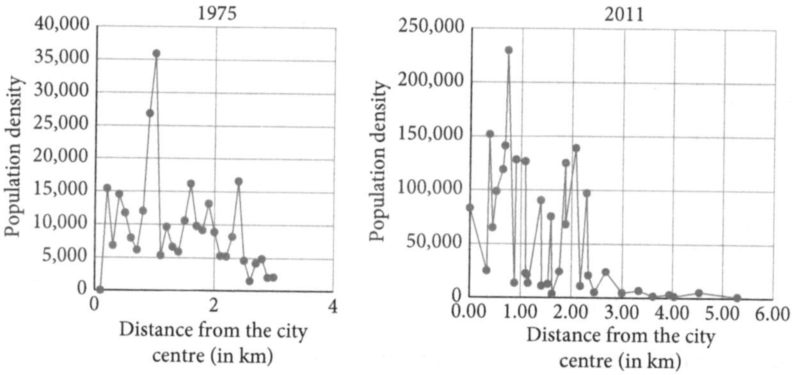

Figure 4.9 Population Density Function, Bellary, 1975 and 2011

Sources: Florczyk et al. (2019), Karnataka Municipal Data Society, Census PCA (2011), and author's analyses.

peak of population density was reached very quickly, within 1 km of the chosen city centre (the city bus stop), whereas in 1975, it reached its peak at exactly 1 km from the identified city centre (its railway station). Nonetheless, this town is largely monocentric, with density rapidly declining thereafter.

Figure 4.10 presents the population distribution for Bijapur in Karnataka. It shows the sprawl that has occurred in the city's spatial area during the four decades from a radius of less than 2 km (taking the city's bus stand as its centre) to more than 5 km in 2011 (considering its municipal office as the centre).

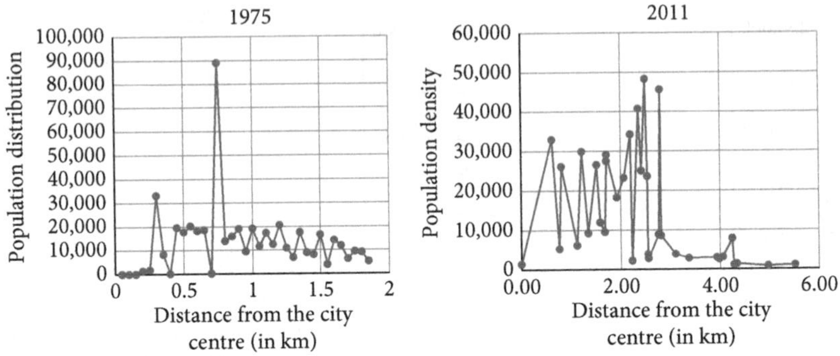

Figure 4.10 Vijayapura's Population Distribution, 1975 and 2011
Sources: Florczyk et al. (2019), Karnataka Municipal Data Society, Census PCA (2011), and author's analyses.

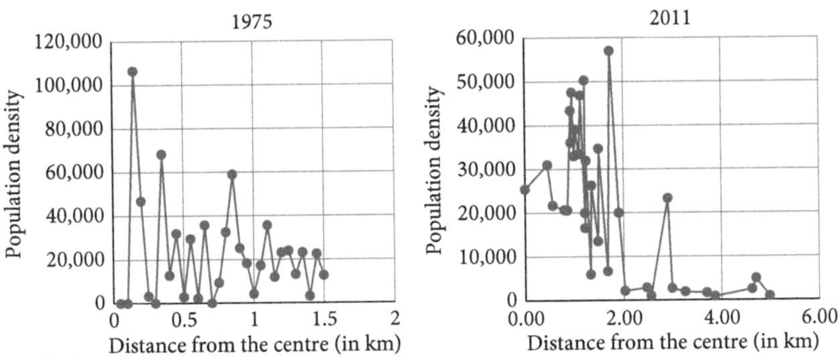

Figure 4.11 Population Density Function, Shivamogga, 1975 and 2011
Sources: Florczyk et al. (2019), Karnataka Municipal Data Society, Census PCA (2011), and author's analyses.

Figure 4.11 presents the population distribution for 1975 and 2011 of a tourist town in Karnataka, Shivamogga, which hosts some famous waterfalls. The figure shows tremendous growth of the town during the four decades, whereby its radius increased from only 1.5 km in 1975 to nearly 5 km in 2011, a more than threefold increase. Similarly its urban form also underwent a change from being predominantly monocentric in 1975 to being polycentric in 2011. Consistent with this, the peak of population density moved from less than 0.2 km from its centre in 1975 (the town's bus stand) to nearly 1.75 km in 2011, when the same centre was considered.

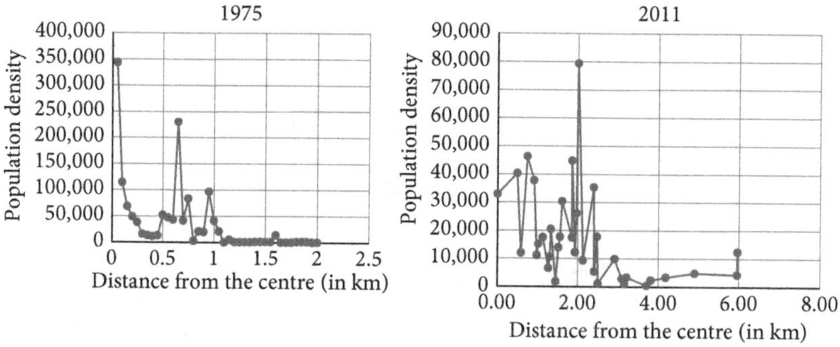

Figure 4.12 Population Density Function, Tumakuru, 1975 and 2011

Sources: Florczyk et al. (2019), Karnataka Municipal Data Society, Census PCA (2011), and author's analyses.

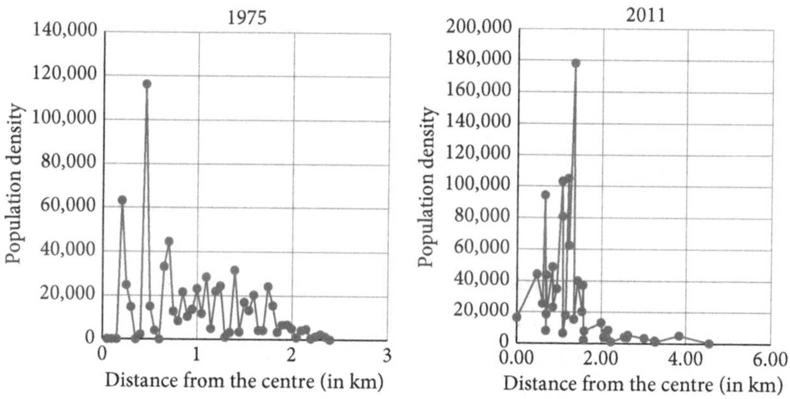

Figure 4.13 Population Density Function, Raichur, 1975 and 2011

Sources: Florczyk et al. (2019), Karnataka Municipal Data Society, Census PCA (2011), and author's analyses.

Figure 4.12 displays the population distribution in 1975 and 2011 of a town which is situated north of Bengaluru, Tumakuru. The town's population distribution resembled closely the negative exponential form in 1975, when its bus stand was considered the centre. In 2011 however, the town grew considerably with its radius increasing to nearly 6 km, and with the peak of population density too shifting rightward towards the edge, at 2 km from its identified core then (the Zilla Panchayat office).

Figure 4.13 summarizes and presents the population distribution of Raichur in northern Karnataka for 1975 and 2011. The spatial sprawl of

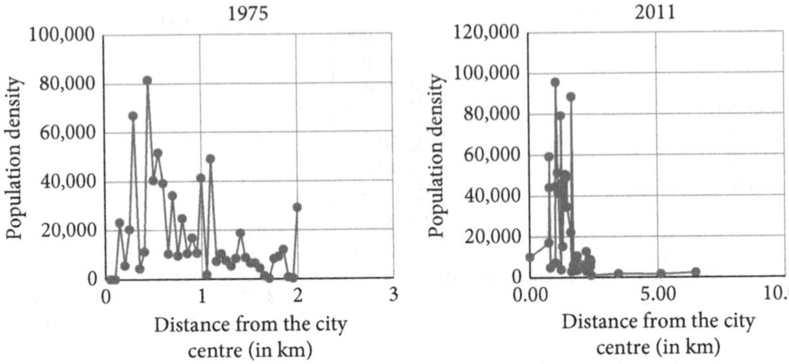

Figure 4.14 Bidar's Population Distribution, 1975 and 2011

Sources: Florczyk et al. (2019), Karnataka Municipal Data Society, Census PCA (2011), and author's analyses.

this town too is quite conspicuous given its radius increased from a mere 2.4 km in 1975 to 4.5 km in 2011, a nearly twofold increase. Consistent with this growth, its peak of population density shifted from less than half a kilometre from the city centre considered in 1975 (its bus stand) to a distance of 1.35 km from its centre in 2011 (the local government office).

Figure 4.14 presents the population distribution for 1975 and 2011 of Bidar, which has a City Municipal Council, even though it is a class I city (with a 2011 population of 214,373). Whereas Bidar's real population density peaked at only 0.45 km in 1975 (considering its railway station as the centre), in 2011, it peaked a bit farther than a kilometre from the chosen city centre, at 1.06 km, even while the city has another peak at 1.67 km from the city core chosen (railway station) in 2011.

4.2.2.1 Suburbanization of Kalaburagi

In terms of the population of cities in Karnataka, Kalaburagi ranks fourth after Bengaluru, Mysuru, and Hubballi-Dharwad in that order. Kalaburagi's population was 543,147 in 2011, as per the Census of India. The city had 58 census wards, and 3 census outgrowths, with an average population per ward of about 9,600. Kalaburagi is an important hub in the Hyderabad-Karnataka region, at about 220 km from Hyderabad and over 600 km north of Bengaluru, and is in that part of the state which is considered lagging, termed Kalyana Karnataka, hence it has been a focus

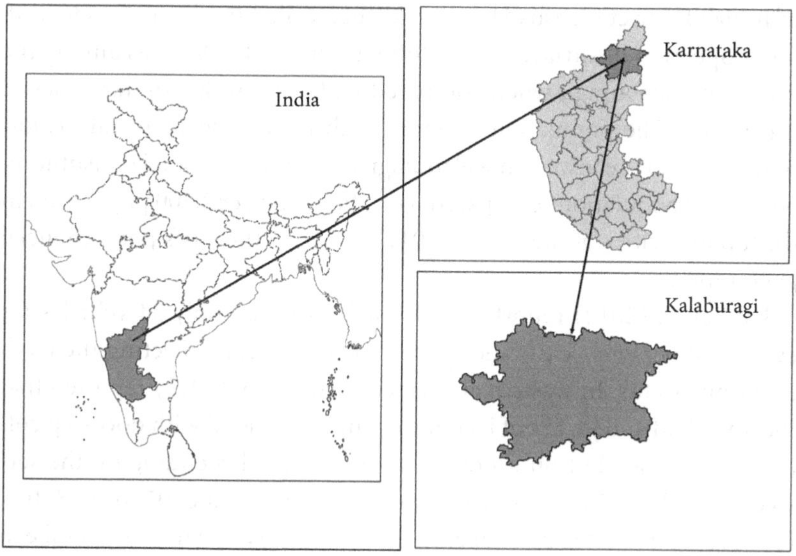

Figure 4.15 Location of Kalaburagi in Karnataka and India
Source: Map of India, Oxford University Press India, 2024 https://kgis.ksrsac.in.

of major policy initiatives for several decades now.[7] Figure 4.15 shows the relative location of Kalaburagi within the country and the state, and its location within the district.

While Kalaburagi's population density increased from 6,673 per sq. km in 2001 to 8,423 per sq. km in 2011, it had the lowest percentage (about 38%) of its population as workforce. Most (91%) of the city's land was utilized for residing purposes, and the rest constituted empty space, demonstrating possibilities for further development, as reported by Paul et al. (2012).

Interestingly, as Paul et al. (2012) pointed out, the city's average investment proposal (a three-year average for the period 2006–07 to 2008–09) was only Rs.670 per capita per year, compared with Rs.28,252, on average, for the state's top-ranking 15 cities, as also documented by Paul et al. (2012). More recent data are not available. Based on the Census

[7] It is instructive to read the report of the Nanjundappa Committee (2010) set up by the government of Karnataka, which may be found at: https://planning.karnataka.gov.in/storage/pdf-files/SUMMARY%20REPORT%20-%20English.pdf, accessed 3 January 2024.

of India's District Census Handbook (then called the town directories), the proportion of surfaced roads to total roads (at 30%) was among the lowest in Kalaburagi, when compared with that in the top ten cities of Karnataka. The population coverage with banks and financial institutions was also the lowest in Kalaburagi, at 1 bank or financial institution per 15,000 population (compared with about one per 2,500 population in the top four cities of the state in 2011), showing the city's poor financial penetration.

Paul et al. (2012) reported that Kalaburagi had only 34 vehicles for every 100 persons, least among the state's 15 cities, reflecting the city's economic status. In waste management, Paul et al. (2012) reported that the town had a mere 5% of its housing units provided with doorstep collection of waste, but on average, the city's capital spending on the service was only Rs.7 per capita (for the period from 2006–07 to 2008–09). However, as reported by Paul et al. (2012), the city had the largest hike in its use of electricity (28% during 2006–09). No doubt the city had poor air quality—its Respirate Suspended Particulate Matter (RSPM) was a whopping 140% of the level deemed permissible by the state's Pollution Control Board (Paul et al., 2012).

Hence, there is plenty of potential for upgradation of municipal amenities and basic services in Kalaburagi. Given a study of sprawl also has several implications for land use and the environment, it is necessary for better deployment of services and environmental sustainability.

In the next sections, I report the density function for Kalaburagi along with its population and job density gradients, as in Sridhar and Narayanan (2016). They made different conjectures about the possible centre of the city. Then they estimated the proximity of the wards to each of the identified centres, associating proximity with the population density at the various points, using Census 2001 and 2011 data.

4.2.2.2 Which is the Centre of Kalaburagi?

A city's Master Plan typically alludes to its centre; however, there is no clear reference to its centre in Kalaburagi's Master Plan. It is essential to have information about the CBD, for purposes of understanding the sprawl, if any. Therefore, Sridhar and Narayanan (2016) first made an attempt to locate Kalaburagi's city centre, defining it as an area of premium land, which is distinguished by its agglomeration of commercial activity, retail services, cinema halls, hotels, and congested traffic, a characterization which was given by the US Census Bureau in 1984. If one were to apply these characteristics of a CBD to Kalaburagi, Sridhar and Narayanan (2016) indicated that each characteristic pointed towards a different part of the city to be considered as its centre. Therefore, they chose many areas to be considered possible centres of the city. This facilitated an understanding of the city's sprawl.

Figure 4.16 summarizes different areas of Kalaburagi—the central bus stand, the railway station, the city's central shopping area, the fortress, the municipal office, and the city's topographic centre—which were considered the city's centre, as done by Sridhar and Narayanan (2016) too. If

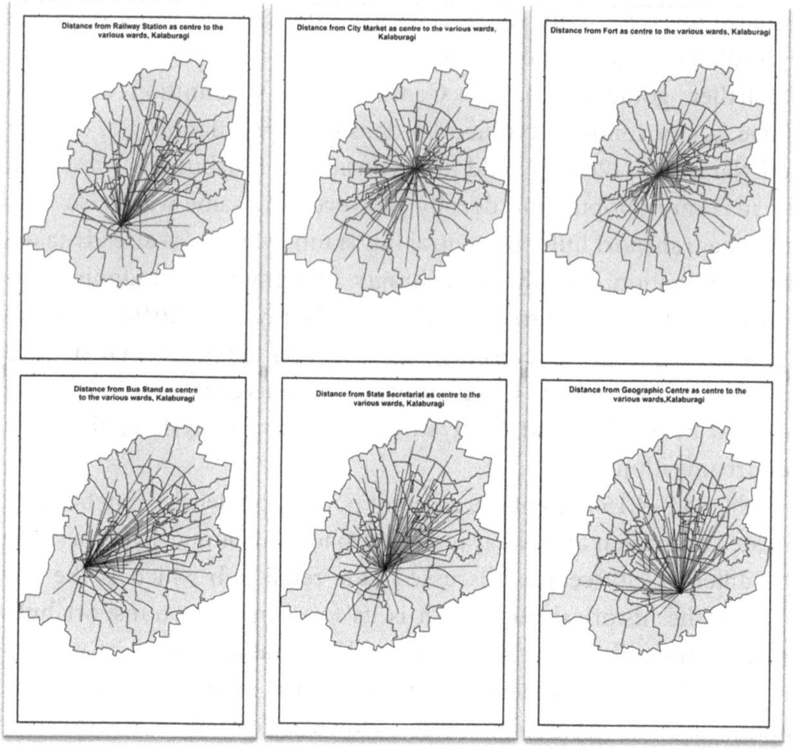

Figure 4.16 Various Assumed City Centres of Kalaburagi and Distances to Each of its Wards

Source: Created by author based on data from https://kgis.ksrsac.in and data in Sridhar and Narayanan (2016).

one considers shopping needs, the city market can be taken as the centre, whereas if recreation is taken as the criterion, the city's historical fortress becomes the centre of the city. As they rightly point out, a city centre responds directly to the formation of the city's new business areas—expanding or contracting, as new businesses are established or old ones relocated, over time. Hence, Kalaburagi's city market was taken as a possible city centre, for analysis by Sridhar and Narayanan (2016). Based on the earlier discussion, the historical fort of Kalaburagi was considered as the second possible city centre.

Major transport pivots in cities are usually taken as the centres, as in Washington, DC, USA and cities in Europe, where extensive public transport networks enable the railway station to be considered as the city's central point. Following that tradition, Kalaburagi's transport hubs, the city railway terminus and its central bus station, were taken as centres by Sridhar and Narayanan (2016).

Further, going by the US Census Bureau's definition discussed above, a city centre is typified by density of population. So, Sridhar and Narayanan (2016) would have considered Kalaburagi's ward with the maximum population density; however, the same ward also consists of a transport hub, the central bus stand, which was already taken for examination. Finally, Kalaburagi's topographical midpoint was considered the city centre by Sridhar and Narayanan (2016) who analysed the city's sprawl, considering six aspects that generated six possible city centres. Figure 4.16 presents the various centres of Kalaburagi selected by Sridhar and Narayanan (2016) for analysis of the city's suburbanization.

Tables 4.8–4.15 present the different population density functions estimated by Sridhar and Narayanan (2016) for Kalaburagi, hypothesizing the different city centres discussed—the retail hub which is the city market, the historical hub which is its fort, the city's transport hubs (namely, the railway station and central bus station), the state government headquarters (located in Vidhan soudha) as done for Bengaluru, and Kalaburagi's geographic centre—shown in Figure 4.16, from Sridhar and Narayanan (2016). The city centres hypothesized and their distance to each of the other wards are also shown in Figure 4.16. It is easy to see visually that the city's fortress or shopping areas are quite at the centre of the town.

Table 4.8 Kalaburagi's Population Density Gradients, 2001–11: City Market as Centre

Dependent variable: natural logarithm of population density		
	Slope coefficient estimate, 2001 (Std. Err.)	**Slope coefficient estimate, 2011 (Std. Err.)**
Access to the city shopping area as centre (in kms)	−0.13 (0.02)***	−0.14 (0.02)***
R^2	0.41	0.46

Source: Created by author based on data from Sridhar and Narayanan (2016).
Intercepts not reported. N = 58 for both years.
***Statistically significant at the 1% level.

Table 4.9 Kalaburagi's Population Density Gradients, 2001–11: Fort as Centre

Dependent variable: natural logarithm of population density		
	Slope coefficient estimate, 2001 (Std. Err.)	**Slope coefficient estimate, 2011 (Std. Err.)**
Distance from city centre (fort)	−0.32 (0.04)***	−0.31 (0.04)***
R^2	0.60	0.59

Source: Created by author based on data from Sridhar and Narayanan (2016).
Intercepts not reported. N = 58 for both years.
***Statistically significant at the 1% level.

As Tables 4.8–4.15 summarize, Sridhar and Narayanan (2016) found evidence for the downward exponentially sloping population density function as a suitable fit for Kalaburagi's urban form. As they noted, all the estimated population gradients were statistically significant in the respective regressions (except a regression in which they took the city's railway terminus as the city centre). This amply demonstrates that Kalaburagi's density was declining in 2011 as one moved away from the centre, no matter which point was considered.

In the estimation which has the city market as Kalaburagi's centre, during the decade 2001–11, there was centralization or compactness, as was observed in a general rise in the modulus of the gradient (see Table 4.8) by Sridhar and Narayanan (2016) who reported a 13% and 14% decrease in Kalaburagi's population density with a unit (1-km) increase in distance from its shopping area, in the two decades, respectively.

When the fortress was taken as Kalaburagi's centre, Sridhar and Narayanan (2016) found a decrease in the modulus of the slope of the population density function during the decade of 2001–11 (Table 4.9), implying greater compression of the city's gradient estimates, denoting sprawl. Judging by Alperovich's (1982) criterion, the population density function for the city, estimated with its fortress as the centre, produced the best goodness of fit (R^2), indicating that the historical fortress is the town's actual centre. Because of this finding, I have higher trust in the compression of the slope of its population density function and the consequent sprawl observed in the city during 2001–11 when the fortress is considered as the city's centre. The other equation that entails a suitable goodness of fit (R^2) is the one in which the city market is assumed as the city centre. The regressions in Tables 4.8–4.15 reported by Sridhar and Narayanan (2016) reaffirm the city's historical fortress as the real centre of Kalaburagi, judging by the benchmark provided by Alperovich (1982), as discussed here.

Sridhar and Narayanan (2016) provided the rationale for why Kalaburagi's fort could be considered the city's real centre. There are several hotels in this area to suit the needs of business as well as leisure travellers, matching various budgets and interests. Furthermore, near the fort, there are diverse accommodation options available for travellers such as resorts, homestays, visitor accommodation, and serviced housing, giving credence to the suggestion of a centre, as per the definition of the US Census Bureau discussed earlier.

Table 4.10 Kalaburagi's Suburbanization, 1975–2015, with Fort as the City Centre

Slope of population function, 1975	–0.69
Slope of population function, 2001	–0.32
Slope of population function, 2011	–0.31
Slope of population function, 2015	–0.51

Sources: Florczyk et al. (2019), Sridhar and Narayanan (2016), and author's analyses.

Table 4.11 Kalaburagi's Population Density Gradients, 2001–11: Railway Station as Centre

Dependent variable: natural logarithm of population density, 2001 and 2011		
	Slope coefficient estimate, 2001 (Std. Err.)	**Slope coefficient estimate, 2011 (Std. Err.)**
Distance from city centre (railway terminus)	−0.05 (0.05)	−0.05 (0.05)
R^2	0.02	0.02

Source: Created by author based on data from Sridhar and Narayanan (2016).

Intercepts not reported. N = 58 for both years.

Table 4.12 Kalaburagi's Population Density Gradients, 2001–11: Bus Stand as Centre

Dependent variable: natural logarithm of population density, 2001 and 2011		
	Slope coefficient estimate, 2001 (Std. Err.)	**Slope coefficient estimate, 2011 (Std. Err.)**
Distance from city centre (bus station)	−0.13 (0.04)***	−0.13 (0.04)***
R^2	0.15	0.15

Source: Created by author based on data from Sridhar and Narayanan (2016).

Intercepts not reported. N = 58 for both years.

***Statistically significant at the 1% level.

Table 4.13 Kalaburagi's Population Density Gradients, 2001–11: State Secretariat as Centre

Dependent variable: natural logarithm of population density, 2001 and 2011		
	Slope coefficient estimate, 2001 (Std. Err.)	**Slope coefficient estimate, 2011 (Std. Err.)**
Distance from city centre (state government headquarters)	−0.14 (0.05)**	−0.13 (0.05)**
R^2	0.11	0.11

Source: Created by author based on data from Sridhar and Narayanan (2016).

Intercepts not reported. N = 58 for both years.

**Statistically significant at the 5% level.

Table 4.14 Kalaburagi's Population Density Gradients, 2001–11, Considering the City's Geographic Centre

Dependent variable: natural logarithm of population density, 2001 and 2011		
	Slope coefficient estimate, 2001 (Std. Err.)	**Slope coefficient estimate, 2011 (Std. Err.)**
Distance from city centre (topographical centre)	−0.15 (0.06)**	−0.15 (0.06)**
R^2	0.09	0.09

Source: Created by author based on data from Sridhar and Narayanan (2016).
Intercepts not reported. N = 58 for both years.
**Statistically significant at the 5% level.

Table 4.15 Kalaburagi's Population Density Gradients, 2001–11: Highest Population Density Ward as Centre

Dependent variable: natural logarithm of population density, 2001 and 2011		
	Slope coefficient estimate, 2001 (Std. Err.)	**Slope coefficient estimate, 2011 (Std. Err.)**
Distance from city centre (ward with the highest population density)	−0.10 (0.04)**	−0.10 (0.04)**
R^2	0.10	0.10

Source: Created by author based on data from Sridhar and Narayanan (2016).
Intercepts not reported. N = 58 for both years.
**Statistically significant at the 5% level.

It should be noted that this ward 33 (containing the fort) is the city centre chosen in the regressions based on data from the Global Human Settlements Layer (GHSL) (Florczyk et al., 2019). Considering the GHSL dataset for 1975 and 2015, and the ward-level data for 2001–11, Kalaburagi's density gradients are summarized and presented in Table 4.10, using the fort as the city centre. Based on this, I find that the city continuously suburbanized during 1975–2011, but centralized thereafter, judging from a rise in the modulus of the city's estimated population gradient during 2011–15.

4.3 Summary of Findings and Conclusions

In this chapter, I have summarized regional disparities in the population suburbanization patterns and trends for cities in south India, treating those in the urbanized and lagging states separately. I find that cities in the south Indian states are much more sprawling when compared with cities all India, for 2015. However, those in the slow-growing states are more compact when benchmarked against cities in all India, and definitely in comparison with the south Indian states. Unsurprisingly, cities the urbanized states follow the sprawling pattern observed in the southern states.

I have studied cities in the south Indian state of Karnataka separately in this chapter. In Karnataka, I have studied the sprawl of Bengaluru, the primate city in the state, with a study of the suburbanization of 11 smaller cities in the state, along with that of an individual city in Karnataka, Kalaburagi in the Hyderabad-Karnataka region. I find that on average, cities in Karnataka, even though they suburbanized during 1975–2015, are far more compact when compared with cities all over India, with a much higher population gradient. Kalaburagi is much more sprawling compared with the cities in Karnataka, with a smaller population gradient. While Bengaluru suburbanized during 1991–2001, it centralized in the period until 2011 and 2015 too, as documented here, possibly because of the annexation of the adjacent urban local bodies, leading to the formation of the merged urban local body called the Bruhat Bengaluru Mahanagara Palike (BBMP).

The pattern of suburbanization of cities in Karnataka is therefore like that of the lagging states, if its primate city Bengaluru is excluded, even though it is classified as an urbanized state. This may be attributed to the fact that Karnataka has many smaller cities, which are more compact, as I have demonstrated with a detailed analysis of the population suburbanization of 11 smaller cities in the state in 1975 and 2011.

The next chapter discusses the employment suburbanization of India's cities.

Appendix 4A.1

Number	City	Population, 2011	Population gradient, 1975	Population gradient, 2011	HH gradient, 2011
1	Bagalkot	111,933	−1.10	0.34	0.31
2	Bengaluru	8,443,675	−0.06	−0.08	−0.07
3	Belagavi	488,157	−1.29	0.09	0.10
4	Bellary	410,445	−0.50	−0.87	−0.88
5	Bhadravathi	151,102	−0.39	−0.75	−0.76
6	Bidar	214,373	−1.35	−0.61	−0.57
7	Vijayapura	327,427	0.36	−0.52	−0.52
8	Chamarajanagar	69,959	−2.38	−0.96	−0.95
9	Channapatna	71,942	−3.33	−0.59	−0.55
10	Chikkaballapur	63,652	−2.45	−1.67	−1.70
11	Chinthamani	76,068	−2.95	−1.99	−2.00
12	Chitradurga	140,206	−2.31	−1.60	−1.63
13	Dandeli	52,069	−1.02	−0.26	−0.26
14	Davanagere	434,971	−1.69	−0.96	−0.95
15	Doddaballapur	84,642	−3.30	−1.58	−1.52
16	Gadag-Betageri	172,612	−1.65	−0.68	−0.68
17	Gangavathi	106,027	−1.08	−0.57	−1.32
18	Gokak	79,121	−2.15	−1.93	−1.89
19	Kalaburagi	533,587	−0.69	−0.51	−0.53
20	Harihar	77,447	−2.48	−0.20	−0.20
21	Hassan	133,436	−3.09	0.09	0.06
22	Hospet	206,167	−1.97	−1.10	−1.10
23	Hubballi-Dharwad	943,788	−0.95	−0.06	−0.06
24	Ilkal	60,242	−2.53	−2.14	−2.16
25	Jamkhandi	68,938	−1.27	−1.68	−1.47
26	Karwar	63,755	−1.16	−0.06	−0.06
27	Kolar	138,462	−2.59	−1.36	−1.37
28	Kollegal	57,149	−3.29	−0.99	−1.01
29	Koppal	79,807	−1.46	−1.08	−1.43
30	Mandya	137,358	−2.43	−0.48	−0.46
31	Mangaluru	479,622	−0.22	0.14	0.12
32	Mysuru	893,062	−0.47	−0.54	−0.56
33	Nippani	62,865	0.38	−1.75	−1.74
34	Rabkavi-Banhatti	77,004	−2.74	−0.29	−0.28

Appendix 4A.1 Continued

Number	City	Population, 2011	Population gradient, 1975	Population gradient, 2011	HH gradient, 2011
35	Raichur	234,170	−1.18	−1.06	−1.01
36	Ramanagaram	95,167	−3.96	−1.08	−1.08
37	Ranebennur	101,248	−2.21	−1.52	−1.49
38	Shivamogga	322,650	−0.41	−0.81	−0.81
39	Sindhanoor	75,837	−2.49	−1.41	−1.43
40	Sira	57,555	−3.24	−1.47	−1.45
41	Sirsi	62,882	−1.86	0.08	0.12
42	Tumakuru	302,143	−2.92	−0.42	−0.41
43	Udupi	125,306	−0.52	−0.11	−0.14
44	Yadgir	74,294	−2.01	−1.19	−1.04

Sources: KMDS, Census of India (2011) Primary Census Abstract, Florczyk et al. (2019), and author's analyses.

5

Have India's Jobs Suburbanized?

5.1 Introduction

It is important to understand the sprawl of employment along with the sprawl of persons and households in cities as one will then know if employment comes after persons or persons go after employment, as Sridhar (2007) investigated. Further, employment sprawl can be serious if the population is centrally located and vice versa and jobs are located in distant peripheries, since it can lead to long commute times and congestion. In this chapter, I outline the sprawl of jobs in India's cities over a period of 20 years, drawing from Sridhar (2007) for 1991, and based on new research for 2011.

Information on jobs disaggregated ward-wise is not easy to get. Such information is not systematically gathered or reported municipal ward–wise in any city of the country, including Bengaluru. There are many such wards in every city. Given the rarity of such data, the job density gradients for all cities (including for Bengaluru) were calculated in Sridhar (2007) taking the help of Mills' two-point method, based on just four data points in each city—jobs in the central city, jobs in the metropolitan area, land area of the central city, and of the metropolitan area. As explained in Chapter 2 on methodology, the empirical work reported in this chapter is somewhat less extensive, compared with the earlier chapters on population suburbanization, as the GHSL does not provide data on jobs, but only on population and built area, along with that on Gross Domestic Product (GDP). Nonetheless, given the importance of jobs for cities, we classify the cities of study as either monocentric or polycentric in this chapter.

It is common knowledge to think of metropolitan areas as those which consist of many job hubs. Nonetheless, if the central city density of jobs is higher than in the suburban areas, the validity of the monocentric

Indian Cities or Suburbs? Kala Seetharam Sridhar, Oxford University Press. © Kala Seetharam Sridhar 2025.
DOI: 10.1093/9780198958147.003.0005

Table 5.1 Suburbanization of Jobs in India, 1991

	% Employment suburban	% Employment suburban, metropolitan cities*
Average	28.84	28.99
Maximum	92.85	56.81
Minimum	0.12	9.93
Std. Dev.	20.11	20.11
Observations	154	4

Source: Created by author based on data from Sridhar (2007).

*Delhi, Mumbai, Kolkata, and Chennai.

urban model holds. Further, as the existing body of work (Small & Song, 1994) argues, I employ the term 'monocentric' here to refer to any distribution which is roughly round-shaped and symmetrical around one central point, and do not confine it to the limited sense of all jobs concentrating in the central part of the city.

Taking a chronological view, Table 5.1 summarizes the proportion of employment that was suburbanized in India's cities as of 1991, from Sridhar (2007), which shows that the metropolitan cities' employment was suburbanized to the same extent (nearly 29%) as that of the other cities on average.[1] However, even the least proportion of jobs suburbanized is quite high in metropolitan cities (at 10% for Delhi) when compared with cities all over India (at only 0.12% of jobs suburbanized in Ujjain). This makes sense because metropolitan cities are likely congested with high demand for land and accessibility to employment and amenities near the centre, hence businesses would like to relocate to the peripheries to take advantage of cheaper land there to cut down on their costs. All over India, the maximum proportion of jobs suburbanized among the four metropolitan areas is in Kolkata (at 57%) in 1991.

Table 5.2 summarizes the employment density gradients for India's cities as of 1991. It is no rocket science to observe that the metropolitan areas' jobs are much more suburbanized than for cities in all India, as is evident from the employment density gradients.

[1] This is based on the general definition of suburbanization we've discussed, rather than the b-suburbanization reported in the forthcoming tables in this chapter.

Table 5.2 Summary of Employment Density Gradients, 1991

Summary statistic	Employment density gradient, all cities	Employment density gradient, metropolitan areas*
Average, all	0.4621	0.2578
Maximum	0.9871	0.3473
Minimum	0.0194	0.1818
Std. Dev.	0.2601	0.0794
Observations	160	4

Source: Created by author based on data from Sridhar (2007).
*Delhi, Mumbai, Kolkata, and Chennai.

Table 5.3 Employment Suburbanization (Density Gradients) of Various Economic Sectors, 1991

	Average	Std. Dev.	Min	Max	Number of cities
Mining	0.4568	0.2593	0.0020	0.9708	81
Family as well as non-family-based manufacturing industry with construction	0.4590	0.2839	0.0191	0.9971	151
Transport and communications	0.4965	0.2621	0.0109	0.9777	126
Retail business services	0.5080	0.2587	0.0403	0.9996	111
Other services	0.4613	0.2652	0.0024	0.9337	136

Source: Created by author based on data from Sridhar (2007).

Further, from Sridhar (2007), I understand the extent of suburbanization of jobs in various employment sub-sectors for 1991. Table 5.3 summarizes the job gradients for cities in the country in various sub-sectors such as construction, family as well as non-family-based manufacturing industry, mining, transport and communications, retail business, and other services.

As reported by Sridhar (2007), given the two-point calculation (rather than the regression-based estimation) technique was used there, it was possible to calculate job gradients for many cities in manufacturing, but not so much for the other sub-sectors. This is partially due to the clustering of jobs in manufacturing relative to employment in other sub-sectors. Table 5.3 shows that, on average, mining and manufacturing jobs were much more sprawling in 1991, relative to jobs in sectors such as transport, storage, communications, retail trade, business, and other services. This is similar to Glaeser and Kahn's (2001) finding for US cities, that sprawl was most observed in manufacturing and least likely in services, as Sridhar (2007) documented as well for Indian cities. Glaeser and Kahn's (2001) results are of relevance for Indian metropolitan areas too, and cities in other countries, as sectors like mining and manufacturing are polluting, hence they locate far from the city's centre, when compared with other jobs. The sector which was most centrally located in India's cities as of 1991 was retail business and trade activity, which is to be expected, given these are mostly non-polluting. This is consistent with what we observe as retail activity is typically concentrated in the city centres. Glaeser and Kahn (2001) found that while human capital influenced the centralization of jobs, residential preferences of workers influenced the decentralization of jobs, which brings us to the question of whether persons go after employment or employment goes after persons, a question with which Sridhar (2007) also engaged.

For this reason, Tables 5.4 and 5.5 provide an interesting summary of the sprawl of both persons and jobs, arranged by cities with varying degrees of central city as compared with suburban density, as reported by Sridhar (2007). Table 5.4 classifies cities by varying degrees of *density in their primary city* relative to *that in their suburbs*:[2] primary city centre density less than that in the peripheries, central city density up to five times greater than in the peripheries, five to ten times greater than in the peripheries, and more than ten times greater than in the peripheries.

While we are interested in the employment suburbanization story in this chapter, Table 5.4 indicates a very interesting finding as of 1991 for India's cities: that it is efficient to encourage high density in the primary city centre. This is because I find, as in Table 5.4, that the employment density gradient keeps increasing (implying the city keeps centralizing) as and when the population density in the city centre is increasing

[2] Sridhar (2007) defined the primary city as referring to the municipal boundaries of the urban agglomeration, whereas suburbs were defined as all areas outside of the municipal corporation limits, but within the urban agglomeration.

Table 5.4 Employment Gradients of Cities, Categories of Population Density in the City Centre Relative to That in Suburbs, 1991

	Gradients for cities with population density in their centre:			
Sub-sector employment slope coefficients (gradient)	**Smaller than in the periphery**	**1–5 times greater than in the periphery**	**5–10 times greater than in the periphery**	**>10 times than in the periphery**
Total	0.05 (0.03)	0.44 (0.25)	0.64 (0.22)	0.78 (0.07)
Mining	0.39 (0.27)	0.46 (0.24)	0.43 (0.35)	0.56 (0.25)
Manufacturing	0.32 (0.28)	0.43 (0.27)	0.64 (0.26)	0.76 (0.18)
Communications	0.28 (0.16)	0.48 (0.26)	0.61 (0.23)	0.80 (0.08)
Trade and commerce	0.44 (0.28)	0.50 (0.26)	0.54 (0.19)	0.89 (0.08)
Other services	0.38 (0.20)	0.44 (0.26)	0.58 (0.29)	0.85 (0.05)

Source: Created by author based on data from Sridhar (2007).
Values in the table are shown as average (standard deviation).

relative to the corresponding density in the periphery. This could be an artefact of the fact that jobs follow people, which is what Sridhar (2007) concluded. Thus, when population centralizes, employment centralizes too, and vice versa. On the other hand, when density in the city centre is less than in the periphery, the sub-sector employment density gradients are lower, indicating sprawl. Therefore, I find densities of persons and jobs move closely together.

I find the same story essentially repeating when we classify cities' central city employment density relative to their suburban employment density. Cities which are less dense in the city centre in terms of employment also are more sprawling, if we read Table 5.5 from right to left. On the other hand, central cities which are highly dense (relative to their suburbs) in terms of employment also have centralized employment in various sectors.

Thus, both Tables 5.4 and 5.5 indicate the need to make central cities vibrant and dense in order to be economically efficient, and limit their overall sprawl, in terms of both population and employment. Nonetheless, Sridhar (2007) found that jobs follow people, as it was found that the sprawl of persons determined the sprawl of jobs, but not vice versa.

Table 5.5 Employment Gradients of Cities, Categories of Job Density in the City Centre Relative to That in Suburbs, 1991

	Gradients for cities with job density in their centre:			
Sub-sector employment slope coefficients (gradient)	Smaller than in the periphery	1–5 times more than in the periphery	5–10 times more than in the periphery	>10 times than in the periphery
Total	NA (NA)	0.44 (0.26)	0.63 (0.25)	0.77 (0.08)
Mining	0.30 (0.25)	0.47 (0.24)	0.48 (0.34)	0.51 (0.27)
Manufacturing	0.31 (0.26)	0.45 (0.28)	0.61 (0.26)	0.81 (0.15)
Communications	0.27 (0.15)	0.48 (0.26)	0.63 (0.23)	0.83 (0.06)
Trade and commerce	0.42 (0.27)	0.50 (0.26)	0.54 (0.19)	0.89 (0.08)
Other services	0.39 (0.20)	0.43 (0.26)	0.68 (0.22)	0.85 (0.05)

Source: Created by author based on data from Sridhar (2007).
Values in the table are shown as average (standard deviation). NA: Not available.

In the next section, I present employment density functions for the 19 cities for which I obtained shape files from the Internet, as explained in Chapter 2 on methodology, for 2011.

5.2 Employment Density Functions of Indian Cities, 2011

I start with understanding the employment suburbanization of Delhi. Figure 5.1 presents the employment density function of Delhi, showing that the country's capital is polycentric with at least four prominent employment centres—one each at 3.3, 10.9 (which represents the peak of its employment density), 13.9, and 18 km away from Sansad Bhavan, assumed to be the city centre. We've identified these areas respectively as Karol Bagh, Nehru Vihar, Darya Ganj, and Rani Khera. These are commercially vibrant wards with rich retail activity which presumably have the most service jobs, hence they are employment centres of the city. Thus, I find that Delhi is polycentric, unlike some of the other cities I study next.

Figure 5.2 displays the employment density function for Bhopal (the capital of Madhya Pradesh), assuming the state assembly's location as

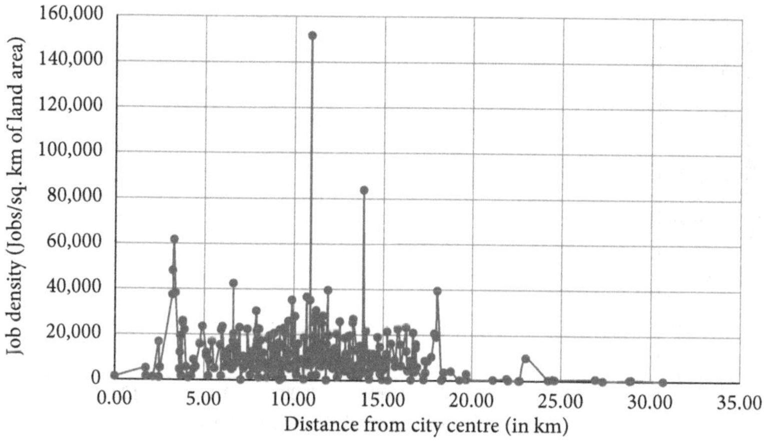

Figure 5.1 Employment Density Function, Delhi, 2011

Sources: Census of India (2011), Delhi's shape file from https://github.com/HindustanTimesLabs/shapefiles/tree/master/city (accessed 30 April 2020), and author's analyses.

the city centre. Employment density peaks at about 2.6 km from the city centre (where the municipal office is located), following which it declines. Although there are many casual observations made that our real cities are not monocentric ones, the case of Bhopal shows that its employment centres are concentrated within about 5 km of the city centre, hence it may be considered monocentric. I have more to say on this towards the end of this chapter.

Figure 5.3 displays the employment density function for Bhubaneswar (Odisha), assuming the Vidhan Soudha's location as the city centre. Employment density peaks at about 3.7 km from the city centre (which is the city's western edge, consisting of educational institutions such as the Indira Gandhi Institute of Pharmaceuticals), following which it declines. The case of Bhubaneswar as well shows that the employment centre is concentrated within about 5 km of the city centre, like what we observe in Bhopal, hence it may reasonably be considered monocentric.

Figure 5.4 shows the employment density function for Chandigarh, assuming centrally located ward 17 (which contains some of the oldest residential and commercial areas) as the city centre. Quite in contrast to Bhopal and Bhubaneswar, employment density peaks at about 6.2

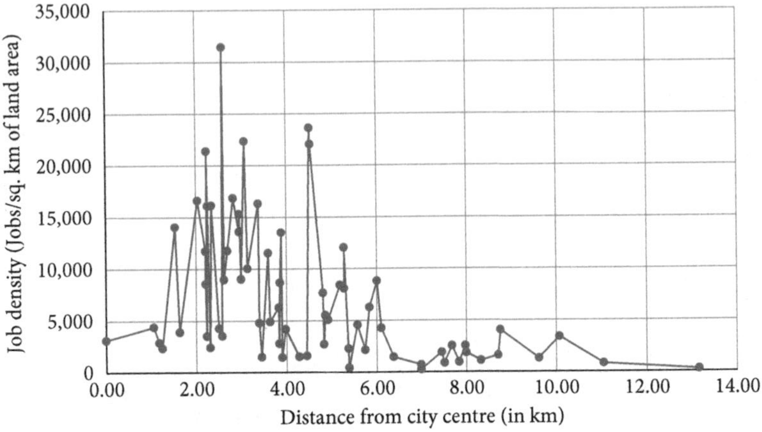

Figure 5.2 Employment Density Function, Bhopal, 2011

Sources: Census of India (2011), Bhopal's shape file from https://github.com/HindustanTimesLabs/shapefiles/tree/master/city (accessed 30 April 2020), and author's analyses.

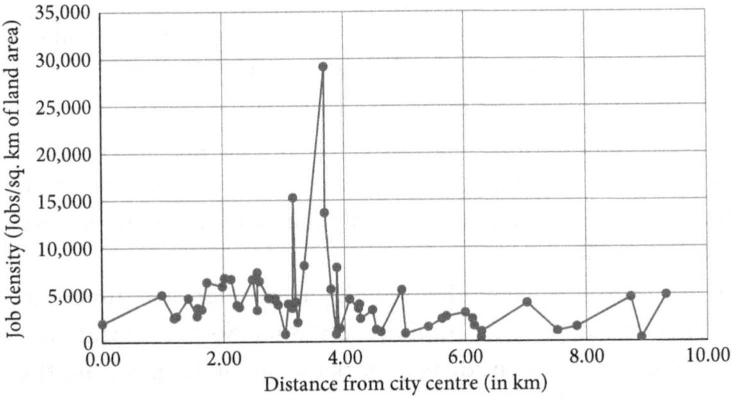

Figure 5.3 Employment Density Function, Bhubaneswar, 2011

Sources: Census of India (2011), Bhubaneswar's shape file from https://github.com/HindustanTimesLabs/shapefiles/tree/master/city (accessed 30 April 2020), and author's analyses.

km from the city centre (ward 5), following which it declines. So, it seems that ward 17 is not the employment centre of the city, rather it is ward 5 which is near the city's western boundary. This makes sense because Chandigarh's ward 5 is economically active consisting of cinemas, temples, mosques, hotels, restaurants, electronics shops,

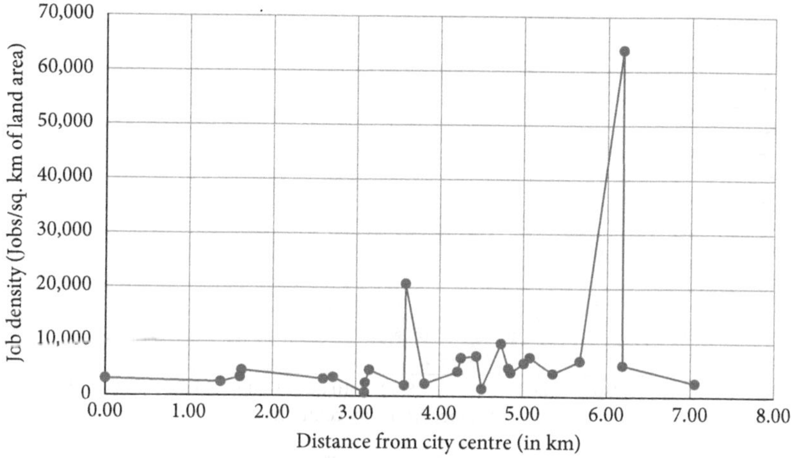

Figure 5.4 Employment Density Function, Chandigarh, 2011
Sources: Census of India (2011), Chandigarh's shape file from https://github.com/HindustanTimesLabs/shapefiles/tree/master/city (accessed 30 April 2020) and author's analyses.

supermarkets, police stations, government offices, schools, and colleges. The employment density function for the city also shows that it is predominantly monocentric, and that its ward 5 may be considered as its real centre.

Figure 5.5 shows the employment density function for Chennai, assuming Parry's Corner as the city centre. Quite in contrast to Chandigarh, and like in Bhopal and Bhubaneswar, employment density in this south Indian city of the most urbanized state peaks at about 4.3 km from the city centre, following which it declines. Thus, it seems that Parry's Corner is not the employment centre of the city, rather it is ward 75 which is located near Purasaiwakkam. This ward is economically vibrant consisting of cinemas, temples, mosques, hotels, restaurants, electronics shops, supermarkets, police stations, government offices, schools, and colleges, thus it is plausible that the job density of this area is the maximum when all wards are considered.

Figure 5.6 displays the employment density function for Coimbatore, the second-biggest city in Tamil Nadu, assuming the ward containing the city's central bus stand as the city centre. Quite like what we find in Chennai, employment density in the textile hub peaks at only about 2 km from the city centre, following which it declines. I find ward 46 is the one

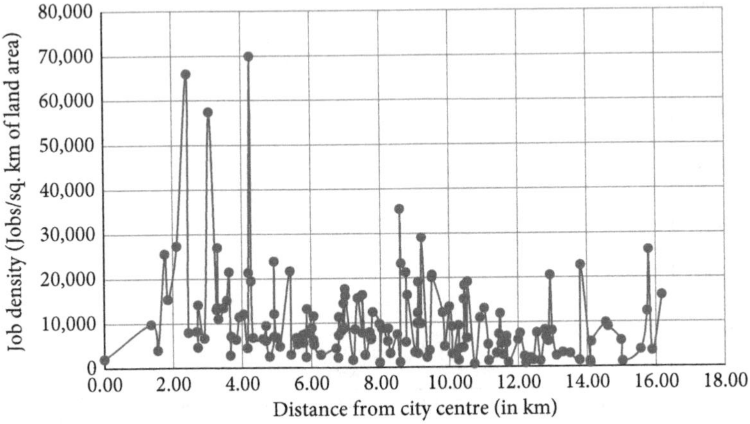

Figure 5.5 Employment Density Function, Chennai, 2011
Sources: Census of India (2011), Chennai's shape file from https://github.com/HindustanTimesLabs/shapefiles/tree/master/city (accessed 30 April 2020), and author's analyses.

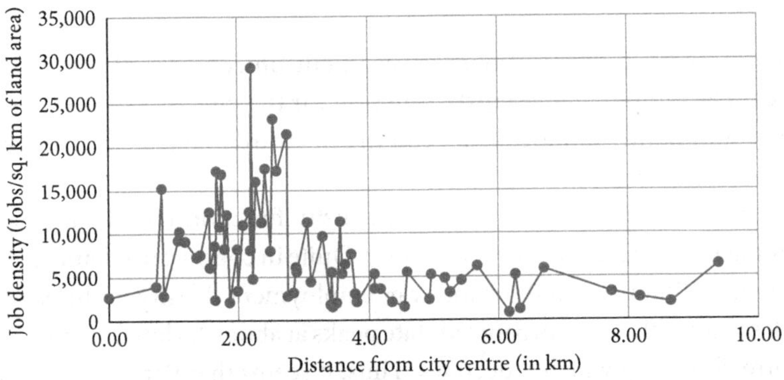

Figure 5.6 Employment Density Function, Coimbatore, 2011
Sources: Census of India (2011), Coimbatore's shape file from https://github.com/HindustanTimesLabs/shapefiles/tree/master/city (accessed 30 April 2020), and author's analyses.

in which employment density peaks: this ward is economically vibrant consisting of cinemas, temples, mosques, hotels, restaurants, supermarkets, police stations, schools, and colleges, therefore it is plausible that the employment density of this area is the highest among all the city's wards. As per the City Development Plan of Coimbatore (2006), this ward has one of the highest population densities as well at 25,001–45,000 persons per square kilometre, hence it is plausible that jobs follow people here.

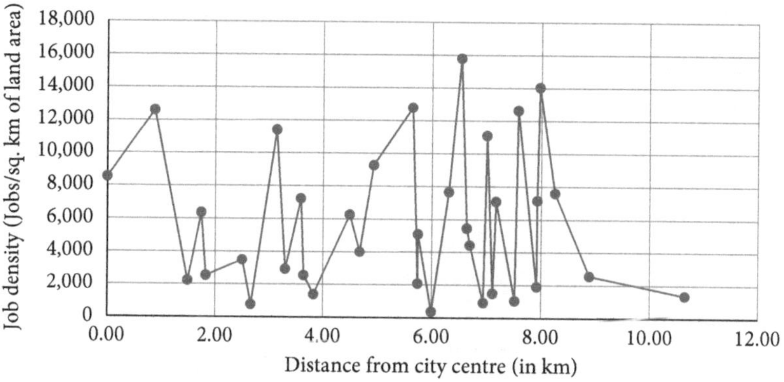

Figure 5.7 Employment Density Function, Faridabad, 2011

Sources: Census of India (2011), Faridabad's shape file from https://github.com/HindustanTimesLabs/shapefiles/tree/master/city (accessed 30 April 2020), and author's analyses.

Figure 5.7 presents the employment density function for Faridabad, Haryana, in the National Capital Region. Faridabad is a strange case because there is no clear employment centre, as we see in Figure 5.7. Clearly Faridabad is polycentric. If one were forced to identify the centre, it would be ward 7, which is geographically the city centre, where employment density peaks at about 15,800 jobs per square kilometre of its land area, at about 6.5 km from the municipal corporation office.

Figure 5.8 presents the employment density function for Hyderabad, a primate city in the newly carved state of Telangana. We may identify multiple employment centres in Hyderabad, at about 2.96 km from the centre, then 5.14 km, 6.87 km, 7.83 km (Talabchanchalam, which is the city's real employment centre, given this ward has the highest employment density[3]), 8.7 km, and finally 20.9 km, at the edge of the city (where the BHEL township is located). I also note that there is a spike in the city's job density towards the edge (at about 21 km from the city centre with an employment density of about 15,620 jobs/sq. km), which is ward 112, Ramachandrapuram, which apparently has good physical (roads) and social infrastructure (with schools and healthcare facilities), making it an

[3] This is the ward containing the famous Charminar monument, which is one of the oldest areas of the city.

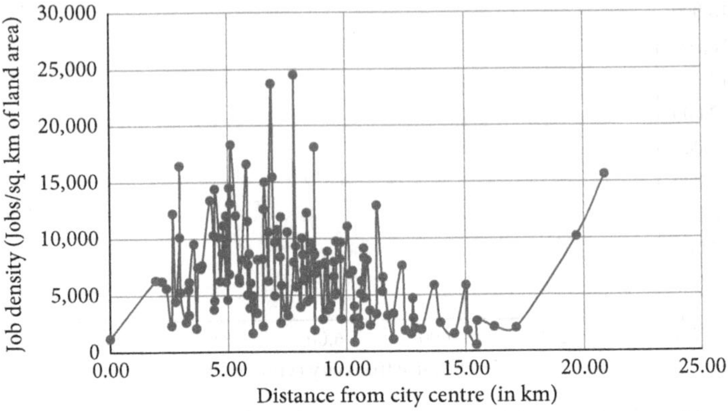

Figure 5.8 Employment Density Function, Hyderabad, 2011

Sources: Census of India (2011), Hyderabad's shape file from https://github.com/HindustanTimesLabs/shapefiles/tree/master/city (accessed 30 April 2020), and author's analyses.

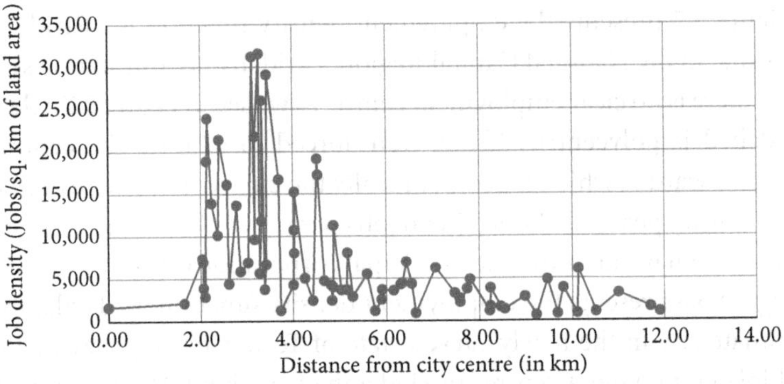

Figure 5.9 Employment Density Function, Jaipur, 2011

Sources: Census of India (2011), Jaipur's shape file from https://github.com/HindustanTimesLabs/shapefiles/tree/master/city (accessed 30 April 2020), and author's analyses.

attractive area to live, so naturally it is another employment centre. I find Hyderabad to be polycentric.

Figure 5.9 presents the employment density function for Jaipur. Similar to what I find in Hyderabad, I identify multiple employment centres in Jaipur too, each at about 3.13 km, 3.28 km (which is the city's real employment centre, given this ward has the highest employment density with several government offices and markets), 3.33 km, and 3.45 km, all within 4 km of the city centre.

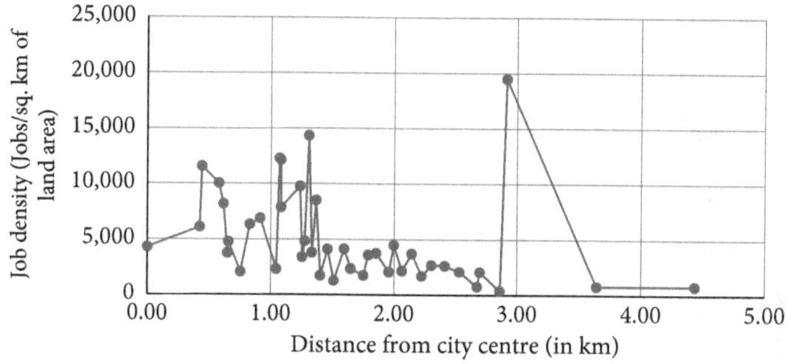

Figure 5.10 Employment Density Function, Katihar, 2011

Sources: Census of India (2011), Katihar's shape file from https://github.com/HindustanTimesLabs/shapefiles/tree/master/city (accessed 30 April 2020), and author's analyses.

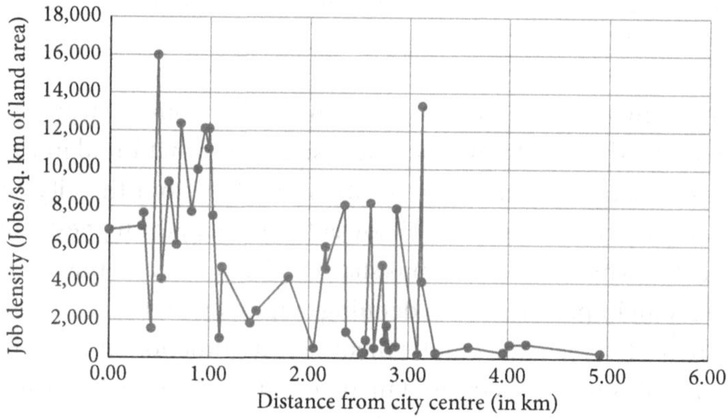

Figure 5.11 Employment Density Function, Kishangarh, 2011

Sources: Census of India (2011), Kishangarh's shape file from https://github.com/HindustanTimesLabs/shapefiles/tree/master/city (accessed 30 April 2020), and author's analyses.

Figure 5.10 presents the employment density function for Katihar in Bihar. It shows the curve of a city which has a single employment centre, ward 6 (which contains the city's bus stand), 3 km away from the chosen city centre containing its municipal office.Katihar's entire city radius is completely within 5 km, thus the employment centre of the city is quite far from the identified central point (which is the municipal office, the Nagar Nigam).

Figure 5.11 presents the employment function for yet another city, Kishangarh, in a lagging state, Rajasthan. As the figure shows, there are

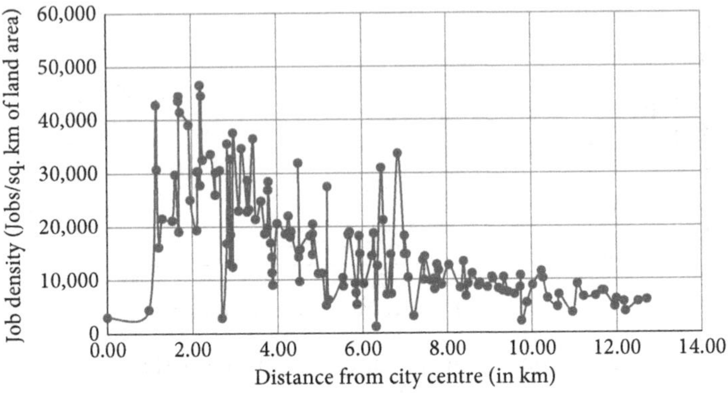

Figure 5.12 Employment Density Function, Kolkata, 2011

Sources: Census of India (2011), Kolkata's shape file from https://github.com/HindustanTimesLabs/shapefiles/tree/master/city (accessed 30 April 2020), and author's analyses.

two employment centres, one at less than half a kilometre from the city centre, where the bus station is located, similar to what I find in Katihar. The second employment centre is about 3.1 km from the city centre, whose employment density is a bit lower than that of the highest employment centre, which has several bus stations. Thus, it seems that transport nodes play an important role in defining employment density.

Figure 5.12 depicts the employment density function of Kolkata, another of India's major metropolitan areas. Similarly to Delhi, Kolkata is also polycentric in employment. The real employment centre of the city with the highest employment density (at 46,606 employed per square kilometre of land area) is about 2.2 km away from the centre (taken as Vidhan Sabha Bhavan). This is ward 49 in the city centre in borough 5, containing parts of the Bowbazaar and Sealdah neighbourhoods. There are also several wards which are closely clustered around this employment centre—these are wards 24, 51, 41, and 39, clustered with several other city wards.

Figure 5.13 shows the employment density of Lucknow, the capital of the most populous state in the country. The employment centre is in ward 2, in the south-eastern part of the city, which is about 8.5 km from the city centre, which contains the Vidhan Sabha. However, there are also a couple of employment centres closer to the city centre, at 1.9 km (in the eastern part) and 2.8 km (also in the eastern part of the town) from the

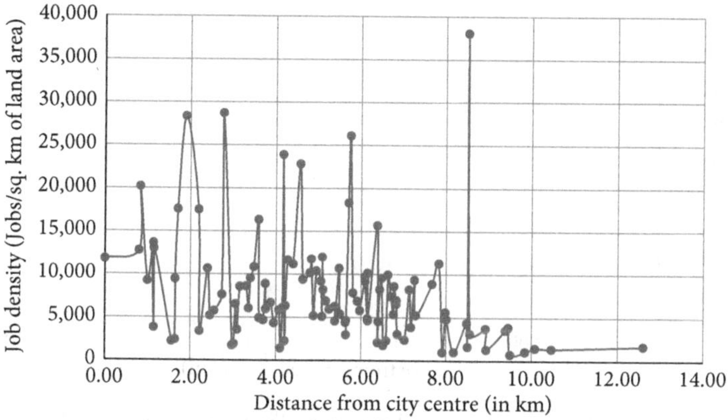

Figure 5.13 Employment Density Function, Lucknow, 2011

Sources: Census of India (2011), Lucknow's shape file from https://github.com/HindustanTimesLabs/shapefiles/tree/master/city (accessed 30 April 2020), and author's analyses.

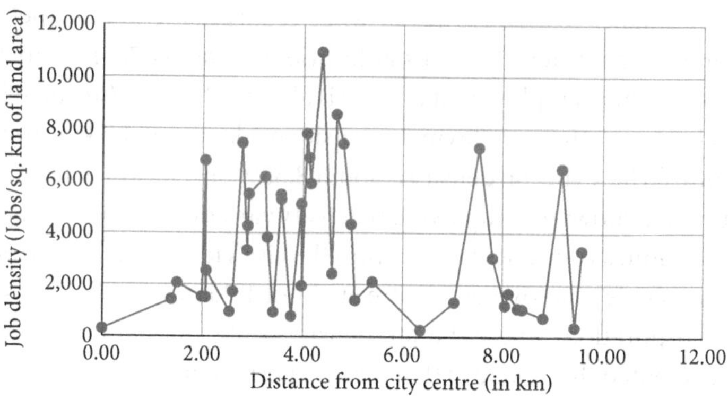

Figure 5.14 Employment Density Function, Purnia, 2011

Sources: Census of India (2011), Purnia's shape file from https://github.com/HindustanTimesLabs/shapefiles/tree/master/city (accessed 30 April 2020), and author's analyses.

centre. Thus, Lucknow is polycentric, even while all employment centres are in the eastern part of the city.

Figure 5.14 shows the job density function of Purnia, in Bihar, and how it changes with distance from its centre, its municipal corporation. While there appear to be multiple job centres as the figure shows, the ward with the highest employment density is ward 26, 4.4 km from the city centre, which consists of at least four bus stations, as is the case with

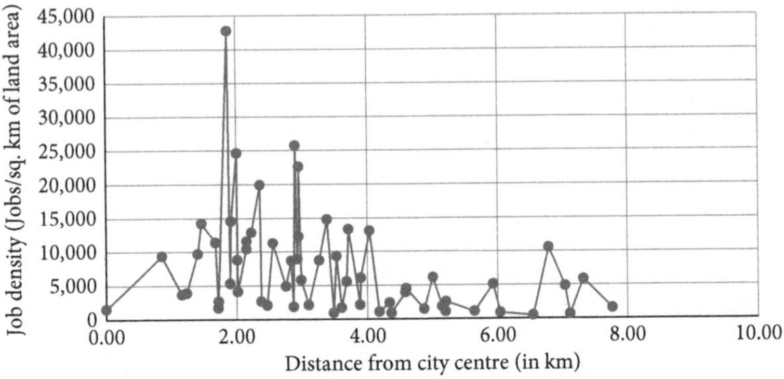

Figure 5.15 Employment Density Function, Tiruchirappalli, 2011

Sources: Census of India (2011), Tiruchirappalli's shape file from https://github.com/HindustanTimesLabs/shapefiles/tree/master/city (accessed 30 April 2020), and author's analyses.

the other smaller towns. However, what is surprising is that there are some employment density peaks at locations as far as 7.5 km from the city centre (where employment density is about 7,283 jobs/sq. km of land area). There are other employment density peaks about 4.7 km from the city centre (where the job density is about 8,539 jobs/sq. km of land area).

Figure 5.15 shows the employment density variations of Tiruchirappalli in Tamil Nadu, as one goes farther from the city's identified central point. There is a single employment centre at about 1.9 km from the city's municipal corporation, where the job density peaks. Ramani et al. (2018) too documented this as one of the wards experiencing high urban sprawl, along with several others in the city.

Figure 5.16 shows the employment density for Vijayawada in Andhra Pradesh. Prima facie, it appears that this is a polycentric city, with multiple employment centres. The primary peak is in ward 6, which is about 1.9 km from the city's centre, the municipal corporation office. The highest job density ward contains a variety of economic activity including hotels, restaurants, cinemas, hospitals, schools, and colleges.

I report the employment density function for Madurai in Tamil Nadu; it is presented in Figure 5.17. This shows that Madurai is monocentric and has only one dominant employment centre where the density of employment is the highest, which is about 3.8 km from the city's centre. This is ward 68 which consists of Dhrowpathi Amman Kovil, a temple. For the

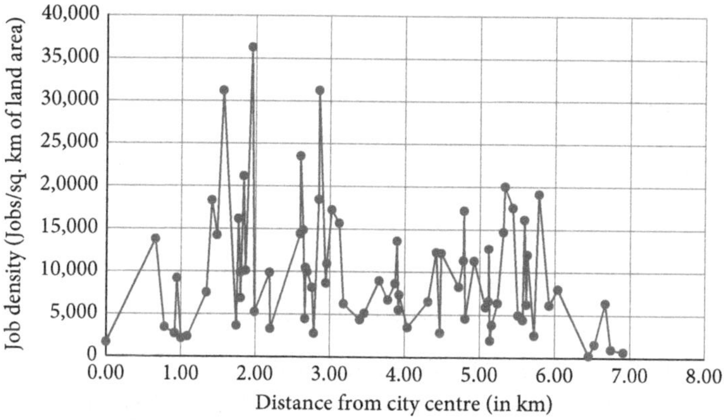

Figure 5.16 Employment Density Function, Vijayawada, 2011

Sources: Census of India (2011), Vijayawada's shape file from https://github.com/HindustanTimesLabs/shapefiles/tree/master/city (accessed 30 April 2020), and author's analyses.

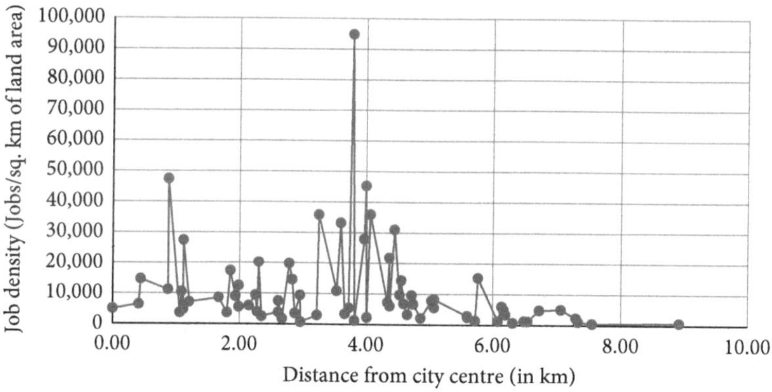

Figure 5.17 Employment Density Function, Madurai, 2011

Sources: Census of India (2011), Madurai's shape file from https://github.com/HindustanTimesLabs/shapefiles/tree/master/city (accessed 30 April 2020), and author's analyses.

temple town that Madurai is, it is no surprise that this is the employment centre of the city.

Figure 5.18 shows the employment density function for a small town in Bihar, Bodh Gaya, where Gautam Buddha is believed to have experienced his enlightenment. As we might expect, for the small town that Bodh Gaya is (with a 2011 population of 38,439), it has clearly only one employment centre. This is ward 12, located at about 1.9 km from the

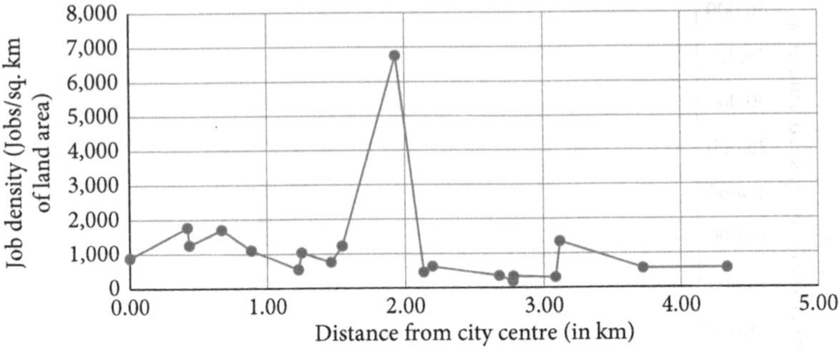

Figure 5.18 Employment Density Function, Bodh Gaya, 2011

Sources: Census of India (2011), Bodh Gaya's shape file from https://github.com/HindustanTimesLabs/shapefiles/tree/master/city (accessed 30 April 2020), and author's analyses.

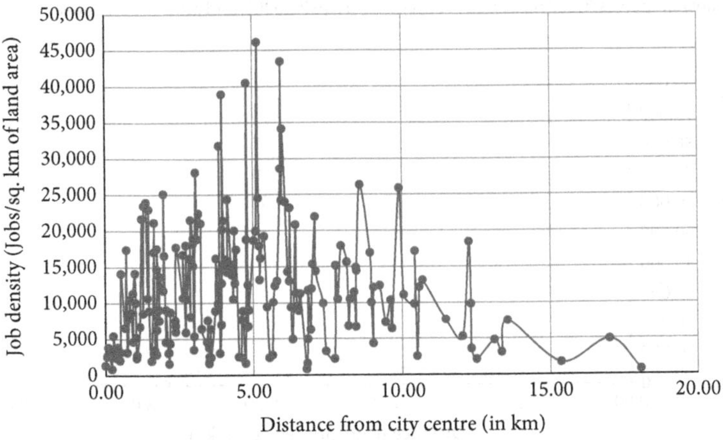

Figure 5.19 Employment Density Function, Bengaluru, 2011

Sources: Census of India (2011) and author's analyses.

city centre, and it consists of several bus stations as we observe in other smaller cities and towns.

Figure 5.19 shows the employment density function of Bengaluru for 2011. Figure 5.19 shows that Bengaluru is polycentric as there are multiple peaks of employment clusters. The maximum job concentration (jobs per square kilometre of land area) is in Kempapura Agrahara, in the heart of the city, 4 km away from the identified centre, which Sridhar (2007) as well reported to be the actual centre of the city, consisting of

Table 5.6 Summary of Estimated Employment Density Gradients, 2011

Employment density gradients, selected Indian cities, 2011		
Average, 19 cities	0.20 (−0.19)*	More decentralized than population (population gradient for 100 cities being 0.32, see Table 3.1)
Maximum	0.73	Kishangarh, Rajasthan
Minimum	0.03	Faridabad, Haryana

Sources: Florczyk et al. (2019), Census of India (2011), and author's analyses.

*This table presents the absolute value of the density gradients estimated. In parentheses is the average value for the cities based on their actual values with sign.

mixed residential uses, with retail activity, small industry, and artisan trades. These are followed by another couple of employment peaks in Padarayanapura in the central part of the city and Nilasandra in the south-eastern part of town (Koramangala). Thus, I find the centre and south of Bengaluru are major job hubs, contributing to its polycentricity.

Table 5.6 presents the employment density gradients whose employment density functions are summarized above. I estimated these employment density gradients by running regressions for the 19 cities in the country, using Census 2011 data. Appendix 5A.1 presents, for each of the 18 cities, the *estimated* employment density gradient for 2011 based on their wards, along with the *calculated* 1991 employment density gradient for the cities, where available. I find that each of these 19 cities' employment suburbanized during 1991–2011, as observed in the significantly declined value of 0.19 in 2011, when compared with its (calculated) 1991 value (its modulus) (0.37).

I find that employment in 2011 is also much more decentralized (with a gradient of 0.19) than population suburbanization in 2015 (with an average gradient of 0.32 for all Indian cities, see Chapter 3, Table 3.1). This is similar to the results in Glaeser and Kahn (2001) who reported that less than one-sixth of jobs were within a 4.8-km compass of the centre of metropolitan areas in the USA. I find this is mostly the case in Indian cities too.

Table 5.7 summarizes the employment concentration in the cities we've studied, by sub-sector and by varying distances from the city centres identified. Various categories of proximity to the city's central point are taken, based on the size of the cities. In large cities the last 5

Table 5.7 Summary of Spatial Distribution of Employment within Selected Cities, by Employment Sub-Sector

Percentage of jobs within a 1-km compass of the identified centre									
Total employment		**Total cultivators**		**Total ag. lab.**		**Total HH industry workers**		**Total other workers**	
Mean	4.75%	Mean	3.59%	Mean	2.67%	Mean	5.00%	Mean	4.94%
Least	0.13%	Least	0.00%	Least	0.00%	Least	0.00%	Least	0.00%
Highest	22.66%	Highest	10.21%	Highest	10.12%	Highest	27.75%	Highest	23.83%
Total observations	18	Total observations	18	Total observations	18	Total observations	18	Total observations	18
Percentage of jobs within a 2-km compass of the identified centre									
Total employment		**Total cultivators**		**Total ag. lab.**		**Total HH industry workers**		**Total other workers**	
Mean	16.91%	Mean	14.32%	Mean	11.89%	Mean	17.14%	Mean	17.27%
Least	0.44%	Least	0.00%	Least	0.00%	Least	0.00%	Least	0.00%
Highest	65.45%	Highest	49.10%	Highest	41.33%	Highest	71.87%	Highest	70.40%
Total observations	18	Total observations	18	Total observations	18	Total observations	18	Total observations	18
Percentage of jobs within a 5-km compass of the identified centre									
Total employment		**Total cultivators**		**Total ag. lab.**		**Total HH industry workers**		**Total other workers**	
Mean	52.25%	Mean	46.29%	Mean	44.55%	Mean	52.25%	Mean	52.13%
Minimum	6.62%	Minimum	10.70%	Minimum	8.38%	Minimum	10.62%	Minimum	8.07%

Maximum	82.13%	Maximum	87.34%	Maximum	78.27%	Maximum	81.86%	Maximum	82.73%
Total observations	15	Total observations	15	Total observations	15	Total observations	15	Total observations	15
Share of employment within the last 5-km radius from the city centre									
Total employment		**Total cultivators**		**Total ag. lab.**		**Total HH industry workers**		**Total other workers**	
Mean	30.32%	Mean	36.42%	Mean	36.04%	Mean	30.70%	Mean	30.27%
Minimum	1.35%	Minimum	2.70%	Minimum	2.86%	Minimum	0.82%	Minimum	1.23%
Maximum	88.78%	Maximum	86.93%	Maximum	89.03%	Maximum	90.72%	Maximum	90.33%
Total observations	13	Total observations	13	Total observations	13	Total observations	13	Total observations	13
Share of employment within the last 2-km radius from the city centre									
Total employment		**Total cultivators**		**Total ag. lab.**		**Total HH industry workers**		**Total other workers**	
Mean	21.36%	Mean	29.71%	Mean	36.86%	Mean	20.40%	Mean	20.74%
Minimum	8.32%	Minimum	6.02%	Minimum	6.23%	Minimum	8.56%	Minimum	8.34%
Maximum	42.85%	Maximum	50.73%	Maximum	63.97%	Maximum	35.25%	Maximum	41.76%
Total observations	4	Total observations	4	Total observations	4	Total observations	4	Total observations	4

Sources: Census of India (2011) and author's analyses.

km continues to have considerable employment, whereas in the smaller cities (e.g. Katihar, Tiruchirappalli, Vijayawada, and Bodhgaya) a 2-km radius was deemed adequate. Delhi is an outlier, hence I had a separate category for employment concentrated within 10 km of the city centre. Appendix 5A.2 shows the extent of concentration of employment for the sub-sectors by varying distances from the city centres, for all the individual cities for which I obtained the data.

In Bengaluru, for instance, about 21% of all employment in the city is within the first 2 km of the city centre. The remaining 79% of employment is scattered across the remaining 16-km radius of the city. For Bengaluru, I also examined the centralization of employment for various sub-sectors for which the data are available. I found that only one-fourth of all household industry jobs were within a 2-km compass of the identified centre as of 2011 (the most recent information applicable at the time this book was being completed), while only 10% each of cultivators and agricultural labourers were within 1 km of the city centre. This may be something to expect as such employment is usually concentrated in areas of raw material or talent availability, proximity to markets, or where the cost of land is lower.

Overall the thing to note is that only 5% of urban employment (represented by domestic manufacturing and other categories of jobs) on average is concentrated in a less than 1-km compass of the city's centre. In less than a 2-km compass of the identified centre, on average, only 17% each of these two urban sectors' employment is concentrated. However, in less than a 5-km compass of the centre, roughly 52% of employment in the urban sectors—household manufacturing and other workers—is concentrated. Considering all the cities, I find that on average, a majority (52%) of *all jobs* are concentrated in less than a 5-km compass of the identified centre (Table 5.7). Similarly, for the 'other workers' who are really the urban workers employed in services such as banks, finance, real estate, insurance, trade, commerce, transport and communications, and related services, the most employment is concentrated within 5 km of the city centre, on average, for the cities considered. Interestingly, on average, a majority (52%) of employment in household industry was also in less than 5 km from the identified centre of the city. In Delhi, 52% of household industry employment was within

10 km of the city centre. In contrast, on average, for all the cities considered, only 46% and 45% respectively of cultivators and agricultural labourers are concentrated within 5 kms of the city centre (Table 5.7). This is natural to expect, as cities are defined primarily based on non-agricultural employment.

Overall, in less than a 2-km compass of the identified centre, on average, only about 17% of jobs in each of household industry and 'other' sectors (services) are concentrated (Table 5.7). However, within the last 5 km from the city centre, on average for all the cities considered, about 30% of employment in each of household industry and other workers is still concentrated. Table 5.7 is convincing evidence of the fact that Indian cities are sprawling as far as urban employment is concerned.

5.3 Are Indian Cities Polycentric?

Based on a study of the employment density functions in several cities, what do we conclude about their monocentricity versus polycentricity? Table 5.8 summarizes the monocentricity versus polycentricity of the cities studied here, based on their employment density functions. More than half of the cities studied (58%) are polycentric.

Since the monocentric cities in Table 5.8 are relatively the smaller ones too, I examined the correlation between city size and polycentricity, and found unsurprisingly that larger cities are characterized by polycentricity, with a positive correlation of 0.54. Further, a paper by Sun et al. (2022) found that multiple employment centres accounted more for the commercial growth of bigger metropolitan areas, taking the case of China. Their findings suggested that strategies to encourage multiple centres were helpful for tackling problems such as congestion and pollution, which typically accompany urban growth.

I analysed the correlations between population, per capita GDP, and polycentricity. What I find is interesting: population and per capita GDP are positively correlated (with a correlation of 0.50), meaning that larger cities are the richer ones too. This makes sense, as large cities are characterized by agglomeration economies (Brueckner, 2011), density, and

Table 5.8 Monocentricity versus Polycentricity of Selected Cities

City, state	Monocentric/Polycentric	Per capita GDP (in PPP$)
Delhi	Polycentric	9,867.86
Bhopal, Madhya Pradesh	Monocentric	2,945.22
Bhubaneswar, Odisha	Monocentric	3,363.75
Chandigarh, Haryana	Monocentric	8,950.28
Chennai, Tamil Nadu	Polycentric	6,028.49
Coimbatore, Tamil Nadu	Monocentric	5,606.90
Faridabad, Haryana	Polycentric	NA
Hyderabad, Telangana	Polycentric	5,204.58
Jaipur, Rajasthan	Polycentric	997.81
Katihar, Bihar	Monocentric	2,265.71
Kishangarh, Rajasthan	Polycentric	1,321.32
Kolkata, West Bengal	Polycentric	4,073.45
Lucknow, Uttar Pradesh	Polycentric	2,380.02
Purnia, Bihar	Polycentric	1,603.04
Tiruchirappalli, Tamil Nadu	Monocentric	6,108.23
Vijayawada, Andhra Pradesh	Polycentric	5,410.69
Madurai, Tamil Nadu	Monocentric	5,296.02
Bodh Gaya, Bihar	Monocentric	1,210.57
Bengaluru, Karnataka	Polycentric	5,579.73

Sources: Census of India (2011), shape files from https://github.com/HindustanTimesLabs/shapefiles/tree/master/city (accessed 30 April 2020), Florczyk et al. (2019), and author's analyses.

NA: Not available.

PPP: Purchasing Power Parity.

productivity increases (Ciccone & Hall, 1993) via sharing, matching, and learning. We find polycentricity and population are positively correlated with a stronger correlation of 0.54. However, polycentricity is weakly negatively correlated with per capita income (with a weak negative correlation of only −0.04). This implies that in the Indian context, cities with multiple employment centres are those with lower per capita GDP. However, the caveats of this finding should be stated. It is possible that monocentric cities such as Chandigarh which have a higher per capita income could be driving these findings. Furthermore, the sample of cities on which these correlations are based is small, at 19.

5.4 Geographic Differences in the Sprawl of Jobs

In this section, I understand geographic differences in the sprawl of jobs in India's metropolitan areas which I have already documented. Given the lack of adequate data, I rely on earlier studies, and combine them with the data I have from the Census for 2011. I first capture regional variations in the employment suburbanization of cities during 1991 and 2011. Then I study employment suburbanization by categories such as urbanized states, south Indian states, and lagging states. This is followed by an analysis of employment suburbanization in Karnataka's cities, since I have data on 44 cities from the Karnataka Municipal Data Society, as indicated in Chapter 2 on methodology. Within Karnataka, I elaborate on the employment suburbanization of Kalaburagi in northern Karnataka, which is traditionally known to be in the lagging region of the state, in the Hyderabad-Karnataka region.

Table 5.9 summarizes the employment density gradients for various regions of the country for 1991, from Sridhar (2007) and the 2011 Census. It should be noted that the employment density gradients for 1991 are *calculated, not estimated*, which they are for 2011. The caveats that accompany *calculated gradients* versus those that are *estimated* (highlighted in Chapter 2 on methodology) should be borne in mind. Having noted this caveat, Table 5.9 summarizes the modulus of the job gradients for various regions of the country for 1991–2011.

Similarly to population (which sprawled in south Indian cities in both 1975 and 2015, see Chapter 4), I find that employment density gradients in the southern region were also lower than the all-India value, implying that employment was sprawling as well in the south Indian cities in 1991 (Table 5.9).

We observe from Table 5.9 that there was a 43% decline in job concentration on average with increasing distance from the identified centre in the south Indian cities, whereas this was 46% for all cities in India in 1991 (Table 5.9).

The most centralized city in terms of jobs in 1991 was Alipurduar in West Bengal (eastern region). The most sprawling (suburbanized) in terms of jobs in 1991 was Alappuzha in Kerala (southern region). I found that Alappuzha's Sprawl Network Disconnectedness Index (SNDI) (which is used for population) was 2.42. As explained by

Table 5.9 Geographic Differences in Employment Density Gradient, India's Metropolitan Areas, 1991–2011

Region	Employment density gradient (absolute value)	
	1991 (calculated)	2011 (estimated)
Mean, South*	0.43	0.14
Mean, East**	0.48	0.25
Mean, North***	0.42	0.14
Mean, West****	0.50	0.47
Average, all Indian cities	**0.46**	**0.20**

Sources: Created by author using data in Sridhar (2007) and Census of India (2011).

*76 cities in Andhra Pradesh, Kerala, Karnataka, Pondicherry, and Tamil Nadu (1991). Vijayawada, Chennai, Coimbatore, Tiruchirappalli, Madurai, Hyderabad, and Lucknow (2011).

**73 cities in Assam, Bihar, Meghalaya, Manipur, Odisha, and West Bengal (1991). Bodhgaya, Katihar, Purnia, Bhubaneswar, and Kolkata (2011).

***99 cities in Chandigarh, Delhi, Himachal Pradesh, Haryana, Uttar Pradesh, and Madhya Pradesh (1991). Delhi, Chandigarh, Faridabad, Bhopal, and Lucknow (2011).

****76 cities in Maharashtra, Goa, Rajasthan, and Gujarat (1991). Jaipur and Kishangarh (2011).

Barrington-Leigh and Millard-Ball (2020), the higher this score, the more the sprawl, as it indicates more disconnectedness of streets. For the 10,137 cities in Barrington-Leigh and Millard-Ball's (2020) dataset (including all cities of the world), the average SNDI was 2.25. If it is assumed that jobs follow people, then higher population sprawl also implies job sprawl.

Table 5.9 shows that the most compact in terms of jobs was the western region of the country in 1991, with the most suburbanized being the northern region. I note that the west is one of the most metropolitanized (along with the southern region); whereas, the northern region is a mixture of states which are highly urbanized (such as Delhi and Haryana), and the most populous and least urbanized, Uttar Pradesh. Therefore, it is easy to believe that the jobs sprawl is due to the influence of Delhi and Haryana in the northern region.

In 2011, I find that jobs sprawled in the cities of south Indian and urbanized states (with an employment density gradient of 0.14 and 0.13, respectively, when compared with 0.20 for all cities for which I have the data) (Table 5.10). This shows that even jobs are not compact in cities of urbanized and south Indian states, similar to what we find with their population (see Chapter 4). This finding is surprising because

Table 5.10 Job Density Gradients for Various Categories of Cities, 2011

Employment density gradients, south Indian cities, 2011		
Average, 7 cities	0.14	More suburbanized than all cities
Maximum	0.25	Tiruchirappalli
Minimum	0.06	Hyderabad
Employment density gradients, cities of lagging states, 2011		
Average, 8 cities	0.30	More compact than all cities
Maximum	0.73	Kishangarh
Minimum	0.05	Purnia
Employment density gradients, cities of urbanized states, 2011		
Average, 11 cities	0.13	Suburbanized compared with all India
Maximum	0.25	Tiruchirappalli
Minimum	0.03	Faridabad
Employment density gradients, all cities, 2011		
Average, 19 cities	0.20	Suburbanized when compared with 1991 (see Table 6.1)
Maximum	0.73	Kishangarh
Minimum	0.03	Faridabad

Sources: Census of India (2011) and author's analyses.

the urbanized states (which are also mostly the south Indian states) experience higher land costs and those associated with urbanization and growth, hence one would expect their costs of sprawl and spreading jobs and people would be high. The actual job sprawl I find in the urbanized states could be because large urban agglomerations such as Delhi have their employment quite spread out as discussed earlier in this chapter.

The employment suburbanization in cities of the urbanized states is still more sprawling (with a job density gradient of 0.13) than that found in the cities of south Indian states (where it was 0.14, see Table 5.10 for the magnitude of relative density gradients across the two sets of states). This reinforces the discussion earlier of how urbanization brings along with it costs that cities would rather avoid—spiralling land and infrastructure development costs, despite which they are sprawling.

Summarizing, I find jobs are more sprawling overall when compared with population which is relatively more centralized (using evidence from Chapters 3 and 4). Jobs in the cities of southern India and in relatively more metropolitanized states are more suburbanized (decentralized) than in the north and less metropolitanized states and all India.

5.4.1 Employment Suburbanization of Cities in Karnataka

In this section, I report the employment density gradients for Karnataka's cities (excluding Bengaluru). These smaller cities from Karnataka were not included in the south Indian cities for which employment density gradients were reported because smaller cities such as Chintamani and Channapatna cannot be included in the same class as Delhi, Chennai, and Bengaluru. Appendix 5A.3 lists the cities in Karnataka for which employment density gradients were estimated for 2011, along with their values.

Table 5.11 presents a summary of the employment density gradients in Karnataka's cities for 2016 (excluding Bengaluru, given it is disproportionately large with an estimated population of more than 10 million as of 2021).

Comparing Tables 5.10 and 5.11, I find that cities and towns in Karnataka are much more centralized in terms of employment, judging from the higher absolute value of its employment density gradient on average (0.87), when compared with those for other south Indian cities (0.14), the urbanized states (which have on average an employment density gradient of 0.13), and cities in all India (0.20). One reason could be the small size of the cities themselves, as they typically do not have much of an employment base to begin with.

I find that Ilkal in northern Karnataka is the most centralized of the cities and towns I study here, with an employment density gradient of 2.04 (Table 5.11). Figure 5.20 depicts the employment density function of this town, which shows that its job density peaks at less than 1 km from the identified centre (its bus stand), but there are other peaks as well, making

Table 5.11 Employment Suburbanization of Karnataka's Cities, 2016

Summary statistic	Absolute value of employment density gradient
Average	0.87
Maximum	2.04 (Ilkal)
Minimum	0.03 (Karwar)
Number of cities	43

Sources: Karnataka Municipal Data Society (KMDS) and author's analyses.

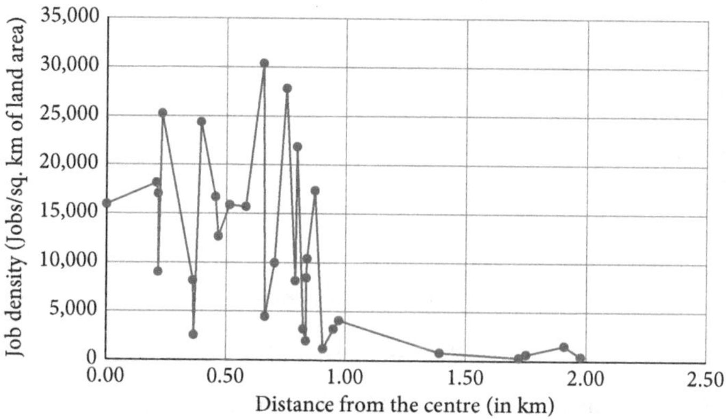

Figure 5.20 Job Density Function, Ilkal, 2011
Sources: KMDS, Census of India PCA (2011), and author's analyses.

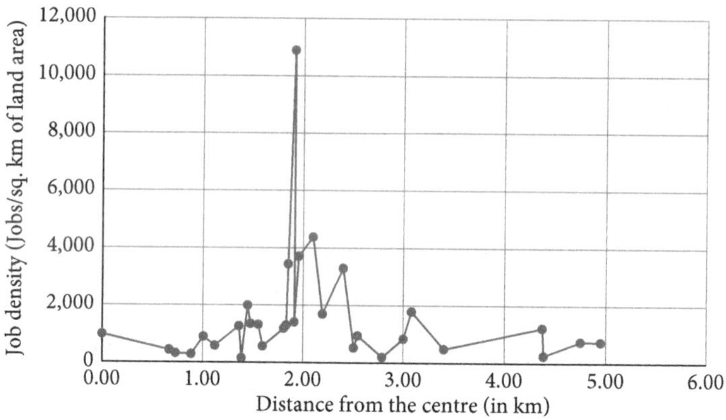

Figure 5.21 Job Density Function, Karwar, 2011
Sources: KMDS, Census of India PCA (2011), and author's analyses.

it polycentric. Ilkal is a small town (known for its brand of sarees); thus, as we expect, the density falls off rapidly with increasing distance from its identified centre, which presumably explains its compactness. Karwar on the western coast of the state is the most suburbanized with an employment density gradient of 0.03 (Figure 5.21). As is documented, Karwar is a naval base on National Highway 66, hence it is natural for us to expect that the highway infrastructure enables its jobs sprawl too, in addition to population sprawl.

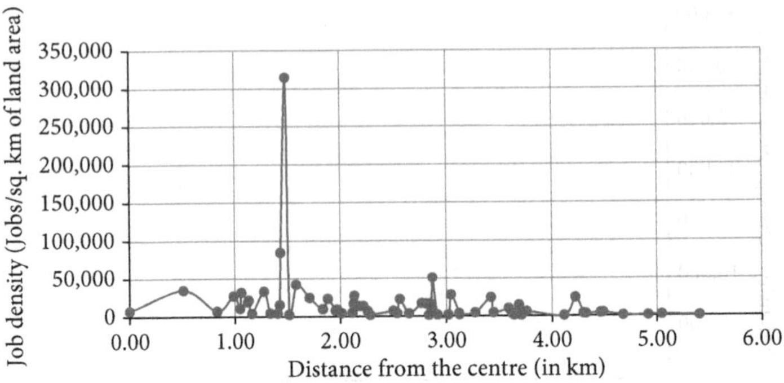

Figure 5.22 Mysuru's Employment Density Function, 2011
Sources: KMDS, Census of India PCA (2011), and author's analyses.

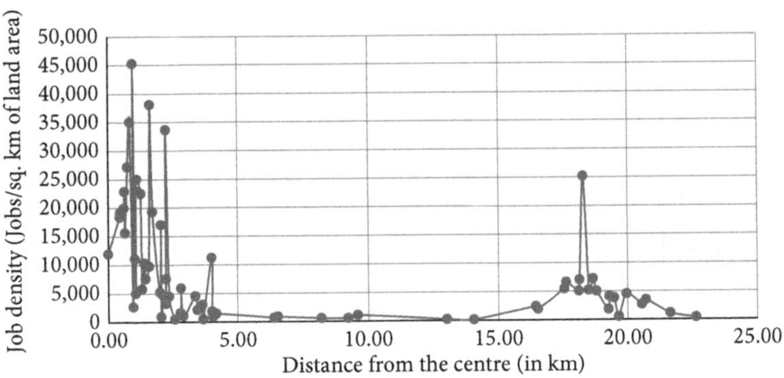

Figure 5.23 Hubballi-Dharwad's Employment Density Function, 2011
Sources: KMDS, Census of India PCA (2011), and author's analyses.

Next, we focus on the employment density functions of the relatively larger (11 of them) cities in Karnataka for understanding their spatial spread. We start with Mysuru's job density function (see Figure 5.22), which shows that the city is primarily monocentric, with its peak of employment density in ward 41, about 1.5 km from the city centre (its railway station). As seen in Chapter 4, this ward also represents the peak of the city's population density, reinforcing that population and jobs co-locate.

Figure 5.23 summarizes and presents the job density function for another major city in the state, Hubballi-Dharwad. In contrast to Mysuru, Hubballi-Dharwad's employment density peaks within less than 1 km

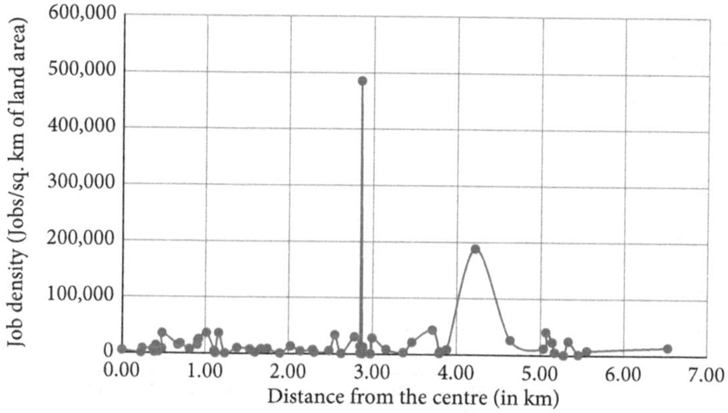

Figure 5.24 Belagavi's Employment Density Function, 2011
Sources: KMDS, Census of India PCA (2011), and author's analyses.

from its identified centre (bus stand). The city also has multiple peaks of employment, unlike Mysuru, which is to be expected given it is a twin city. The city's employment density follows the standard negative exponential form, save for a peak which is at 18 km from the identified centre, in ward 11 in the eastern part of town.

Figure 5.24 presents the job density function of Belagavi, another important town in the state.Figure 5.24 shows that the town is predominantly monocentric in terms of having a single centre of employment, which is nearly 3 km from the identified centre (the bus stand). This is also the ward of the highest population density, which implies that jobs and people follow each other.

Figure 5.25 displays the job density function of the coastal city, Mangaluru, which is clearly polycentric with several employment density peaks. However, I find that the peak of employment density, at more than 7,560 jobs per square kilometre of land area, is attained only at about 3.92 km from the identified centre (the city corporation office), in ward 46 in the southern part of town. There is also another employment peak closer to the city centre, at about 3.2 km from there. In addition, job density peaks somewhat at about 12 km from the centre, in the northern part of town.

Figure 5.26 displays the job density function of Davanagere, another class I city in the state. The city is monocentric as far as employment

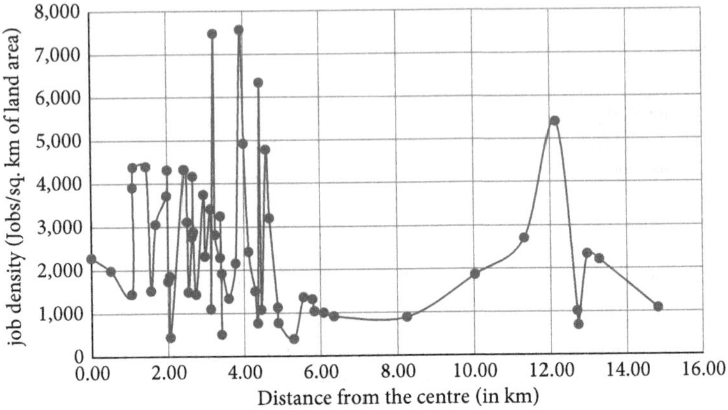

Figure 5.25 Mangaluru's Employment Density Function, 2011
Sources: KMDS, Census of India PCA (2011), and author's analyses.

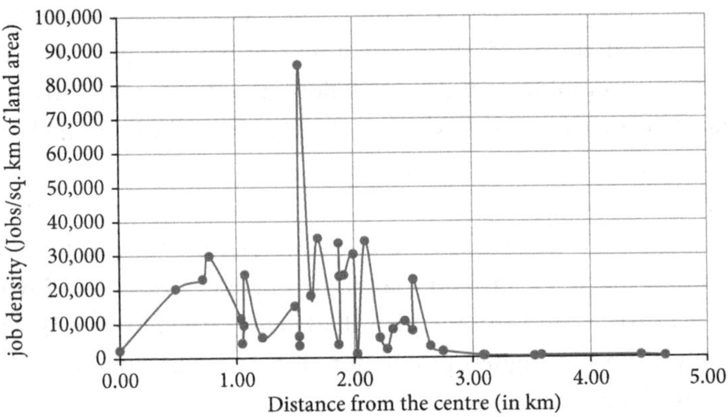

Figure 5.26 Davanagere's Employment Density Function, 2011
Sources: KMDS, Census of India PCA (2011), and author's analyses.

is concerned, with its density peaking at 1.5 km from the centre (city railway station and municipal office). This is ward 7 (Azad Nagar) which is primarily residential, reinforcing the idea that population and jobs co-locate.

Figure 5.27 shows the employment density function of Bellary. This is primarily a monocentric city, with its dominant peak of employment within less than 1 km from the identified centre (the city's bus stand).

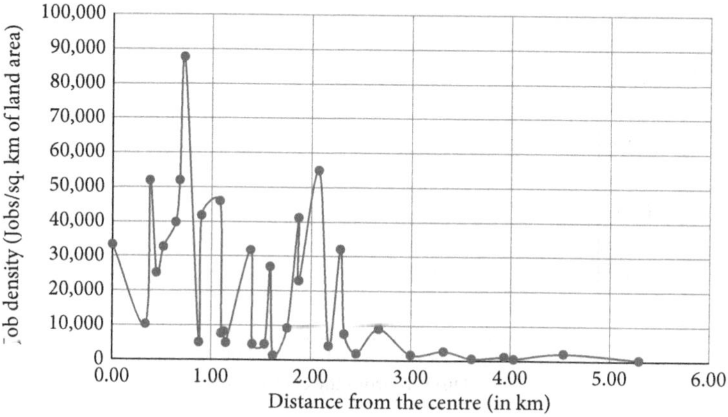

Figure 5.27 Bellary's Employment Density Function, 2011
Sources: KMDS, Census of India PCA (2011), and author's analyses.

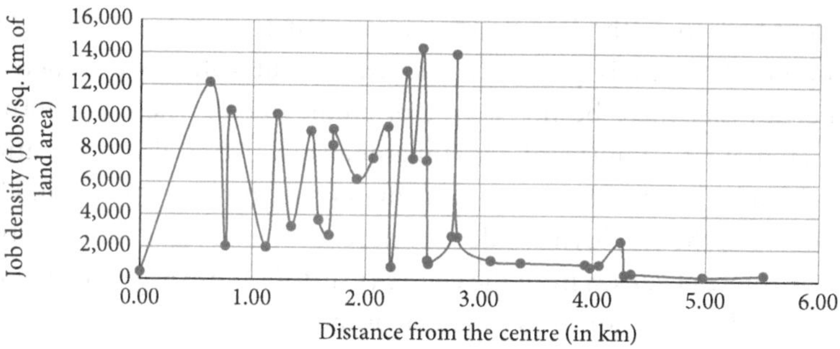

Figure 5.28 Vijayapura's Employment Density Function, 2011
Sources: KMDS, Census of India PCA (2011), and author's analyses.

Ward 17 is the area where employment density peaks and is again a residential area (Nijalingappa colony).

Figure 5.28 summarizes and presents Vijayapura's job density function in 2011. The small town has multiple employment centres, with the primary peak in ward 18, at about 2.5 km from its centre (its municipal office). The several employment density peaks occur until 2.8 km from its centre.

Figure 5.29 depicts the job density function of another town in central Karnataka, Shivamogga. Prima facie, it has at least three centres of peaking employment density, with its tallest peak being 1.2 km from

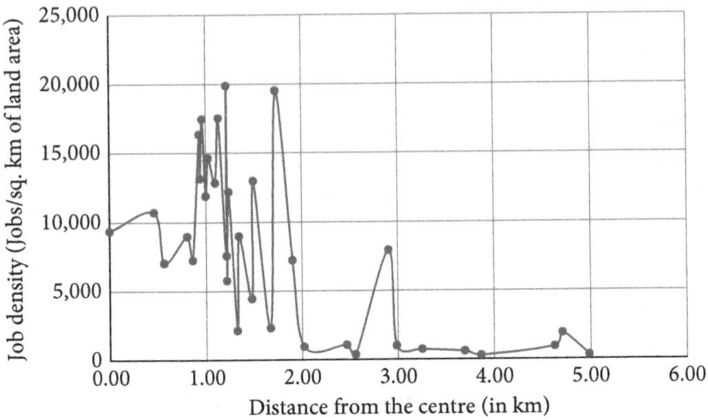

Figure 5.29 Shivamogga's Employment Density Function, 2011
Sources: KMDS, Census of India PCA (2011), and author's analyses.

its identified core (the bus stand), representing ward 18 (Appaji Rao Compound) which is primarily residential, but with 14 commercial properties that must be the source of employment. There is another peak at about 1.7 km (ward 24, Himambada, which is also residential, but with a higher number—29—of commercial properties that could be the source of the employment density observed), one right at the centre, and one more at 2.9 km from the centre (ward 17, Vidyanagar, again primarily residential, with 19 commercial properties).[4]

Figure 5.30 depicts the job density function of Tumakuru, north of Bengaluru. The town is primarily monocentric as far as its employment density is concerned, with a single peak at 2 km from the centre identified (Zilla Panchayat office). This is ward 11 (Melekote, Gangasandra), which is primarily residential, along with some 60 commercial properties.[5]

Figure 5.31 displays the employment density function of Raichur in the northern part of the state. It is predominantly monocentric with a single employment density peak at 1.2 km from its centre (its local government

[4] http://shivamoggacity.mrc.gov.in/ is the source of information on commercial properties, and was accessed on 20 October 2024.

[5] http://tumakurucity.mrc.gov.in/ is the source of information on commercial properties, and was accessed on 20 October 2024.

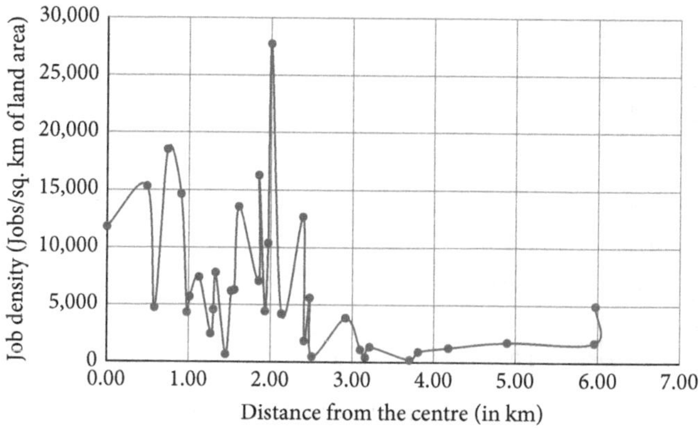

Figure 5.30 Tumakuru's Employment Density Function, 2011
Sources: KMDS, Census of India PCA (2011), and author's analyses.

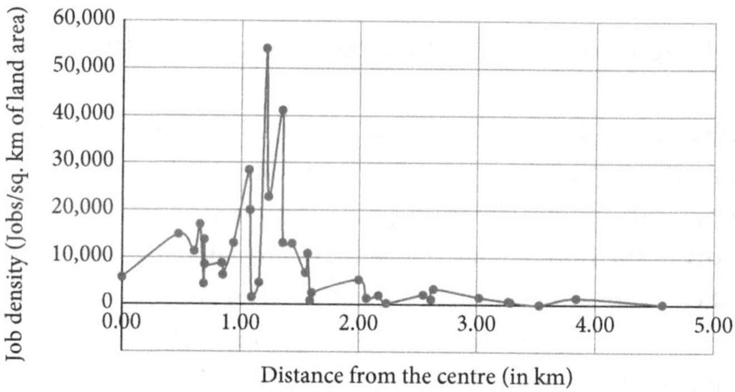

Figure 5.31 Raichur's Employment Density Function, 2011
Sources: KMDS, Census of India PCA (2011), and author's analyses.

office). The only other peak of employment density is in a ward which is 1.35 km from its centre.

Figure 5.32 summarizes the job density function of a class I city, Bidar, for 2011, which shows a couple of peaks of its employment density, one each at 1 km (the highest one) and 1.6 km from its centre (its railway station).

I now specifically focus on the suburbanization of employment in Kalaburagi during 2001–11, in the backward Hyderabad-Karnataka region. This section draws heavily upon Sridhar and Narayanan (2016).

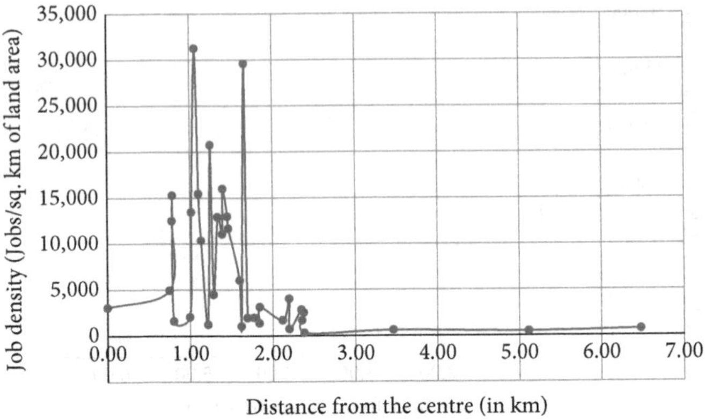

Figure 5.32 Bidar's Employment Density Function, 2011
Sources: KMDS, Census of India PCA (2011), and author's analyses.

5.4.2 Employment Suburbanization of Kalaburagi, 2001–11

As Sridhar and Narayanan (2016) did, this section reports parameter estimates of the job density function for a small city in Karnataka, Kalaburagi, estimating equation [2.2], equipped with information on job density at the disaggregated level of the municipal ward.[6] This is accomplished by making varying conjectures about the city's central point, then computing the proximity of each of the municipal wards to each of the conjectured centres, in 2001 and 2011. The disaggregated information on jobs, the extent of their concentration at various points in the city, is a valuable dataset with which Sridhar and Narayanan (2016) identified various points within the city as its central point. This facilitated an examination of the sprawl of the town over the two decades of study. Tables 5.12–5.18 report the employment suburbanization of Kalaburagi during 2001–11, taking different and appropriate parts in the city as possible centres, based on the empirical job density functions estimated.

[6] We have considered only the primary jobs (defined as those workers who were employed for six months or more in the preceding year) in the town to empirically evaluate the job density function, since marginal jobs are relatively fewer and do not alter the findings in a significant way.

Table 5.12 Empirical Job Density Functions, Kalaburagi, 2001–11: City Market as City Centre

	Slope coefficient estimate, 2001 (Std. Err.)	Slope coefficient estimate, 2011 (Std. Err.)
Proximity to city market as city centre (in km)	−0.31 (0.03)***	−0.30 (0.03)***
R^2	0.61	0.58

Source: Created by author based on data from Sridhar and Narayanan (2016).
Intercepts not reported. N = 58 in both year regressions.
***Statistically significant at the 1% level.

Table 5.13 Empirical Job Density Functions, Kalaburagi, 2001–11: Fort as City Centre

	Slope coefficient estimate, 2001 (Std. Err.)	Slope coefficient estimate, 2011 (Std. Err.)
Proximity to fort as city centre (in km)	−0.32 (0.03)***	−0.31 (0.03)***
R^2	0.62	0.61

Source: Created by author based on data from Sridhar and Narayanan (2016).
Intercepts not reported. N = 58 in both year regressions.
***Statistically significant at the 1% level.

Jobs suburbanized in Kalaburagi over the decade (observed in the insignificant decrease in the modulus of the job gradient, see Table 5.12) when the city market was considered the city's centre. The regression estimates show that there were, respectively, a 31% and a 30% decline in the job concentration when moving a unit distance (1 km) farther from the considered centre, the city's primary shopping area, in both decades. Even when taking the historical fortress as the city's central point, there is an insignificant decrease in the modulus of the job gradients from 0.32 to 0.31 (Table 5.13), implying sprawl of jobs in the city from the fort outwards. Quite strikingly, the estimation with the fortress as the centre also has the maximum R^2 for the employment suburbanization equation (see Table 5.13), showing that the location of the fortress is the actual employment centre, given by the guideline provided by Alperovich (1982),

Table 5.14 Jobs Suburbanization in Kalaburagi, 2001–11: City Railway Station as City Centre

	Slope coefficient estimate, 2001 (Std. Err.)	Slope coefficient estimate, 2011 (Std. Err.)
Proximity to railway station as city centre (in km)	−0.06 (0.05)	−0.06 (0.04)
R^2	0.03	0.03

Source: Created by author based on data from Sridhar and Narayanan (2016).
Intercepts not reported. N = 58 in both regressions.

Table 5.15 Jobs Suburbanization in Kalaburagi, 2001–11: Bus Stand as City Centre

	Slope coefficient estimate, 2001 (Std. Err.)	Slope coefficient estimate, 2011 (Std. Err.)
Proximity to bus stand as city centre (in km)	−0.13 (0.04)***	−0.13 (0.04)***
R^2	0.16	0.17

Source: Created by author based on data from Sridhar and Narayanan (2016).
Intercepts not reported. N = 58 in both regressions.
***Statistically significant at the 1% level.

yielding the best goodness of fit for employment density too, in addition to population density, as demonstrated in Chapter 4.

Sridhar and Narayanan (2016) also considered the public transport hubs in the city—the railway station (Table 5.14) and bus stand (Table 5.15)—as its city centre. The city's railway station represents the weakest part for use as the city centre, as the R-squared is very low with this specification (Table 5.14). Relatively, the bus stand is far more centrally located compared with the railway station, from the viewpoint of jobs, judged from the R-squared (Table 5.15).

Sridhar and Narayanan (2016) also considered other locations as possible city centres for jobs. The first of these is the state government headquarters, similar to what I have used in Bengaluru. This indicates the assumption that the state secretariat serves as a job centre. Table 5.16

Table 5.16 Jobs Suburbanization in Kalaburagi, 2001–11: State Government Headquarters as City Centre

	Slope coefficient estimate, 2001 (Std. Err.)	Slope coefficient estimate, 2011 (Std. Err.)
Proximity to state's government headquarters as city centre (in km)	−0.14 (0.05)**	−0.14 (0.05)**
R^2	0.12	0.13

Source: Created by author based on data from Sridhar and Narayanan (2016).
Intercepts not reported. N = 58 in both regressions.
**Statistically significant at the 5% level.

Table 5.17 Jobs Suburbanization in Kalaburagi, 2001–11: Topographic Central Point as Core

	Slope coefficient estimate, 2001 (Std. Err.)	Slope coefficient estimate, 2011 (Std. Err.)
Proximity to the town's topographic central point (in km)	−0.15 (0.06)**	−0.16 (0.06)**
R^2	0.09	0.11

Source: Created by author based on data from Sridhar and Narayanan (2016).
Intercepts not reported. N = 58 in both regressions.
**Statistically significant at the 5% level.

shows that the employment suburbanization of Kalaburagi, when taking the state government headquarters as the centre, stayed stable during 2001–11, with a 14% decline in its job concentration as one went 1 km away from the state secretariat.

When one considers the topographic centre as the city's central point (see Table 5.17), as Sridhar and Narayanan (2016) did, there was an increase in the employment centralization of the city during 2001–11. This implies that when the topographic centre was considered the city centre, the city became somewhat compact in the spatial distribution of its jobs during the decade.

Table 5.18 summarizes the job gradients estimated for the town, assuming the area with the maximum population density as its core. This

Table 5.18 Jobs Suburbanization in Kalaburagi, 2001–11: Maximum Density Area as Core

	Slope coefficient estimate, 2001 (Std. Err.)	Slope coefficient estimate, 2011 (Std. Err.)
Proximity to the maximum population density area (in km)	−0.10 (0.04)**	−0.10 (0.04)**
R^2	0.11	0.12

Source: Created by author based on data from Sridhar and Narayanan (2016).
Intercepts not reported. N = 58 in both regressions.
**Statistically significant at the 5% level.

is not an unrealistic assumption, because jobs often follow people, as Sridhar (2007) found. Table 5.18 shows that the employment suburbanization of Kalaburagi remained stable during 2001–11, registering a 10% decline in job density for every kilometre of distance from the city's highest population density ward.

5.5 Summary of Findings and Conclusions

I examined employment suburbanization in India's cities over a 20-year period, drawing from Sridhar (2007) for 1991, and based on new research in this chapter for 2011. I find that as of 1991, the metropolitan areas' jobs were much more suburbanized than for cities in all India, as evident from the employment density gradients. Overall, I find that employment in mining, quarrying, and industrial sectors was much more sprawling (in the specific sense of a decline in their employment density gradient) in 1991, as opposed to their services (telecommunications, logistics, retail and business activity, and other services) counterparts. The most compact jobs in India's cities as of 1991 were in retail and business activity, which is natural to expect given they are somewhat skilled jobs. This is consistent with what we observe as retail activity is typically concentrated in the city centres.

I find that the employment density gradient keeps increasing (implying the city keeps centralizing) as and when the density of persons in the city core increases relative to density in the peripheries. When population centralizes, employment centralizes too, and vice versa. On the other hand, when the density of persons in the city core is less than in the peripheries, the employment sub-sector density gradients are lower, indicating sprawl. Thus, I find that both the density of persons and that of jobs moved closely together in 1991.

I estimated the job density functions for several urban areas for which the data are available for 2011. I examined the correlation between city size and polycentricity, and found unsurprisingly that larger cities are characterized by polycentricity, with a positive correlation. I found population and per capita GDP are positively correlated, meaning that larger cities are the richer ones too. However, polycentricity is weakly negatively correlated with per capita income. This implies that in the Indian context, cities with multiple employment centres are those with lower per capita GDP. However, the negative correlation is only weak.

I find that employment is much more decentralized (with a gradient of 0.21 as of 2011) than population (with a density gradient of 0.32) in 2015. Considering all the cities, I find that on average, a majority (52%) of *total employment* is concentrated within a 5-km radius of the core of the urban area. Within the last 5-km radius of its core, on average 30% of employment in other sectors or household industry employment is concentrated. Similarly, for the 'other workers' who are really the urban workers employed in services such as banks, finance, real estate, insurance, trade, commerce, transport and communications, and related services, most employment is concentrated within 5 km of the city centre, on average, for the cities considered. Interestingly, on average, a majority (52%) of employment in household industry was also located within 5 km of the core of the urban area. Overall, in less than a 2-km compass of the core of the urban area, on average, only about 17% of jobs in each of household industry and 'other' sectors (services) are concentrated, showing the job sprawl in Indian cities.

I have summarized in this chapter the employment suburbanization patterns and trends for the states by geographic region, cities in the southern part of the country, towns in the urbanized states, and those in the lagging states. Like in the case of population, I find that jobs in cities of the south and metropolitanized states are suburbanized to a greater extent when compared with cities in all India, and cities in the country's slow-growing regions, in 2011.

Urban areas in the lagging states are more compact as far as their jobs are concerned, compared to the all-India cities and definitely in comparison with the south Indian and the urbanized states. Unsurprisingly, cities in the urbanized states follow the sprawling pattern observed in the southern states.

I have also studied employment suburbanization of the 11 biggest cities in Karnataka separately in this chapter, and that of an individual city in Karnataka, Kalaburagi, in the Hyderabad-Karnataka region. I find that on average, the employment suburbanization of cities in Karnataka is far more compact when compared with cities in all India, with a much higher modulus of the job gradient (at 0.87 compared with 0.67 for all cities (including those in Karnataka)), when estimated at the ward level. Kalaburagi is much more sprawling in its jobs compared with the average city in Karnataka, having a lower slope of the employment gradient.

The type of employment suburbanization of cities in Karnataka is therefore similar to that of the lagging states, even though it is classified as an urbanized state. This may be attributed to the fact that Karnataka has many smaller cities, which are far more compact.

Summarizing then, this chapter provides convincing evidence that Indian cities are sprawling in their urban employment. This naturally leads to the enquiry as to what the trajectory is of post-industrial development in India's cities.

It is now common belief that India bypassed manufacturing to move directly to become a service-oriented economy from being an agricultural one, quite in contrast to what the Lewis model of development shows: the shift from agriculture to manufacturing to services. In the case of India, I find that individual cities which led industrial development in the beginning of the post-independence period have now deindustrialized. There is a Kolkata Jute mills project which documents the decline of the jute industry in West Bengal and makes an attempt to study its remediation.[7] The assumption behind the rehabilitation efforts was that the land locked up in jute mills can be useful for unlocking for purposes of affordable housing in the city. However, rehabilitation has its own challenges with obsolete land laws and lack of adequate capital for investment. Another example of a deindustrialized Indian city is Mysore

[7] https://dusp.mit.edu/projects/kolkata-jute-mills

(now called Mysuru), which once hosted the Ideal Jawa factory. However, unable to bear the onslaught of the Japanese motorcycle industry, Ideal Jawa in Mysuru closed in 1996, as also to abide with environmental regulations.

India's government since 2014 has also advocated a Make in India call to industry to increase investment in manufacturing, to boost the industrial base of the country. Despite many milestones, this has not been very successful because the physical infrastructure (roads, highways, supply chain and logistics management, and renewable energy/power) needed for post-industrial development is not adequate.

The next chapter makes an attempt to explain the suburbanization of population in India's cities.

Appendix 5A.1 Employment Density Gradients, Selected Cities, 1991–2011

State	City	Population, 2011	Estimated employment density gradient, 2011	Calculated employment density gradient, 1991
Andhra Pradesh	Vijayawada	1,021,806	−0.12	−0.4983
Bihar	Bodh Gaya	38,439	−0.31	NA
Bihar	Katihar	226,261	−0.58	NA
Bihar	Purnia	282,248	−0.05	−0.2936
Delhi	Delhi	15,118,073	−0.10	−0.1818
Haryana	Chandigarh	961,587	0.18	NA
Haryana	Faridabad	1,414,050	−0.03	NA
Karnataka	Bengaluru	84,43,675	−0.08	−0.3785
Madhya Pradesh	Bhopal	1,798,218	−0.25	NA
Odisha	Bhubaneswar	840,834	−0.15	NA
Rajasthan	Jaipur	3,046,163	−0.21	**−0.2392**
Rajasthan	Kishangarh	154,886	−0.73	NA
Tamil Nadu	Chennai	4,646,732	−0.07	**−0.3011**
Tamil Nadu	Coimbatore	1,050,721	−0.17	**−0.3944**
Tamil Nadu	Tiruchirappalli	847,387	−0.25	−0.6474
Tamil Nadu	Madurai	1,017,865	−0.24	−0.8084
Telangana	Hyderabad	6,715,216	−0.06	**−0.2787**
Uttar Pradesh	Lucknow	2,817,105	−0.14	**−0.2918**
West Bengal	Kolkata	4,496,694	−0.14	**−0.1429**
Average		**2,583,016**	**−0.19**	**−0.37**

Sources: Census of India (2011), shape files from https://github.com/HindustanTimesLabs/shapefiles/tree/master/city (accessed 30 April 2020), and Sridhar (2007).

NA: Not available.

Appendix 5A.2 Spatial Distribution of Employment within Selected Cities, by Employment Sub-Sector

	Total employment	Total cultivators	Total ag. lab.	Total HH industry workers	Total other workers
Bengaluru					
1-km radius	9.53%	10.21%	10.12%	12.13%	9.45%
2-km radius	20.84%	22.02%	19.03%	23.86%	20.77%
5-km radius	53.74%	52.43%	52.46%	52.16%	53.81%
Last 5 km	3.40%	6.94%	4.27%	2.18%	3.38%
Bhopal					
1-km radius	0.77%	0.34%	0.24%	0.30%	0.80%
2-km radius	6.61%	4.49%	3.92%	5.27%	6.74%
5-km radius	56.82%	53.84%	48.31%	53.47%	57.16%
Last 5 km	14.29%	11.64%	15.39%	13.71%	14.32%
Bhubaneswar					
1-km radius	2.91%	1.33%	0.80%	2.86%	2.95%
2-km radius	14.43%	16.31%	23.60%	13.13%	14.37%
5-km radius	72.01%	67.10%	72.96%	70.30%	72.14%
Last 5 km	35.56%	38.34%	35.77%	36.44%	35.48%
Chandigarh					
1-km radius	2.76%	3.49%	1.90%	2.58%	2.43%
2-km radius	11.22%	13.07%	10.97%	9.28%	9.67%
5-km radius	72.42%	66.26%	54.00%	69.04%	65.59%
Last 5 km	88.78%	86.93%	89.03%	90.72%	90.33%
Chennai					
1-km radius	0.65%	0.28%	0.37%	0.81%	0.65%
2-km radius	2.86%	2.31%	1.95%	2.27%	2.89%
5-km radius	25.05%	23.05%	29.80%	25.65%	25.01%
Last 5 km	25.85%	31.40%	25.87%	29.02%	25.74%
Coimbatore					
1-km radius	3.17%	5.17%	2.76%	2.85%	3.17%
2-km radius	20.71%	21.45%	16.43%	17.18%	20.85%
5-km radius	80.00%	87.34%	77.82%	81.86%	79.92%
Last 5 km	29.17%	27.44%	41.52%	25.99%	29.18%

(continued)

Appendix 5A.2 Continued

	Total employment	Total cultivators	Total ag. lab.	Total HH industry workers	Total other workers
Delhi					
1-km radius	0.13%	0.00	0.00	0.00	0.00
2-km radius	0.44%	0.00	0.00	0.00	0.00
5-km radius	6.62%	10.70%	8.38%	10.62%	8.07%
10-km radius	39.15%	44.46%	44.66%	52.74%	45.62%
Last 5 km	1.35%	4.17%	3.70%	0.82%	1.23%
Faridabad					
1-km radius	5.43%	4.88%	5.55%	7.95%	5.27%
2-km radius	15.83%	10.75%	12.04%	18.38%	15.83%
5-km radius	40.42%	30.65%	25.97%	39.78%	40.96%
Last 5 km	59.58%	69.35%	74.03%	60.22%	59.04%
Hyderabad					
1-km radius	1.08%	0.88%	1.53%	1.21%	1.07%
2-km radius	1.92%	1.94%	2.20%	1.86%	1.92%
5-km radius	28.40%	23.24%	22.75%	29.49%	28.57%
Last 5 km	2.89%	2.70%	2.86%	2.65%	2.90%
Jaipur					
1-km radius	0.93%	0.18%	0.44%	1.73%	0.91%
2-km radius	1.76%	0.28%	0.74%	2.65%	1.75%
5-km radius	42.11%	12.43%	23.78%	50.46%	42.48%
Last 5 km	39.52%	82.21%	64.74%	34.17%	38.62%
Katihar					
1-km radius	17.16%	7.03%	5.82%	12.64%	19.98%
2-km radius	65.45%	49.10%	41.33%	71.87%	70.40%
Kolkata					
1-km radius	0.58%	0.52%	0.38%	0.34%	0.60%
2-km radius	6.30%	9.46%	10.14%	4.94%	6.30%
5-km radius	39.73%	40.32%	37.30%	37.14%	39.84%
Last 5 km	31.16%	29.27%	27.17%	42.11%	30.77%
Lucknow					
1-km radius	2.90%	1.84%	0.73%	3.07%	2.96%
2-km radius	7.94%	5.12%	3.54%	7.89%	8.10%
5-km radius	34.10%	23.48%	22.25%	34.07%	34.60%
Last 5 km	25.96%	46.47%	46.53%	23.94%	25.22%

Appendix 5A.2 Continued

	Total employment	Total cultivators	Total ag. lab.	Total HH industry workers	Total other workers
Purnia					
1-km radius	2.38%	2.38%	2.25%	2.31%	2.29%
2-km radius	8.81%	8.81%	9.25%	9.05%	9.12%
Last 5 km	36.64%	36.64%	37.62%	37.17%	37.33%
Tiruchirappalli					
1-km radius	2.47%	5.26%	0.47%	1.00%	2.53%
2-km radius	17.29%	12.59%	3.39%	16.86%	17.63%
5-km radius	75.81%	53.30%	46.74%	76.58%	76.60%
Last 2 km	16.29%	34.76%	44.64%	19.05%	15.45%
Vijayawada					
1-km radius	3.63%	4.49%	3.54%	2.77%	3.66%
2-km radius	30.85%	24.99%	23.46%	25.55%	31.31%
5-km radius	82.13%	72.70%	67.46%	81.27%	82.73%
Last 2 km	17.99%	27.34%	32.59%	18.74%	17.40%
Bodh Gaya					
1-km radius	22.66%	8.99%	7.06%	27.75%	23.83%
2-km radius	50.19%	39.49%	17.00%	57.91%	52.18%
Last 2 km	42.85%	50.73%	63.97%	35.25%	41.76%
Madurai					
1-km radius	6.39%	7.38%	4.15%	7.71%	6.32%
2-km radius	20.88%	15.51%	15.07%	20.62%	20.93%
5-km radius	74.35%	77.54%	78.27%	71.89%	74.40%
Last 2 km	8.32%	6.02%	6.23%	8.56%	8.34%

Sources: Census of India District Census Handbook (2011) and author's analysis.

Appendix 5A.3 Karnataka's Cities and their Employment Suburbanization, 2011

City	Population, 2011	Estimated employment density gradient, 2011
Bagalkot	111,933	0.32
Belagavi	488,157	0.09
Bellary	410,445	−0.87
Bhadravathi	151,102	−0.75
Bidar	214,373	−0.60
Vijayapura	327,427	−0.54
Chamarajanagar	69,959	−0.97
Channapatna	71,942	−0.55
Chikkaballapur	63,652	−1.64
Chinthamani	76,068	−1.90
Chitradurga	140,206	−1.60
Dandeli	52,069	−0.27
Davanagere	434,971	−0.97
Doddaballapur	84,642	−1.51
Gadag-Betageri	172,612	−0.66
Gangavathi	106,027	−1.00
Gokak	79,121	−1.94
Kalaburagi	533,587	−0.52
Harihar	77,447	−0.22
Hassan	133,436	0.11
Hospet	206,167	−1.09
Hubballi-Dharwad	943,788	−0.06
Ilkal	60,242	−2.04
Jamkhandi	68,938	−1.48
Karwar	63,755	−0.03
Kolar	138,462	−1.31
Kollegal	57,149	−0.94
Koppal	79,807	−1.43
Mandya	137,358	−0.51
Mangaluru	479,622	0.14
Mysuru	893,062	−0.55
Nippani	62,865	−1.71
Rabkavi Banhatti	77,004	−0.25
Raichur	234,170	−1.03

Appendix 5A.3 Continued

City	Population, 2011	Estimated employment density gradient, 2011
Ramanagaram	95,167	−1.07
Ranebennur	101,248	−1.52
Shivamogga	322,650	−0.81
Sindhanoor	75,837	−1.34
Sira	57,555	−1.27
Sirsi	62,882	0.12
Tumakuru	302,143	−0.42
Udupi	125,306	−0.08
Yadgir	74,294	−1.16

Sources: Census of India (2011), Karnataka Municipal Data Society, and author's analyses.

6
Explaining India's Suburbanization of Population

6.1 Introduction and Motivation

In the previous chapters, I tried to understand if persons, families, and jobs have sprawled in Indian cities; the answer to this was a definitive yes. Further, I documented the regional patterns of such sprawl in India's cities, given the data availability. In terms of population, employment, and households, I found that the urbanized states, fast-growing states, and south Indian states sprawl much more than their less urbanized, lagging, and north Indian counterparts with significant regional variations. In this chapter, I examine the factors associated with India's suburbanization, primarily of population, as the dataset was not big enough to understand the suburbanization of households or jobs, as discussed in Chapter 2. Thus, this chapter deals with factors which explain the population suburbanization of India's cities. I deal with each of these explanatory factors to understand their significance in driving suburbanization.

Conventional city models show that rises in earnings of residents and city size increase sprawl, as Mieszkowski and Mills (1993) pointed out. Specifically, as income increases, population and households would like to suburbanize to consume more land and housing. While this is generally true for the USA and advanced countries, in emerging economies such as India, recently the trend is not only the above one observed in the USA, as Sridhar (2007) pointed out, but also one of increasing peripheralization of the poor. Evidence based on 2,700 surveys in Bengaluru shows that the income and expenditure of the households in the periphery are lower than in the core of the city (see Sridhar & Smitha, 2018). If this were to be the case, then the suburbs of Indian cities would consist of primarily low-income households, similar to cities in Europe (such as

Indian Cities or Suburbs? Kala Seetharam Sridhar, Oxford University Press. © Kala Seetharam Sridhar 2025.
DOI: 10.1093/9780198958147.003.0006

Paris and Rome), China, and Brazil, where the relatively richer households locate centrally and poorer households locate in peripheral parts of cities. While it would have been a pathbreaking exercise to understand the spatial distribution of income of households by their location for Indian cities, unfortunately, at the time of finishing this manuscript, it was not considered feasible to have access to such information, even based on nighttime satellite data.

It is logical that when a city's population becomes large, the declining slope of its density function becomes stronger as it suburbanizes, with households moving out to consume more land, which is now more expensive in the city's central areas. Given this, it is consistent to observe that metropolitan cities such as Bengaluru, Chennai, Delhi, Hyderabad, Kolkata, and Mumbai are much more sprawling than their smaller counterparts such as Pune or Mysuru.

Further, as explanations of suburbanization, the evidence has been that wherever highways exist, they facilitate lowering the transport cost, as the review in Chapter 1 summarizes. Since it is more likely for large cities to also have good highway infrastructure, such cities are more likely to suburbanize by enabling the spreading out of households and population. It should be mentioned that the mere existence of highways is no guarantee of suburbanization as the transport costs also may be high. What theory predicts is that, when the costs of transport are lower, a metropolitan area suburbanizes.

Tiebout's (1956) theory of voting with the feet implies that there is central city flight from poor social and economic conditions such as high crime, pollution, high unemployment, traffic congestion, high taxes, poor public services, and space congestion in general in the city core, that in turn results in movement of both population and jobs to the suburbs, as Mieszkowski and Mills (1993) discussed.

Further, India's land use controls are extraordinary, and I discuss next their significance in determining sprawl.

Finally, considering the technological evolution which has taken place in terms of convergence of mobile and computer communications, and proliferation of smart phones everywhere, they are bound to change the physical commute and bypass highway infrastructure, facilitating sprawl. In the "computer-mediated economy" (Varian, 2001), communications has a substantial influence on sprawl. Existing studies (e.g. Gaspar &

Glaeser, 1998; Negroponte, 1995) speculated about how communications can lead to a decrease in the necessity for residents to agglomerate in the form of a city. They predicted how improvement in technology will result in a 'spaceless world', influencing the development and evolution of cities.

I next discuss the empirical evidence about Indian cities as far as market-based factors such as income and transport costs are concerned, and flight from poor central city socio-economic conditions as explanations of suburbanization in Section 6.2, primarily drawing on findings from Holian and Sridhar (2017), followed by the importance of land use regulations in Section 6.3. Then Section 6.4 focuses on the role of technology in enabling suburbanization and sprawl of cities in general. Section 6.5 presents the findings from this empirical research on the determinants of suburbanization. The final section of the chapter summarizes and concludes.

6.2 Market-Based Factors, Central City Problems, and Suburbanization

As discussed earlier, Mieszkowski and Mills (1993) pointed to central city social and economic problems as possible causes of suburbanization. In the context of Indian cities, Holian and Sridhar (2017) studied the effect of roads or air pollution on sprawl, while Holian (2014) studied the effect of socio-economic development on air quality in Indian cities. Roads which facilitate faster travel are an important factor which make possible location outside of the city core where jobs are presumably located. Poor air quality in Delhi and other Indian metropolitan areas, attributed to vehicular pollution, has now attracted attention for its health hazards. But, as Mieszkowski and Mills (1993) pointed out, it is not clear if traffic congestion in the central city, and the air pollution to which it has led, have resulted in greater suburbanization of Indian cities.

Considering the standard urban model and the conventional reasons for sprawl, Holian and Sridhar (2017) examined the effect of roads along with air quality on the sprawl of India's urban areas. They also attempted to understand if the sprawl characterizing India's urban agglomerations, which Sridhar (2007, 2010) documented, was persisting, and if that was the case, what associated factors were leading to the same.

Holian and Sridhar (2017) calculated population gradients, based on information from the Indian Census of 2001,[1] and extended the work on the sprawl of Indian urban areas to include indicators of air quality and roads. As found by Holian and Sridhar (2017), the higher slope (0.6) in 2001 of the population density function for India's cities indicated that they had centralized, compared with that in 1991 (when the slope coefficient, the density gradient, was only 0.55); however, the percentage of employment suburbanized in India's cities in 2001 was 37%, much higher than that (22%) found by Sridhar (2007). It should be noted that the suburbanization extent for both population and employment is determined by Holian and Sridhar (2017) based on the municipal corporation limits rather than any other scientific definition, like I use here. Their findings enabled an understanding of suburbanization as associated with socio-economic conditions like comparative disparities in employment opportunities, education in the central part of cities vis-à-vis that in the peripheral areas, along with other factors, as summarized by Mieszkowski and Mills (1993).

Attempting to understand market-based factors such as metropolitan area–wide income and transport cost as reasons of suburbanization, Holian and Sridhar (2017) used three different measures of income: one as used by Sridhar (2007), from the NCAER, and a second measure representing the mean per capita expenditure at the district level (based on the assumption that people may not be honest about their income, but are likely to be candid about their expenditure). The other income measure used by Holian and Sridhar (2017) was the relative spending in cities compared to that in villages, which could indicate differences in the central/suburban quality of living. They found on average 1.6 times more spending in cities relative to that in villages, which was to be expected.

Holian and Sridhar (2017) examined socio-economic conditions in the core of Indian urban agglomerations relative to those in their peripheries to understand if that was a cause of the observed suburbanization. They found that joblessness in the city core was lower, at somewhat

[1] Analogous information on the geographic area of cities was not published by the Indian Census in 2011.

more than half of that in the city periphery, which indicated that the job situation in the city core was better. This reflected improving quality of life there (although they found the highest unemployment ratio was 1.9, showing that in some cities the unemployment rate in the primary city was 1.9 times higher than in the periphery); it is instructive to note also that Sridhar (2007) found a joblessness ratio (for the primary city compared to that in the periphery) of 1.5 in 1991.

When Holian and Sridhar (2017) examined other conditions of the core of Indian cities, they found the proportion of the oppressed communities,[2] in the core of Indian cities versus that in the peripheral areas, was 0.91 on average in 2001, higher than found by Sridhar (2007) at an average of 0.80 in 1991. Further, Holian and Sridhar (2017) found that the relative literacy in the core to that in the peripheries was on average 0.93, implying that the central parts of the cities were less literate than the suburbs in 2001. This contrasts with a comparable proportion of 1.05 on average in 1991, found by Sridhar (2007), showing that the core of Indian urban agglomerations became literate to a smaller extent in 2001 compared to what they were in 1991. This is likely due to the annexing, into the central folds, of peripheral areas, which are ostensibly less literate. As found by Holian and Sridhar (2017), overall then, in 2001, in terms of socio-economic conditions, while the central city had worsened in terms of education and the prevalence of oppressed social groups, its economic opportunities had improved, relative to corresponding conditions in the city's periphery, since 1991.

On average, there were only 2.9 governing urban local bodies in the typical metropolitan area, as reported by Holian and Sridhar (2017), which was significantly lower than the 6.3 local urban governments on average per urban agglomeration in 1991, as documented by Sridhar (2007). This is compatible with the consolidation of urban administration, as I have discussed above. Holian and Sridhar (2017) as well reported that land use regulations such as the floor space index (FSI) are conservative in India's urban agglomerations, as originally documented in Sridhar (2010) and further shown in Brueckner and Sridhar (2012).

[2] In India, Scheduled Castes and Scheduled Tribes are oppressed and are often subject to discrimination (an example of which is that they are not allowed into temples etc.), which typically lead to conflicts.

Holian and Sridhar (2017) found that population size had the anticipated negative effect on the gradient, demonstrating that big urban agglomerations are more suburbanized, confirming the impact of natural evolution (city size) on sprawl. The percentage of employment which is suburbanized was observed by Holian and Sridhar (2017) to have an inverse impact on the suburbanization of persons, (contradictory to Sridhar (2007) who did not find it to be statistically significant), which lends credence to the fact that people follow jobs.

Holian and Sridhar (2017) also found support for population's flight from poor socio-economic conditions in the central parts of cities: for example, it was found that the greater the education levels in the city core relative to those in the periphery, the lesser the degree of sprawl. The number of urban local governments in a metropolitan area were found to be significant in influencing suburbanization, but with a positive effect, implying that multiple local governments fundamentally show the importance of the main urban local body in the metropolitan area which leads to centralization of population around the primary central city. This is compatible with the existing body of work which reports the same. The historical suburbanization of the city has a positive effect on current suburbanization, reflecting the dominance of past spatial distribution trends (Chakravorty (2000) found the same with respect to his study of Kolkata).

The primary findings of Holian and Sridhar (2017) were that large cities, and those with a higher percentage of employment suburbanized, were associated with more population sprawl, despite accounting for the historical pattern of population suburbanization in the previous decade. Besides, a better quality of living, reflected in higher relative central city literacy rates, was found to be associated with greater centralization. Their results showed evidence of both evolution-based and flight-from-socio-economic-conditions explanations of sprawl in India's cities. That study by Holian and Sridhar (2017) demonstrated progress over previous work, by including road infrastructure, air quality, and central city/suburban income ratios in the explanation of suburbanization. They found that sprawl was higher in cities with better roads. Their results regarding the effect of air quality on sprawl were not, however, as per expectations.

It has been widely believed that the upgradation of highway infrastructure caused the sprawl observed in US cities (as also pointed out by Baum-Snow, 2007). Thus, I anticipated road density to have a direct impact on population suburbanization. However, Holian and Sridhar (2017) found a positive effect since roads represent access, basing their finding on the density of surfaced roads (called *pucca* roads) to land area disaggregated for the city core and periphery. The way in which this variable is defined serves as a test of both the market-based evolution theory and the flight away from poor socio-economic conditions. It should be noted that the market-based natural evolution theory would predict the sign on these variables to be negative, as transport upgradations decrease the cost of travel, which tends to increase sprawl. The flight from poor socio-economic conditions framework for understanding sprawl predicates a direct effect on the central city indicator (which means good road infrastructure in the centre implies little or no movement to the periphery) and a negative sign expected on the suburban measure of roads (poorer roads in the city imply more movement to the suburbs). Both these expectations were found to be correct in the actual model estimated. A final variable was used by Holian and Sridhar (2017) which measures the proportion of highway infrastructure in the centre to that in the periphery, to examine flight from poor socio-economic conditions, which predicates a positive effect—a higher proportion suggests better roads in the centre compared with those in the periphery. Persons would be attracted to the centre with better roads and the gradient would be higher. Even this variable was found to be statistically significant by Holian and Sridhar (2017) in the empirical model estimated.

However, Holian and Sridhar (2017) found that when the time lag of the gradient was incorporated in their model, all highway infrastructure variables retained their expected signs as per the above discussion, but lost their statistical significance, showing the dominance of historical trends in the distribution of population. Conversely, the proportion of literacy rate in the centre relative to its value in the periphery had a direct impact on sprawl, as was expected, but only when the time lag of the gradient was incorporated additionally in the estimation.

Interestingly, Holian and Sridhar (2017) also examined the effect of air quality on sprawl in India's urban areas. Given data constraints, they were unable to disaggregate air quality in the centre and suburbs separately, but nonetheless incorporated a city-wide measure of air quality to forge synergy between the literature on cities and the environment in India.

Their hypothesis regarding air quality was that urban areas with poorer air quality would sprawl more (implying an inverse impact on the gradient), representing flight from poor socio-economic conditions.

Holian and Sridhar (2017) also revisited the significant role played by policies affecting land use (read the FSI) in India's urban agglomerations, found by Sridhar (2010) and Brueckner and Sridhar (2012) who empirically found that the conservative floor area ratios (FARs) in India's urban areas led to their unrestrained expansion. Holian and Sridhar (2017) included different indicators of land use, the hypothesis being that more relaxed FARs will result in more compact cities.

They found that two of the four air pollution indicators they included had a direct impact on the gradient, indicative of the fact that the higher the relative pollution in the centre, the higher the extent of centralization of the city. They provided the rationale for the unforeseen result. First, the population may not be sensitive to pollution in the centre of the city. Second, the measure of air quality used by Holian and Sridhar (2017) was not a ratio relating carbon emissions in the core to those in the periphery. Even assuming the population was sensitive to air quality, pollution may be equally high in the central and suburban parts of the studied cities, which were not measured by them separately. Further, there could be a selection bias, in the sense of job opportunities being available aplenty in the centre, which may lead to not only poorer air quality in the centre but also more concentration of population there.

Summarizing, Holian and Sridhar (2017) found that India's urban agglomerations became compact over the decade from 1991 to 2001, judging by the average density gradient during the two periods. This correlates with our observation because many Indian cities became large during the period, with their surrounding urban bodies being annexed into the central city for what was deemed better overall metropolitan governance. They found support for the market-based theory (indicated by city size, i.e. population) and flight away from socio-economic conditions (as reflected in the proportion of literates in the centre to those in the periphery), similar to what earlier studies found for India.

For whatever reasons, the 2011 Census of India PCA stopped publishing data on land area, which renders the task of computing density gradients for Indian cities an impossible task. It is plausible that the observed sprawl in the periphery of India's urban agglomerations could be related to public expenditure in these areas (the formulation of fresh innovative or industrial plazas) or to 'show-off' luxury (as in Delhi's farmhouses), or the emergence of entirely new smart towns (such as New Town in Kolkata) with partnerships between the government and other actors.

6.3 Policies Governing Land Use in India's Urban Areas

I would fail in the assessment of the explanation of suburbanization if I did not account for the highly significant role of policies governing the use of land in India's urban areas (which Sridhar (2010) focused on) and the urban land ceiling, which are discussed here. Indian cities have strong land use regulations, given their socialistic approach. I primarily consider regulations such as the FSI, a measure of the capital to land area which is permissible in an urban area. This refers to the proportion of the constructed area to the area of the parcel of land on which it sits, with lower values showing conservatism whereas higher values of the FSI indicate relaxed regulations. Sridhar (2010) showed how Indian cities have had highly conservative FARs compared with cities in the rest of the world such as Singapore, the USA, and China. One would expect the FSI to have a positive effect on cities' sprawl. That is, if the FSI is higher, it will lead to compact cities (implying a higher gradient) and a direct impact.

Given the overwhelming influence of policies governing land in the country's urban areas, I deal with that, since they have undesirable effects on the city's sprawl and the use of spatial area by households, along with implications for the deployment of infrastructure by the local government for providing basic urban services. I note that the utilization of area per capita in the largest of India's urban areas like Mumbai is a mere 5 sq. m., among the lowest household consumption of space utilized anywhere (Patel, 2013), and nearly 50% of that metropolitan area's population reside in what are designated as squatter settlements. In Bengaluru, the floor area consumption was 19.35 sq. m. per capita, based on primary surveys (Sridhar et al., 2018), which compares with 43.9 sq. m. per capita in

Copenhagen (Denmark), 41 sq. m. per capita in Stockholm (Sweden), and 37.9 sq. m. per capita in Berlin (Germany) as reported by Bertaud (2004).

Brueckner and Sridhar (2012) examined the effect of policies governing land use like the FSI and took it to the next level, finding that if cities had a lower value of the FAR, their spatial area increased. Relaxing the FAR by one unit, they found, led to a reduction in the cities' spatial area by about 20%, which resulted in welfare gains of about Rs.106 million for a typical Indian city, assuming less commuting (less time and less fuel) for its residents.

The goal of land use regulations in all countries is to guarantee well-formulated growth of urban areas such that basic infrastructure may be provided as per the city's master plan. The intensity of such regulations is usually set by local seismic, technical, socio-economic, and environmental factors. Thus, even while such controls are intended to prevent negative effects at a highly disaggregated level such as the neighbourhood, they inadvertently affect the urban form of the agglomeration, the effectiveness with which the highly inelastic factor (land) is used, and the city's low-income households, all in an unfavourable manner, not considered by such policy frameworks, as pointed out by Bertaud (2014).

Sridhar (2010) and Sridhar (2018, 2019) describe several policies which govern the use of land in India's urban areas including the FSI, rent control, and the urban land ceiling act. Sridhar (2010) examines the effect of the FSI and other regulations in India's urban areas on their suburbanization. Sridhar (2018) investigates rent control and finds that it does not only theoretically lead to a restricted supply of rental housing, but also leads to problems from an implementational point of view in most Indian states and cities. Sridhar (2019) examines the effect of FARs on population and household density, considering the standard urban model, taking Bengaluru, finding that FARs impact (both population and household) density negatively. The finding is that with respect to Bengaluru, the Karnataka rent control Act essentially renders itself ineffective. In the context of Mumbai, Sridhar (2019) examines anecdotal evidence regarding the FAR, where its associated effects are further aggravated by the existence of other distortions such as rent control and urban land ceiling legislation (repealed in 1999), which I discuss next.

6.3.1 Urban Land Ceiling

It is recognized that land use regulations have costs and benefits from a public services or citizen's perspective. It is no rocket science to know that when benefits outweigh costs of a regulation, it must be retained. Conversely, when the opposite is true, the legislation must be reformed or revoked. The Urban Land Ceiling and Regulation Act (ULCRA) of 1976 was enacted in India with good intentions of redistributing land from the rich to the poor, stipulating that persons or enterprises could not own vacant land beyond a limit (which varied across cities). If individuals or firms owned vacant land beyond the stipulated limit, they had to 'declare' the excess land and sell it at a price lower than its market value to the government, which used the land for distribution amongst the urban poor, for accommodating them in housing, or for 'other public purposes' (hospitals, schools) from which the urban poor were expected to benefit.

The law was accepted by several states[3] where the local urban authorities used it to accumulate a sufficient inventory of scarce land for identified 'public' purposes like widening of roads, expanding open spaces, and improving 'public' amenities. There is no substantive evidence if the surplus land 'taken' by the government was indeed utilized for serving real 'public' objectives. But it was clear that the implementation of the law superficially constrained the availability of land in cities, raising its value manifold, which led to corrupt practices, as Joshi and Little (1996) pointed out. As Bertaud (2002) indicated, the primary impact of this law was to lock up big swathes of land in litigation, since these lands could not be utilized for any useful purpose. Another unfavourable effect of the act was that it also prevented private firms and real estate developers from assembling land for future redevelopment. For these reasons, the act effectively decreased the availability of land in cities. Due to this and various other reasons, in India, there is now general agreement that the sociological, political, and economic costs of ULCRA outweighed the benefits such policies were expected to bestow (Bertaud, 2002). Therefore,

[3] Indian states which enacted the land ceiling act were the then undivided Andhra Pradesh, Assam, Bihar, Gujarat, Haryana, Himachal Pradesh, Karnataka, Madhya Pradesh, Maharashtra, Manipur, Meghalaya, Orissa, Punjab, Rajasthan, Tripura, Uttar Pradesh, and West Bengal.

ULCRA was repealed by most states in 1999, following the economic reforms of 1991. With the infamous act's repeal, it was estimated that 25,000 acres of land were unlocked in Mumbai alone,[4] out of which 10,000 acres were estimated to be in zones with the potential to be developed, with the rest in restricted territory like coastal zones and forest lands.

While a majority of the Indian states have revoked the pernicious law, at the time of finishing this book, it continues in some.[5] As discussed above, the effect of this act has been to artificially create a scarcity of urban land, and lead cities to sprawl much more than they would otherwise, a hypothesis which is empirically testable. Excessive suburbanization, which I have documented here, has adverse effects on affordable accommodation in the city core and the employment centres, where real estate increases in value. This also increases travel time for the urban poor who are forced to move out of the central city to the peripheral areas, as we find in Indian cities (see Sridhar & Smitha, 2018).

6.3.2 Floor Area Ratio

Rules and regulations pertaining to buildings have been in operation in the world's urban areas for many centuries, whose objective was meant to 'control' unplanned growth, protect neighbours, and prevent congestion in cities. But as Bertaud (2002) points out, most city-level policies in the country are fundamentally reduced to the simple idea of 'reducing central city congestion'.

FAR, also called FSI, is the most common indicator of the relative use of capital to land, in terms of their relevance for the factors of production. The higher this use, the higher the FAR/FSI is and vice versa. One of the predictions of the standard framework is that FARs decrease when one moves away from the city centre. The reason for such a downward-sloping FAR/FSI curve is clear: if jobs were to agglomerate in the city core, minimal commuting costs associated with land near the centre would result

[4] https://www.business-standard.com/article/economy-policy/law-repeal-may-free-up-25-000-acres-in-mumbai-107041901101_1.html, accessed 27 September 2024.

[5] These states which continued to enforce the pernicious law as of 2024, when this book was being completed, are Andhra Pradesh, Assam, Bihar, Maharashtra, Odisha, and West Bengal.

in higher land prices, which would make a way for higher capital land proportions (measured by the FAR as described above). This is the opposite of what one sees in India's urban agglomerations, with rising FSI towards the city's suburban areas where land is comparatively cheaper.

In India's urban areas, the FSI influences the constructed area on a piece of land, based on guidelines such as the following, provided by the Government of India's Town and Country Planning Organization (TCPO, 1999):

a. Land use (residential/commercial/industrial);
b. Plot size (higher plots have greater permissibility for higher built areas);
c. Road width (higher road widths entail higher FAR/FSI);
d. Setbacks (higher setbacks allow higher FSI);
e. Availability of parking (greater availability of parking permits higher FSI).

However, given the above guidelines, the stipulated FAR/FSI cannot be attained in the core of India's urban areas as most of the specified requirements such as plot size (larger plots have higher FSI), parking availability, or width of road (broader roads typically permit higher FSI), subject to the use to which land is put, cannot be met there. In the suburbs of Indian cities, alternatively, the stipulated requirements can be met, but there is no demand there for a higher FAR/FSI as there is in the centre. So, overall, Indian cities have a uniformly low FAR which is consumed throughout the city.

Due to the above, the extraordinarily low FSI continuing in the core part of India's urban areas is a highly conservative land use regulation.[6] The highest permissible FSI is a mere 1.33 in Mumbai's core city (e.g. Nariman Point). In mega urban regions across the globe, the FSI ranges between 5 and 15 in the city centre, declining to roughly 0.5, or less, in the peripheral areas (as pointed out by Bertaud, 2004).[7] Ideally everywhere,

[6] An FAR/FSI of 1.5 implies that a mere 1.5 sq. ft of space (on several storeys if applicable) can be constructed on 1 sq. ft of a plot. An FAR of 2, for example, would allow the construction of space to the extent of two times the plot area.

[7] As an example, Manhattan in New York has an FSI of 15, one of the tallest anywhere across the globe, which is allowed for domestic, retail, and manufacturing uses.

as technological improvements occur and public amenities improve, the capital labour ratio, the FAR/FSI in the central city, also should steadily increase.[8] The evidence worldwide is that the intensity of the regulation is negatively related with size of the city. That is, the larger the city, the less severe the regulation would be, in theory.

However, if one were to go by the TCPO's 1999 guidelines, existing infrastructure such as parking is inadequate, thus higher population, employment, or household density (resulting from a relaxed FSI) may not be accommodated easily. We should note that, as Sridhar (2010) points out, with a higher FSI, the density of persons, households, or jobs will decline. As pointed out by Sridhar (2010), this counter-intuitive finding is observed because a more relaxed FSI is usually correlated with a greater floor area per person or job (commercial or industrial FAR) and vice versa. Whether or not population, household, or job density increases or decreases with a higher or lower FSI is subject to the demand response of FAR/FSI with respect to constructed space. If in response to a relaxation in the FAR, a greater than commensurate rise in constructed space is observed, then the density of persons, households, and/or jobs is higher. The requisite deployment of infrastructure is to be upgraded in areas where a steeper rise in FSI is predicted. If on the other hand, the resulting use of space were lower than the FSI relaxation, then population, household, and job density should decline.

[8] Quite in contrast to the cross-country comparison, the FSI in Mumbai has continuously declined for the past six decades: it was initially permitted to be above 4 in its central business district (to cover the construction costs of the developer), while it is now 1.33. Many buildings in Nariman Point were built before the 1.33 FSI was imposed and so entail an FSI greater than this. So, any renovation of rehabilitated structures entails losing further constructed space, to abide by the new FSI, which is financially unviable due to the exorbitant value of built space in the metropolitan area. When old buildings had to be renovated, the metropolis' urban local body, the Municipal Corporation of Greater Mumbai (MCGM), permitted the FAR to be raised to greater than 3 (as pointed out by Phatack, 2003), recognizing the impracticality of keeping the residents in their current location while keeping the FSI the same.

Nonetheless, an exchange of FSI is permitted in the metropolis, frequently called the transfer of development rights (TDRs), which the MCGM permitted in lieu of the land or amenities it could not afford or construct. However, this was largely discretionary or random, and failed to ameliorate the adverse effects of a conservative FSI throughout the central part of the metropolis. As has been shown by previous work, TDRs are not the best method by which the effectiveness of land can be increased, but one by which a source-starved urban local body (ULB) can raise higher revenues, which also has become a charter for corruption not just here but in other cities around the world.

In most cities across the world, the FAR/FSI tends to increase over time. This monotonic improvement in the consumption of FAR/FSI has two objectives, as Bertaud (2004) highlights:

1. Such a progressive policy allows persons, households, and firms to absorb more floor area when their economic conditions improve, without the need to move to the periphery.
2. A higher FAR/FSI leads to a decline in spatial area of the city, and reduces commuting and associated expenditures, as shown by Brueckner and Sridhar (2012) taking the case of Indian cities. Besides, in most cities, planners set the regulated FAR/FSI for future buildings higher than for current ones. Such a convention supports the renovation of dilapidated structures at taller heights than before.

Frequently real estate projects are not economically viable without a higher FAR. Thanks to restrictive FARs, a small number of structures get refurbished, and the metropolitan area ends up with an accumulation of wasted area. With restrictive FARs, the city horizontally spreads without a good reason and in areas wherever higher FARs are permitted and achieved. As argued by Bertaud (2004), the horizontal expansion of the city leads to economic unviability of mass transit in thinly populated places and renders it inaccessible for commuters, the marginalized, and the vulnerable. I find many examples of this reality in Indian cities where public transport is restricted to only the core of cities, leaving the periphery out.

The unduly restrictive FAR/FSI in Indian cities has resulted in a superficial rise in rental and land prices, adversely affecting housing affordability, due to which residents are forced to live in spaces considered very small by international standards (see Bertaud, 2004). The poorer and vulnerable households are the most affected as they cannot bid high prices to match the consumption of housing by the richer households. Thus, the impoverished are steadily moved out of conventional housing into squatter settlements or footpath encroachments. It has been in fact persuasively argued by Bertaud (2004) that a relaxation of the FSI in Mumbai's municipal corporation limits would increase twofold the floor area consumed over a decade (as accomplished in Shanghai).[9]

More relaxed FSIs are allowed usually in the peripheral areas of the country's urban areas, like the case of Hyderabad (where there is no limit of FAR, but an FAR of 7 is allowed as per the World Resources Institute). But they are typically low in the city's central parts, which I perceive as poor public economics; land with basic amenities such as water pipelines, sewage networks, and other facilities, which exist in the central city but are not fully utilized, represents a cost on the city government and the tax-paying public (as pointed out by Bertaud, 2002). Bertaud and Brueckner (2005) estimated, taking Bengaluru, that welfare loss from FSI restrictions represented anywhere from 3% to 6% of the expenditure of families. Further, Brueckner and Sridhar (2012) estimated that a unit relaxation in the FSI led to reducing the spatial area of a city by 20%, which led to a reduction in commutes and savings in the form of fuel and time. Adding credence to this idea, Savage and Dasgupta (2006) reported that the time for a one-way commute to work in Bengaluru rose steadily from about 20 minutes to roughly double the duration, during 1991–2001. Besides, I also note that the unduly restrictive FSIs in India's cities have led to poor compliance with these regulations.[10]

Therefore, I have compelling reasons to lend credence to how restrictive land use regulations (read the FAR/FSI) rather than market forces give way to the observed density patterns, unaffordability of decent houses, and sprawl in the country's metropolitan areas. Noting the

[9] It is documented that in 1984, Shanghai consumed floor area of only a little more than 3 sq. m. per capita. Its city government then perceived that upgrading the consumption of floor area was its prime concern. So, it increased the FSI there radically. Two decades later, the built area consumed in the metropolis was greater than 13 sq. m. per capita on average, as pointed out by Bertaud (2004).

[10] Defiance of building regulations is quite common practice in Indian cities such as Bangaluru, where the evidence is that nearly 85% of all structures built during 2020–21 violated the bye-laws, as per a survey by the municipal government in Bengaluru (https://www.deccanherald.com/india/karnataka/bengaluru/85-of-new-buildings-violated-bylaws-bbmp-survey-1051161.html, accessed 21 September 2023). As per the engineers, most of these transgressions of bye-laws in Bengaluru were found in low-rise residential buildings. It is understandable that with a restricted FAR, it is difficult to afford space, hence the owner is forced to infringe on the bye-laws, with unapproved construction and inclusion of additional floors, which yields rental income. Boob and Rao (2012) found large-scale violations of the development control rules in Yavatmal district of Maharashtra. Conducting a perception survey of homeowners, they found that 85% stated that the breach was due to the high price of real estate, to which the restrictive FSI undoubtedly contributes.

significance of these regulations, I study the theoretical effect of such regulations on suburbanization in India.

6.3.2.1 The Theoretical Effects of FAR/FSI

Brueckner (2009) shows the theoretical effects of FARs on the city's spatial limits. Figure 6.1 from Brueckner (2009) demonstrates these effects. H is the building curve of the city in the absence of FARs. When an FAR limit is imposed, it constrains the city's building heights (indicated by H_{FAR}), mandated in the city up to *X**. Naturally, buildings which do not adhere to the limit should be reconstructed within conforming heights, once the regulation is in place. So, the FAR restriction decreases the supply of housing space to *X**. Real estate projects can construct without restriction beyond *X**, indicated by the H_{FAR} curve. The scarcity in housing leads to a situation of excess demand given the shortfall in supply, which increases the price of housing everywhere in the city. It follows that developers are not in a position to use land to its maximum extent within *X** (until which the regulation is enforced). Nonetheless, given inflated prices of housing increase their profits, tougher bidding happens for land everywhere in the city, leading to higher land prices in all locations. Therefore, families move beyond city limits looking for lower land prices, which causes the city to grow spatially and sprawl.

Next, I understand the effect of technology on suburbanization.

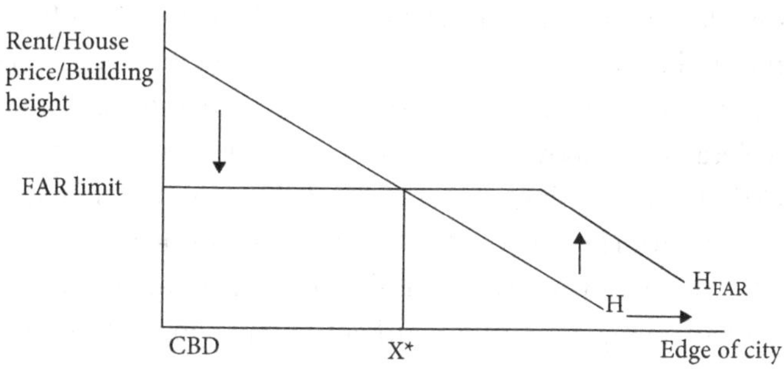

H-Building height contour in pre-FAR city
H_{FAR}-Building height contour in post-FAR city
X*-Limit up to where FAR restriction binding

Figure 6.1 The Theoretical Effects of FAR on City Limits
Source: Created by author from data in Brueckner and Sridhar (2012).

6.4 Technology and its Effects on Suburbanization

Quantum jumps in telecommunications brought about by smart phones which are continually progressing in their capabilities (5G, 6G, and so on) and seamless computer connectivity powered by the Internet that permits work from home and other remote locations may be referred to as technological change. The integration of technologies in desktop computers, tablets, laptops, and smart phones has enabled users to keep in touch with their contacts seamlessly across locations around the world. Undoubtedly, progress made in wireless technologies has increased the physical and geographical movement of persons and their capability to supply their labour from anywhere. Thus, there is every incentive for households to locate away from employment centres where their employers are located.

The natural corollary of the relative ease of access to wireless technology is telecommuting: accomplishing one's work-related tasks through communications rather than in person. It refers to work from home, non-conventional places, or office subsidiary branches, as pointed out by previous work (e.g. Shin et al., 2000). Such a phenomenon implies the limited or full replacement of technological devices for work instead of physically commuting to the workplace. Desktops, tablets, public Wi-Fi or digital infrastructure providing connectivity to the Internet, smart phones, broadband connectivity, and router networks have eliminated the geographical constraints that previously necessitated workers to be physically present in their workplaces.

Even while Mokhtarian and Henderson (1998) found in the case of California, and Irani et al. (2000) documented evidence of teleworking in Mumbai, as early as the 1990s, nobody can deny that the coronavirus of 2020 accelerated the move towards such communications, with Zoom/Webex/MS Team meetings, Google Meet links, and WhatsApp video calls. Working from home, which is quite common since the pandemic in India's cities, as everywhere else, has the potential to bestow a number of substantive advantages on firms, workers, and the population, since they reduce lengthy travel times for workers.[11] Besides, it improves worker

[11] Had the required data been available, we would have been able to say conclusively if the population would like to reside in suburbs and work from home provided the availability of suitable devices and technologies.

efficiency, as it decreases the commute to work and permits them to focus on work when they are in their best position to do so.

National Panasonic reported that half of their workers' time in subsidiary locations was on routine activity that was not very effective. Thus, for these workers in its subsidiary locations, National Panasonic actively explored the work from home concept to increase worker output.[12] It was documented as early as 2002 that in the United Kingdom, every week, traffic bottlenecks accounted for 2.5 hours' extra work-related travel. Another firm, British Telecom (BT), started using teleconferencing in the United Kingdom in lieu of 30% of its regular meetings. At BT, three-fourths of all such meetings became substitutes for in-person meetings. Research that examined the long-run effects of this policy reported that BT decreased CO_2 emissions by more than 50,000 tonnes that year, in addition to conserving more than 10 million litres of vehicle fuel, translating into approximately £10 million, attributable to a decrease of greater than 200 million miles of commutes and more than 1,700 years of employee time compared to the previous year.

As must be evident, remote work benefits not only workers but also employers who can potentially reduce their workspace costs. As Kurland and Egan (1999) reported, the technology giant IBM documented substantial cost reduction of more than $70 million in expenditure on office space due to its employees working remotely. Further, when remote work is considered, it should be noted that firms' option of shopping for skills becomes wider to include even the physically disadvantaged. Quite in contrast to the popular view, work from home has the potential to indeed improve worker involvement in institutional activities. BT reported that the mean conference call included eight attendees; if physical meetings were conducted, on average, only five persons travelled to the same.[13]

Sridhar and Sridhar (2003) found, using the Internet Usage Data supplement of the US Bureau of Labor Statistics (1998) and the Survey of Income and Program Participation (1996) that, on average, remote workers constituted only 3% of the US population in 1995–96, while nearly 33% of households on average used the Internet in their home for

[12] "No more morning rush, office is at home", *Economic Times*, 2 April 2001, Bennett, Coleman & Co. Ltd.

[13] "Ringing in healthier ways", *Economic Times*, 21 July 2002, Bennett, Coleman & Co. Ltd.

attending to office-related work. Sridhar and Sridhar (2003) performed independent regressions of population and household suburbanization in US cities measured by their (calculated) density gradients, to understand the effect of remote work, using alternative indicators for the same. They used an infrastructure variable which facilitates remote work, in addition to the proportion of employees who partly clocked in their hours from both their residence and workplace, as the telecommuting indicator to understand its effect on US suburbanization. While the hypothesis was that cities with a greater percentage of remote workers were mostly suburbanized, they found that the relevant (*mixed workers*) variable had a positive effect on suburbanization, indicating greater population centralization with higher work from home, which suggested that remote work led to cities becoming more compact. This showed that communications technology and face-to-face interactions which cities facilitate complement, not substitute, each other.

Further, Sridhar and Sridhar (2003) used an alternative measure of remote work, referring to those that used the Internet at home for work-related activity. This variable was predicted to have an inverse effect on suburbanization, since the higher the percentage that used such infrastructure in their residence for work, the higher would be the flexibility to locate far from their place of work and the higher would be the degree of suburbanization. However, they found that this measure was not statistically significant. They also highlighted that this measure could be biased if traditional office-goers brought home their work partially. In such an event, their dependence on such communication infrastructure at their residence for work will not result in a decreased commute to work. From this viewpoint, Sridhar and Sridhar (2003) argued that this indicator could not be considered a good measure of the intended effects of remote work to understand its effects on sprawl.

Summarizing, Sridhar and Sridhar (2003) found that among all the work from home variables, mixed workers in fact lived closer to the city centre (where their jobs were presumably located) rather than the opposite which had been expected. This showed that communications made possible by devices (smart phones, tablets, laptops) are not an alternative for personal interactions and urban densities, as we may imagine, but complementary, like what Gaspar and Glaeser (1998) found.

These findings are similar with those from other studies (see, e.g. Kurland & Egan, 1999) that acknowledge the caveats of working from home, and the necessity for steady surveillance of the employee in an organizational context, which explains why working from home could increase the city's compactness, as opposed to suburbanization. For the same reasons, work from home implies challenges for the employer and employee, while mere online participation may constrain the worker's chances for, and participation in, highly appreciated institutional activity. It may also present a challenge to the company to guarantee the standard of its products and their timely supply (Mitter, 2000). Additionally, Giuliano (1998) warned that the effect of communications in leading to spatially distributed activity is beset with technological and organizational barriers. Ng and Jin (2000) indicated that work from home requires a major reform in work culture, confidence of employee supervisors, *suo moto* stimulation of workers, synergy with team members, and collaboration. Once these challenges are overcome, work from home is an inclusive way of involving the disadvantaged and women in the workforce, who, given their constraints, may be unable to engage productively in the economy otherwise. The degree to which communications affect urban form is determined not only by adeptness of its use by workers and organizations alike, but also by a change in organizational culture.

We should remember the caveat that remote work need not be always home-based, it refers to work from anywhere. As Mitter (2000) predicted, now remote work has progressed to include gig employees on the move such as salespersons, delivery workers or those that are 'on site', such as electricians, plumbers, construction workers, and so forth. The primary feature of such workers is that they imply multiplicity in the workplace and decrease travel time.

Since the pandemic, the effect of technology that has suburbanized Indian office work is unquestionable. A significant takeaway of Sridhar and Sridhar (2003) is that the location decisions of persons and households, and their effect on urbanization growth, are complicated. Attributing them to the mere influence of technology is naïve and simplistic.

The next section now summarizes the empirical findings from this research, as far as the causes of suburbanization of Indian cities are concerned.

6.5 Empirical Findings from This Research

I estimated the population gradient for 2015 obtained from the regressions reported in Chapter 3, and change in the gradient during the four decades, 1975–2015, for 100 Indian cities, as dependent on several factors, as shown by the theory, and other empirical evidence, summarized by the above literature review, subject to the constraints of data availability. It may be recalled that Mills (1992) did a similar estimation for US metropolitan areas. In these equations, I included exogenous variables representing the city size and income, and central city socio-economic conditions such as the proportion of literacy, Scheduled Castes/Scheduled Tribes (SC/ST), and unemployment rate in the city core relative to their values in the periphery. I included FAR as the measure of land use regulations. Unfortunately, I could not use any measure of technology or work from home to understand their impact on suburbanization. Sridhar et al. (2018) found that the proportion of employees who were telecommuting was negligible in Bengaluru, which is reasonable, given it was the pre-pandemic period. Thus, the lack of a measure of technology to indicate work from home in the pre-pandemic period is not a problem.

Tables 6.1 and 6.2 summarize the regression results of the change in the population density gradient and population gradient of 2015, respectively. In both these tables, city size (measured by population) and GDP per capita are indicators of the natural evolution or market-based theory of suburbanization. Both encourage sprawl (with a lower gradient) as per the market-based theory of natural evolution, thus they are expected to negatively impact the density gradient. The 1975 core density (measured in terms of population per square kilometre area of the central city) is meant to be a control for the pressure on its infrastructure, such that if this core density were to be high, it would encourage suburbanization (a negative effect). The relative proportions of the socially oppressed communities, SC/ST, literacy rate, and unemployment rate, all in the core to those in the periphery, are meant to reflect the flight from socio-economic conditions and expected to negatively affect the density gradient. The urbanizable land is a control variable because cities which do not have much urbanizable land (due to water bodies, hills, and/or mountains) cannot sprawl; alternatively more urbanizable land enables greater sprawl (leading to a lower value of the gradient). Thus, I expect a negative relationship between urbanizable land and the gradient. The FAR is included as an indicator of land use regulation, which is shown by existing studies to impact suburbanization (Sridhar, 2010; Brueckner & Sridhar, 2012). Specifically, higher FARs are expected to lead to higher values of the population density gradients and vice versa. Hence, the relationship is expected to be positive. Finally, the 1975 gradient is included as a lagged variable, to understand the effects of the city's past evolution on the current dispersion of inhabitants in the city. It is expected to exert a positive effect.

Table 6.1 shows that the change in the sprawl of India's urban areas during the four decades is sensitive to central cities' economic conditions. Specifically, the greater the unemployment rate disparities between the city core and the periphery, the higher the degree of suburbanization (lower value of the dependent variable). This means that job-seeking residents tend to flee the city core when joblessness is high there relative to what they find in the periphery. None of the other variables have a statistically significant effect on the variations in the population gradient during the four decades.

The model unsurprisingly explains only 15% of the variation in the population gradient during the four decades. This is because while the dependent variable captures the variation in the gradient during the four decades, most of the independent variables are from a single year: 1975, 2011, or 2015. This possibly explains the poor fit of the model.

Table 6.2 shows the regression of the 2015 population density gradient as associated with the same factors as in Table 6.1. The fit of this model is far better than the earlier model as observed in its R^2 of 0.45. This is easy to understand as population gradient (the response variable) is from 2015, and all the exogenous regressors are from either 1975 (lagged), 2011 (the flight from socio-economic conditions variables), or 2015 (the city GDP per capita). Therefore, the fit is far better. I find that urbanizable land has a negative association with the 2015 density gradient, showing that cities with greater amounts of urbanizable land sprawl more (with a smaller gradient), as per expectation. Thus, it may well be the case that cities with less urbanizable land are more efficient with their use of land, and centralized. The positive influence of the lagged 1975 population gradient is overwhelming on the 2015 population density gradient. This also explains much of the goodness of fit of the 2015 population gradient. The values of the variance inflation factor in Table 6.2, as in Table 6.1, show that multicollinearity is not a problem.

Table 6.3 presents the correlations between the variables in the regression analysis. No correlations are alarming enough to suggest strong multicollinearity or linear dependency.

Table 6.1 Association of Change in Population Suburbanization with Various Factors

	Coefficients	Std. Err.	Normalized coefficients	T statistic	Significance	Variance inflation factor	Variable mean
Intercept	−11.94	12.62		−0.95	0.35		
Population, 2011 (in millions)	0.41	0.43	0.13	0.96	0.34	1.61	2.00
City per capita GDP (in 1,000s of Rs), 2015	0.18	0.54	0.04	0.33	0.74	1.44	4.36
1975 city core density (in 1,000s of persons/sq. km of area)	−0.02	0.11	−0.02	−0.16	0.87	1.65	13.92
Proportion of SC/ST in the core city to that in the suburbs, 2011	0.04	0.10	0.05	0.43	0.67	1.24	2.03
Proportion of literacy rate in the core to that in the periphery, 2011	5.44	11.80	0.06	0.46	0.65	1.33	1.04
Proportion of unemployment rate in the core to that in the periphery, 2011	−2.11**	0.88	−0.29	−2.39	0.02	1.16	1.08
Urbanizable land area (%)	5.16	5.68	0.11	0.91	0.37	1.25	0.90
Floor Space Index, 2015	0.71	0.63	0.13	1.13	0.26	1.05	3.88
Population gradient, 1975	0.01	2.76	0.00	0.00	1.00	1.63	−0.38
Dependent variable mean							0.27
R-squared	**0.15**						
F value	**1.34**						
Number of observations	**79**						

Source: Florczyk et al. (2019), Census of India Primary Census Abstract (2011), and author's computations.

Response variable: change in population gradient, 1975–2015. This is computed as below:

$$\frac{\left[\text{Gradient Value 1975} - \text{Gradient Value 2015}\right]}{\text{1975 Gradient}}.$$

Table 6.2 Regression of the 2015 Population Density Gradient

	Coefficients	Std. Err.	Normalized coefficients	T statistic	Significance	Variance inflation factor	Variable mean
Intercept	−0.11	0.31		−0.36	0.72		
Population (in millions)	0.01	0.01	0.06	0.53	0.59	1.61	−0.28
City per capita income (in 1,000s of Rs)	0.02	0.01	0.12	1.14	0.26	1.44	2.00
1975 central city population density (in 1,000s per sq. km of land area)	0.00	0.00	−0.16	−1.39	0.17	1.65	4.36
Proportion of SC/ST in the core city to that in the suburbs, 2011	0.00	0.00	0.12	1.24	0.22	1.24	13.92
Proportion of literacy rate in the core to that in the periphery, 2011	0.12	0.29	0.04	0.42	0.68	1.33	2.03
Proportion of unemployment rate in the core to that in the periphery, 2011	0.00	0.02	−0.01	−0.12	0.91	1.16	1.04
Urbanizable land area (%)	−0.24*	0.14	−0.17	−1.69	0.10	1.25	1.08
Floor Space Index, 2015	0.00	0.02	0.00	−0.02	0.98	1.05	0.90
Population gradient, 1975	0.29***	0.07	0.49	4.29	0.00	1.63	3.88
Dependent variable mean							−0.28
R-squared	**0.45**						
F value	**6.29**						
Number of observations	**79**						

Sources: Florczyk et al. (2019), Census of India Primary Census Abstract, (2011) and author's computations.

*Statistically significant at 10% level. ***Statistically significant at 1% level.

Table 6.3 Correlation Matrix of Variables

	Urbnland	PG2015	FAR	PG1975	SCST ratio	Lit ratio	Unratio	PopMns	PCI000	CCden75000	CHG7515
Urbnland	1.00	−0.36	−0.09	−0.24	0.05	0.13	0.09	−0.18	−0.37	0.06	0.02
PG2015	−0.36	1.00	0.05	0.59	−0.01	−0.08	−0.04	0.26	0.28	−0.37	−0.03
FAR	−0.09	0.05	1.00	0.13	0.01	0.19	−0.08	0.10	0.04	0.01	0.17
PG1975	−0.24	0.59	0.13	1.00	−0.11	−0.10	0.05	0.34	0.20	−0.45	−0.01
SCSTratio	0.05	−0.01	0.01	−0.11	1.00	−0.32	0.12	−0.03	−0.12	0.22	−0.01
Litratio	0.13	−0.08	0.19	−0.10	−0.32	1.00	−0.25	−0.02	0.12	0.07	0.15
Unratio	0.09	−0.04	−0.08	0.05	0.12	−0.25	1.00	−0.03	−0.29	−0.04	−0.31
PopMns	−0.18	0.26	0.10	0.34	−0.03	−0.02	−0.03	1.00	0.33	0.19	0.12
PCI000	−0.37	0.28	0.04	0.20	−0.12	0.12	−0.29	0.33	1.00	−0.04	0.12
CCden75000	0.06	−0.37	0.01	−0.45	0.22	0.07	−0.04	0.19	−0.04	1.00	0.05
CHG7515	0.02	−0.03	0.17	−0.01	−0.01	0.15	−0.31	0.12	0.12	0.05	1.00

Sources: Florczyk et al. (2019), Census of India Primary Census Abstract (2011), and author's computations.

Note on variables used:

Urbnland: Urbanizable land in city i

PG2015: Population gradient, 2015 of city i

FAR: Floor Area Ratio of city i

PG1975: Population gradient, 1975, of city i

SCSTratio: Ratio of SC/ST population in the central city to that in the suburbs, of city i

Litratio: Ratio of literacy rate in the central city to that in the suburbs, of city i

Unratio: Ratio of unemployment rate in the central city to that in the suburbs, of city i

PopMns: Population of city i (in millions)

PCI1000: Per capita income of city i (in 1000s of PPP$)

CCden75000: Central city density in 1975 in 1000s of persons per sq km of land area of city i

$$\text{CHG7515: } \frac{[\text{Gradient Value 1975} - \text{Gradient Value 2015}]}{\text{1975 Gradient}} \text{ of city i}$$

6.6 Summary and Conclusions

Summarizing what has been accomplished in this chapter, I have reviewed the existing literature on the factors explaining suburbanization. Based on that, I understood natural evolution, central city socio-economic conditions, land use regulations, and technology as determining the extent of suburbanization/sprawl.

I then analysed the factors which have led to the observed sprawl in India's cities. Given the data constraints, I associated the 2015 and the change in the 1975–2015 population gradients, with a variety of exogenous socio-demographic factors. I find that the time-lagged population gradient has a powerful association with the 2015 gradient and changes in the density gradient (over 1975–2015), showing the influence of the historical spatial distribution of population. Besides, poor central city economic conditions (such as the unemployment rate) push residents away to the suburbs. Finally, the urbanizable land has a direct influence on the 2015 population gradient, partly because bigger cities grow without natural constraints and suburbanize when compared with those cities with constraints such as water bodies or mountains.

Whereas this chapter has taken an entirely quantitative approach to understanding suburbanization of India's cities, the next chapter focuses on qualitative perceptions of the phenomenon based on discussions with several stakeholders, and, wherever possible, correlates them with the findings from this chapter.

7
Qualitative Perceptions of Suburbanization

As discussed in Chapter 2 on methodology, in addition to the quantitative approach taken to achieve the objectives of this research on suburbanization, I supplemented the empirical estimations of the standard urban models presented in the earlier chapters with qualitative views from experts. Towards accomplishing this goal, I conducted a seminar on suburbanization in November 2021, at the Institute for Social and Economic Change, in which subject experts, policy makers, and well-known real estate developers were invited to share their views regarding suburbanization. The objectives of the seminar were to understand, from their perspective, responses to the research questions below, which are a subset of the questions representing the focus of the quantitative work, central to this book.

1. Are Indian cities suburbanized?
2. Are there geographic differences in the sprawl of India's urban areas? Why do you think so?
3. What are the causes of suburbanization of Indian cities?

In addition to the above, the speakers were asked to reflect on additional questions regarding land use regulations and if they perceived the floor area ratio (FAR) to be a problem in Indian cities which has led to sprawl.

The chapter is structured as follows: Section 7.1 provides a brief introduction to the urbanization process in the country as captured in the seminar of experts. Then Section 7.2 presents an overview of the qualitative discussions of whether Indian cities have suburbanized, followed by

Indian Cities or Suburbs? Kala Seetharam Sridhar, Oxford University Press. © Kala Seetharam Sridhar 2025.
DOI: 10.1093/9780198958147.003.0007

an explanation of the causes of suburbanization in Section 7.3.[1] Section 7.4 focuses on the significant part played by regulations affecting land use in the sprawl of India's urban agglomerations. Section 7.5 transitions to a discussion of sprawl against the background of megacity governance. The final section of this chapter concludes with policy suggestions for sprawl and the trade-offs involved.

7.1 Introduction

The possibility of accomplishing a five-trillion-dollar economy for India which is now discussed in policy circles requires that the Gross Domestic Product (GDP) of the country should grow at a minimum of 10.5% per annum, so also to enable it to become a higher-income country ('Viksit Bharat') by 2047. The Indian economy is expected to leapfrog in the next couple of years to morph into a different one, with the income levels significantly higher, quality of life much better, and poverty levels mitigated.

Only about 3% of India's land is covered by urban areas which contain 35% of the urban population and which make a huge contribution (estimated to be 60%) to the GDP. Thus, it is clear that cities offer high economic returns. As the economy gets more industrialized, tractors and equipment are bringing about mechanization in agriculture; it follows that in reality we need fewer people to do the same amount of farming. The surpluses families are growing in the villages must be the creation of employment not originating from agriculture in the rural areas and that's happening in many places, thus we have created industrial towns. This is nothing but the standard Lewis two-sector model, where it is possible to increase agricultural output by removing surplus labour out of agriculture (with mechanization) into non-farm activities and cities.

In the early days after Independence, there was heavy investment in rural areas and smaller towns when it was thought that investment should take place in the rural rather than in the urban areas; this was necessary, to look at the poorer segments of society, and this was the appropriate

[1] Unfortunately, there was not much discussion in the seminar about if and whether there are geographic variations in the extent of suburbanization of India's cities, for which I primarily rely on the quantitative analyses in earlier chapters. Where it was discussed in the seminar, it is elaborated.

direction in which to go at that point in time. But now a majority of our GDP is created in cities, thus it is only the concentration which matters for economic efficiency and scale economies (see Brueckner, 2011)—whether it is industrialization, or retailer specific services such as information technology, all these segments have leapfrogged, just like growth which has taken place in Bengaluru, Hyderabad, Mumbai, and Gurgaon.

Residents of rural areas now migrate into cities and towns and, in the process, inadvertently increase the GDP of the country. Hence, following India's well-known Jawaharlal Nehru National Urban Renewal Mission (JNNURM) and the Urban Infrastructure Development Scheme for Small and Medium Towns (UIDSSMT) (which is now the Atal Mission for Rejuvenation and Urban Transformation—AMRUT), the next policy emphasis on urbanization in India was to create 100 smart cities. These programmes facilitated the creation of urban infrastructure at a faster pace to absorb migrants from villages to cities, who presumably settle in the periphery of the cities, which leads to what is commonly understood suburbanization.

7.2 Are Our Cities Suburbanized?

We slowly find now that the Central Business Districts of cities are losing their prominence. For instance, half the business in the legendary MG Road in Bengaluru has moved out, presumably to avoid land leasing costs. Similarly, in many cities, the traditional zones where the business and economic activities used to locate have migrated to the suburbs. This must explain some advantages of suburbs of which there are three: first, lower transportation time with highways; second, better standard of living; and third, a very secure sense of the aggregate economy, which is driving many of our cities ahead.

Therefore, Indian cities are suburbanized depending on the extent and spread of such economic activity. Regional variations exist in suburbanization across states of the country for obvious reasons such as the extent of urbanization, per capita income, size of cities, and their distribution. Taking the case of Karnataka, it is moderately urbanized at about 40%, and it would have been about 55% urban if the criterion used for defining urban areas—of 5,000 population—were to be relaxed (Sridhar, 2020).

Karnataka's cities have a mix of urbanization in both their central and peripheral areas. This could be due to several reasons: there is core economic activity which can be either in services or the agricultural sector. In and around Bengaluru for instance, there is the robust industrial sector due to which suburbanization is happening now. Similarly, most Indian cities have suburbanized depending on the extent that their economy is dependent on manufacturing versus services.

The above qualitative explanation is somewhat consistent with the quantitative analyses in the previous chapters, whereby I found that based on the general definition of suburbanization, Kolkata is the most suburbanized with nearly 99% of its population in both 1975 and 2015 suburbanized, owing to its manufacturing prowess (the jute mills). Cities dependent on polluting manufacturing processes tend to suburbanize as these activities cannot locate in the centre. Mangaluru was the most centralized in 1975 (at 83% of its population centrally located), presumably because it has a large number of services—primarily banking and educational institutions, which tend to locate centrally.

7.3 Causes of Suburbanization

Two major forces are drivers of suburbanization. One originates from rural areas in the context of agriculture. There is now a tremendous decline in the employment opportunities in villages (despite the Mahatma Gandhi National Rural Employment Guarantee programme), thus there has been forced diversification; people are not able to get productive job opportunities within agriculture and allied activities. Therefore, they are resorting to petty activities in the rural non-agricultural sectors. The rural non-agricultural sector in the Indian context did not replicate the East Asian model, rather it is the proliferation of low-productivity activities to a large extent. Thus, as a result, what we get is that the rural space is now unable to retain agriculture as the dominant activity and, at the same time, non-agricultural activities are not as productive as their urban counterparts. However, because a sizable percentage of the workforce is in non-farm activities, these areas are undergoing a major reclassification from being agrarian to the municipal, even though the government does not recognize them as urban areas; this is now one important source of suburbanization.

The other source of suburbanization is that which originates from the city itself. The migration from rural areas to cities, along with the natural rate of growth of urban population, have continued to occur and are continuing, thus city centres logically get congested and hence peripheral areas/suburbs of the cities have developed. There are limitations of the city centre in providing affordable housing or office spaces.[2] Real estate values have increased significantly at the city centre, whereas the suburbs are comparatively safer and cheaper in terms of real estate (see Sridhar (2004) for a description of the disparities in real estate process between the central city and suburbs of Indian cities) and it is very conducive to raising the family there. Hospitals, schools, and a number of new facilities coming up have moved to the suburbs and suburbs are becoming more like urban areas.

As economic growth takes place within the city, we see increasing competition for space between builders, residents, industrialists, and corporate bodies. It is important to understand if such growth is industry-led or services-led. If industry-led, the largest cities, specifically the million-plus ones, and the class I cities too, where it may not be obvious, have witnessed to some extent this suburbanization process. As urban areas get saturated, the second-best solution for a new firm, resident, or a new migrant to locate would be the peripheral and agrarian parts of the bigger cities. By locating in the rural hinterland of the bigger cities, one can reduce the input costs of the raw materials and land, but simultaneously retain access to the resources available within the city.

So, one can identify the above sources to explain the suburbanization process. In fact, data from the 2011 Census indicate that within the decade of 2001–11, nearly 2,500 census towns emerged. These census towns are nothing but an outcome of this suburbanization process. They are obviously not recognized by the Government of India because they do not have any urban statutory body, but in terms of all other criteria, these spaces resemble urban characteristics. If we were to understand the location of these 2,500 census towns which emerged in the decade

[2] One of the richest cities in India, Mumbai, provides the least in terms of housing. Nearly 50% of Mumbai's population lives in slums and half of them could afford a house of the size which they are currently consuming, if it were supplied. So, although there are people moving into suburbs continuously, there are unauthorized settlements giving shelter to 50% of the population in Mumbai.

of 2001–11, one cluster is seen in the neighbourhoods of the very large metropolitan and classified cities which are expanding fast. So, some of the activities and residents are shifting to the rural hinterland of these big cities. Another cluster of such census towns may be identified in the remote rural areas, where there is no dynamism. There is no activity which can provide momentum for economic growth and therefore, in these remote parts, the workforce is, by force, engaged in petty activities in the non-farm sector and that is how some of these towns are emerging.

It is interesting and surprising to note that the above qualitative explanation of the causes of suburbanization is also consistent with the econometric analyses where we mostly found that the historical hangover of cities determines the extent of their current urban sprawl (as shown by the significant effect of the time-lagged density gradient on its current value).

7.4 Role of Land Use Regulations in Suburbanization

As shown by the existing body of work and policy debates, land use policies like zoning, rules governing height restrictions of buildings, primarily the floor space index, and others significantly affect urban sprawl and the way in which cities develop. Certain important points must be considered in planning for a city to limit its sprawl: first, the administrative setup; second, the legal framework. The first is an administrative question which relates to whether the town planners of Indian cities are competent enough to plan for a city, a town, or a rural area. This is part of the current debate on the discipline itself in India—that there are not enough competent town planners and more need to be trained.

With respect to the legal framework, zoning regulations and change of land use from farming to non-agricultural purposes (residential, industrial, or commercial), Karnataka, for example, has removed the alienation clause which otherwise makes transfer of land/property more difficult. A piece of land which is bought for certain purposes is deemed conversion the approval for which should be granted fast; but the decision should respect the zoning laws—whether it is commercial, residential, industrial, or mixed use—but how it affects a particular area depends on certain local conditions, as well as citizen feedback and economic activity. The pace of approvals also determines the extent of suburbanization of a city. The faster the approvals, the greater the extent of urbanization and suburbanization too, assuming land conversion deals happen in the peripheral areas.

The FAR becomes extremely important as with other regulations, as they regulate the city's spatial growth. Hyderabad is the only Indian city which has in fact removed restrictions on the FAR, with the result that its FAR is at 7 (the highest among Indian cities). If the theory had been right, then Hyderabad must have been highly compact. However, I have documented in the earlier chapters that Hyderabad was the most suburbanized in 1975, and its population and households have continued to suburbanize. In terms of employment, I find Hyderabad to be polycentric as documented in Chapter 5, despite its higher FAR. In Bengaluru, a builder can build as much as s/he can, subject to parking, fire brigade requirements, and civil aviation regulations. However, in contrast to Hyderabad, Bengaluru has become centralized as seen in the preceding chapters, based on the quantitative evidence, which is consistent with the theory. So, the issue of FAR is fungible and this will completely change in the next couple of years. As the city needs more water, sewage, schools, hospitals, roads, and transportation, we also cannot just unilaterally increase FAR without collateral infrastructure.

On average, Indian cities have quite low FSI when set against the global standards, as demonstrated previously (Sridhar, 2010). That being the case, whatever infrastructure is provided also is being underutilized. Looking at this from the developers' perspective implies not only increasing the FSI, but also doing justice to the infrastructure. Optimizing the infrastructure requires coordinated integration between certain departments at the periphery. The FSI must be higher on transit-oriented developmental activities.

The reader should recall that the FAR/FSI did not have the expected effect on the density gradient (Chapter 6); these results are qualitative.

7.5 Suburbanization and Metropolitan Governance

Suburbanization has many implications for urban governance because many urban agglomerations in India have multiple urban local bodies

(ULBs). It is important to understand which is the dominant central city and what is the role of consolidating metropolitan governance versus fragmented metropolitan government in suburbanized cities like Kolkata and Bengaluru.

A suburb is well defined if it is within the boundary governed by the ULB laws—the municipalities or the Municipal Corporation Act. If it is outside the boundaries of the city or town, it is governed by the rural local body act as we call it, but the Town and Country Planning Act is applicable for both rural and urban areas. We declare it a Local Planning Authority (LPA). We find many times that the boundary of the town is mimicked by or overlaps with that of the LPA but there are times in many cases where it extends beyond the limits of the LPA. Also, this is more often seen in the jurisdiction of the Urban Development Authorities (UDAs). Other than this, to have balanced development, there are regional development authorities, which are special authorities created for metropolitan governance. Yet there is always a question as to whether we are taking away the statutory powers which are constitutionally vested in a rural local body or ULB. But worldwide experience shows us that there is necessity for regional planning, like the New York and the New Jersey transport Metropolitan Authority, to get the best economic potential from urbanization.

7.6 Policy Suggestions for Suburbanization

There are several negative effects of suburbanization, as I demonstrate in the next and final chapter, which is why we want to ask how far a city can grow and if there are limits to growth.

One important challenge which came to the fore during the seminar was the new construction happening in the peripheries because of new residential developments due to suburbanization.

Most of the cities are required to do a huge catch-up in terms of not only new construction but also unauthorized construction in the peripheral areas. It is a challenge to bring in more appropriate management of construction debris in addition to unauthorized construction in the peripheral areas, because such land parcels are not within the jurisdiction of the municipal area, and they lack municipal authenticity. In the suburbs of cities, it is also clear that there is a requirement for various kinds of amenities, with the need for a great deal of coordination and co-working between the private parties and the government involved. But lakes are disintegrating and disappearing in some areas because of suburbanization due to the residential developments and construction happening. In most of the cities, such coordinated efforts do not happen, and citizen groups take this task upon themselves, as has happened in the case of Bengaluru.

Based on the qualitative analyses, an investment strategy is recommended: in the 'suburbs' which are in the neighbourhood of the large metropolitan areas or other class I cities, there is tremendous scope for exploiting the agglomeration economies with investment in transport and housing. Then such urban sprawl can be made liveable and be connected to the agglomeration economies of the large cities, which is consistent with what other studies find as well (Brueckner, 2011; Sridhar, 2011).

However, when one compares the living conditions across measures of space, we find that the suburbs of large metropolitan cities offer better living conditions compared to the 'small towns' in the outskirts of metropolitan areas (also called suburbs). Slums exist in the suburbs of large cities, but if we compare the status of residents of squatter settlements in a large city suburb vis-à-vis a 'small town suburb', we find that the well-being for the slum dwellers in the suburbs of large metropolitan cities is much better compared to the well-being of their counterparts in the 'smaller towns suburbs'. By the same token, smaller and secondary 'suburbs' in the form of census towns are also growing but they are not growing with the wealth and standard of income we see in the metropolitan cities. So, what we are looking for is a higher GDP growth per capita in the smaller town suburbs (census towns). These findings tend to suggest that there is a huge role for the state to play, if we were to take the census towns as an indicator for urban sprawl.

So, one important policy intervention could be in terms of controlling the money-laundering activities which go on in terms of land speculation in the suburbs and peripheral areas of large cities. Land speculation will have to be controlled and more organized activities will have to be initiated. In the case of advanced sprawl, new growth dynamism will have to be created and new activities will have to be generated, so that such urban sprawl becomes self-sufficient in nature. The nexus between political parties and builders will have to be broken, and land scams will have to be stopped, which implies land use regulations such as the FSI must be relaxed and simplified considerably. Finally, subsidiary economic activities in the edge of cities will need to have a strong association with the main activities within the city, such that the main city and their suburbs should work as a continuum, otherwise it is not possible to make these spaces productive. Thus, it is possible that central areas of cities will become important and be reclaimed with better infrastructure.

However, there is a problem with infrastructure in the suburbs, as most of our planning is oriented towards the central city. The central parts are also presumably the ones included in the city master plans, hence they are covered with good public services like highways, extensive water and sewer pipelines, and public transport networks. But there is a problem with traffic and mobility, communications, and urban infrastructure in the peripheral areas/suburbs. Most of the developed countries have created urban infrastructure in advance of bringing in suburbanization. In various developed countries of the world like China, smaller countries like Singapore, or world-class cities such as Dubai, every suburb is facilitated by roads, metro, and other urban amenities like schools, colleges, hospitals, and police stations. In India, we have not been able to match the growth of urbanization and the provision of infrastructure in suburbs of cities.

The city of Mumbai constructed 390 km of suburban railway in the last 60 years but has added only 19 km recently. There are 2,342 suburban trains ferrying about 7.5 million passengers daily, which represents the world's largest suburban train system. To catch up, Mumbai is constructing 300 km of suburban and city metro rail in the next five years. It is adding a cross-harbour bridge which will open up enough land to be equivalent to half of Mumbai; at the time this book was being completed, a new airport in Panvel Mumbai was expected to be commissioned, as well as a coastal road across the western side of Mumbai, and a water project (called the Pinjal River Project) which will give 24-7 water to the city and its suburbs. All these five projects together have an investment of Rs.3 lakh crores. Of course, there is no denial of the fact that there is a dual responsibility of the private sector to deliver internal infrastructure while the government typically provides the external planning and design for purposes of the increasing burgeoning and ambitious population, which is intellectually serving not only India but the rest of the world. Thus suburban India, similar to its central city counterpart, deserves a good quality of life with investments in infrastructure.

Indian urbanization is generating enough money (the largest cities of the country—Delhi, Mumbai, Chennai, and Bengaluru—generate the most tax revenue for the exchequer), and there is no doubt that there is a surplus of money for good projects; it is up to private investors really to take up the development of this infrastructure and design a good quality of life. The governments must expedite the work on roads and national highways. The Government of India at the time of completing this book (in 2023–24) was completing 35 km of national highway per day. Such seamless connectivity improves economic efficiency and productivity undoubtedly, but it also leads to sprawl.

The next and final chapter presents the environmental implications of sprawl and suburbanization in India, summarizes the findings of this pioneering work, and concludes with prospects for next steps in this research agenda.

8
What are the Outcomes of Suburbanization?

8.1 Introduction

As documented in the earlier chapters, suburbanization/sprawl implies the horizontal expansion of cities, leading to many questions regarding the effective delivery of services, especially in the peripheral/suburban areas. It is instructive to note here that electricity access by Brihanmumbai Electricity Supply and Transport (BEST) in Mumbai is confined to the Mumbai city area and excludes the suburbs. Similarly in Varanasi, which I have found here to be one of the most suburbanized cities of the country, the areas under the core city have excellent sewerage connections or a piped sewer system. The outcome of suburbanization I examine in this chapter entails an assessment of the geographic variations in the provision of basic services such as educational facilities, healthcare, water, and sanitation in Bengaluru, against norms specified by the Government of India's Ministry of Housing and Urban Affairs (MoHUA). This assessment derives from the surveys of families representative of the urban area, as Sridhar et al. (2021) did. I understand if the city's sprawl has resulted in the delivery of inadequate basic amenities in the suburbs, relative to those in the centre, on which Sridhar et al. (2021) report.

In this chapter, I examine two outcomes of excessive sprawl and spatial inequality in the distribution of public amenities like water, and access to healthcare and educational facilities (based on primary surveys in Bengaluru), and poor air quality due to excessive carbon emissions (based on secondary data from all cities for which the data are available). This chapter first presents evidence regarding the spatial inequality in the distribution of services, which is investigated taking the case of

Indian Cities or Suburbs? Kala Seetharam Sridhar, Oxford University Press. © Kala Seetharam Sridhar 2025.
DOI: 10.1093/9780198958147.003.0008

Bengaluru. Then this chapter focuses on air quality, based on data for most of the 100 cities for which the various suburbanization analyses have been presented in the previous chapters.

The structure of this chapter is as described here. The next section, Section 8.2, summarizes the existing research on Bengaluru and urban services in general (which are not covered elsewhere in this book), following which the findings of the specific research on urban services reported in this chapter are described in Section 8.3—with respect to access to healthcare, educational facilities, water, and sanitation facilities and waste management—using the surveys described in Sridhar et al. (2021). Taking the case of Bengaluru, I present spatial disparities across its central and peripheral areas, for the selected services. Given the limited available empirical research on the extent of intra-city disparities in the provision of public services in other Indian cities, intra-urban disparities with regard to the provision of various basic urban services in an Indian city should be especially invaluable.

Following the description of spatial inequality, in Section 8.4 the evidence on urban sprawl and air quality is summarized, based on secondary data sources, for most of the Indian cities studied, as found in this research. Then the last part of this chapter, Section 8.5, summarizes all findings of the book and points to further directions for research.

8.2 Existing Studies

City surveys are periodically done everywhere. If we take the case of water supply, the MoHUA specifies the availability of 135 litres per capita daily (LPCD) as a benchmark for India's cities. It is instructive to note that in this context, Paul et al. (2012) documented in Bengaluru, actual consumption of only 124 LPCD during 2007–10. More recently, based on a pilot in a ward, Sridhar et al. (2017) reported actual usage of about 80 LPCD of water supply on average, which was even lower (at 59 LPCD) for slum households of the pilot ward. If representative, this is a cause for concern, as these data from different sources imply that the availability of potable water has been decreasing since 2007 in Bengaluru. The Smart Cities Mission concept note of the Government of India specifies that all households in cities must be covered with a sewerage network, but Paul et al. (2012) found only a little more than half of families in the metropolis had access to a sewer network over the period from 2008 until 2010.

Rao and Tewari (1979) provided insights into Bengaluru's pattern of growth for the first time ever. The study found a lopsided development of population and city area with the former overtaking the latter, leading to crisis with respect to basic amenities including housing.

The Bengaluru-based Public Affairs Centre (PAC) developed a unique way of assessing the accountability of the government departments to citizens: citizen report cards (CRCs), which were used as a means of peer review of government departments by citizens. These CRCs were started in Bengaluru and Hubballi-Dharwad in Karnataka, and rolled out in other Indian cities—Delhi, Mumbai, Pune, and Ahmedabad. These were deemed to be successful in improving service delivery in these cities.

However, recognizing the inadequacy of authentic economic information disaggregated at the level of the city (most such data were available only up to the district level), Paul et al. (2012) developed several indicators to measure the economy of a city; they reported that Bengaluru led the pack of cities in Karnataka, examining fresh data on the investment proposals approved for the city, and outstanding credit at the city level. Bengaluru accounted for nearly 85% of all new investment proposals in to the 11 cities they examined. However, the other, smaller cities in the state were found to be superior to Bengaluru on other economic indicators such as banking accessibility (measured by banks per 100,000 persons) and revenue gathering (which Paul et al. (2012) measured by the efficiency with which property taxes were collected). Besides, the smaller cities were much better than Bengaluru in their delivery of basic urban facilities such as the provision of water supply connections to households, collection of garbage at the doorstep, and sanitation in their slums. In 2011, based on Census data, the proportion of Bengaluru's families with sanitation improved to 97% from 91% in 2001. Interestingly, despite such high private access to toilets, Paul et al. (2012) reported that Bengaluru was characterized by a greater number of public parks than public toilets as of 2009, which showed the priority of the urban local body (ULB).

Due to the paucity of data, there is sparse research which throws light on the sub-city distribution of basic services, as suburbanization continues to occur. Here, I document the findings of a study demonstrating the spatial distribution of basic services in Bengaluru.

8.3 Spatial Inequality in the Distribution of Basic Services

After missing many rounds of the competition, Bengaluru became a 'smart city' in 2017, as part of which the city's ULB, the BBMP, got access to Rs 1,700 crore to improve its infrastructure. While Chapter 4 described the historical development of the spatial pattern of Bengaluru, here I focus on the spatial distribution of basic services and question if that is a fallout of the sprawl of the city. In the context of the observed suburbanization, this chapter analyses the current level of basic services in Bengaluru and compares it against the norms specified by the MoHUA for health, water, and sanitation, as simple information about basic services does not exist for India's cities.

8.3.1 Methodology and Data Sources

Since there are no disaggregated secondary data on service delivery for areas within the city, to understand their distribution in Bengaluru, I draw upon data from primary surveys of about 1,500 households, reported in Sridhar et al. (2021). A total of 27 representative city wards were covered by the primary surveys, which covered all central and peripheral areas of the metropolitan area. Some 56 households were sampled from each ward to understand the various aspects of public services.

The next sections elaborate findings with respect to the basic services—healthcare, availability of water supply, and access to waste collection—across the centre and suburbs of the metropolitan area.

8.3.2 Spatial Disparities in Availability of Healthcare

Regarding availability of healthcare infrastructure, which is a major aspect mentioned in the Government of India's smart cities mission concept note, Sridhar et al. (2021) found that nearly two-thirds (64%) of respondents from the primary survey had access to primary health centres (PHCs) within a short distance; however, significantly fewer, less than half, went there for care. The remaining desired non-government hospitals on obvious grounds, including long distance to PHCs (21%), among others.[1] In terms of the distance travelled to avail of healthcare, the private hospitals provided the best access. As Sridhar et al. (2021) noted, nearly half (47%) of those who were surveyed had access to non-government healthcare within less than 1 km; about 49% had a non-government healthcare facility available anywhere from 1 to 5 km away, showing fair coverage even in the face of sprawl.

The spatial analysis of primary healthcare across Bengaluru by Sridhar et al. (2021) indicated that the East Zone ranked the top in access to such facilities, followed by the South and West zones of the city, which were defined to be centrally located (see Figure 8.1). When proximity to either government or private healthcare was taken into account (Figure 8.2), Sridhar et al. (2021) reported that Jayanagar (which is a centrally located ward) ranked the best in availability of healthcare followed by three peripheral wards in the next positions, which meant that they had either a private hospital or a government PHC very near, within 1.5 km (Figure 8.2).

8.3.3 Spatial Disparities in Water Supply

The Government of India includes 'quality and adequate' water supply as part of its definition of a smart city. The benchmark with respect to water supply stipulates 24-7 supply of water to residents and full coverage of all housing units in the metropolitan area with the necessary network, and assurance of 135 LPCD in terms of quantity. Sridhar et al. (2021) noted that none of these benchmarks were satisfied in the city (Table 8.1). When compared with the stipulated 100% metering of all household water connections, only 81% of connections were metered in Bengaluru (Table 8.1). Part of the reasons for not being able to connect all households with water connections is sprawl. The city's outlying 110 villages were included within the fold of the ULB in 2006, with the result that they were long deprived of a municipal water supply. Only recently, after the

[1] Sridhar et al. (2021) reported that in slums, the percentage of those visiting public healthcare facilities was greater (48%), but they found that more than half of families in these squatter settlements also visited both public and non-government healthcare facilities.

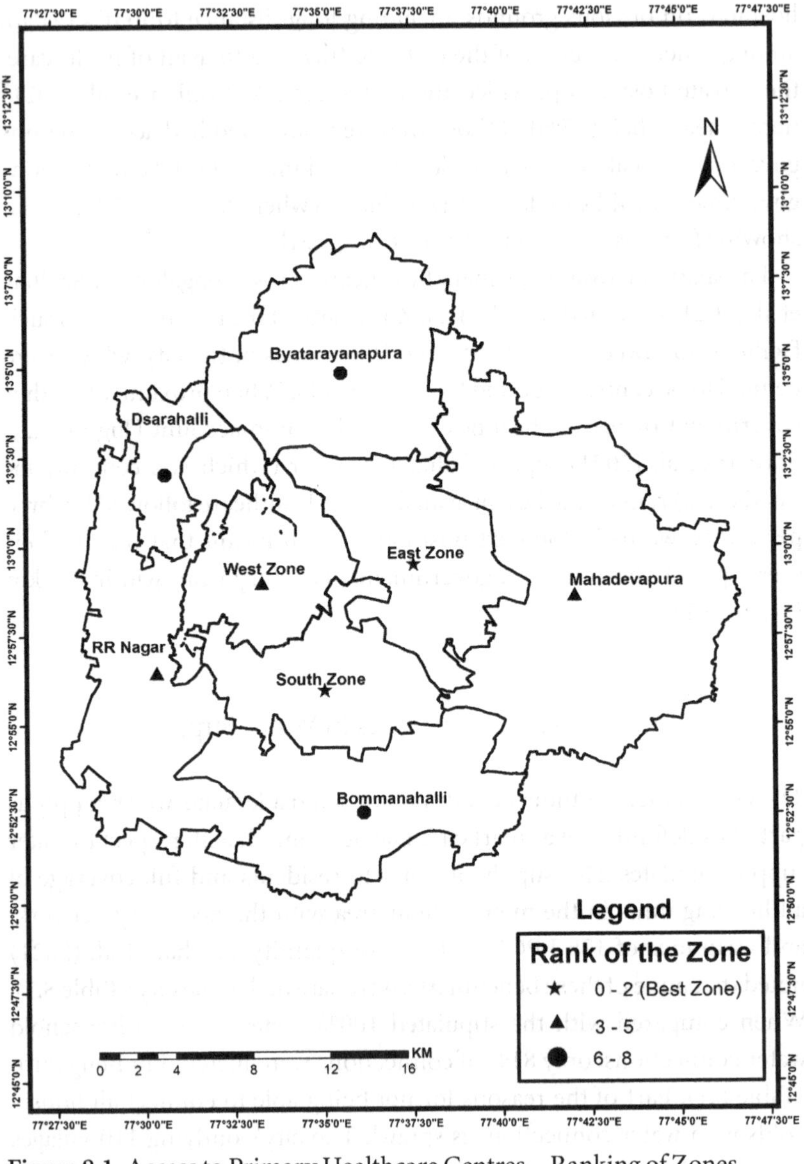

Figure 8.1 Access to Primary Healthcare Centres—Ranking of Zones, Bengaluru

Source: Created by author based on data in Sridhar et al. (2021).

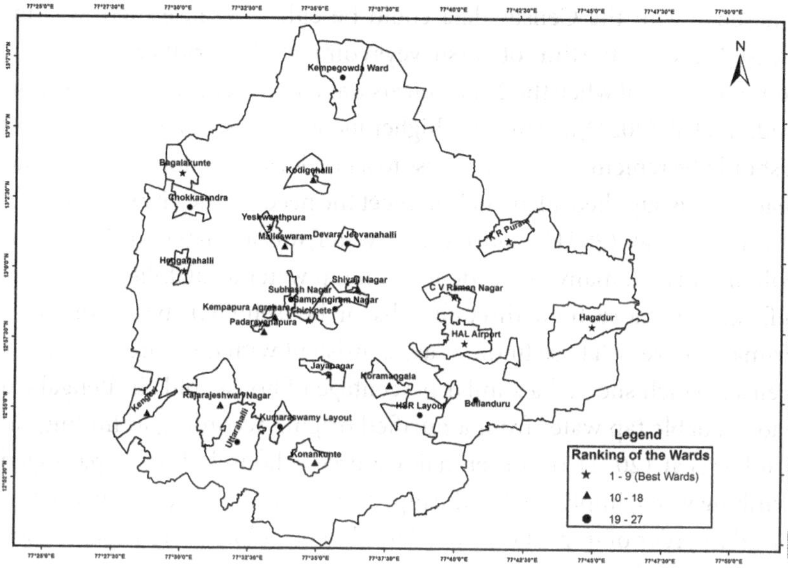

Figure 8.2 Distance to Any Healthcare Facility at the Ward Level, Bengaluru

Source: Created by author based on data in Sridhar et al. (2021).

Table 8.1 Service Level Standards for Water Supply

Service level standard	Bengaluru's actual service delivery
Round-the-clock water supply	Not met
All housing units with a connection	Not met
Availability of 135 LPCD	Not met (70 litres)
100% metering	Not met (81%)
100% effectiveness in gathering charges	Not met

Sources: https://smartcities.gov.in and Sridhar et al. (2021).

2015 household surveys were conducted, were households in the outlying areas of Bengaluru connected to the municipal water supply network.

On the accessibility to tap water, Sridhar et al. (2021) found that the majority, i.e. 90%, of the households had a tap within their premises, consistent with data from the 2011 Census of India which reported a slightly lower percentage of families as having a tap within their compound. The difference with the Census data could be either because there was increased access at the time of the surveys completed by Sridhar et al. (2021) compared to that when the 2011 Census was conducted, or the sampling in Sridhar et al. (2021) was more of higher income households. Nonetheless, it should be remembered that access to a tap does not automatically mean that water is supplied adequately to meet the needs of the city's families.

Sridhar et al. (2021) reported that water was available in the metropolitan area via many antecedents with tap water availability being significant (in more than three-fourths of households), based on their primary surveys. These findings are consistent with those from the 2011 Census which showed a similar percentage of households in Bengaluru had available tap water from a purified origin. According to findings in Sridhar et al. (2021), the other major source to households was packaged drinking water, implying that the piped supply was of insufficient quality. Third in order of importance was found to be public stand posts (which 6.7% of households, mostly the poor, depended on), even while 4.5% of households obtained their water supply from borewells. Among the localities of Bengaluru, households in a central ward in western Bengaluru (Kumaraswamy layout) had the best access to piped water supply at 96.4%, as reported by Sridhar et al. (2021), compared with the 2011 Census which reported access for this ward at 97.6%.

Overall, as reported by Sridhar et al. (2021), about 9% of the city's households were able to access water from within a 100-m. distance and a small proportion (1.0%) were able to get their water from anywhere between 100 and 500 m. away.

Comparing the data in Sridhar et al. (2021) with corresponding data from the Census of India 2011 shows consistency across the two when water supply sources within the premises (the first panel in Figure 8.3), near the premises (the middle panel in Figure 8.3) and away from the premises are considered (the last panel in Figure 8.3). Figure 8.3 indicates that the suburban and peripheral wards contain the households with their water supply likely to be away from the premises, demonstrating the consequences of sprawl.

Interestingly, all the top wards with the highest LPCD reported were peripheral, based on the analysis of Sridhar et al. (2021). But many of these wards were not even connected to the municipal system (provided by the Bangalore Water Supply and Sewerage Board (BWSSB)) at the

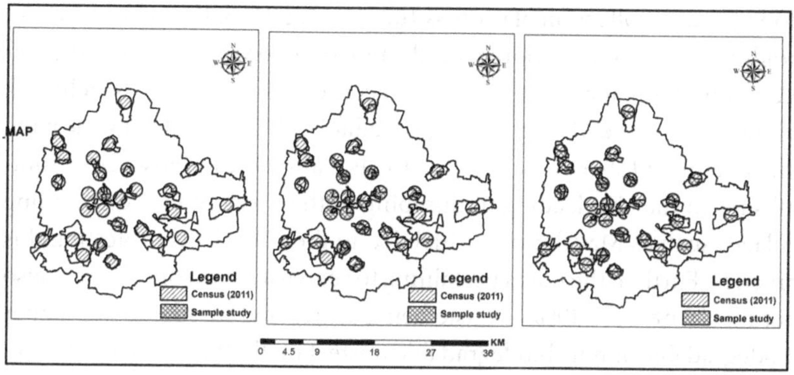

Figure 8.3 Water Supply Sources in Bengaluru
Source: Created by author based on data in Sridhar et al. (2021).

time research was completed by Sridhar et al. (2021). So, the quantity of water received by these wards may be reflective of the fact that they depended on water tankers. Hence, excessive sprawl leads to a rise in the price of basic services for residents of suburban and peripheral areas.

Sridhar et al.'s (2021) study of perceptions about access to water indicated that a majority were satisfied with the services provided (which nearly half the respondents rated as excellent or good) and water supply was dependable (43%) and on time (one-third of respondents). Nonetheless, several respondents were unhappy with the water supply because of infrequency of supply (15%) or inadequacy (9%). These findings from Sridhar et al. (2021) imply spatial inequalities in water access across the city, which are much greater in the peripheral parts.

8.3.4 Spatial Disparities in Access to Solid Waste Management

Urbanization brings along with it changes in lifestyles which lead to increased generation of all kinds of waste. Undoubtedly therefore concerned with the public health implications, the Government of India's MoHUA, as part of their guidelines for smart cities, came up with certain benchmarks based on effective solid waste management (summarized in Table 8.2). I note that no benchmark for solid waste specified in Table 8.2 is satisfied by Bengaluru. While the coverage benchmark for door-to-door collection of waste is 100%, only 50% of Bengaluru's households were covered by doorstep collection of solid waste. As far as the collection of municipal waste itself is concerned, as against the benchmark of 100% set by the MoHUA, Bengaluru had only 85% collection, leaving the remaining 15% of waste on the streets. I also note the absence of landfill sites in the city, leading to dumping of the waste in the surrounding villages such as Mavallipura, which led to their residents protesting this practice. Further, the norm pertaining to segregation of solid waste is also not met, with only 30% of waste being segregated by source into either biodegradable or non-biodegradable waste. Finally, the norm of 100% recycling of waste is not met (Table 8.2).

Of the benchmarks presented in Table 8.2, I note that the failure to meet the first two benchmarks is possibly due to sprawl. As the municipal area and suburbanization keep increasing, the local body finds it difficult to provide doorstep collection of services in the peripheral or suburban areas. In fact, this is confirmed from actual observation in the peripheral parts where loads of solid waste are left on the roadside, compared to the relatively clean central parts of the city.

Sridhar et al. (2021) reported, judging from their surveys, that a majority (92.3%) of households who were surveyed in the city generated anywhere between 1 and 2 kg of waste each in 2018. This is not inconsistent with estimates of its ULB, the BBMP, which show the garbage creation per capita to be 309 gms, but lower per capita at 300 gms in slums (https://site.bbmp.gov.in/departmentwebsites/swm/ accessed February 5, 2025).

Table 8.2 Norms for Municipal Solid Waste

Norms	**Bengaluru's actual level of solid waste management**
All households to be covered by door-to-door collection of municipal solid waste every day	Not met (50% households covered)
100% gathering of municipal solid waste	Not met (85% municipal solid waste collected)
Complete separation of waste at source, i.e. wet, dry, and other waste	Not met (30% segregated at source)
100% recycling of solid waste	Not met

Source: Created by author using data in Sridhar et al. (2021).

Bengaluru has a unique challenge with its management of trash, since residences contribute more than half (58%) to the city's total garbage creation, which is the maximum among the various generators, as per the BBMP (https://site.bbmp.gov.in/departmentwebsites/swm/ accessed February 5, 2025). Most of the trash (97.5%) thus created was collected largely by the local authority and the periodicity of waste gathering was daily in the case of two-thirds of households. A big army of roughly 20,000 workers (called *pourakarmikas*) engage in doorstep gathering of solid waste, cleaning of litter on roads, and transporting the same to its destination. In addition, community-based informal associations who mutually help, citizen associations at the neighbourhood level, also participate in waste gathering at the doorstep, segregate waste as per the standard norms, and assist in decentralized composting in some areas, even with help from private firms. However, some households primarily in the peripheral areas pointed out that waste gathering happened only less frequently like once weekly, once a month, or even every 15 days, leading to offloading of their waste on the corners of roads.

Sridhar et al. (2021) attempted to understand the efficiency with which the waste so generated was collected. More than half of the households were satisfied, rating the solid waste collection as either excellent (10.8%) or good (41.8%). About 39.1% of respondents were satisfied with the reliability of services (34.7%). However, residents in the peripheral areas were of the view that it was dissatisfactory, poor, or substandard (Figure 8.4). They pointed to untimely services, as well as pile-ups of waste on the roads leading to challenges for public well-being. This shows the spatial inequality across Bengaluru in garbage management, putting the suburbs and peripheral wards in a disadvantageous position. Figure 8.4 shows that the satisfaction levels of residents in the central areas are higher, as these wards also rank better with respect to solid waste management. In contrast, the peripheral areas rank low.

Table 8.3 summarizes disparities in the provision of urban amenities across the centre and suburban parts of the metropolitan area. A higher percentage (78%) of families have tap water in the centre of the city, relative to a mere 74% in the suburbs (Table 8.3). The availability of water supply (in LPCD) is similar across the central and peripheral wards as may be seen in the table. In respect of education and healthcare, even

Figure 8.4 Ranking of Wards Based on SWM

Source: Created by author based on data in Sridhar et al. (2021).

Table 8.3 Disparities in Amenities, Centre and Periphery of Bengaluru

Amenity	Average, centre	Average, periphery
Tap water on premises (% of housing units)	78	74
Proximity to primary, secondary, or high school (in km)	1.48	1.52
Proximity to higher educational institution (college) (in km)	2.81	3.24
Proximity to healthcare (in km)	1.60	1.56
Water supply—LPCD	69	70

Source: Created by author using data in Sridhar et al. (2021).

considering access provided by private providers, central parts of the city enjoy shorter distances to each of these facilities.

So, as Sridhar et al. (2021) found, a greater proportion (78%) of households in Bengaluru's central wards had tap water on the premises, compared to those in the peripheral wards. The consumption of water is similar across the central and peripheral wards at an average of 70 LPCD, which is nonetheless acutely short of the 135 LPCD norm stipulated by the MoHUA. In terms of access to schools and colleges, the centrally located wards were found to be better, with closer proximity of a km distance to the facilities. With respect to availability of healthcare facilities (private and public), as Sridhar et al. (2021) reported, central wards have better access with more than 70% of households being able to access these within 1 km. So, Sridhar et al. (2021) find that central wards are better than peripherally located wards with respect to social services such as health and education, which should enable the BBMP and private actors to fix the geographic disparities. Sridhar et al. (2021) also found that public amenities do not satisfy the norms specified by the Government of India, which should be a rude awakening to all cities which have been suburbanizing.

Summarizing, when I consider access to a variety of basic services, central parts of the city are superior to their peripheral counterparts. This must motivate us to limit the suburbanization of Indian cities and encourage more compact urban growth, which is expected to lead to much better delivery of basic services.

8.4 Urban Sprawl and Air Quality

As many studies have argued, a city which is characterized by sprawl emits more carbon and has poorer air quality, when compared to a city which is centralized. This is because settlements which are diffuse and spread out imply larger single-family units, requiring greater amounts of energy than their tinier counterparts and concentrated homes in centralized cities (Arifwidodo (2014) contains corroboration of this from a city in Indonesia, Bandung). Therefore, the assumption is that urban areas which are more decentralized also lead to higher carbon emissions and have poorer air quality, compared with cities which are more centralized. Sridhar (2018) lends support to this in India's urban areas, finding a positive association between suburbanization and carbon footprint per person. This shows that the greater the extent to which a city is compact, the smaller will be its carbon footprint, like what Arifwidodo (2014) found, and the lower would be the particulate matter (PM 2.5), making the city's air safer. The reverse is also true.

I have data on air quality measured by PM 2.5 for the reference epochs 2000, 2005, 2010, and 2014 from the same database used for measuring sprawl of the 100 cities (Florczyk et al., 2019). I compute the correlation between each of these air quality measures, and urban sprawl indicated by the gradients for 2015 and 1975.

Table 8.4 summarizes the correlations between the gradients and the PM 2.5 values. For all the reference epochs 2000, 2005, 2010, and 2014, I found that Aligarh (in Uttar Pradesh) had the maximum values of PM 2.5, indicating serious concerns with its air quality, which must have worsened since 2014. I note that this was a city which suburbanized significantly during 1975–2015 as may be seen from its estimated density gradient value of −0.64 in 1975, which was only −0.59 in 2015 (indicating flattening if I consider its absolute value). On the other hand, when I consider the reference epoch 2000, Mangalore (Mangaluru now) was the one with the least PM 2.5 at only 23.20 micrograms per cubic meter; this city also suburbanized during the four decades of study, but its population was less than 500,000 as of 2011. In contrast, Aligarh was a city with a million-plus population in 2011. In terms of the minimum, Thiruvananthapuram (Kerala), was the one with the least PM 2.5 (at 21.82 micrograms per cubic meter) in the reference epochs 2005, 2010, and 2014, as per data

Table 8.4 Correlation between Suburbanization and PM 2.5, Indian Cities

	PG2015	PG1975	PM2000	PM2005	PM2010
PG2015	1.00	0.59	−0.11	−0.13	−0.14
PG1975	0.59	1.00	−0.06	−0.09	−0.09
PM2000	−0.11	−0.06	1.00	0.99	0.99
PM2005	−0.13	−0.09	0.99	1.00	1.00
PM2010	−0.14	−0.09	0.99	1.00	1.00
PM2014	−0.16	−0.07	0.98	0.98	0.99

Sources: Florczyk et al. (2019) and author's analyses.
PG: Population gradient. PM: Particulate matter.

from Florczyk et al. (2019) which centralized during the four decades (with an increase in the absolute value of its population gradient from 0.15 to 0.19), showing the virtues of compactness.

Thus I undoubtedly find, as Sridhar (2018) had found, that the population density gradient and the PM 2.5 for various reference epochs—2000, 2005, 2010, and 2014—are negatively correlated. The strongest is that between the population density gradient 2015 and the PM 2.5 for 2014 at −0.16 (which however is not statistically significant), suggesting that cities which were sprawling in 2015 (with lower values of the gradient) were also the ones which had higher levels of PM 2.5 in 2014 (the years are close enough). Similarly, the population density gradient for 1975 was negatively correlated with the PM 2.5 for 2005 and 2010, implying that cities that were more suburbanized in 1975 were the ones with poorer air quality as late as 2005 and 2010 (with higher values of PM 2.5). However, even these correlations were not statistically significant. Nonetheless, given the long-lasting effects of PM 2.5 on public health, the negative correlation strongly suggests that our cities should be compact (with a high value of the density gradient) to emit less carbon and have lower PM 2.5.

8.5 Summary and Conclusions

In this book I have covered a lot of ground asking the question of whether India's urban areas have suburbanized over 1975–2015. First, I have found that the downward-sloping population density function is appropriate for understanding the structure of India's cities.

Second, in response to the question of whether or not India is suburbanized, the answer to that was a resounding yes. This is because while India was 31% urban in 2011 and estimated to be 35% urban in 2020, it was 82% suburban in 2015, beyond a compass of 1 or 2 km from the city core, which is significantly higher than its urbanization. Indian cities have also sprawled in terms of their boundaries predicted based on concentric circles I have drawn around a designated city centre, even while there are significant regional variations in this spatial sprawl as I have demonstrated. While the earlier evidence is that compact cities are those which are characterized by higher central city densities, recent evidence shows that Indian cities are increasing their central city density and suburbanizing at the same time. Thus, one way to encourage compact growth is to further increase central city densities by improving central city infrastructure.

Based on the limited evidence available regarding the suburbanization of households, I further found that households suburbanized nearly to the same extent as population. I find that cities in the south Indian states are a lot more sprawling when compared with cities in all India, for 2015. However, those in the slow-growing states are compact relative to cities in the entire country and definitely in comparison with the south Indian states. Unsurprisingly, cities in the urbanized states follow the sprawling pattern observed in the southern states. I find the pattern of population suburbanization of cities in Karnataka is similar to that of the lagging states, if its primate city Bengaluru were to be excluded, even though it is classified as an urbanized state. This may be because Karnataka has many smaller cities, which tend to be more compact.

I find that employment is a lot more decentralized than population suburbanization in 2015. Considering all the cities, I find that on average, a majority (52%) of *all jobs* are concentrated in a 5-km compass of the core. Similarly, for the 'other workers' who are really the urban workers employed in services such as banks, finance, real estate, insurance, trade, commerce, transport and communications, and related services, most employment is concentrated within 5 km of the city centre, on average, for the cities considered. Interestingly, on average, a majority (52%) of employment in household industry was also located within 5 km of the core of India's cities. Overall, in a 2-km compass of the core of the country's cities, on average, only about 17% of jobs in each of household industry and 'other' sectors (services) are concentrated, with the remaining 83% of jobs suburbanized.

Like population, jobs in urban areas of the southern and in the metropolitanized states are more suburbanized relative to cities in the slow-growing states and those in the entire country, for 2011. I find that on average, the employment suburbanization of cities in Karnataka is a lot more compact when compared with cities in all India, with a much higher job gradient (at 0.87 compared with 0.67 for all Indian cities for which ward-level data are available (including those in Karnataka)). The pattern of employment suburbanization of cities in Karnataka is therefore similar to that of population suburbanization, again that of the lagging states, if its primate city Bengaluru were to be excluded, even though it is classified as an urbanized state. This could be because Karnataka has many smaller cities, whose employment is also a lot more compact.

In this book, I have analysed the factors which lead to population suburbanization. Given the data constraints, estimating the population density function in 2015 and change in the gradient over 1975–2015 for 100 large Indian cities, I find that the time-lagged gradient has a powerful association with the 2015 population gradient and changes in the density gradient during the four decades, showing the influence of the historical spatial distribution of population. Besides, poor central city economic conditions (such as the unemployment rate) push residents away to the suburbs. Finally, the urbanizable land has a negative association with the 2015 population gradient, partly considering the fact that cities, once big, grow without natural constraints, and suburbanize when compared with those cities with constraints such as water bodies or mountains.

The qualitative discussions with academics, policy makers, and developers demonstrated that suburbanization stems from the forces of urbanization itself, but could also originate in rural areas, which appear to be the basis of census towns in India. I distinguish the superior standard of public services in the suburbs of metropolitan areas when compared with their counterparts in rural areas (census towns) where these services leave much to be desired. Nonetheless, even in the suburbs of cities, real estate developers recognize the importance of upgrading municipal infrastructure rapidly to support the urbanization process, given their higher productivity and rapid augmentation of economic output. Broadly, most of the findings from the qualitative discussions captured with the experts were generally consistent with those based on the quantitative analyses as reported here.

As far as land use regulations are concerned, it was recognized by the developers who participated in the discussion that the floor area ratio (FAR) is going to be fungible and must completely change in the next couple of years. As the city needs more water, sewage, schools, hospitals, roads, and transportation, it is acknowledged that one can't just unilaterally increase the FAR without collateral infrastructure.

Suburbanization has a lot of implications for urban governance because many urban agglomerations in India have multiple ULBs. It is important to understand which is the dominant central city and what is the role of consolidating metropolitan governance versus fragmented metropolitan government in suburbanized cities like Kolkata and Bengaluru.

The discussions also recognized that suburbanization has a number of ecological effects in the sense of lakes in the periphery of cities getting polluted due to construction debris and poor air quality, which need to be managed with better coordination across agencies responsible for these services at various spatial levels.

In the final chapter, this book discussed the effects of suburbanization: one instance taken was the delivery of services in the centre and periphery of metropolitan Bengaluru, and another example considered was air quality taking into account all the cities selected for the study. Taking the case of Bengaluru, the book presented disparities in access to a variety of amenities, like tap water, solid waste management, and schools and colleges, which showed that central parts of the city are superior to their peripheral counterparts. This must motivate us to limit the suburbanization of Indian cities and encourage more compact urban growth, which is expected to lead to much better delivery of basic services.

Examining air quality, as I did in this chapter, I find, as Sridhar (2018) had found, that the population density gradient and the PM 2.5 for various reference epochs—2000, 2005, 2010, and 2014—are negatively correlated. The strongest is that between the population density gradient 2015 and the PM 2.5 for 2014 at −0.16 (which however is not statistically significant), suggesting that cities which were sprawling in 2015 were also the ones which had higher levels of PM 2.5 in 2014 (the years are close enough). Similarly, the population density gradient for 1975 was negatively correlated with the PM 2.5 for 2005 and 2010, implying that cities that were more suburbanized in 1975 were the ones with poorer air quality as late as 2005 and 2010.

Hence, as climate change continues to occur and developing countries find the need to urbanize more to grow economically, suburbanization seems like an inevitable phenomenon, based on evidence presented in this book. However, if cities can grow in a compact way by putting in place better central city infrastructure, we can have the cake and eat it too. This book has demonstrated this in a modest way.

8.6 Caveats and Scope for Further Research

I acknowledge that the research reported here has some limitations, like all new ideas. Our analyses based on the standard urban model depended on a 1- or 2-km compass for determining the central part of the urban area and the extent of suburbanization. This distance may seem small for large cities. There are also no clear-cut answers for why this would be the right number. I have not been able to apply different thresholds to differently sized cities. I also do not know if these spatial extents make sense for both 1975 and 2015.

This research has used the GHSL for understanding the extent of suburbanization of 100 of India's major urban areas. This dataset uses satellite data to locate urbanizable area, which it then matches with corresponding Census of India data on population, measured to a precision of 1-km square grids, superimposed on urbanizable area. A caveat to be noted is that the contours of the GHSL map may not correspond exactly with a city's administrative boundaries. I take the example of Pune whose population in 1975 was 1,750,000 as per the GHSL. According to the Census of India 1971 (which is the closest corresponding year to the GHSL), the city's population was less than 1,000,000. A further additional reality check lies in the fact that several of India's urban areas (Vasai-Virar, Hubballi-Dharwad, and Hyderabad-Secunderabad are some examples) are located next to each other as twin cities. For instance, Vasai-Virar is a 'suburb' of Mumbai but is considered as a separate city in the GHSL. Such problems could distort the measurement of suburbanization of not only Mumbai, but also of Vasai-Virar.

Another corollary of using the GHSL is that different estimates of suburbanization might be obtained if we were to use other nighttime satellite data such as VIIRS, Google Earth, or those from NASA.

On the explanation of suburbanization, I use income from the GHSL, but that may not be a precise depiction of the economic activity happening in the urban areas. Further, on measuring land use regulations, I have been able to control for only the FAR. Even there, I used estimates of the actual FAR consumed from the WRI, from a few years ago. Current actual FARs consumed may have changed since then. Further, as discussed earlier, I could not use any measure of technology or work from home to understand their impact on suburbanization. This may have been a significant limitation in the post-pandemic world where many employees continue to work from home or have resorted to hybrid models of work.

Future research should fix the problems above, although that is easier said than done. The above problems should not undermine the value of the extensive research attempted to understand the suburbanization of India's cities at such a granular level, for the first time. The next steps of this research can fix the individual problems highlighted above and refine estimates of the extent of suburbanization and its causes for India's cities, such that we may formulate sustainable policies to limit sprawl and support the delivery of better urban services to citizens.

Appendix

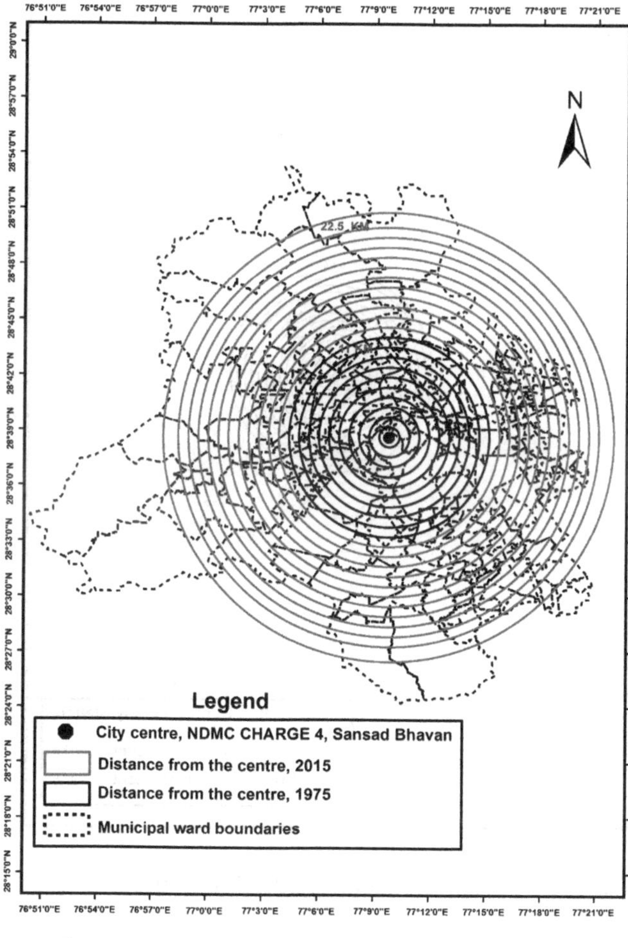

Delhi's Boundaries with Concentric Circles, 1975 and 2015

Sources: Florczyk et al. (2019) and author's analysis.

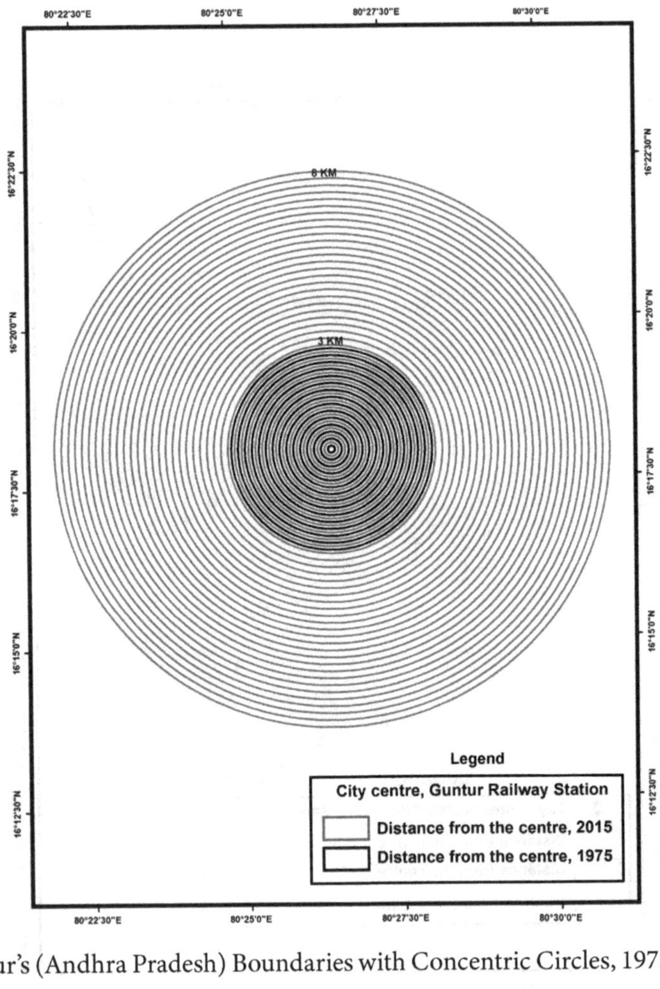

Guntur's (Andhra Pradesh) Boundaries with Concentric Circles, 1975 and 2015

Sources: Florczyk et al. (2019) and author's analysis.

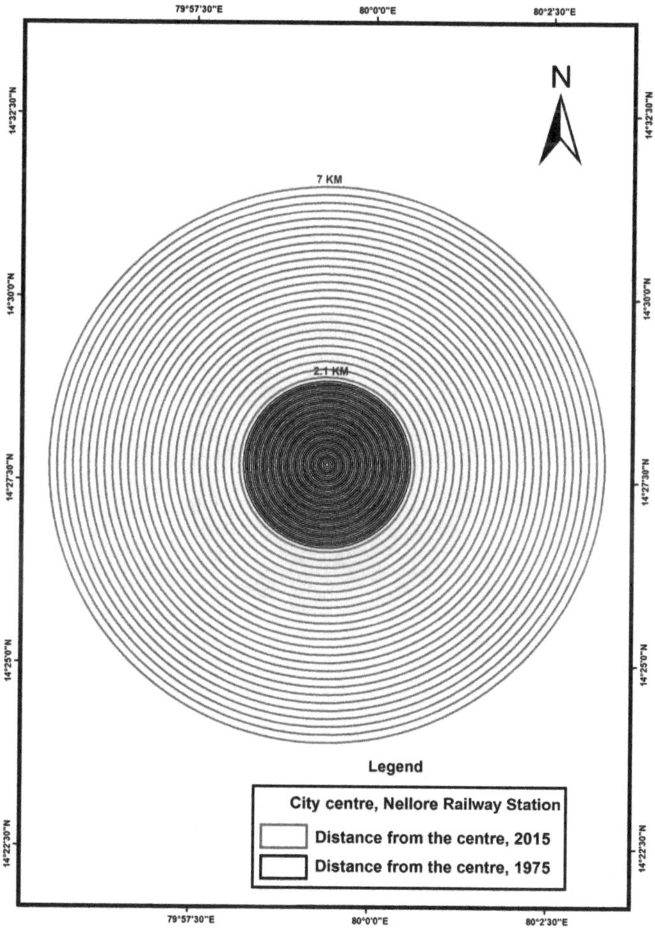

Nellore's (Andhra Pradesh) Boundaries with Concentric Circles, 1975 and 2015

Sources: Florczyk et al. (2019) and author's analysis.

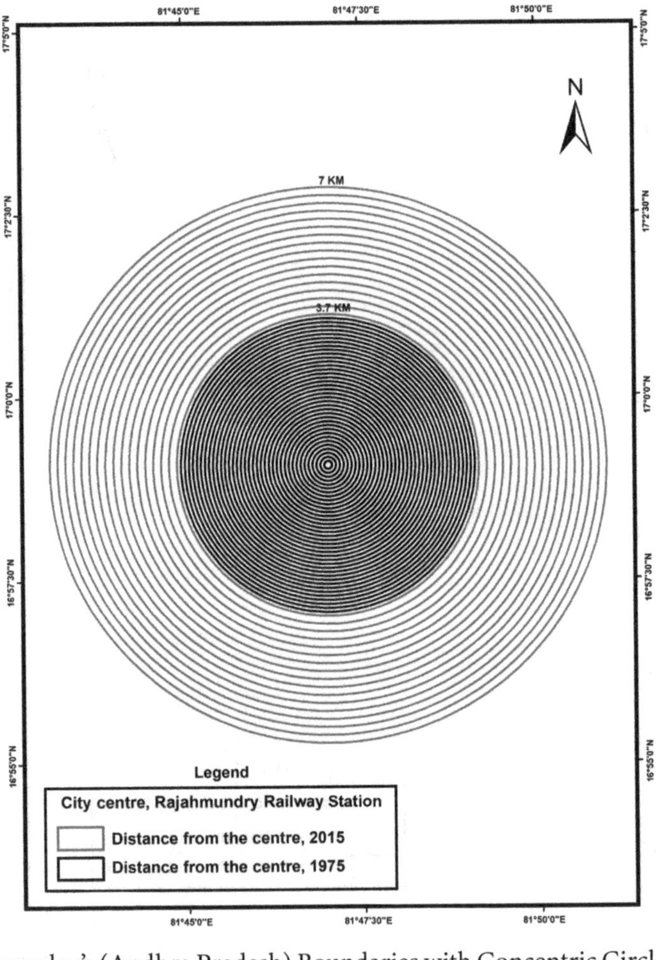

Rajahmundry's (Andhra Pradesh) Boundaries with Concentric Circles, 1975 and 2015

Sources: Florczyk et al. (2019) and author's analysis.

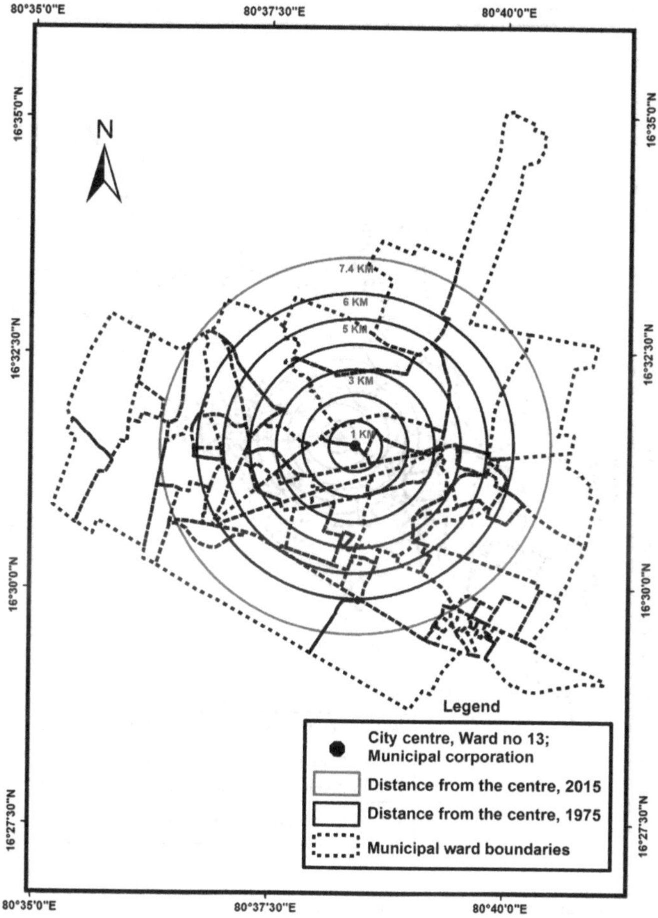

Vijayawada's (Andhra Pradesh) Boundaries with Concentric Circles, 1975 and 2015

Sources: Florczyk et al. (2019) and author's analysis.

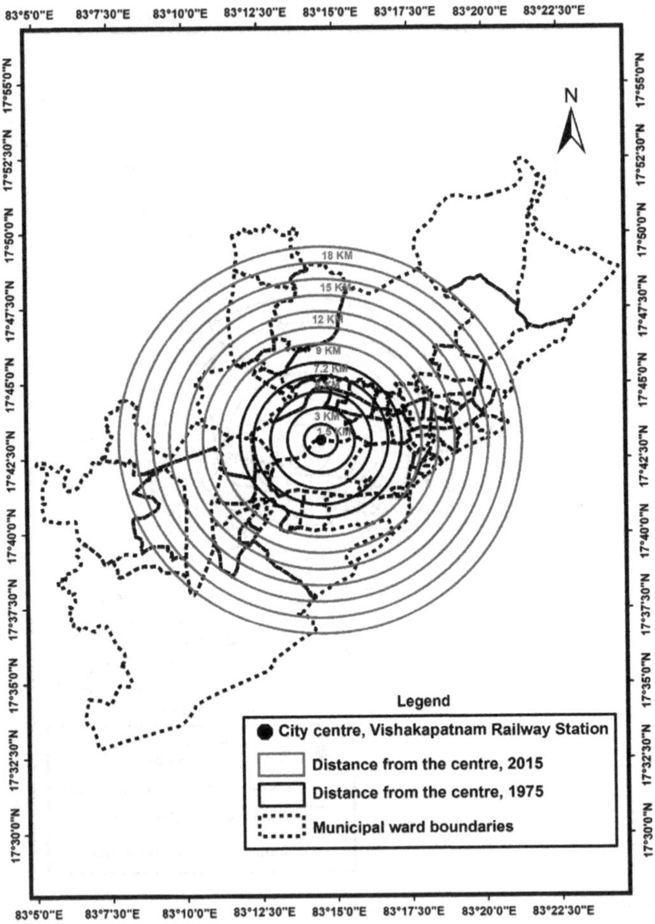

Visakhapatnam's (Andhra Pradesh) Boundaries with Concentric Circles, 1975 and 2015

Sources: Florczyk et al. (2019) and author's analysis.

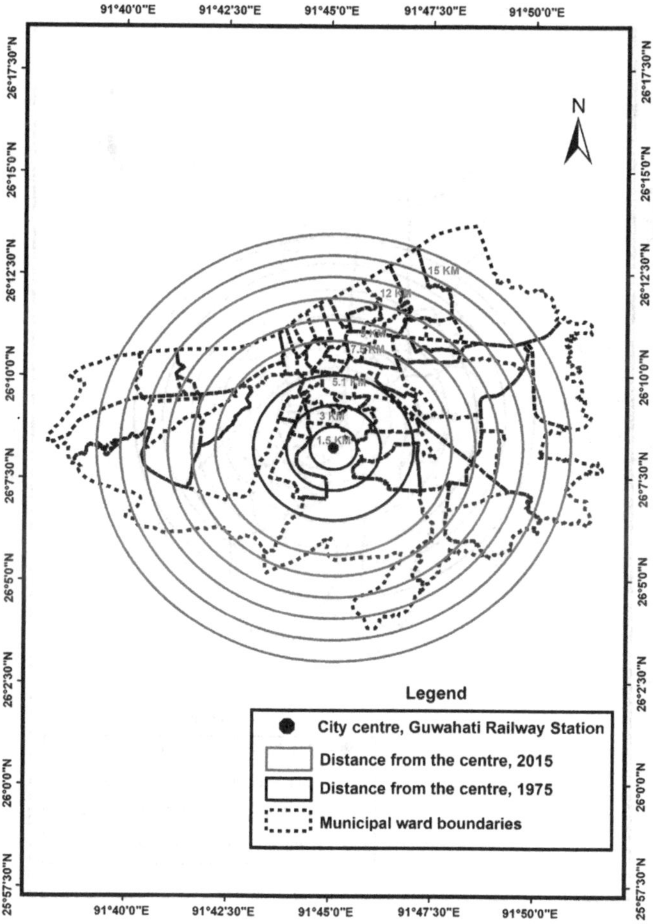

Guwahati's (Assam) Boundaries with Concentric Circles, 1975 and 2015

Sources: Florczyk et al. (2019) and author's analysis.

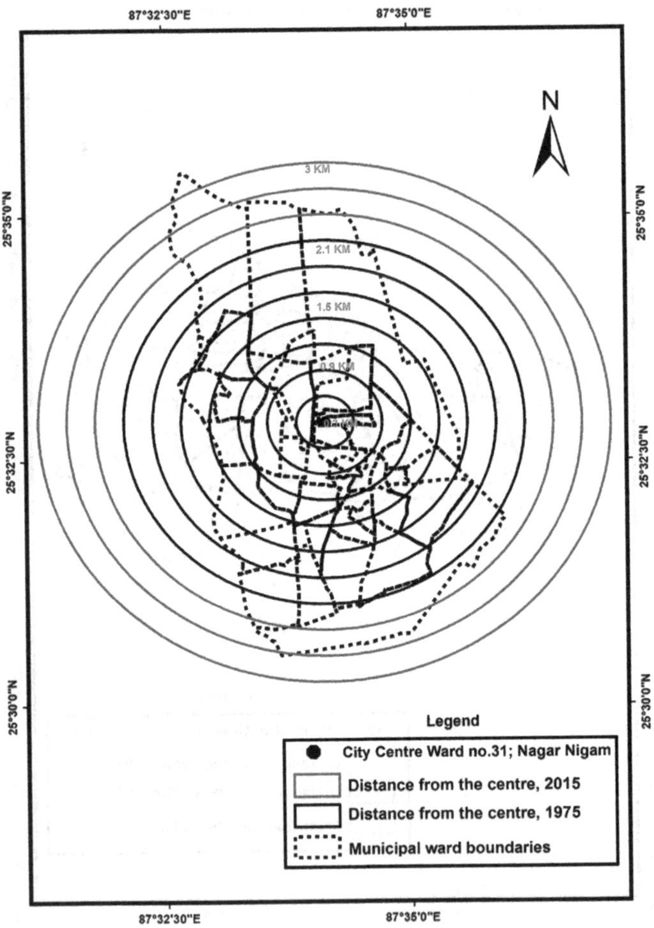

Katihar's (Bihar) Boundaries with Concentric Circles, 1975 and 2015

Sources: Florczyk et al. (2019) and author's analysis.

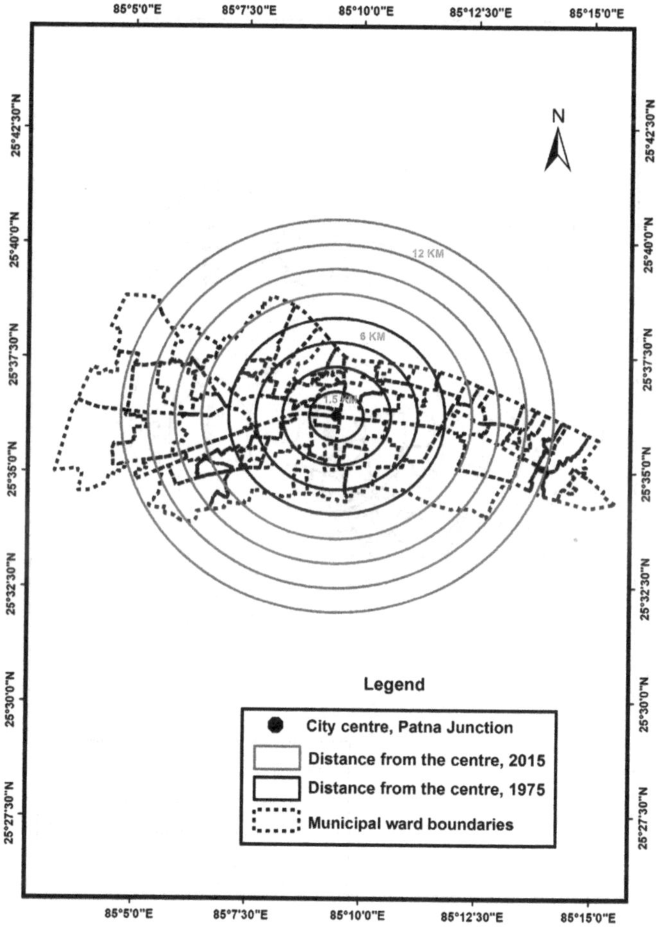

Patna's (Bihar) Boundaries with Concentric Circles, 1975 and 2015

Sources: Florczyk et al. (2019) and author's analysis.

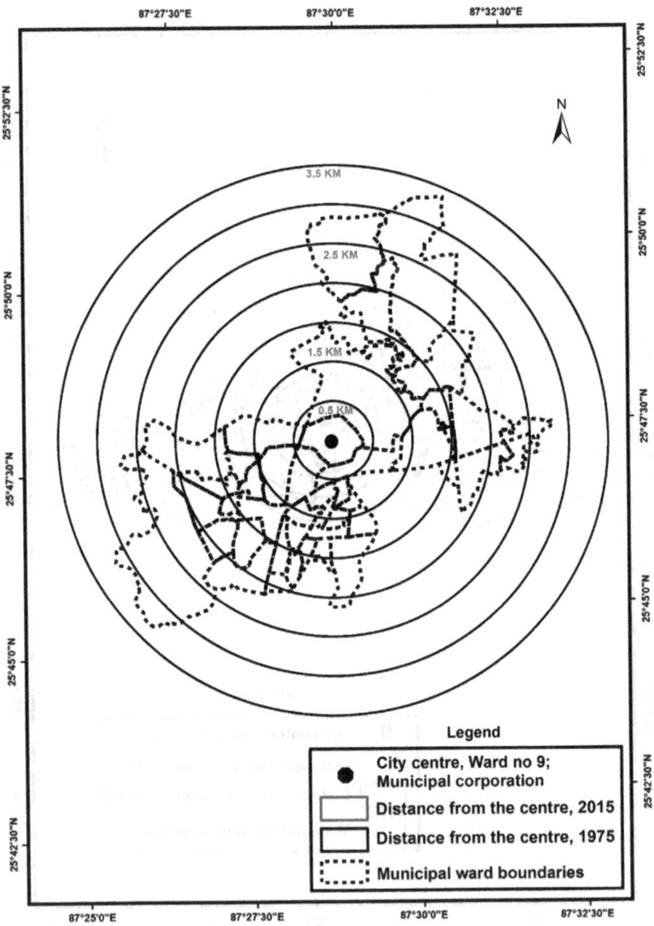

Purnia's (Bihar) Boundaries with Concentric Circles, 1975 and 2015

Sources: Florczyk et al. (2019) and author's analysis.

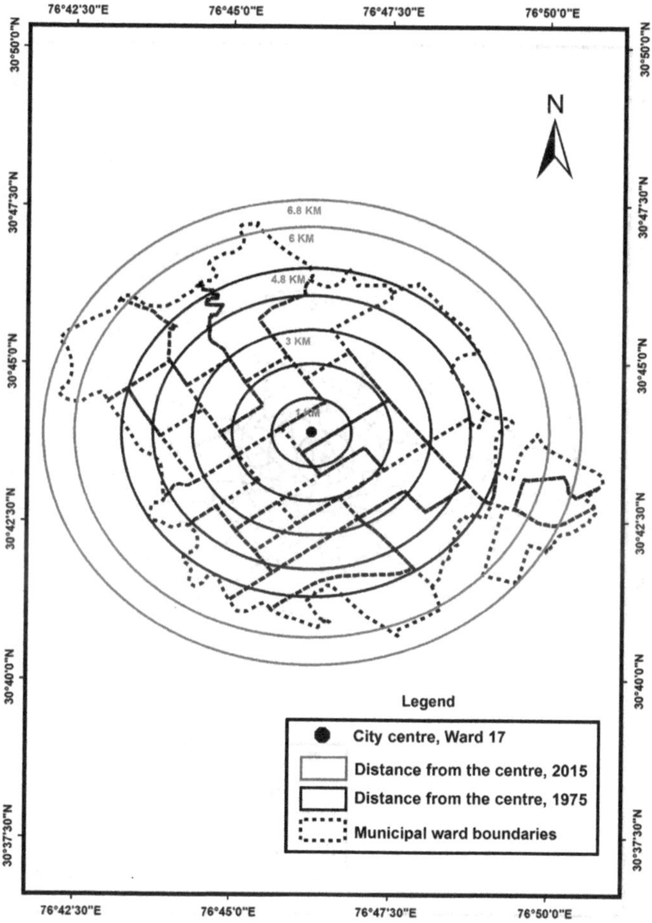

Chandigarh's (Chandigarh) Boundaries with Concentric Circles, 1975 and 2015

Sources: Florczyk et al. (2019) and author's analysis.

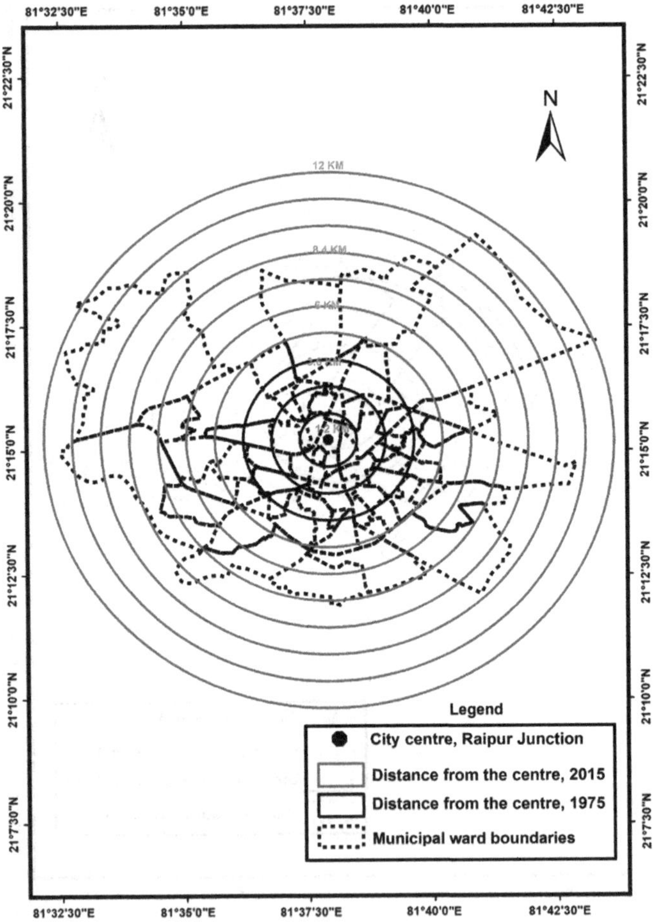

Raipur's (Chhattisgarh) Boundaries with Concentric Circles, 1975 and 2015

Sources: Florczyk et al. (2019) and author's analysis.

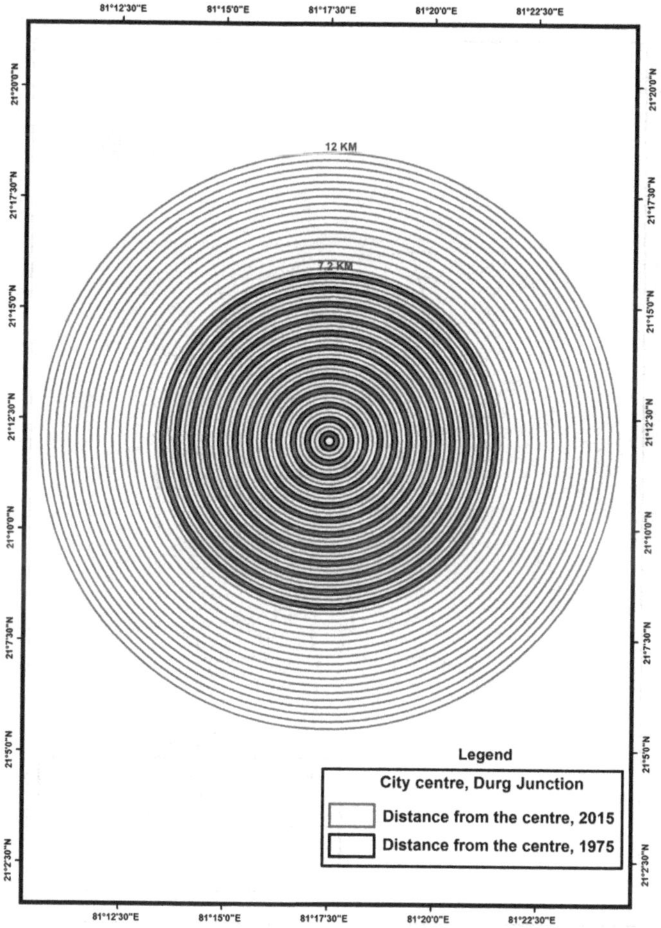

Durg-Bhilai's (Chhattisgarh) Boundaries with Concentric Circles, 1975 and 2015

Sources: Florczyk et al. (2019) and author's analysis.

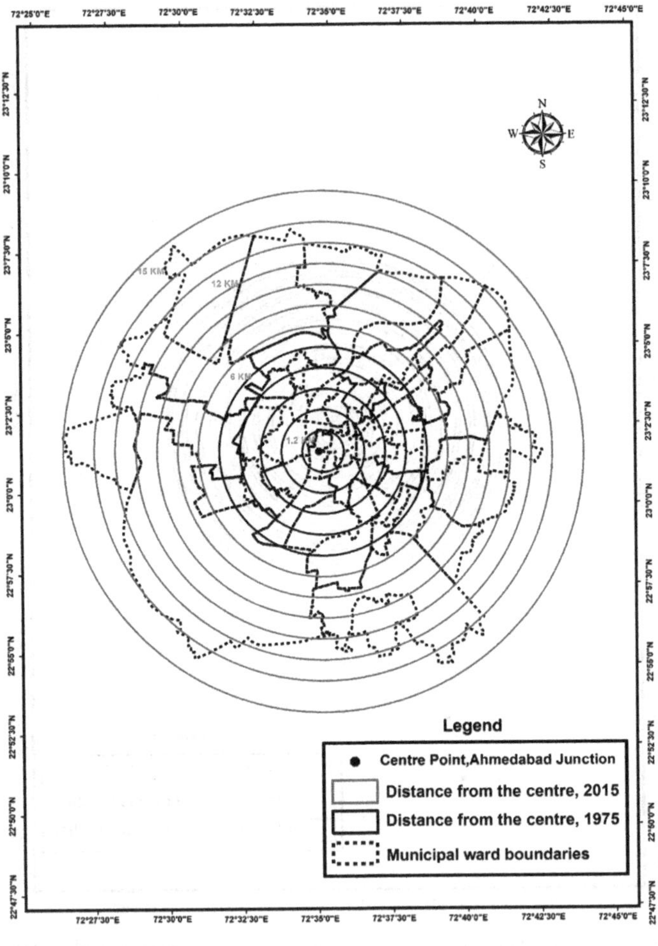

Ahmedabad's (Gujarat) Boundaries with Concentric Circles, 1975 and 2015

Sources: Florczyk et al. (2019) and author's analysis.

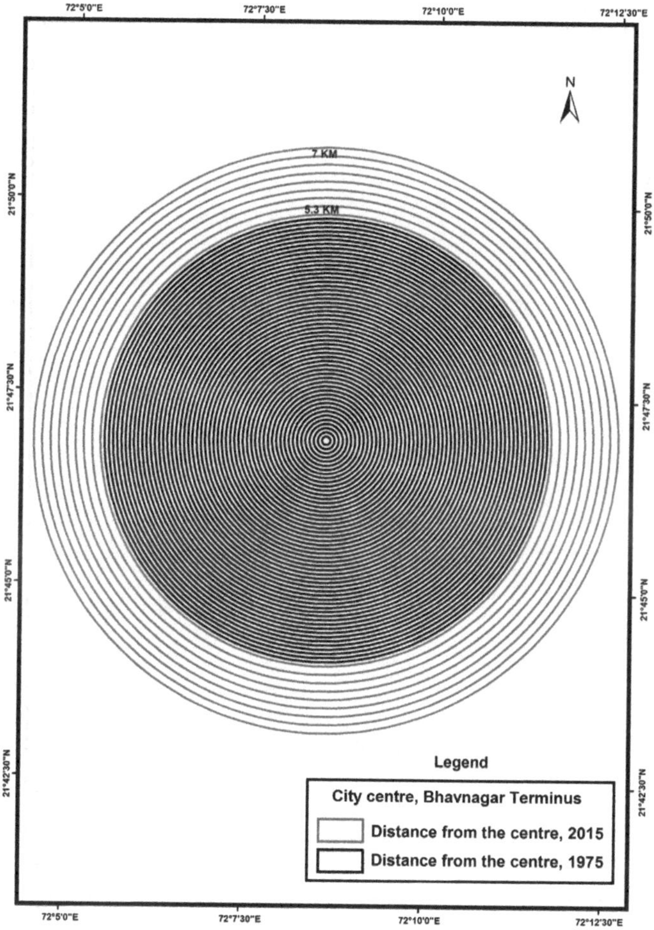

Bhavnagar's (Gujarat) Boundaries with Concentric Circles, 1975 and 2015

Sources: Florczyk et al. (2019) and author's analysis.

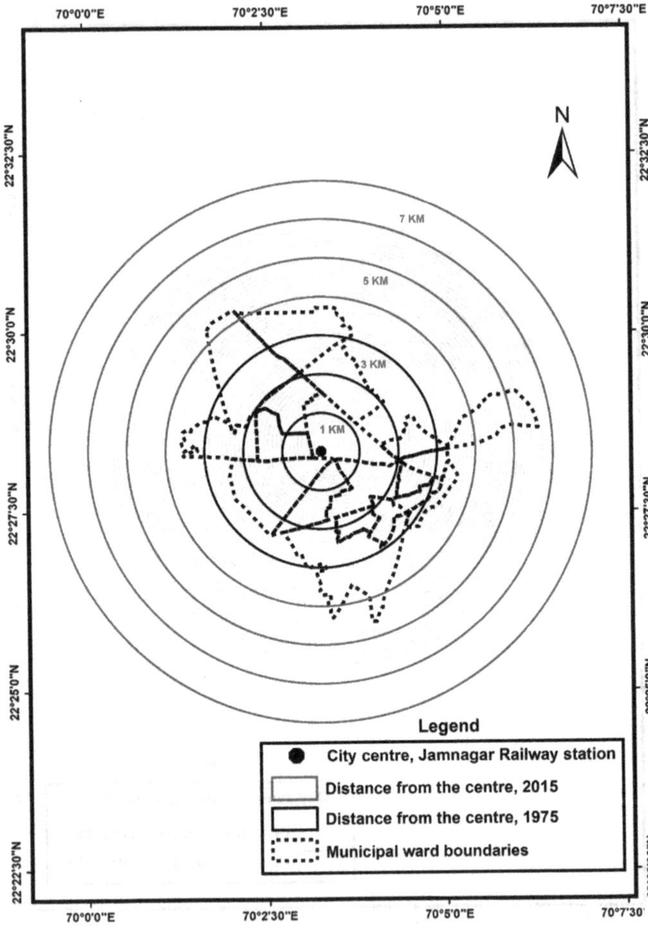

Jamnagar's (Gujarat) Boundaries with Concentric Circles, 1975 and 2015

Sources: Florczyk et al. (2019) and author's analysis.

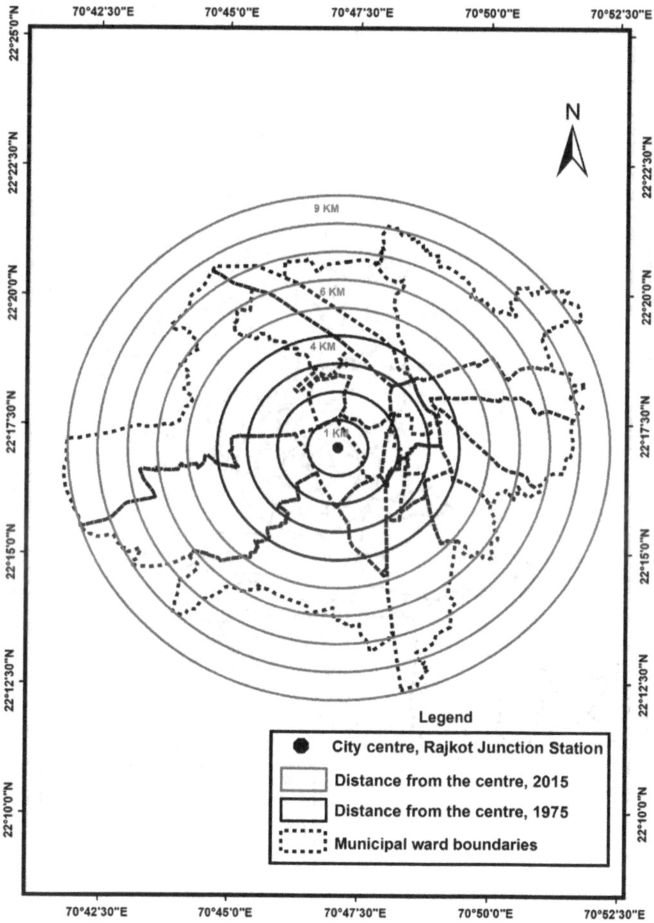

Rajkot's (Gujarat) Boundaries with Concentric Circles, 1975 and 2015

Sources: Florczyk et al. (2019) and author's analysis.

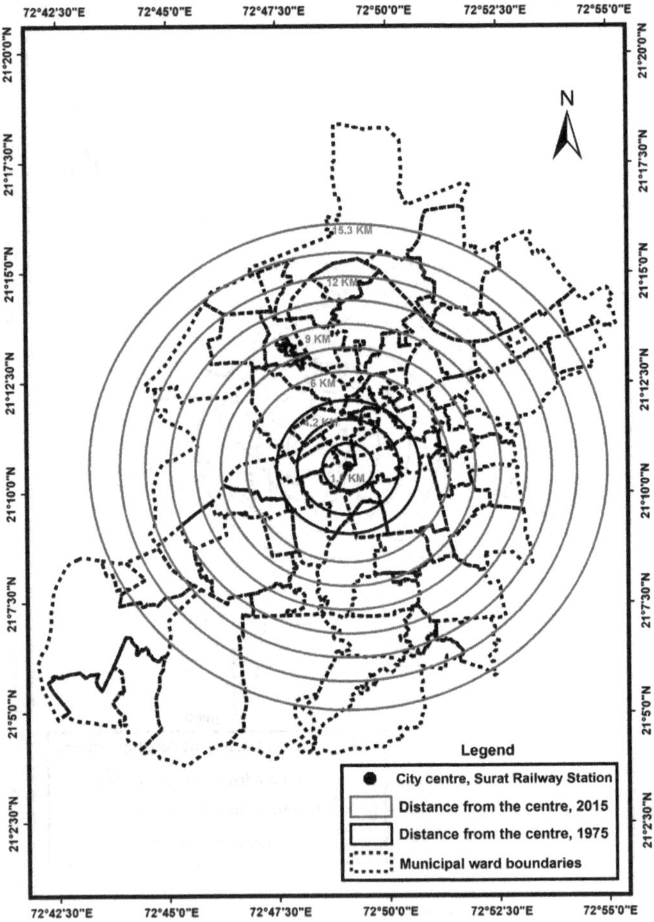

Surat's (Gujarat) Boundaries with Concentric Circles, 1975 and 2015

Sources: Florczyk et al. (2019) and author's analysis.

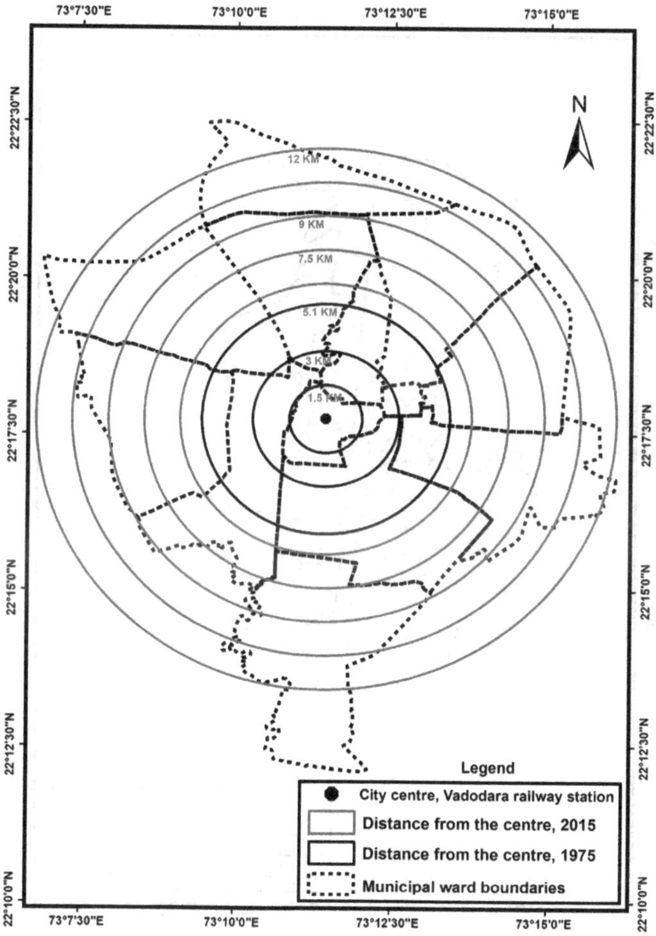

Vadodara's (Gujarat) Boundaries with Concentric Circles, 1975 and 2015

Sources: Florczyk et al. (2019) and author's analysis.

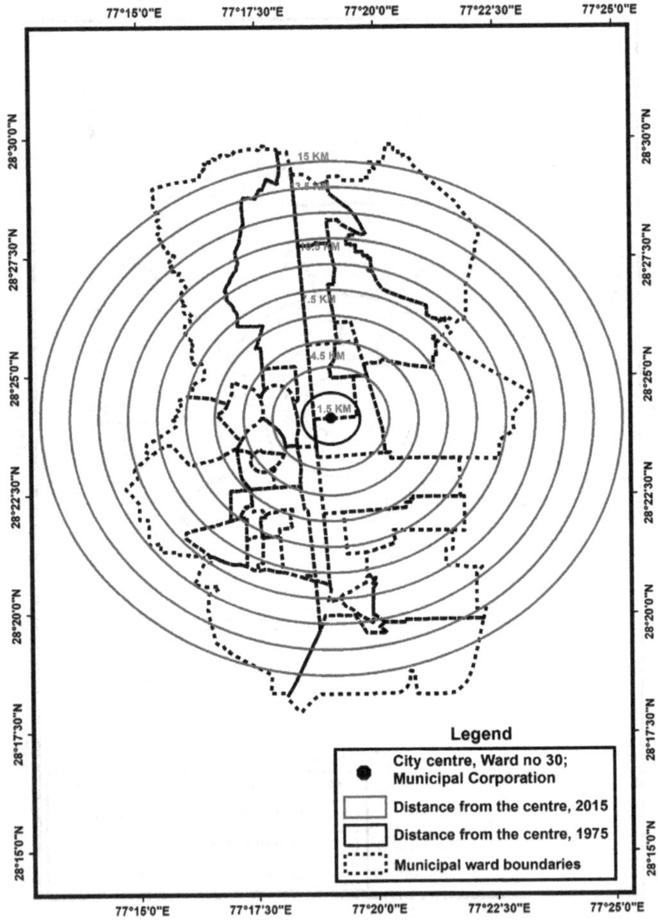

Faridabad's (Haryana) Boundaries with Concentric Circles, 1975 and 2015

Sources: Florczyk et al. (2019) and author's analysis.

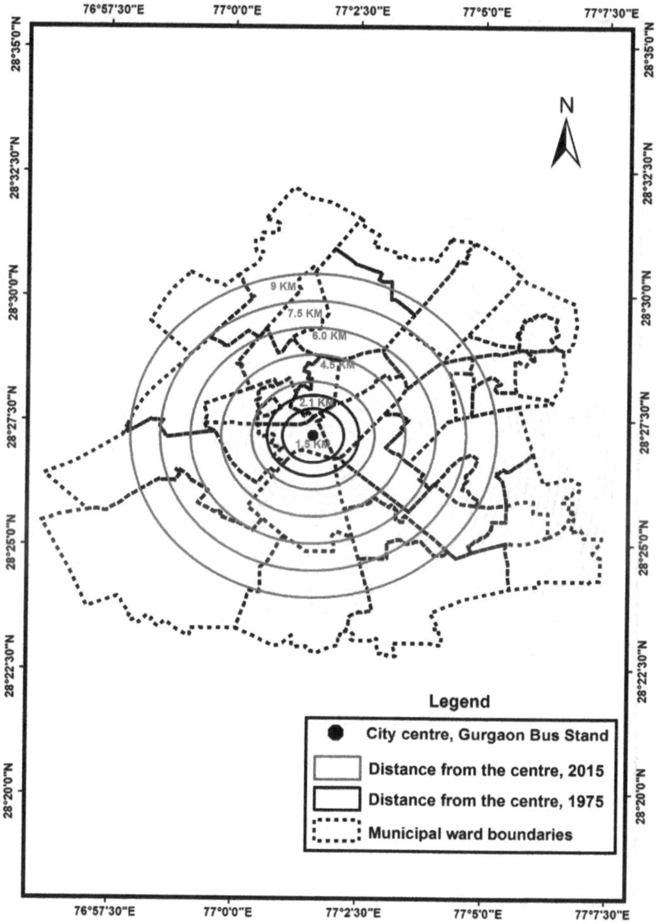

Gurgaon's (Haryana) Boundaries with Concentric Circles, 1975 and 2015
Sources: Florczyk et al. (2019) and author's analysis.

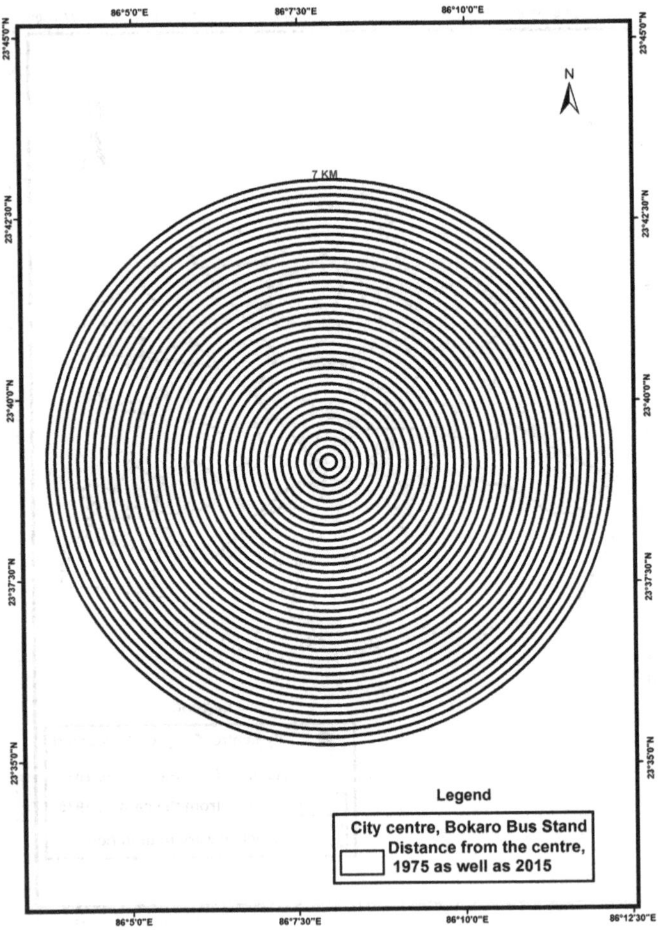

Bokaro's (Jharkhand) Boundaries with Concentric Circles, 1975 and 2015

Sources: Florczyk et al. (2019) and author's analysis.

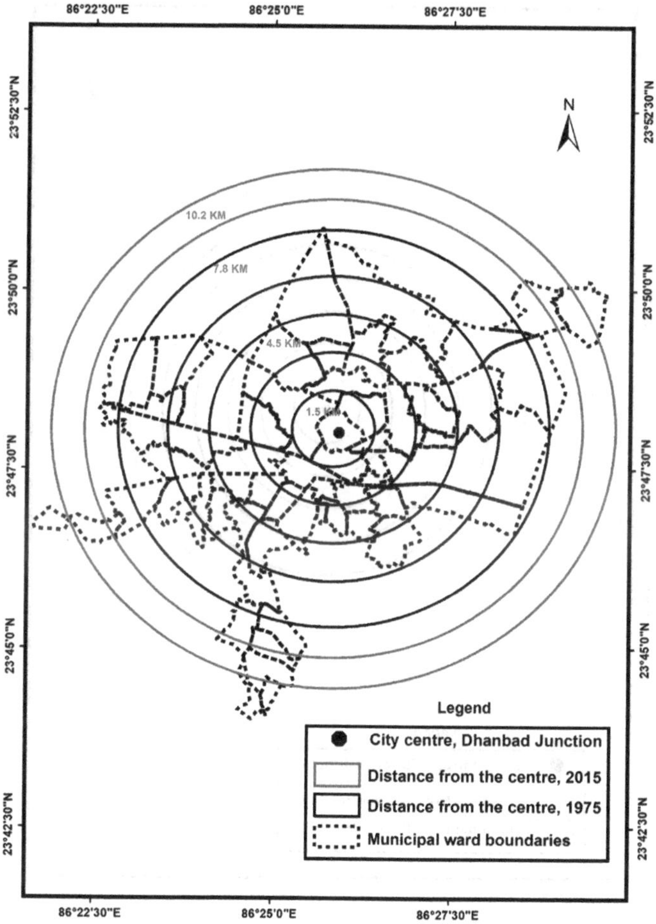

Dhanbad's (Jharkhand) Boundaries with Concentric Circles, 1975 and 2015

Sources: Florczyk et al. (2019) and author's analysis.

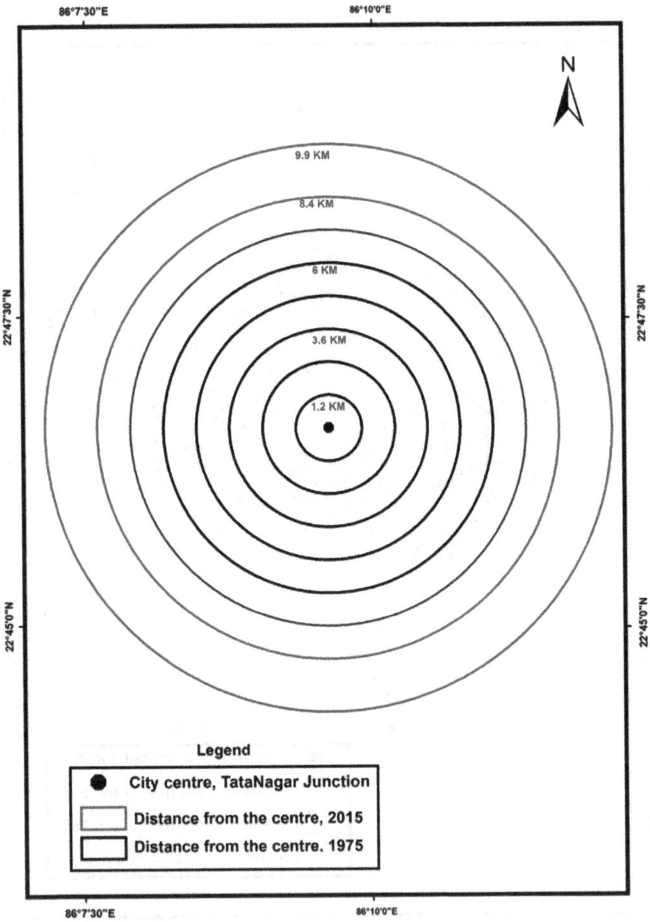

Jamshedpur's (Jharkhand) Boundaries with Concentric Circles, 1975 and 2015

Sources: Florczyk et al. (2019) and author's analysis.

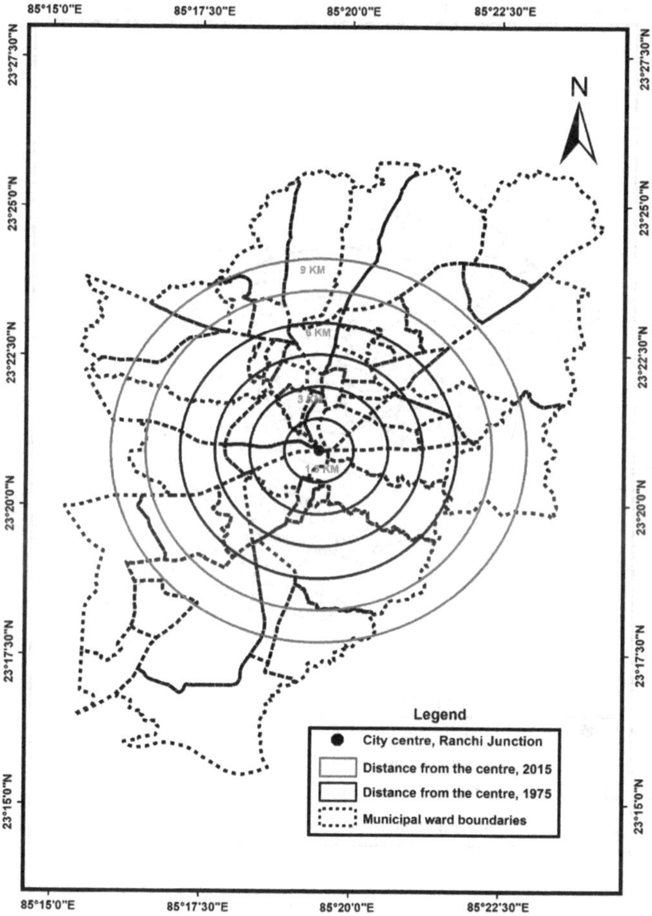

Ranchi's (Jharkhand) Boundaries with Concentric Circles, 1975 and 2015

Sources: Florczyk et al. (2019) and author's analysis.

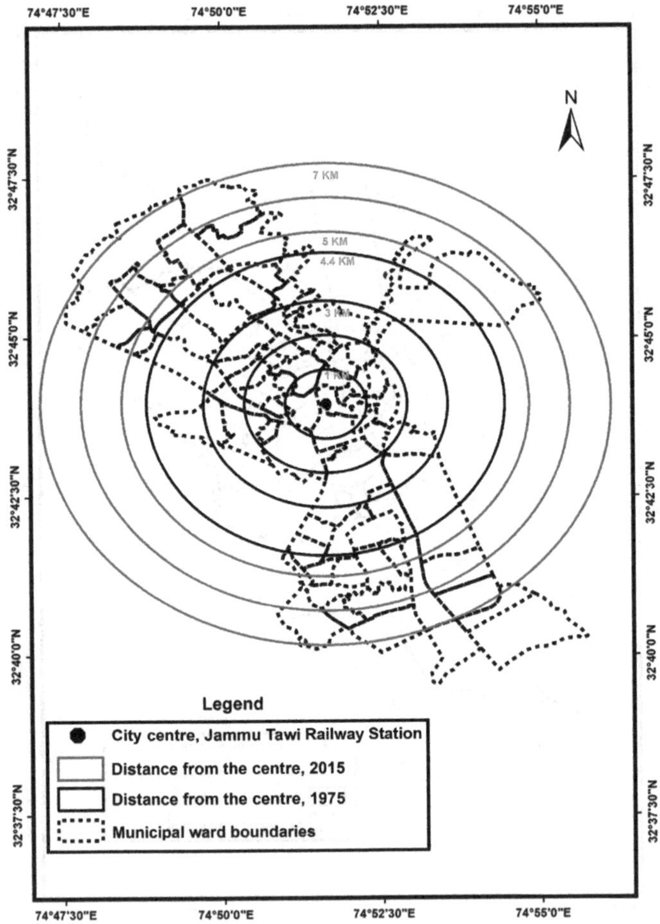

Jammu's (Jammu and Kashmir) Boundaries with Concentric Circles, 1975 and 2015

Sources: Florczyk et al. (2019) and author's analysis.

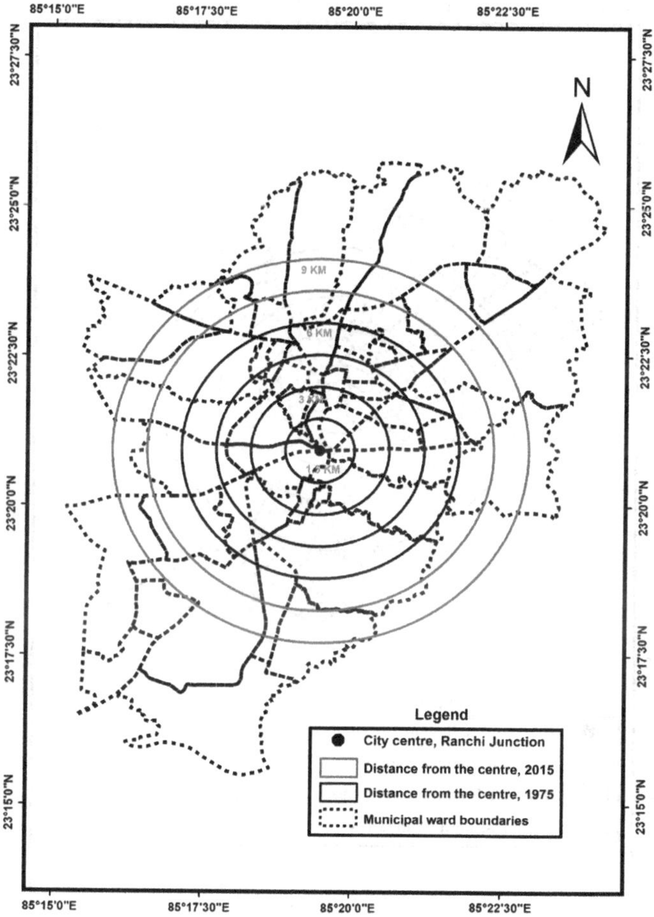

Ranchi's (Jharkhand) Boundaries with Concentric Circles, 1975 and 2015
Sources: Florczyk et al. (2019) and author's analysis.

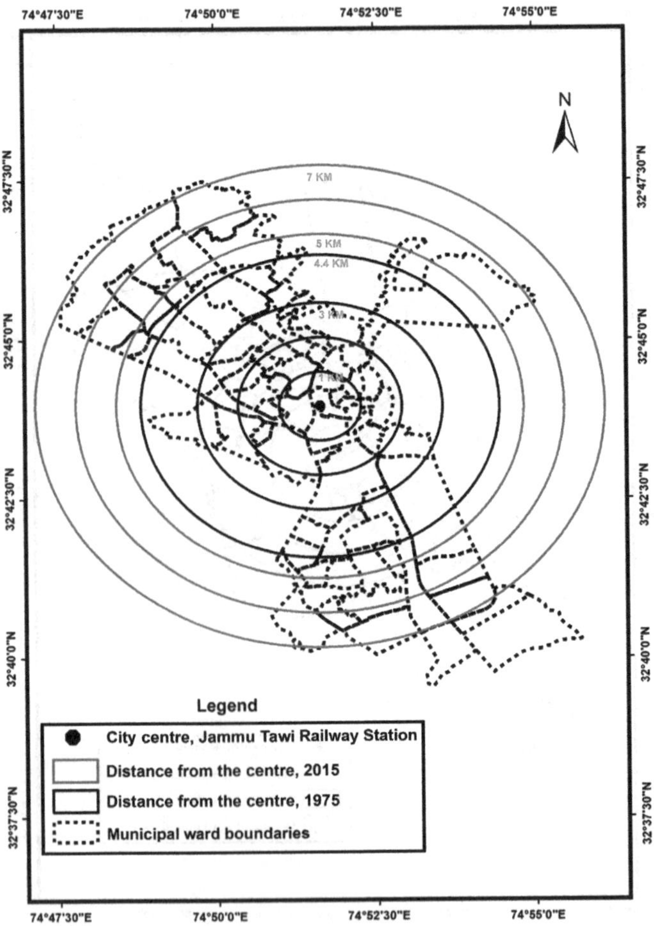

Jammu's (Jammu and Kashmir) Boundaries with Concentric Circles, 1975 and 2015

Sources: Florczyk et al. (2019) and author's analysis.

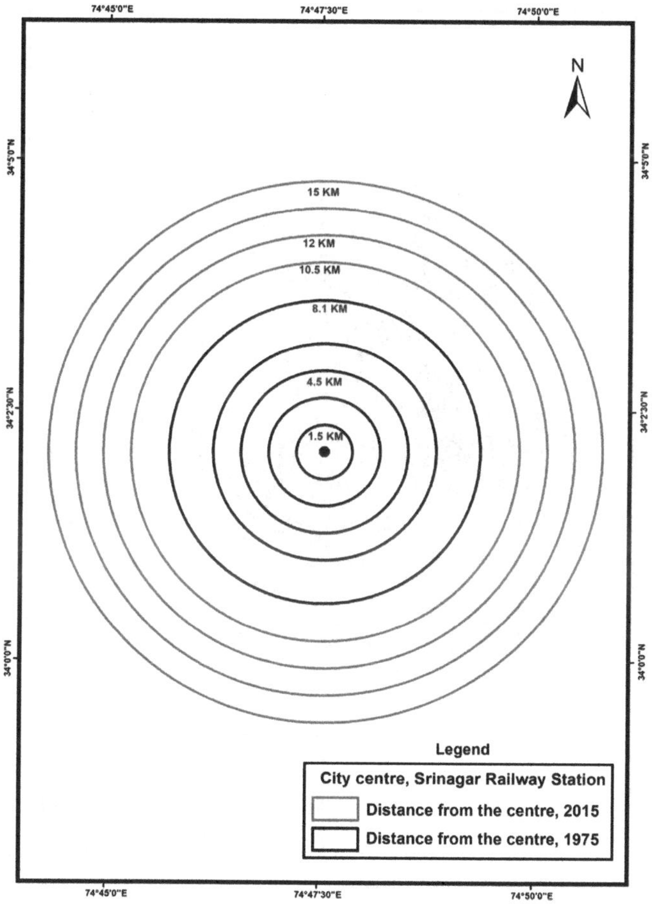

Srinagar's (Jammu and Kashmir) Boundaries with Concentric Circles, 1975 and 2015

Sources: Florczyk et al. (2019) and author's analysis.

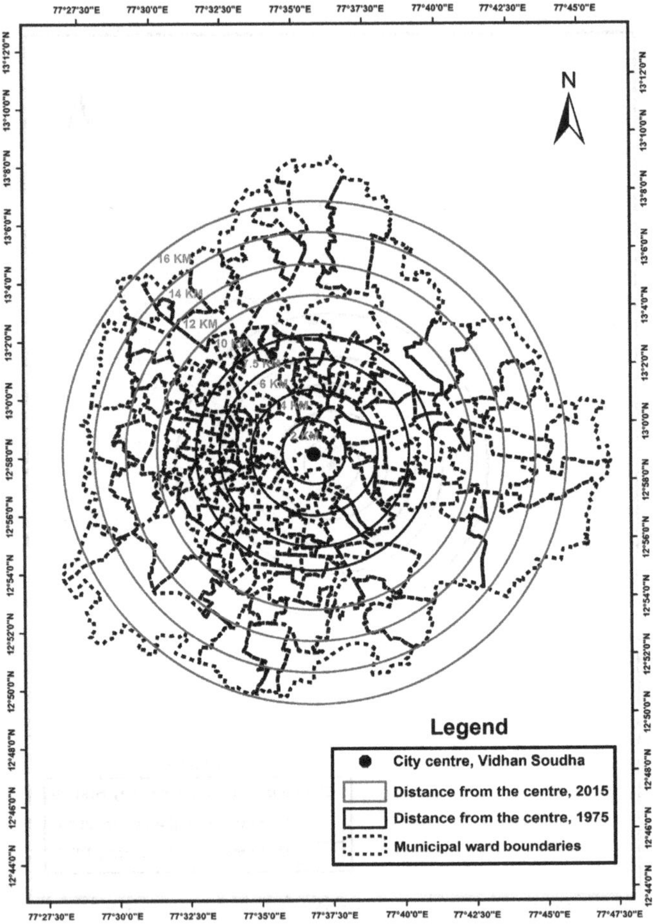

Bengaluru's (Karnataka) Boundaries with Concentric Circles, 1975 and 2015

Sources: Florczyk et al. (2019) and author's analysis.

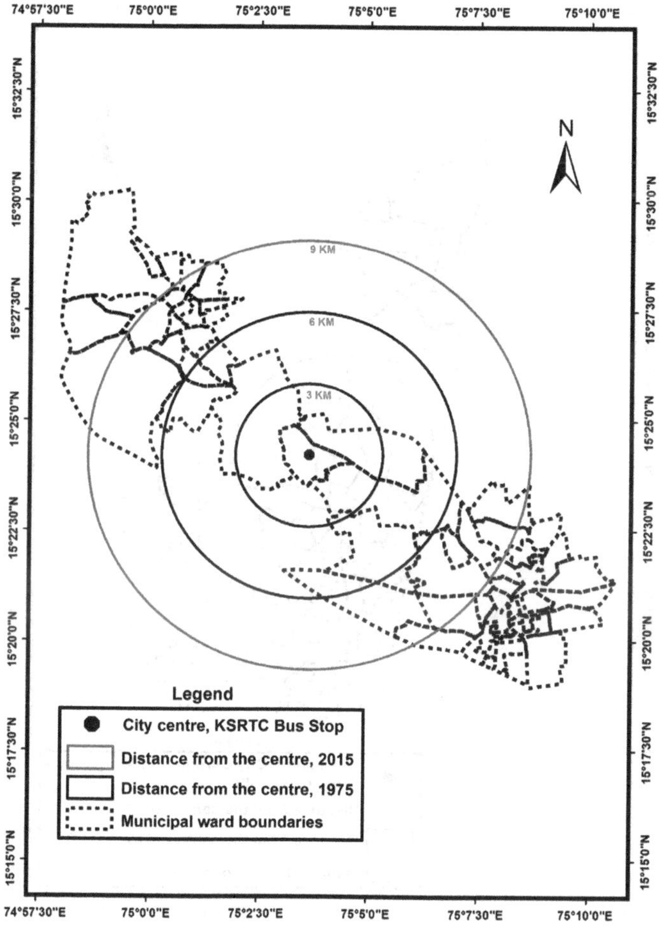

Hubballi-Dharwad's (Karnataka) Boundaries with Concentric Circles, 1975 and 2015

Sources: Florczyk et al. (2019) and author's analysis.

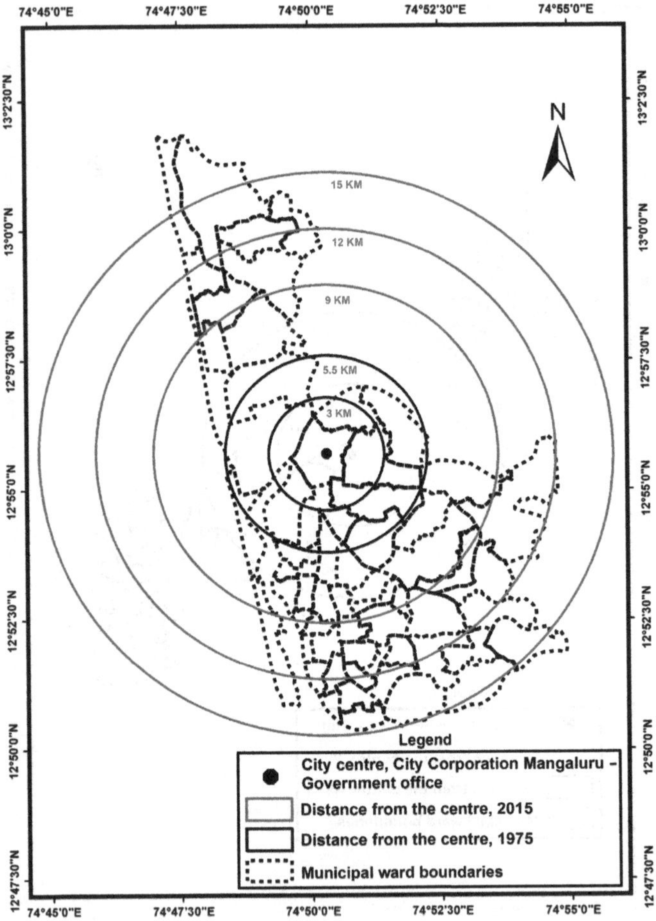

Mangaluru's (Karnataka) Boundaries with Concentric Circles, 1975 and 2015

Sources: Florczyk et al. (2019) and author's analysis.

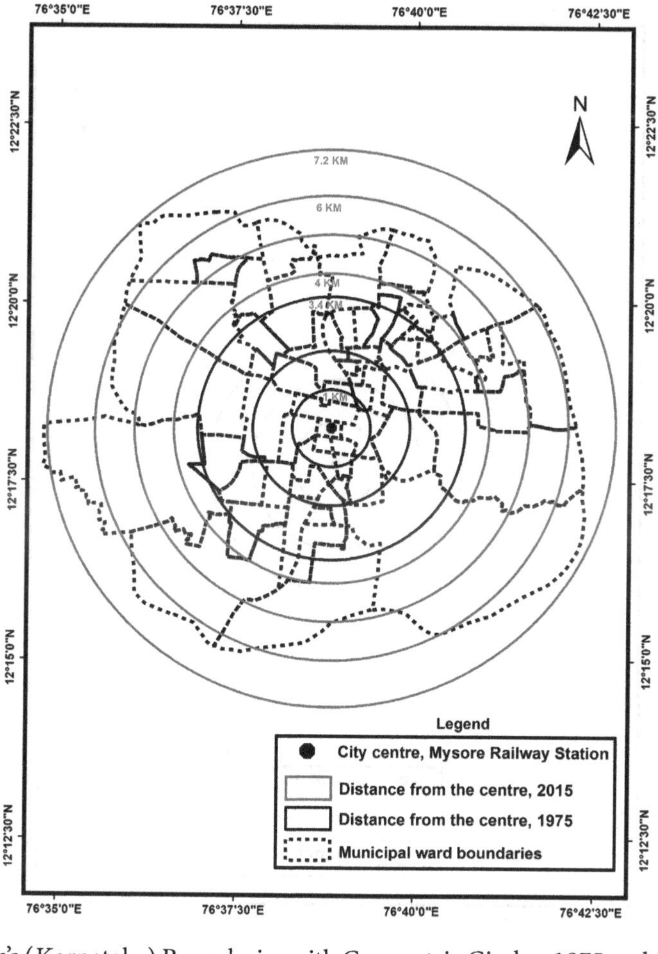

Mysuru's (Karnataka) Boundaries with Concentric Circles, 1975 and 2015

Sources: Florczyk et al. (2019) and author's analysis.

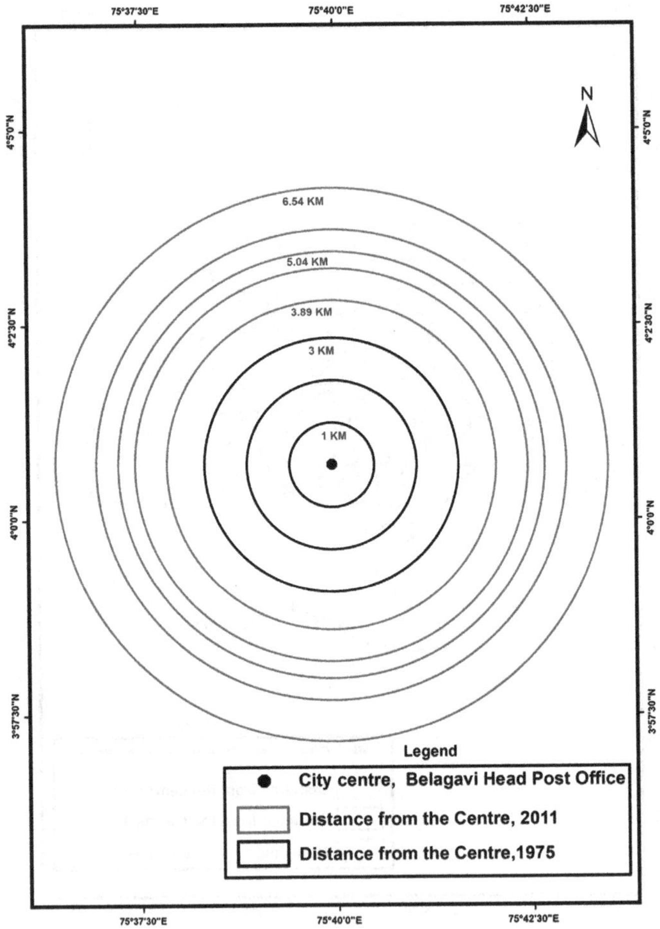

Belagavi's (Karnataka) boundaries with concentric circles, 1975 and 2011

Sources: Florczyk et al. (2019), KMDS and author's analysis.

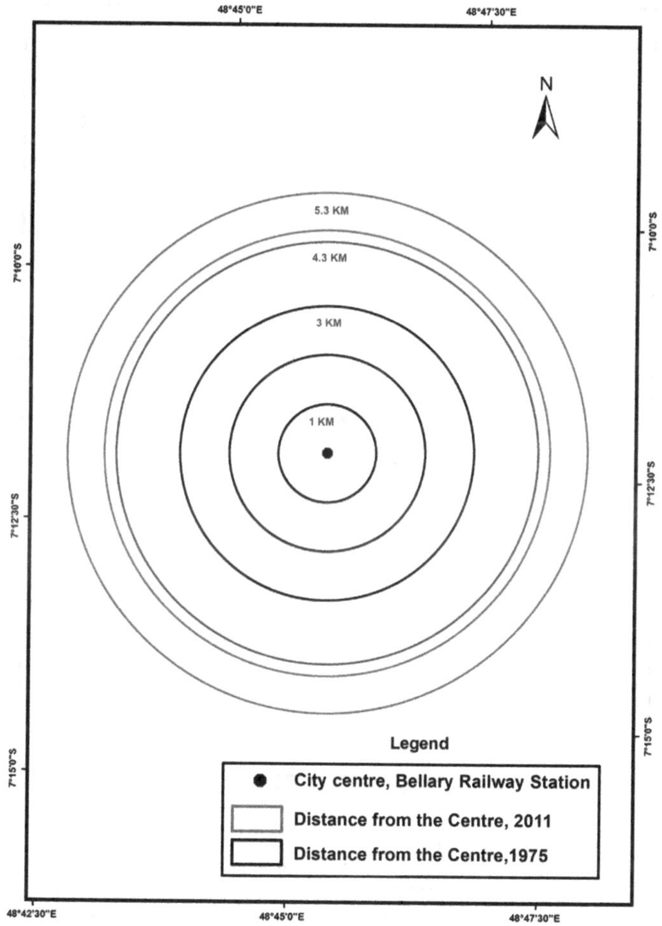

Bellary's (Karnataka) boundaries with concentric circles, 1975 and 2011

Sources: Florczyk et al. (2019), KMDS and author's analysis.

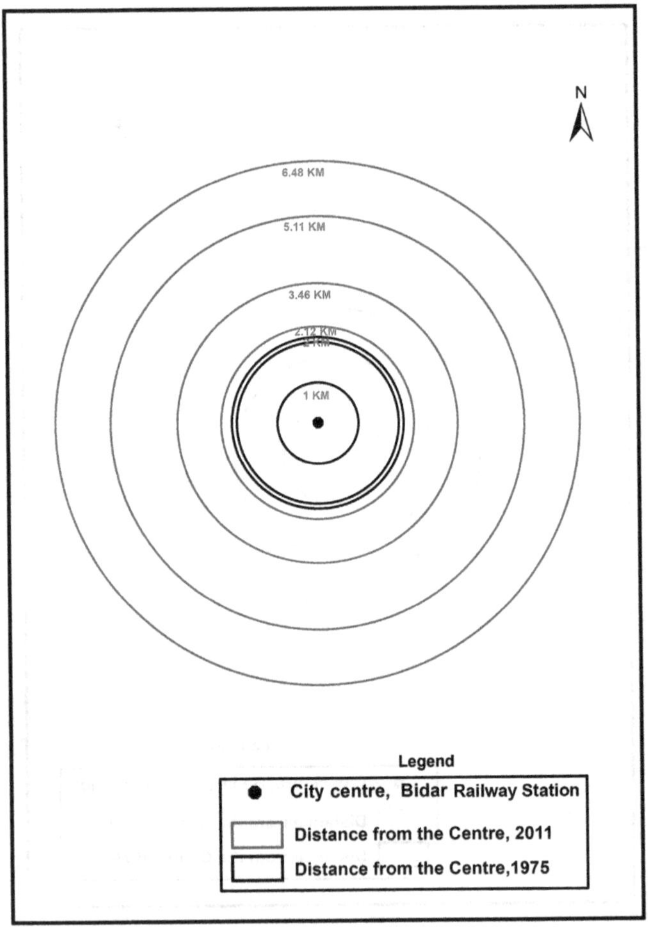

Bidar's (Karnataka) boundaries with concentric circles, 1975 and 2011

Sources: Florczyk et al. (2019), KMDS and author's analysis.

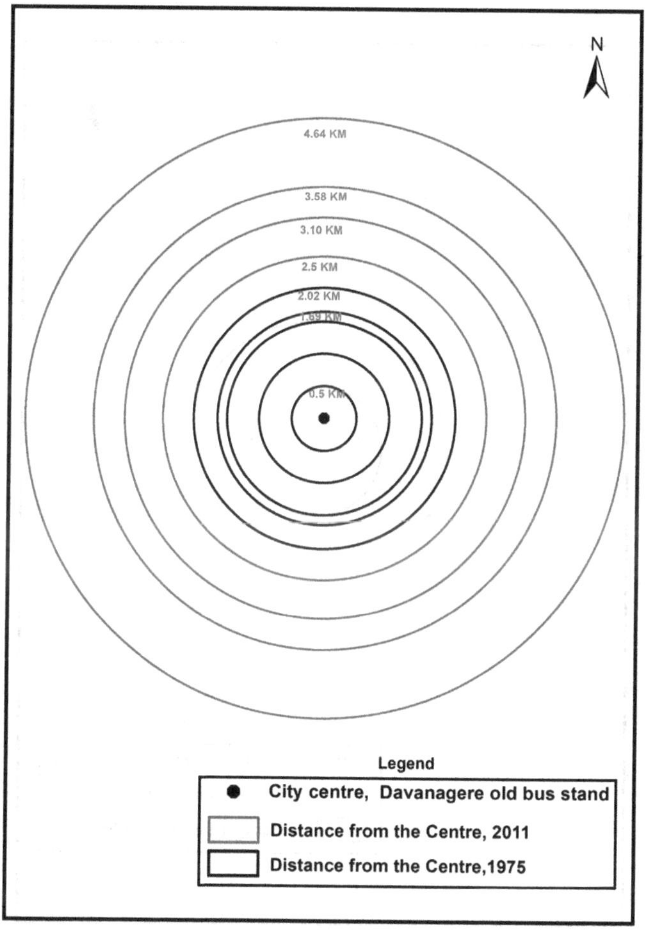

Davanagere's (Karnataka) boundaries with concentric circles, 1975 and 2011

Sources: Florczyk et al. (2019), KMDS and author's analysis.

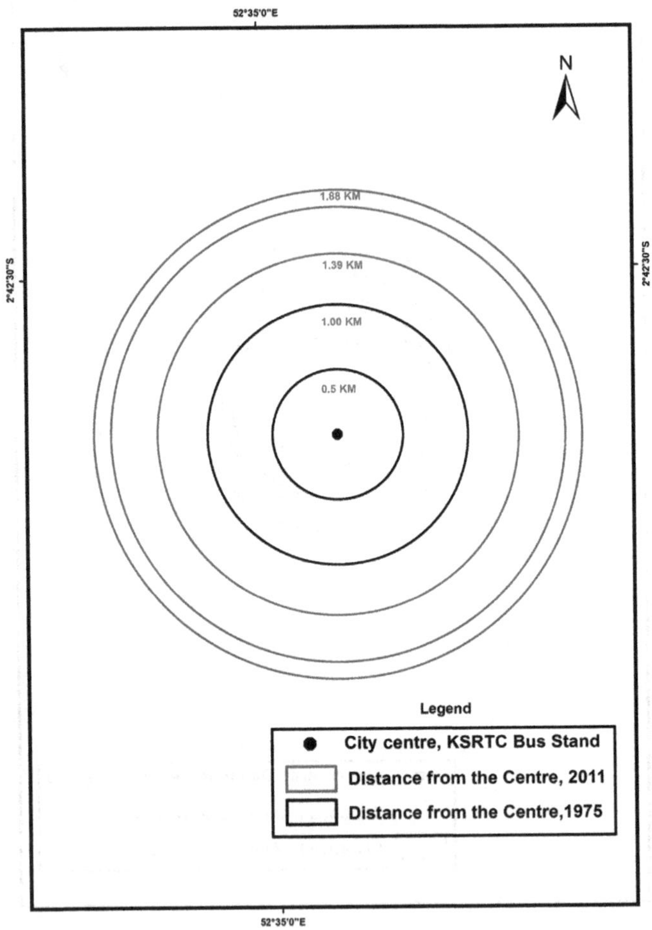

Ilkal's (Karnataka) boundaries with concentric circles, 1975 and 2011

Sources: Florczyk et al. (2019), KMDS and author's analysis.

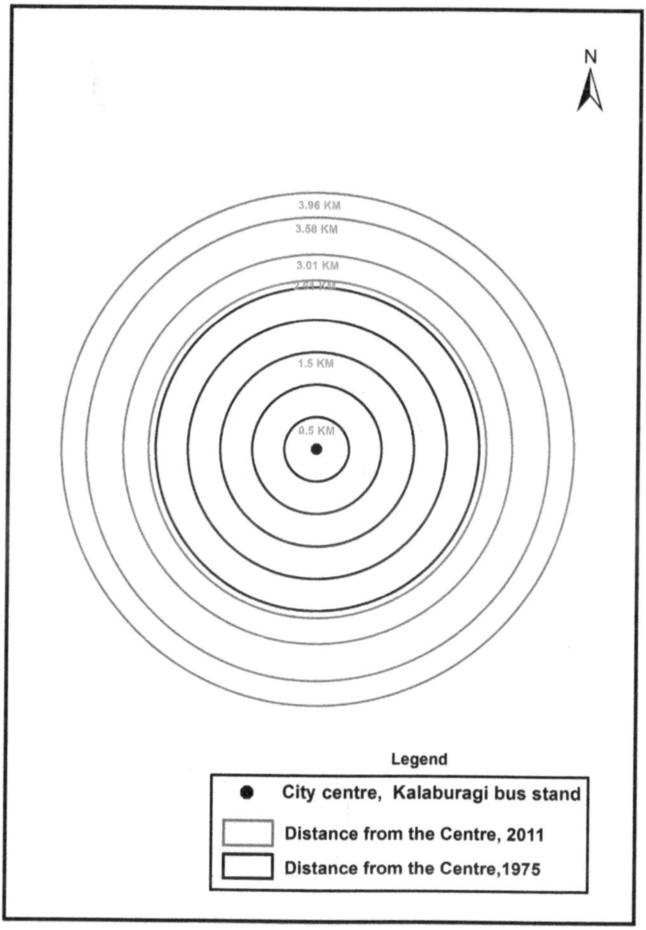

Kalaburagi's (Karnataka) boundaries with concentric circles, 1975 and 2011

Sources: Florczyk et al. (2019), KMDS and author's analysis.

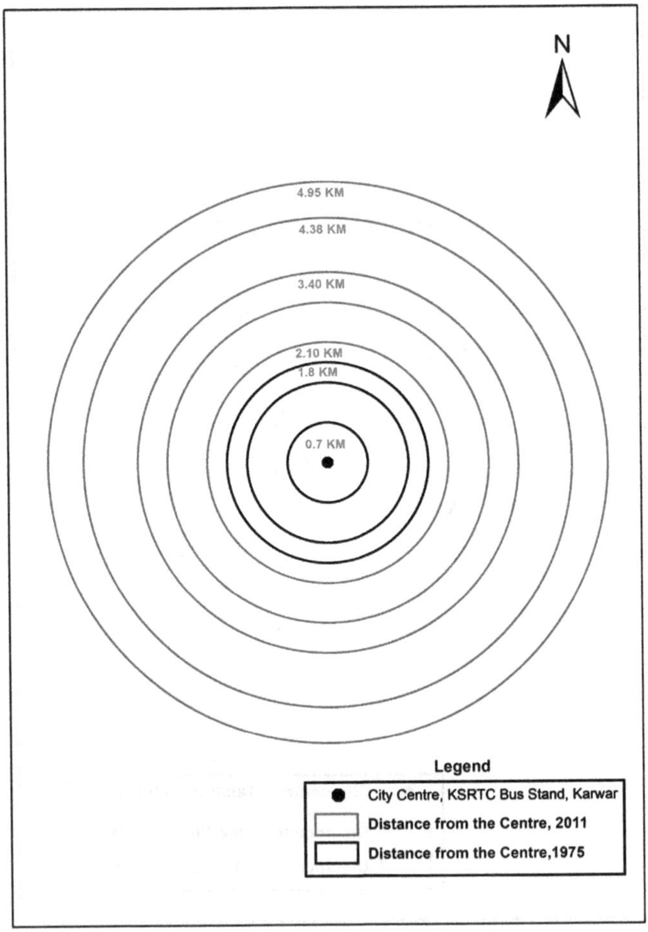

Karwar's (Karnataka) boundaries with concentric circles, 1975 and 2011

Sources: Florczyk et al. (2019), KMDS and author's analysis.

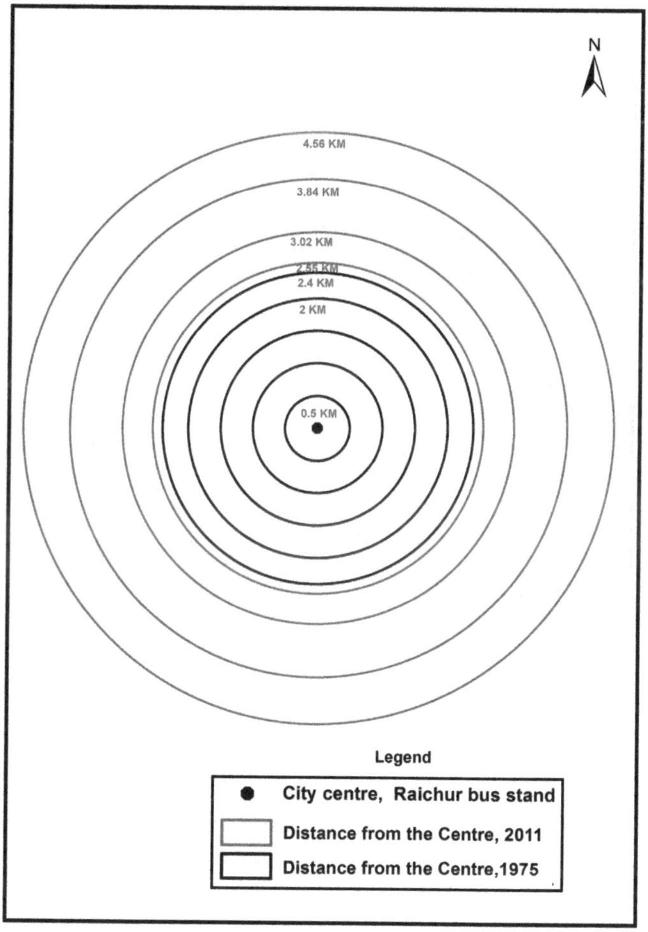

Raichur's (Karnataka) boundaries with concentric circles, 1975 and 2011

Sources: Florczyk et al. (2019), KMDS and author's analysis.

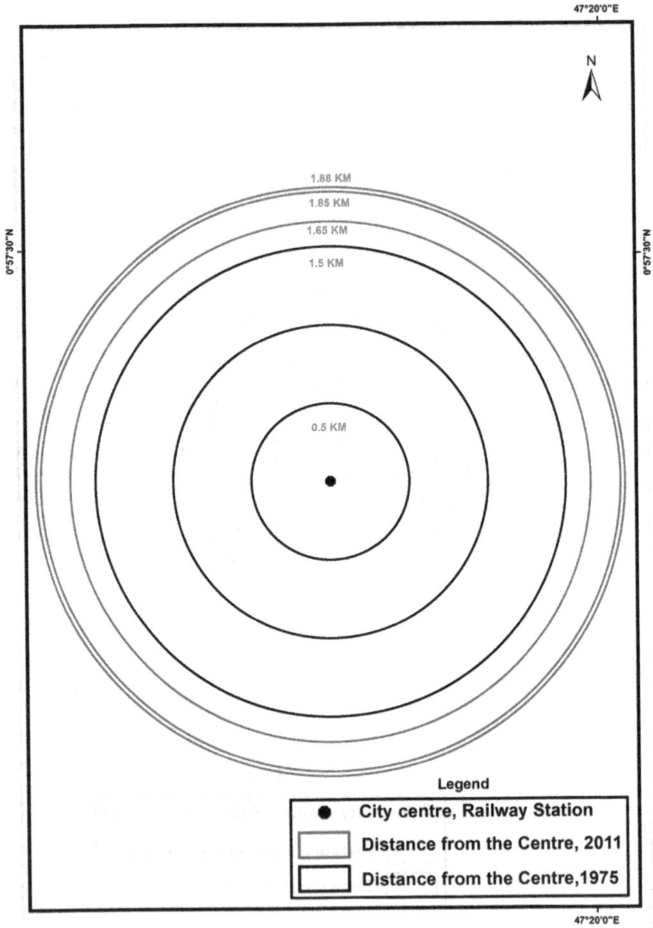

Ramanagaram's (Karnataka) boundaries with concentric circles, 1975 and 2011

Sources: Florczyk et al. (2019), KMDS and author's analysis.

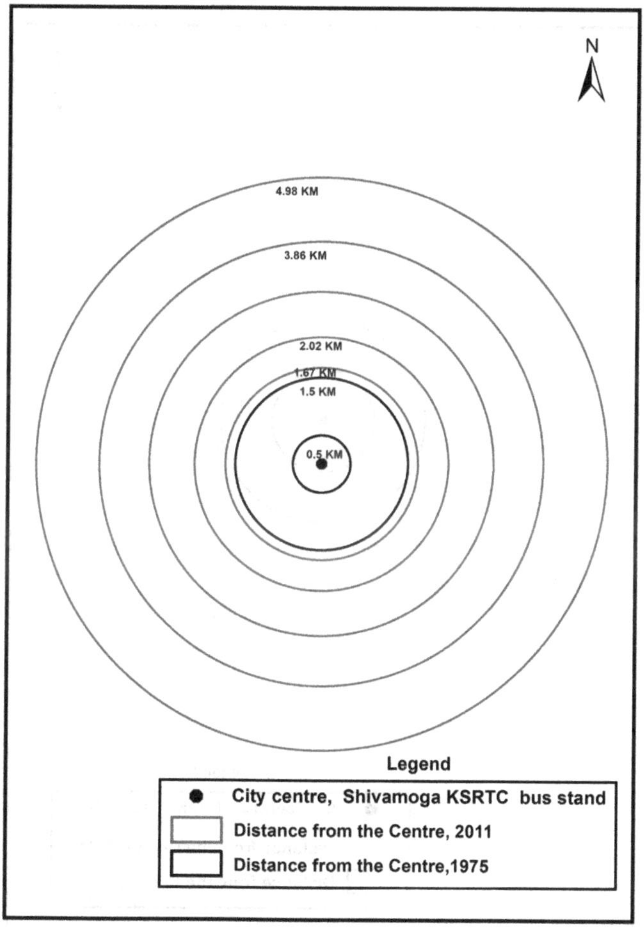

Shivamogga's (Karnataka) boundaries with concentric circles, 1975 and 2011

Sources: Florczyk et al. (2019), KMDS and author's analysis.

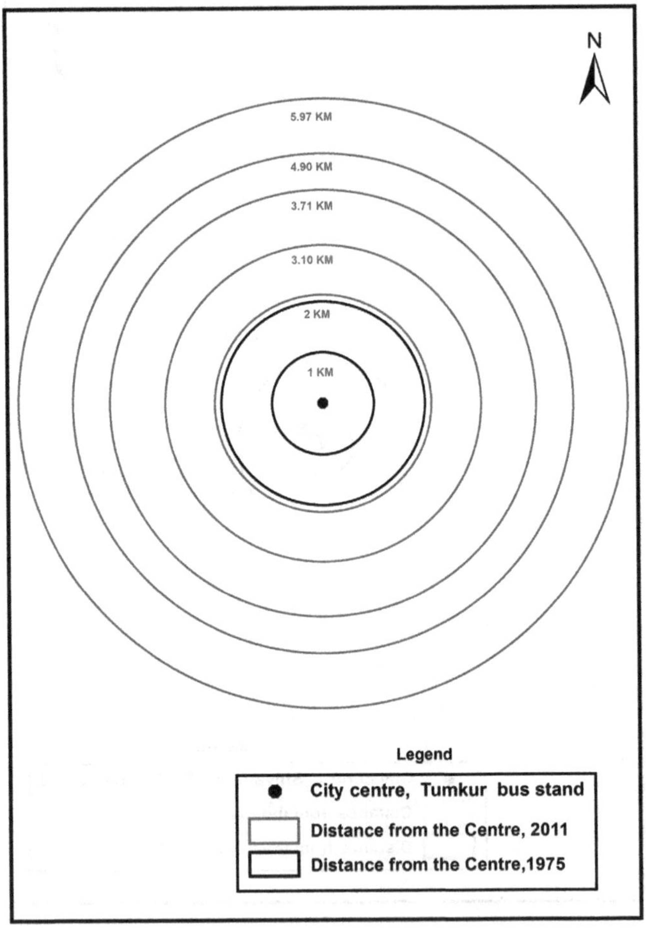

Tumakuru's (Karnataka) boundaries with concentric circles, 1975 and 2011

Sources: Florczyk et al. (2019), KMDS and author's analysis.

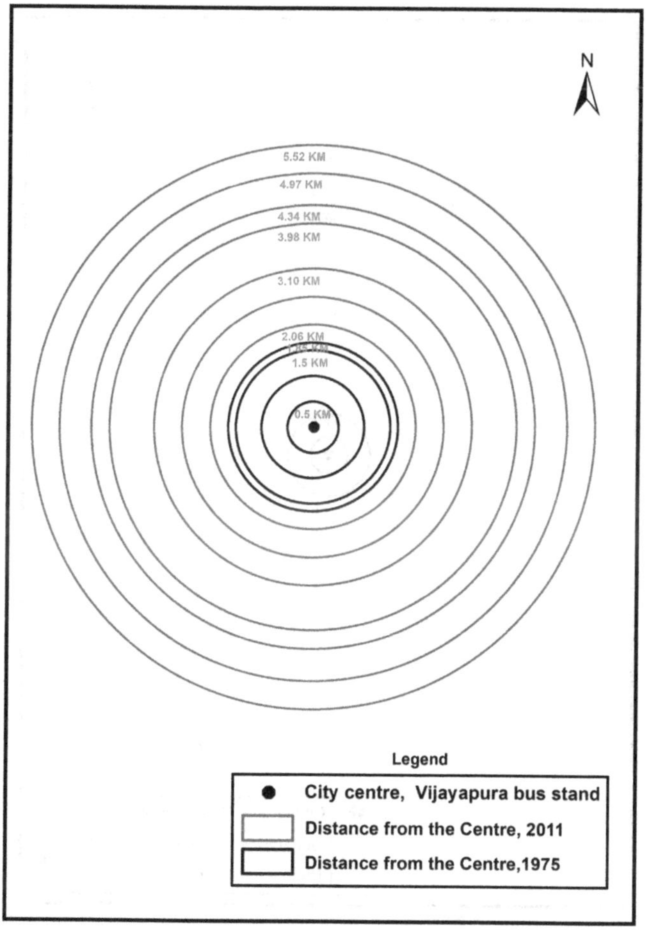

Vijayapura's (Karnataka) boundaries with concentric circles, 1975 and 2011

Sources: Florczyk et al. (2019), KMDS and author's analysis.

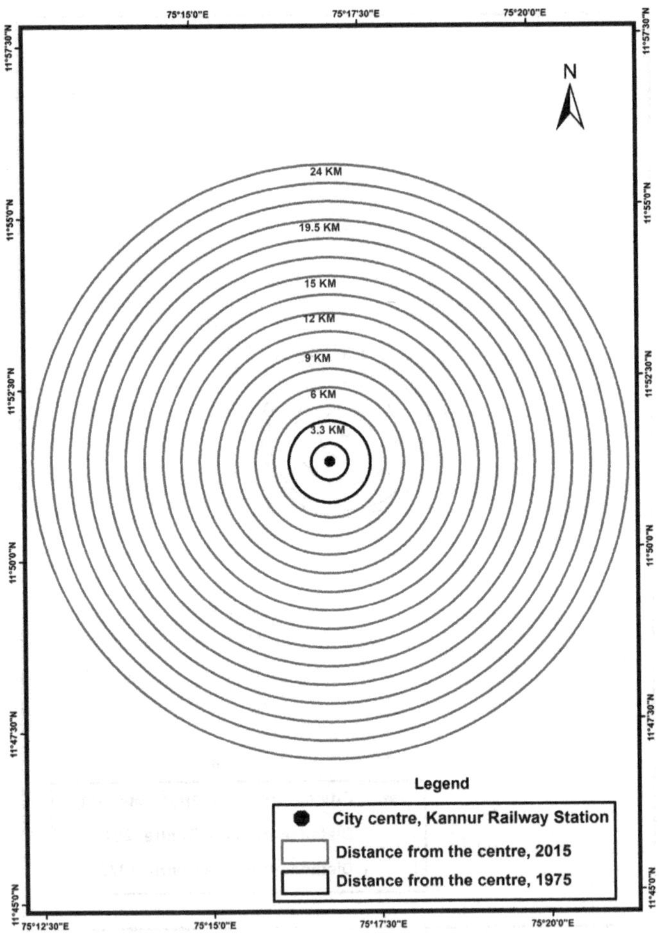

Kannur's (Kerala) Boundaries with Concentric Circles, 1975 and 2015

Sources: Florczyk et al. (2019) and author's analysis.

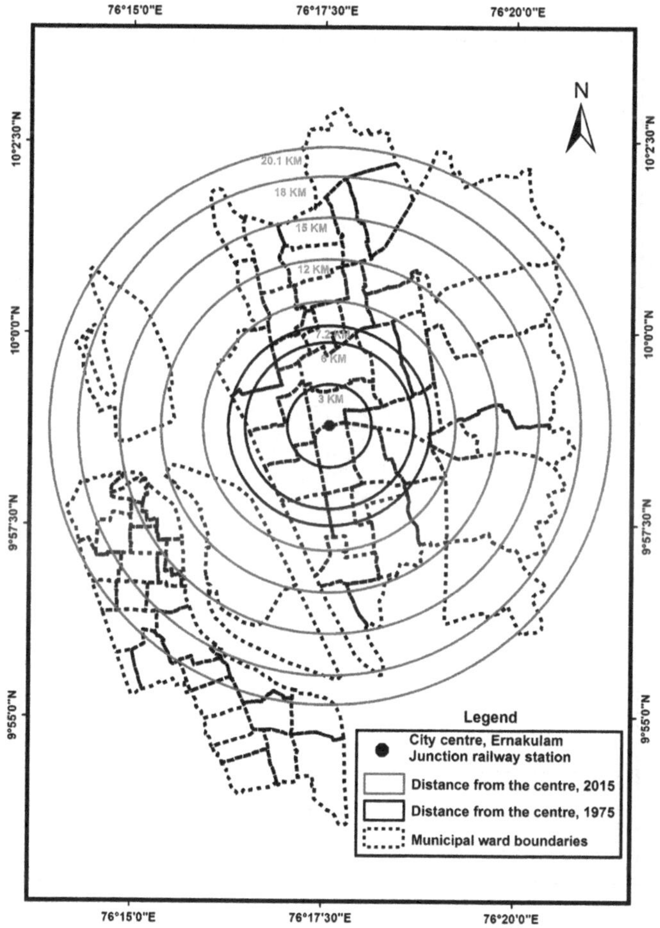

Kochi's (Kerala) Boundaries with Concentric Circles, 1975 and 2015

Sources: Florczyk et al. (2019) and author's analysis.

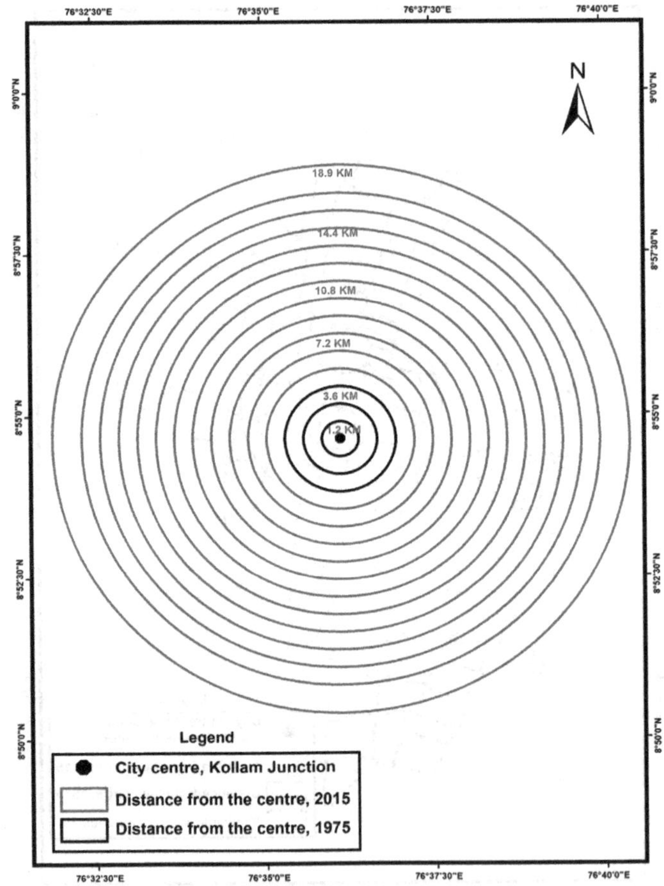

Kollam's (Kerala) Boundaries with Concentric Circles, 1975 and 2015

Sources: Florczyk et al. (2019) and author's analysis.

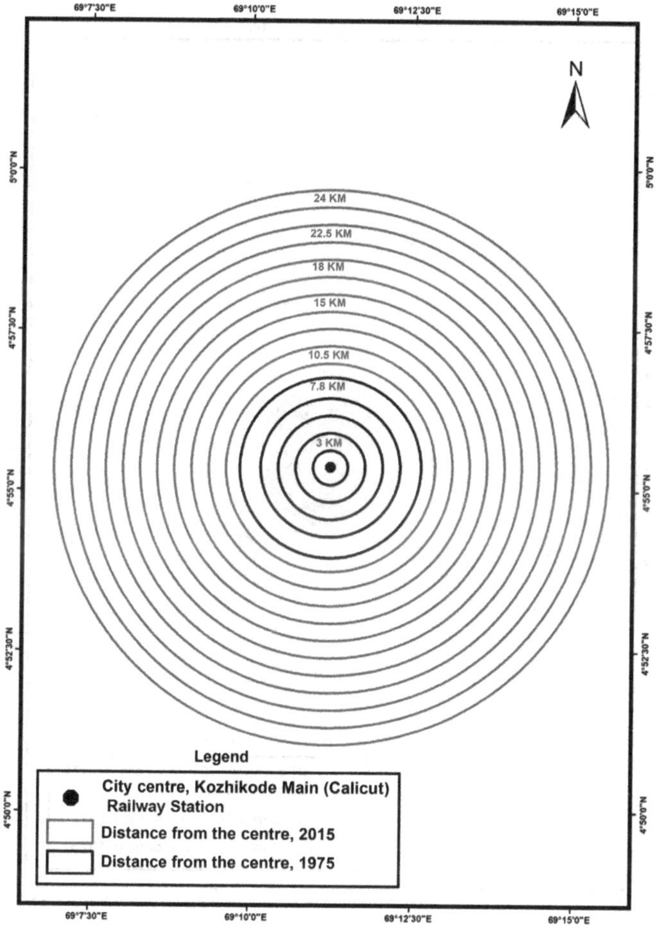

Kozhikode's (Kerala) Boundaries with Concentric Circles, 1975 and 2015

Sources: Florczyk et al. (2019) and author's analysis.

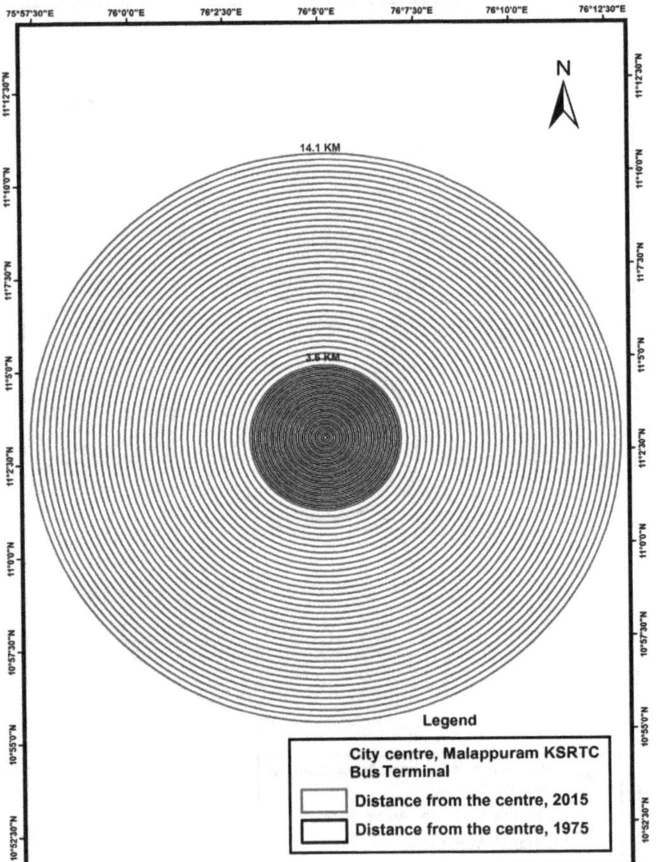

Malappuram's (Kerala) Boundaries with Concentric Circles, 1975 and 2015

Sources: Florczyk et al. (2019) and author's analysis.

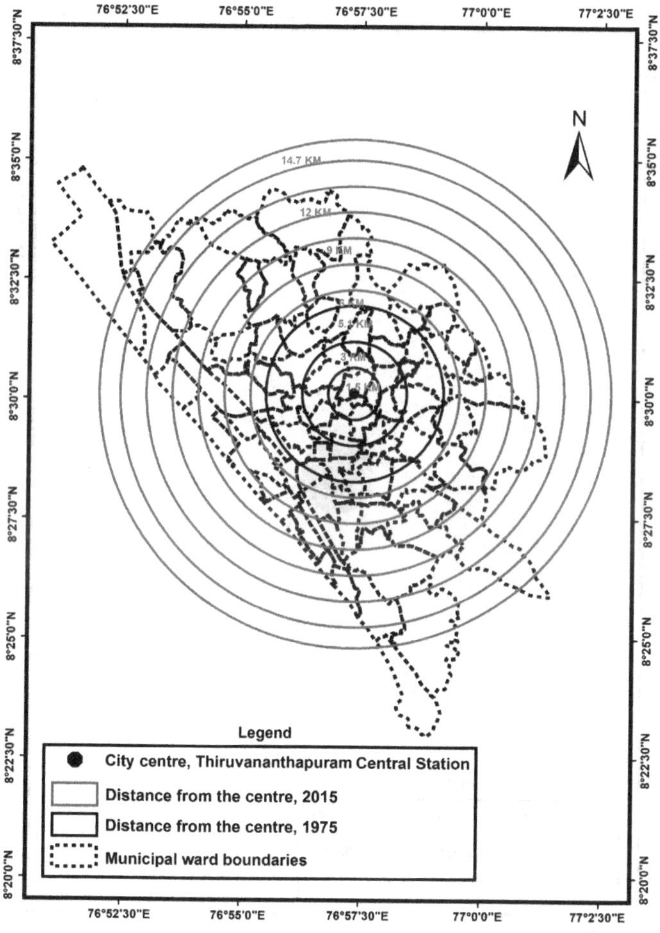

Thiruvananthapuram's (Kerala) Boundaries with Concentric Circles, 1975 and 2015

Sources: Florczyk et al. (2019) and author's analysis.

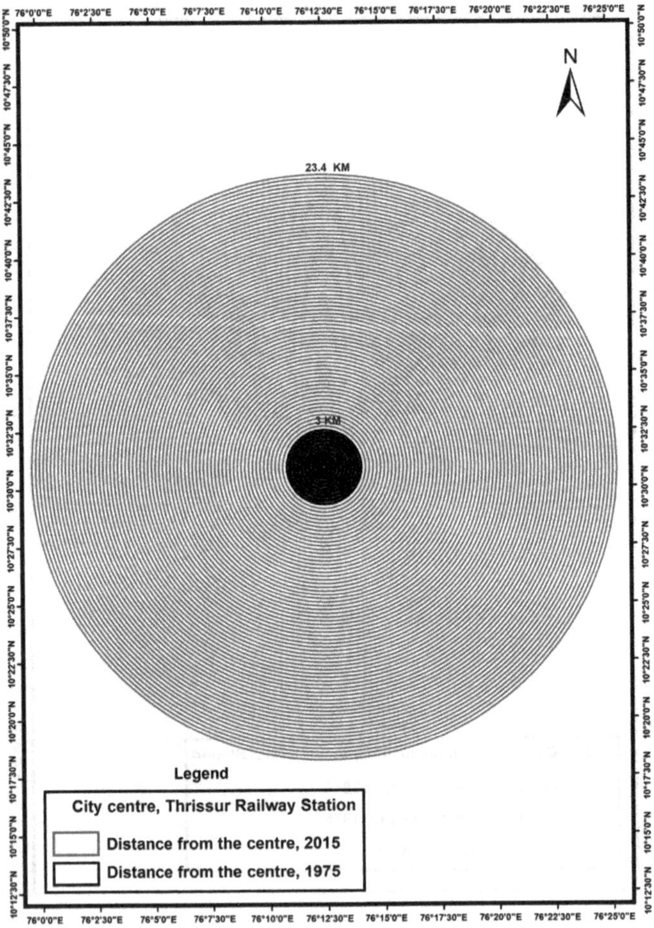

Thrissur's (Kerala) Boundaries with Concentric Circles, 1975 and 2015

Sources: Florczyk et al. (2019) and author's analysis.

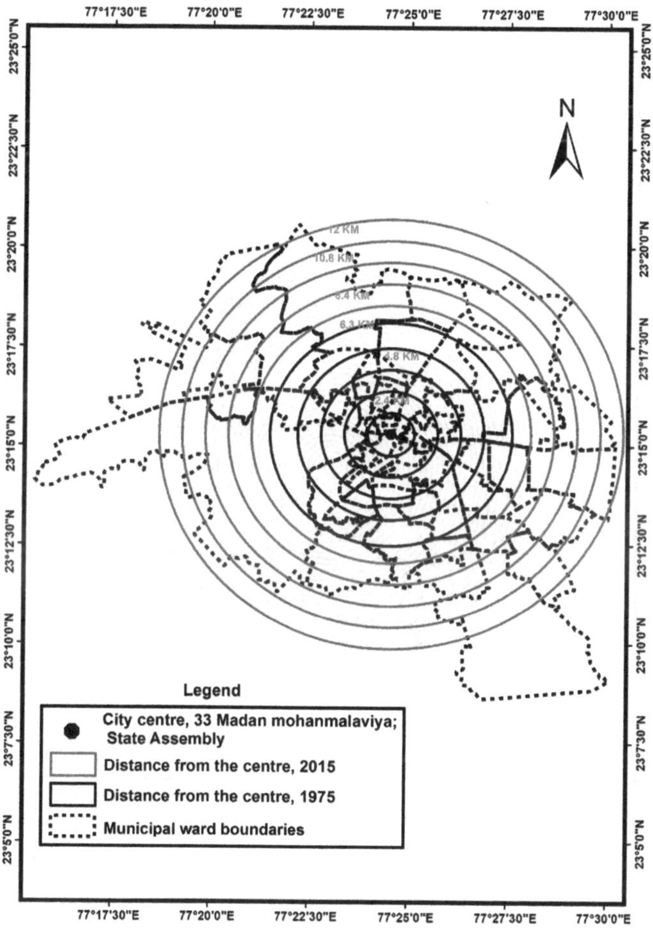

Bhopal's (Madhya Pradesh) Boundaries with Concentric Circles, 1975 and 2015

Sources: Florczyk et al. (2019) and author's analysis.

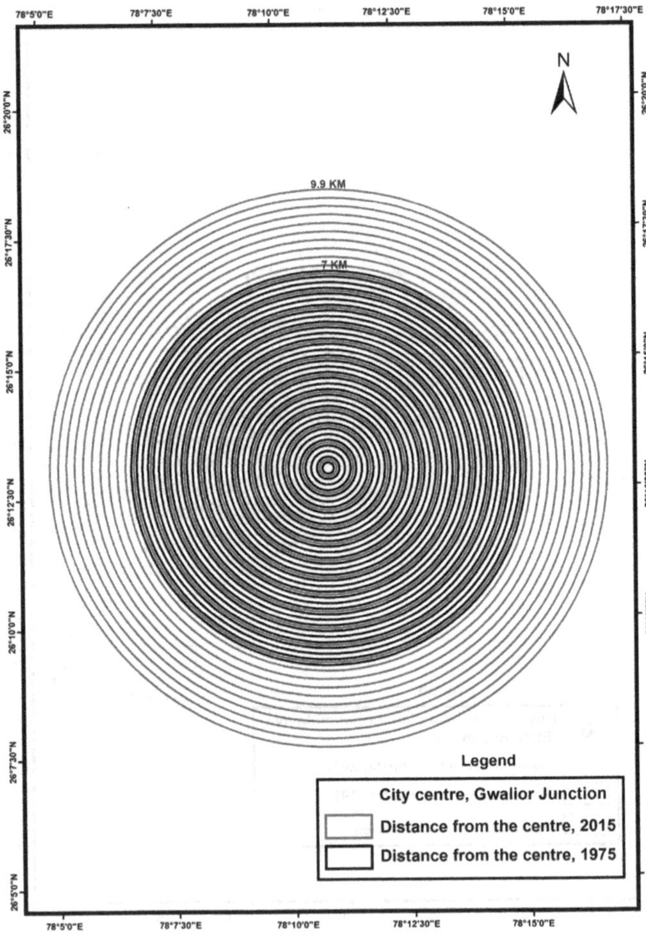

Gwalior's (Madhya Pradesh) Boundaries with Concentric Circles, 1975 and 2015

Sources: Florczyk et al. (2019) and author's analysis.

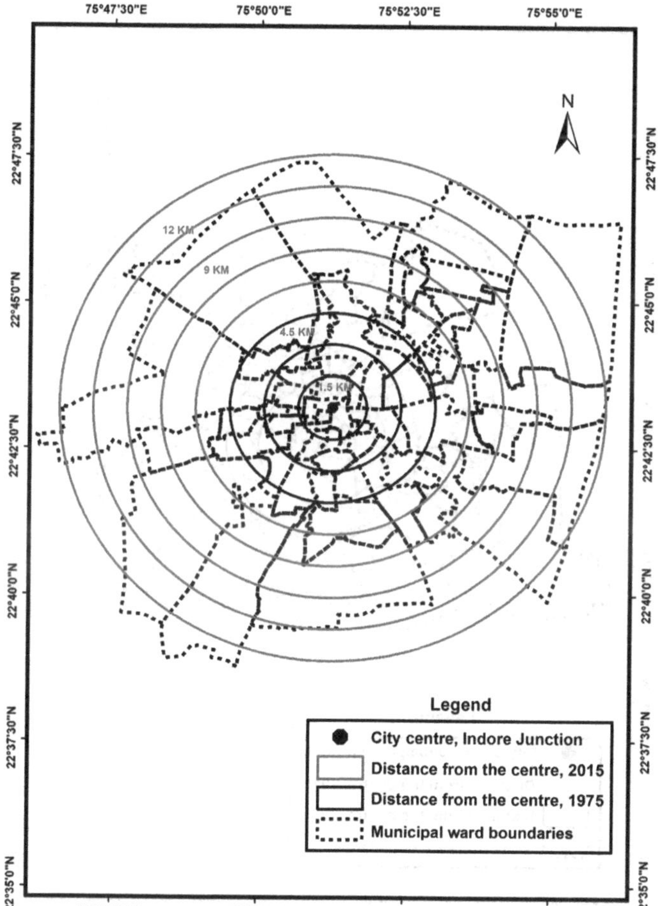

Indore's (Madhya Pradesh) Boundaries with Concentric Circles, 1975 and 2015

Sources: Florczyk et al. (2019) and author's analysis.

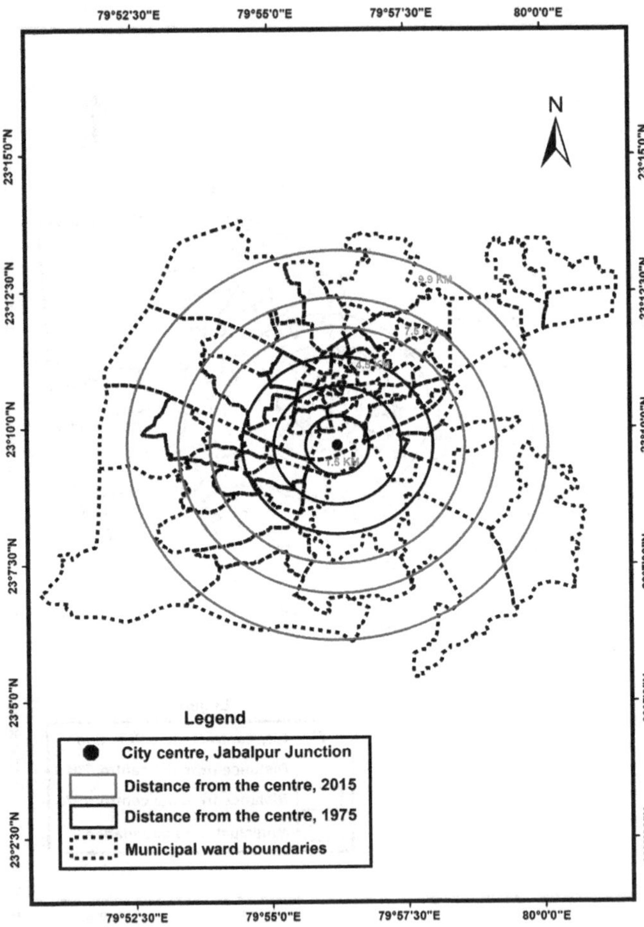

Jabalpur's (Madhya Pradesh) Boundaries with Concentric Circles, 1975 and 2015

Sources: Florczyk et al. (2019) and author's analysis.

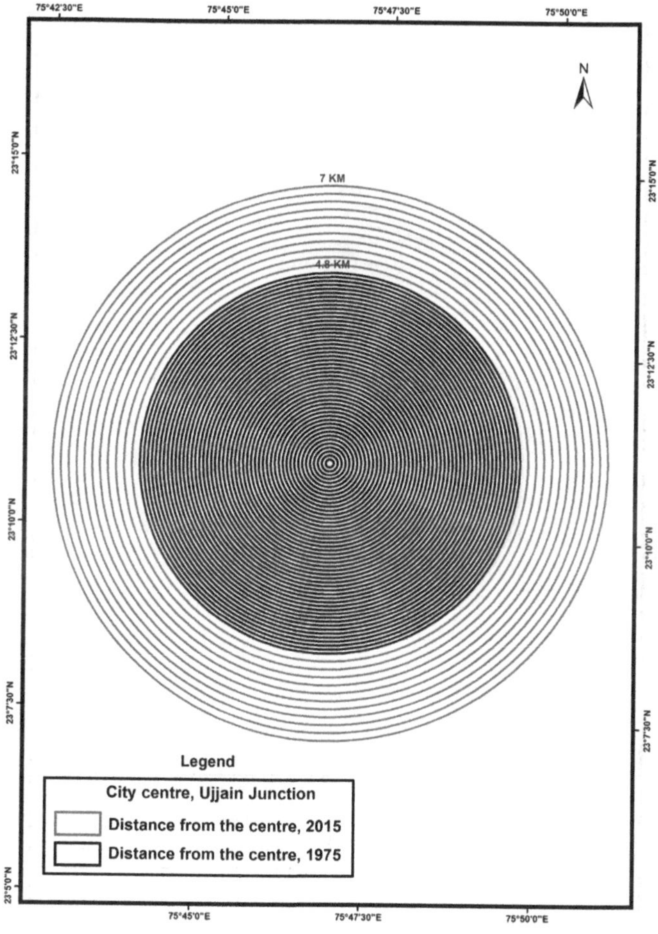

Ujjain's (Madhya Pradesh) Boundaries with Concentric Circles, 1975 and 2015

Sources: Florczyk et al. (2019) and author's analysis.

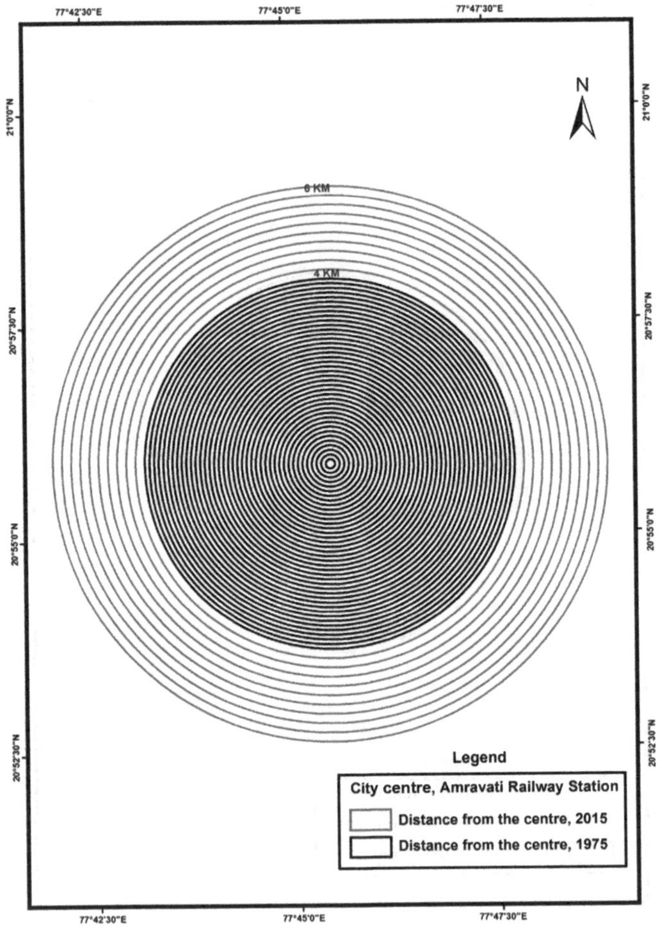

Amravati's (Maharashtra) Boundaries with Concentric Circles, 1975 and 2015

Sources: Florczyk et al. (2019) and author's analysis.

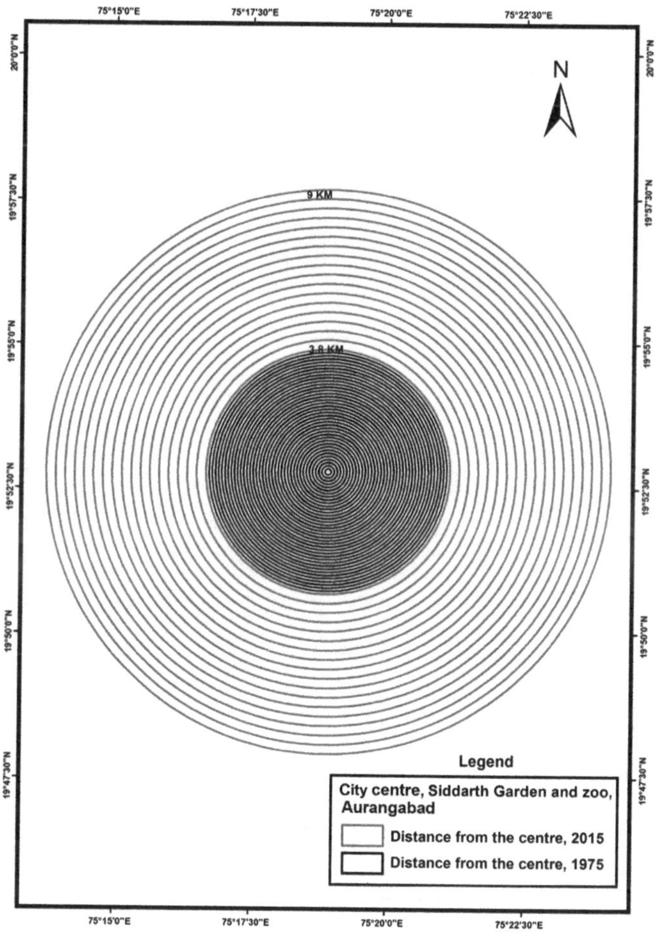

Aurangabad's (Maharashtra) Boundaries with Concentric Circles, 1975 and 2015

Sources: Florczyk et al. (2019) and author's analysis.

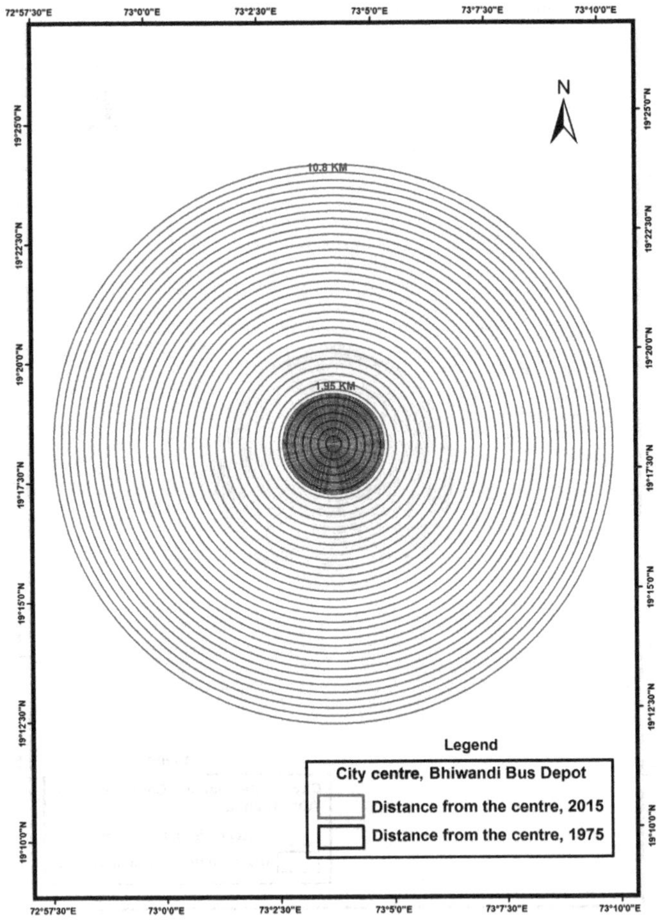

Bhiwandi's (Maharashtra) Boundaries with Concentric Circles, 1975 and 2015

Sources: Florczyk et al. (2019) and author's analysis.

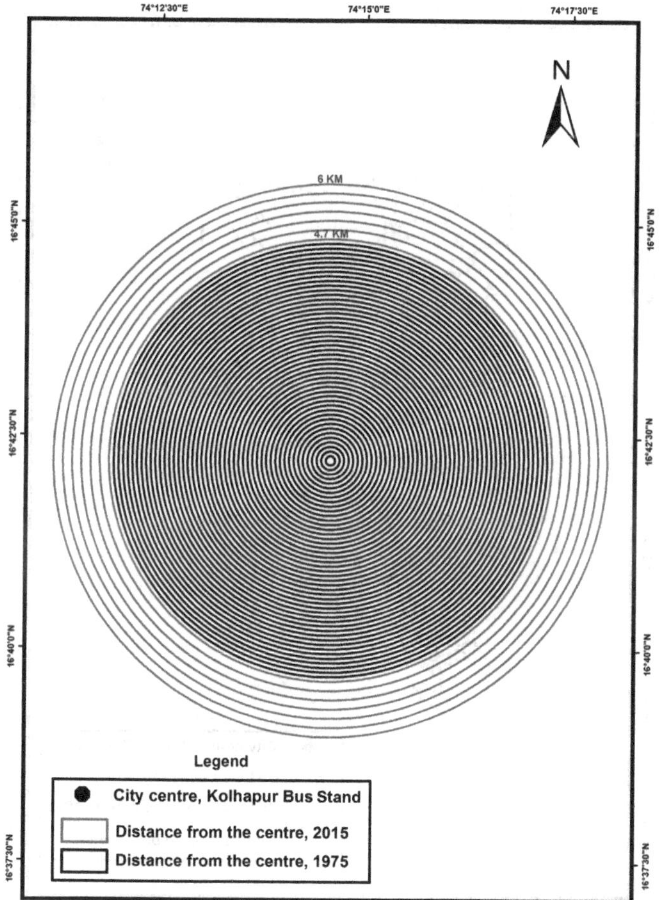

Kolhapur's (Maharashtra) Boundaries with Concentric Circles, 1975 and 2015

Sources: Florczyk et al. (2019) and author's analysis.

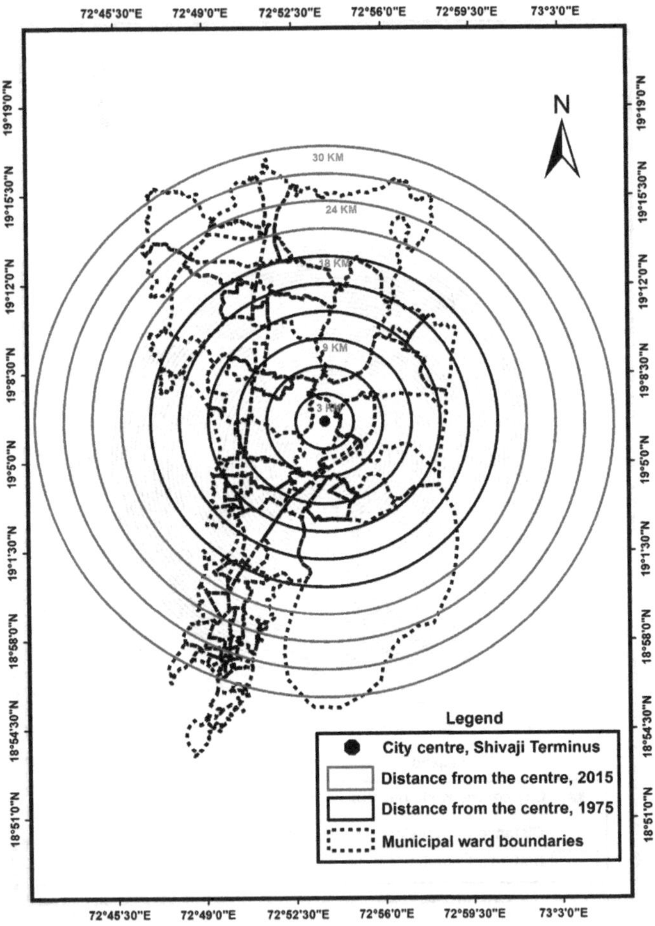

Mumbai's (Maharashtra) Boundaries with Concentric Circles, 1975 and 2015

Sources: Florczyk et al. (2019) and author's analysis.

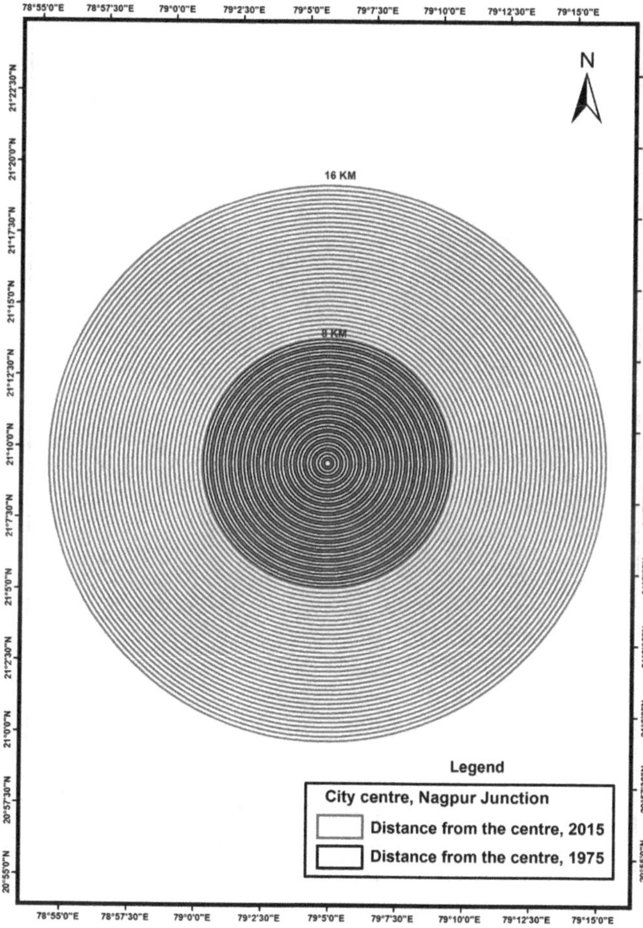

Nagpur's (Maharashtra) Boundaries with Concentric Circles, 1975 and 2015

Sources: Florczyk et al. (2019) and author's analysis.

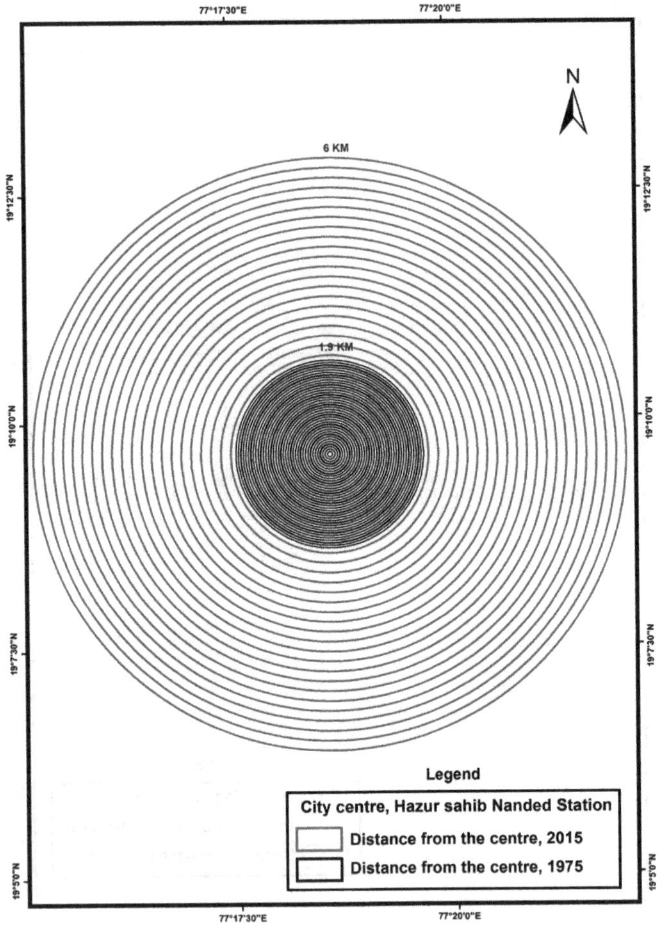

Nanded-Waghala's (Maharashtra) Boundaries with Concentric Circles, 1975 and 2015

Sources: Florczyk et al. (2019) and author's analysis.

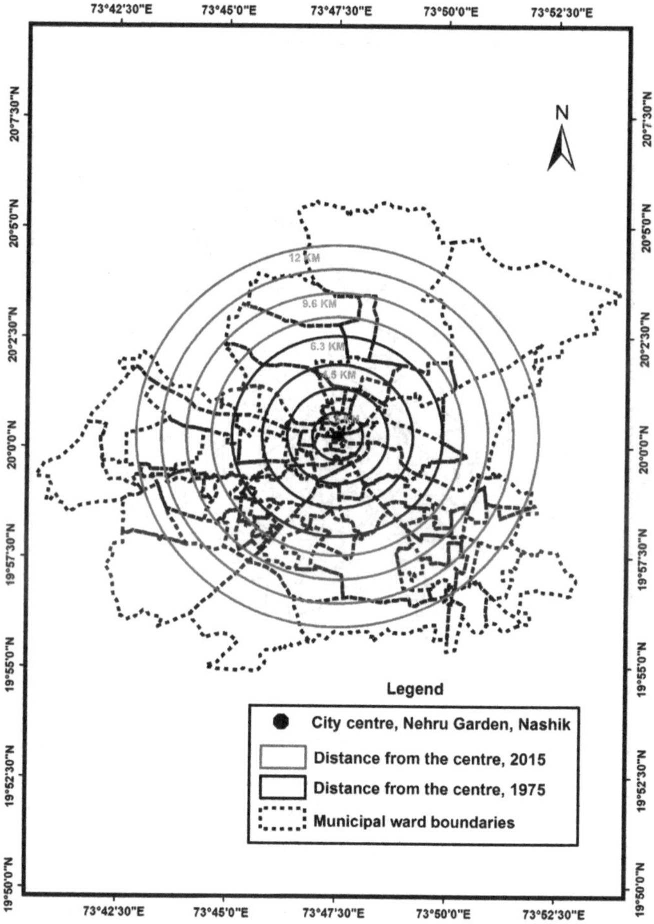

Nashik's (Maharashtra) Boundaries with Concentric Circles, 1975 and 2015
Sources: Florczyk et al. (2019) and author's analysis.

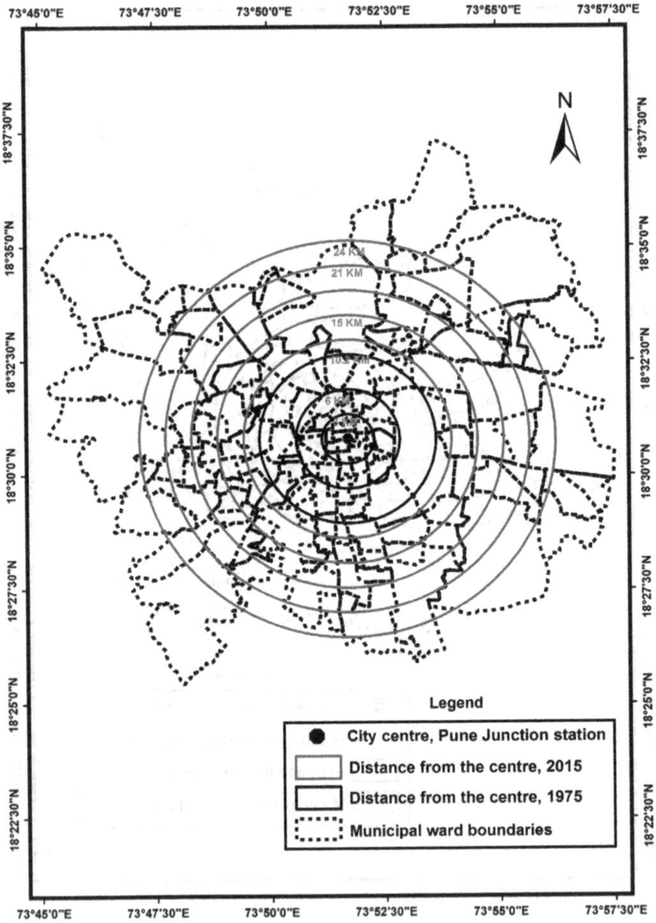

Pune's (Maharashtra) Boundaries with Concentric Circles, 1975 and 2015

Sources: Florczyk et al. (2019) and author's analysis.

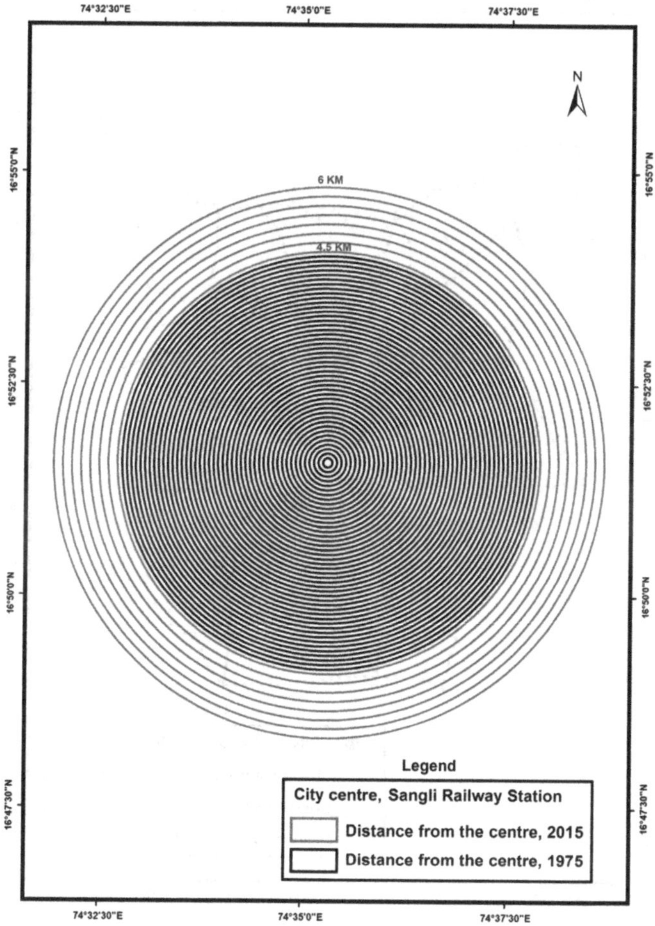

Sangli's (Maharashtra) Boundaries with Concentric Circles, 1975 and 2015
Sources: Florczyk et al. (2019) and author's analysis.

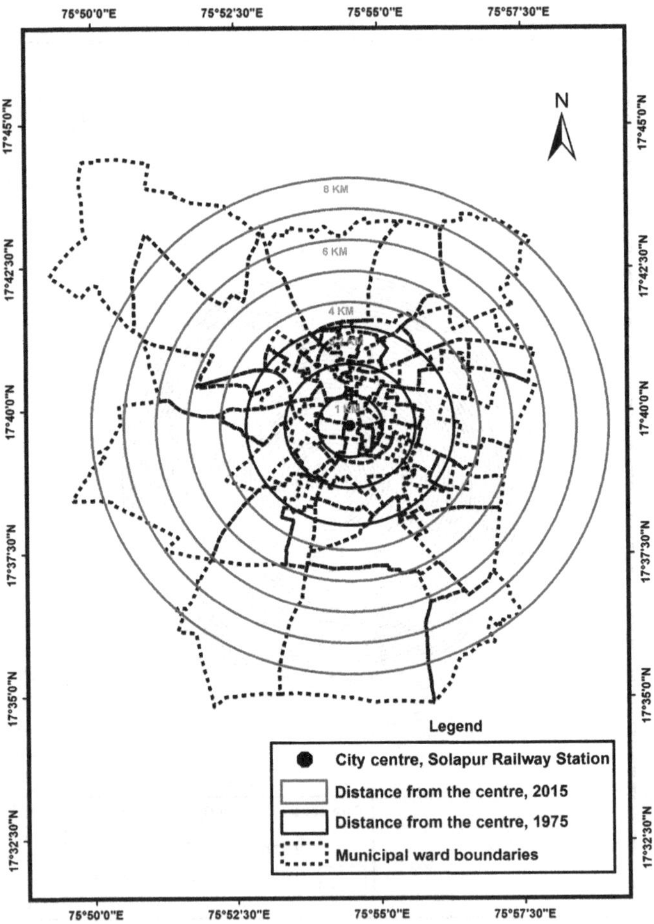

Solapur's (Maharashtra) Boundaries with Concentric Circles, 1975 and 2015

Sources: Florczyk et al. (2019) and author's analysis.

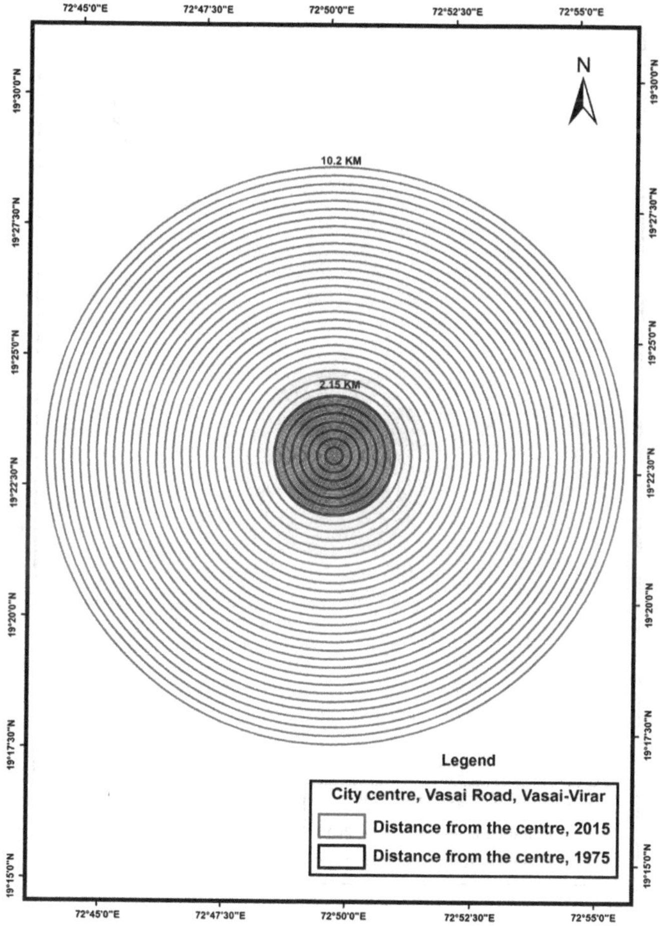

Vasai-Virar's (Maharashtra) Boundaries with Concentric Circles, 1975 and 2015

Sources: Florczyk et al. (2019) and author's analysis.

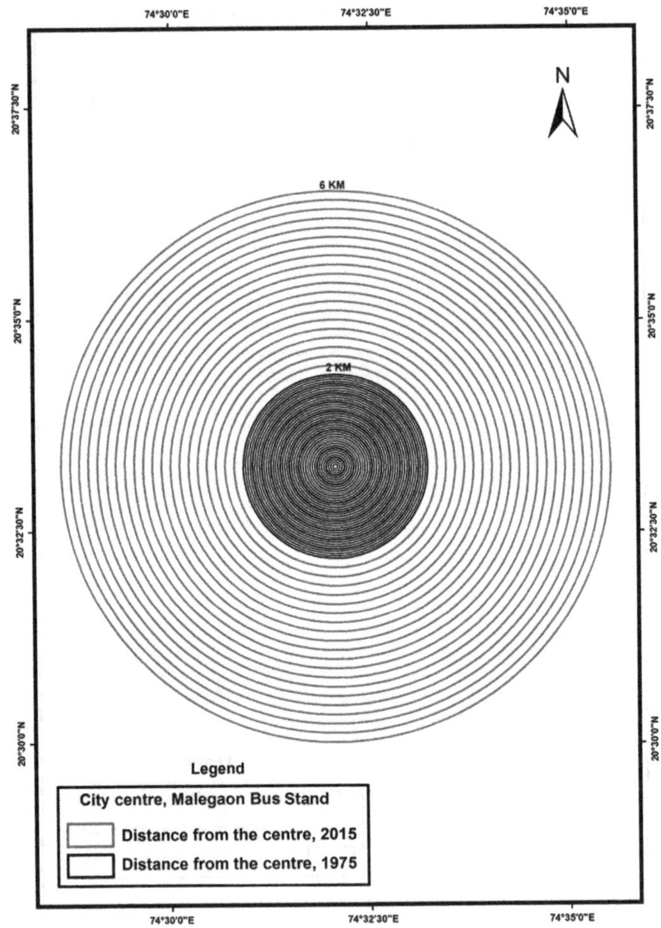

Malegaon's (Maharashtra) Boundaries with Concentric Circles, 1975 and 2015

Sources: Florczyk et al. (2019) and author's analysis.

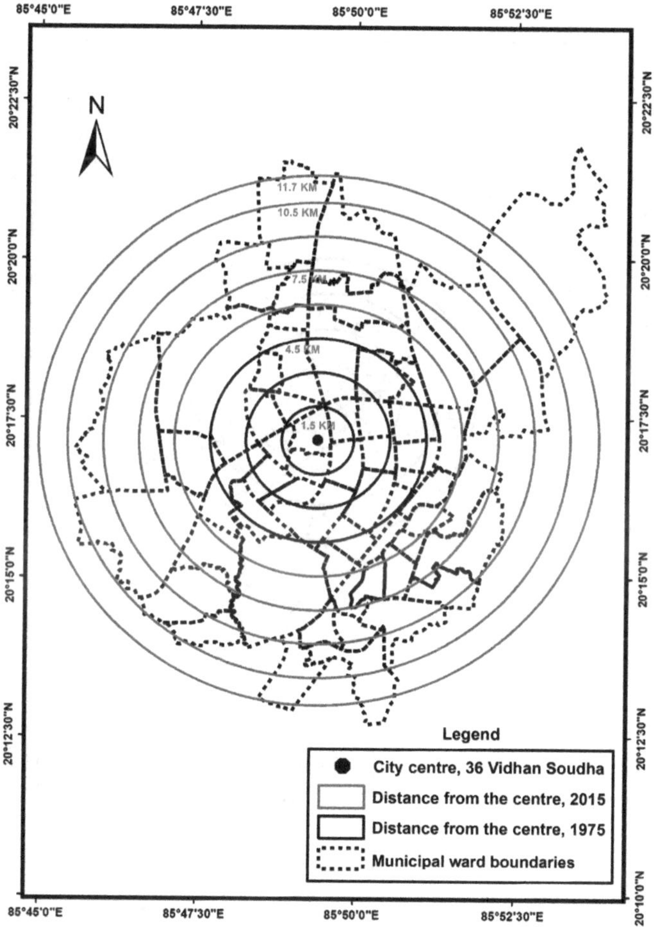

Bhubaneswar's (Odisha) Boundaries with Concentric Circles, 1975 and 2015

Sources: Florczyk et al. (2019) and author's analysis.

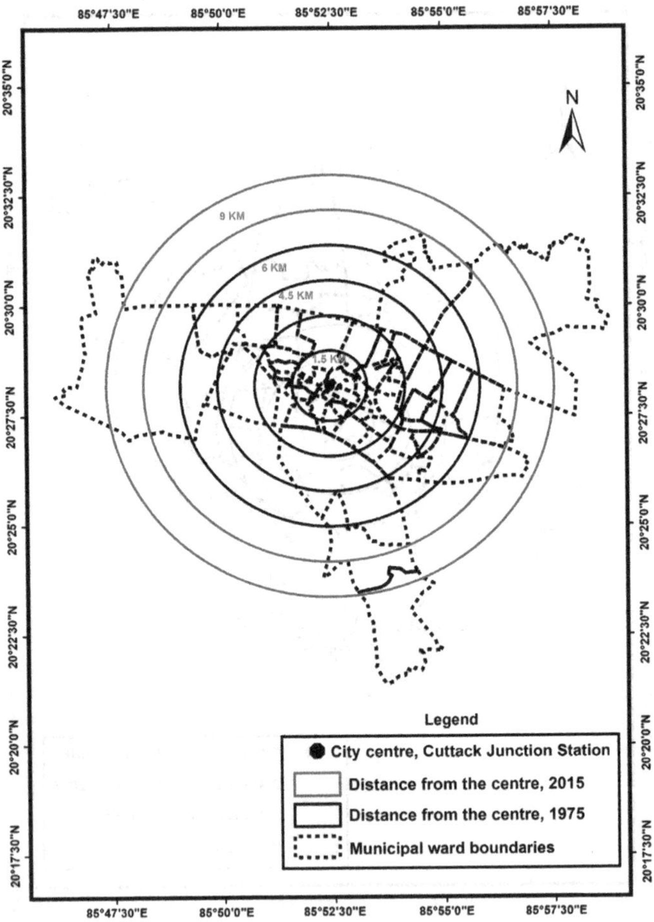

Cuttack's (Odisha) Boundaries with Concentric Circles, 1975 and 2015

Sources: Florczyk et al. (2019) and author's analysis.

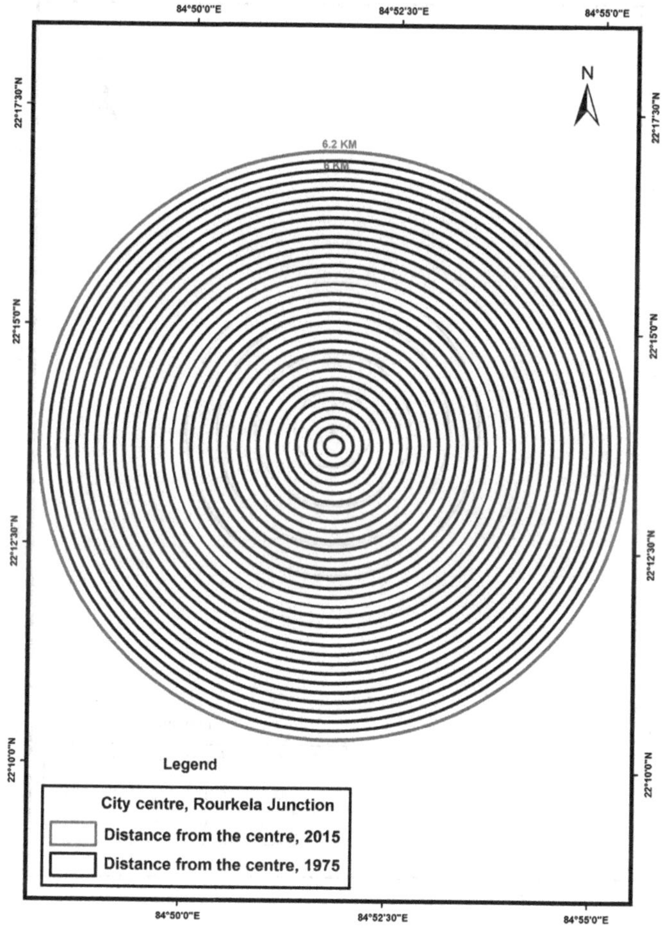

Rourkela's (Odisha) Boundaries with Concentric Circles, 1975 and 2015

Sources: Florczyk et al. (2019) and author's analysis.

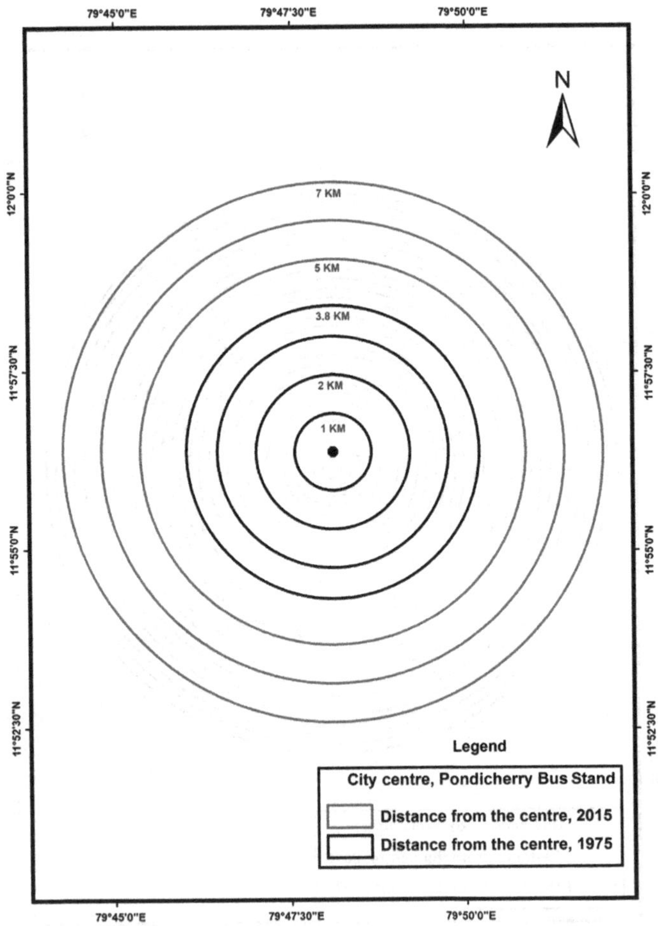

Puducherry's (Puducherry) Boundaries with Concentric Circles, 1975 and 2015

Sources: Florczyk et al. (2019) and author's analysis.

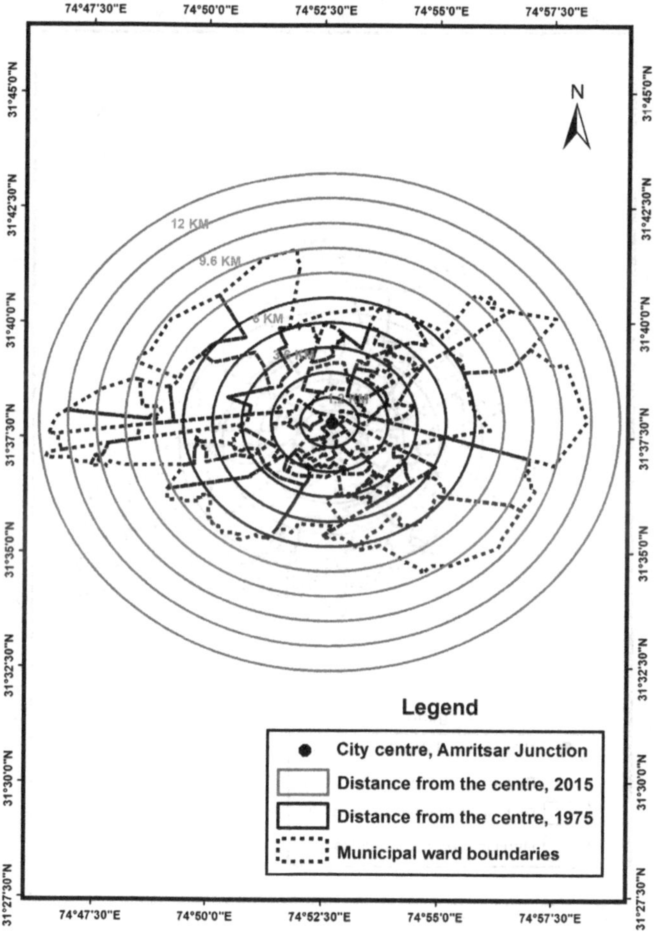

Amritsar's (Punjab) Boundaries with Concentric Circles, 1975 and 2015

Sources: Florczyk et al. (2019) and author's analysis.

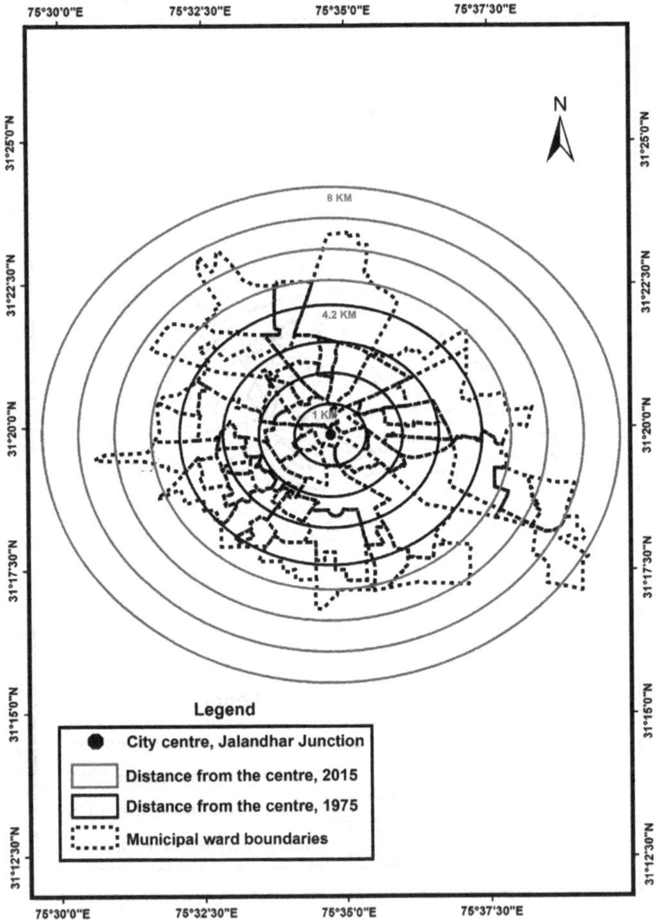

Jalandhar's (Punjab) Boundaries with Concentric Circles, 1975 and 2015

Sources: Florczyk et al. (2019) and author's analysis.

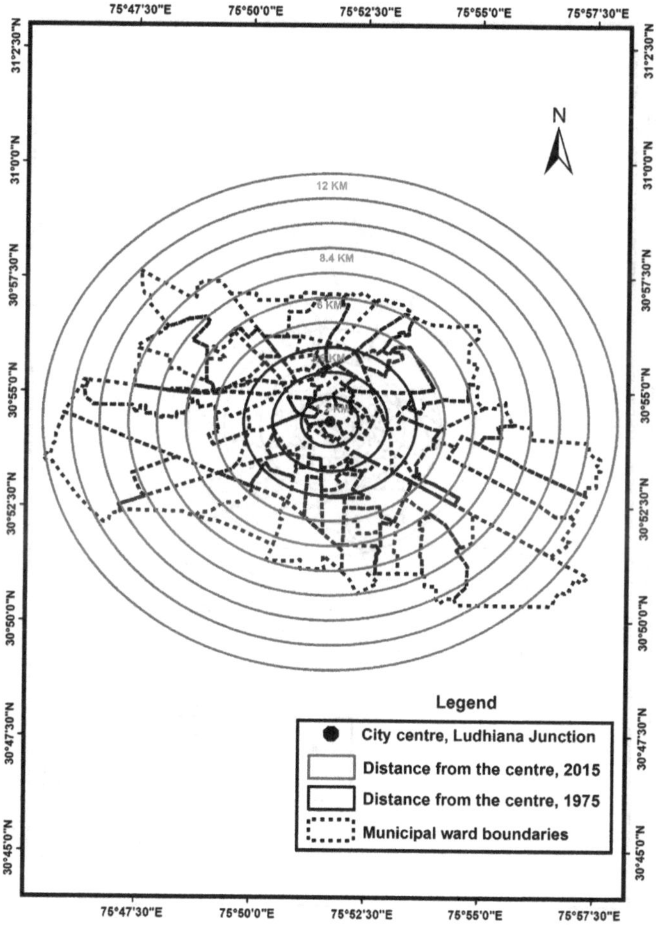

Ludhiana's (Punjab) Boundaries with Concentric Circles, 1975 and 2015
Sources: Florczyk et al. (2019) and author's analysis.

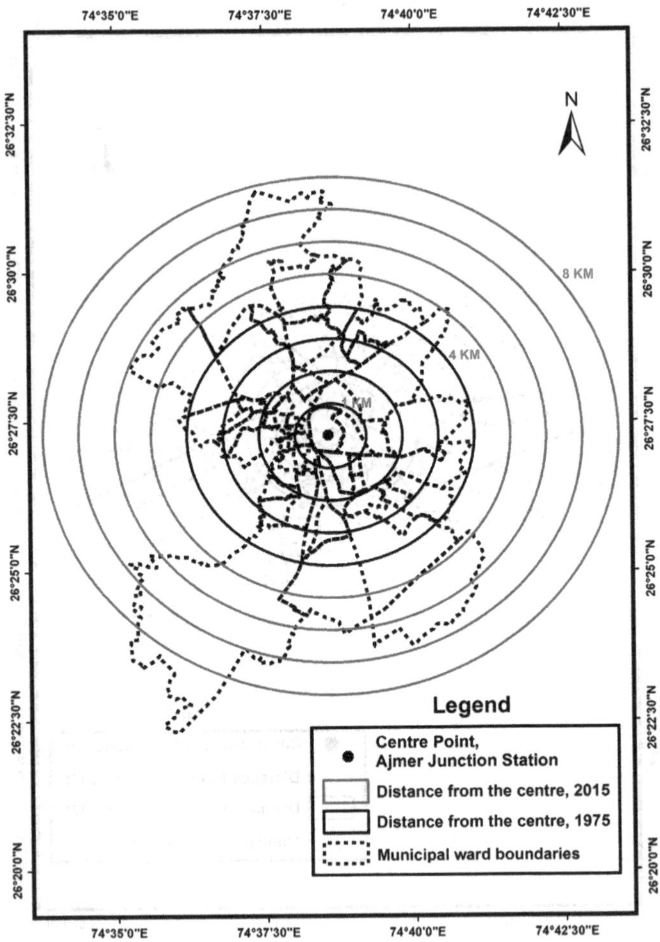

Ajmer's (Rajasthan) Boundaries with Concentric Circles, 1975 and 2015

Sources: Florczyk et al. (2019) and author's analysis.

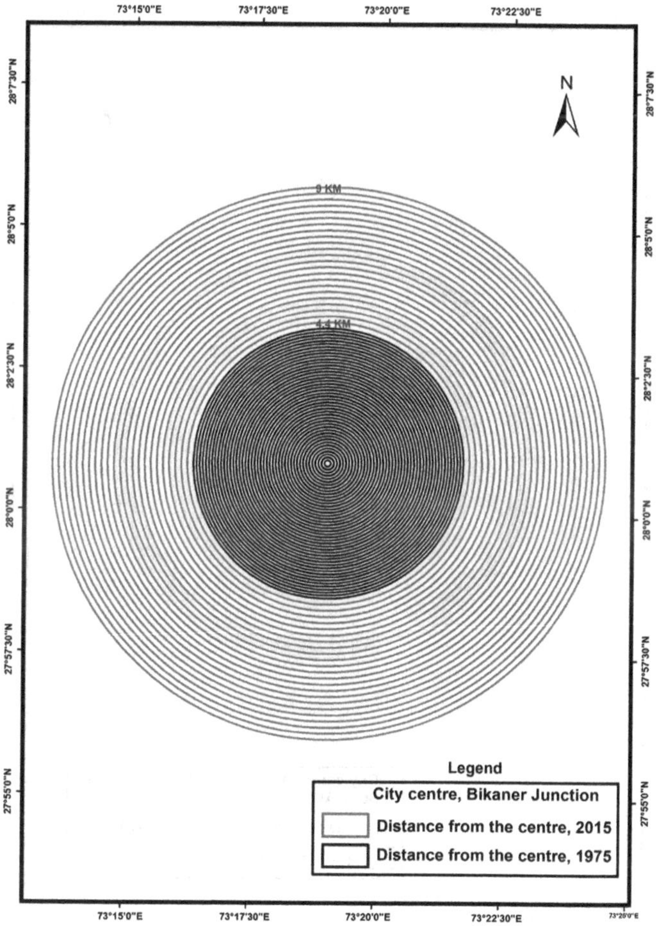

Bikaner's (Rajasthan) Boundaries with Concentric Circles, 1975 and 2015
Sources: Florczyk et al. (2019) and author's analysis.

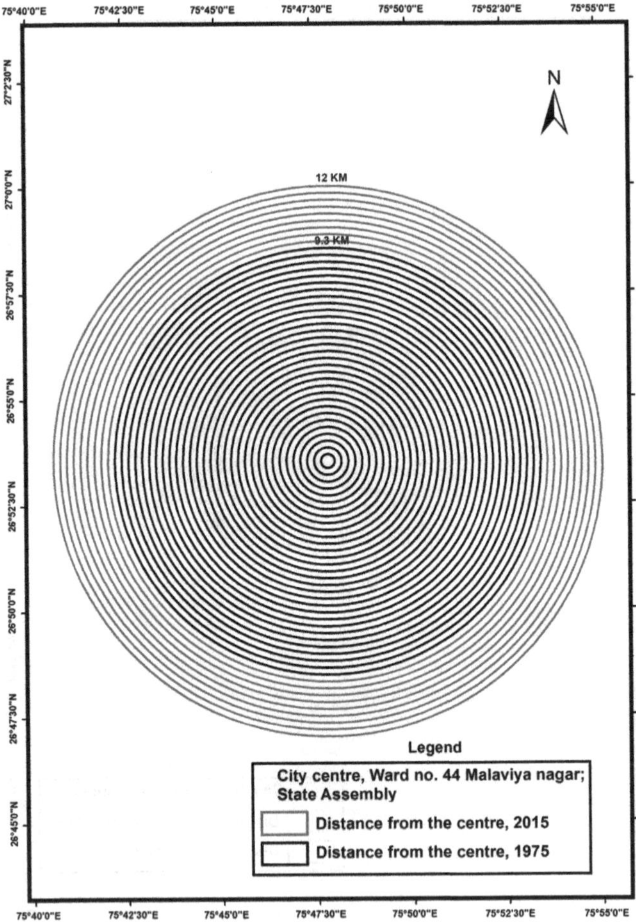

Jaipur's (Rajasthan) Boundaries with Concentric Circles, 1975 and 2015

Sources: Florczyk et al. (2019) and author's analysis.

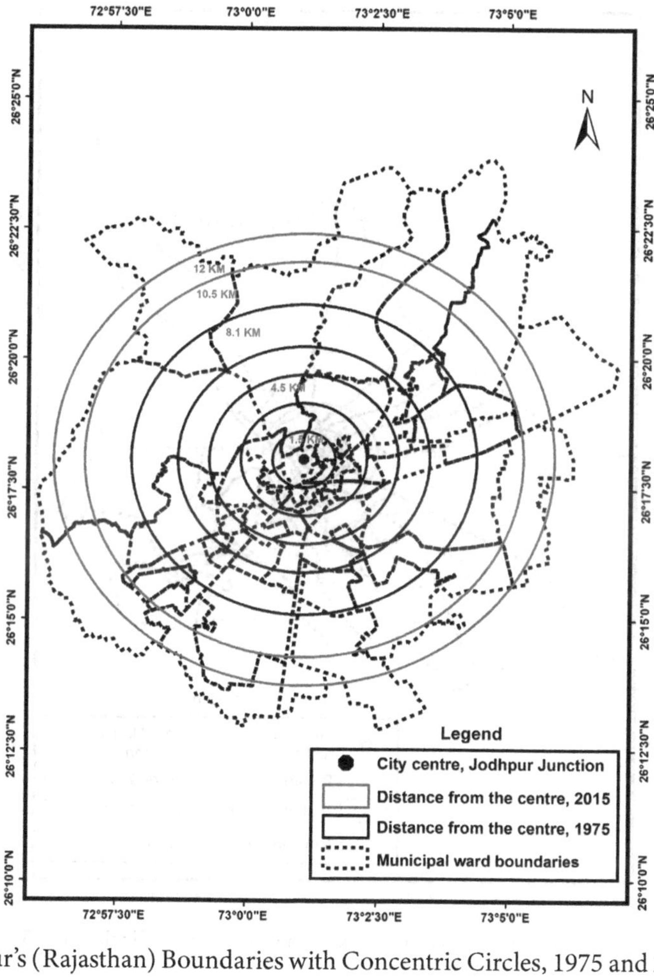

Jodhpur's (Rajasthan) Boundaries with Concentric Circles, 1975 and 2015

Sources: Florczyk et al. (2019) and author's analysis.

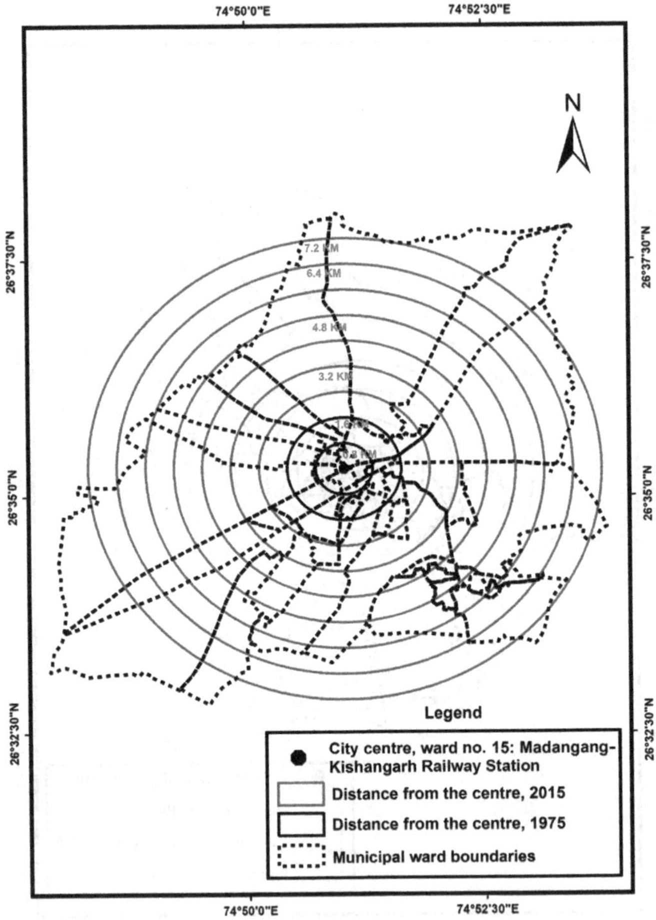

Kishangarh's (Rajasthan) Boundaries with Concentric Circles, 1975 and 2015

Sources: Florczyk et al. (2019) and author's analysis.

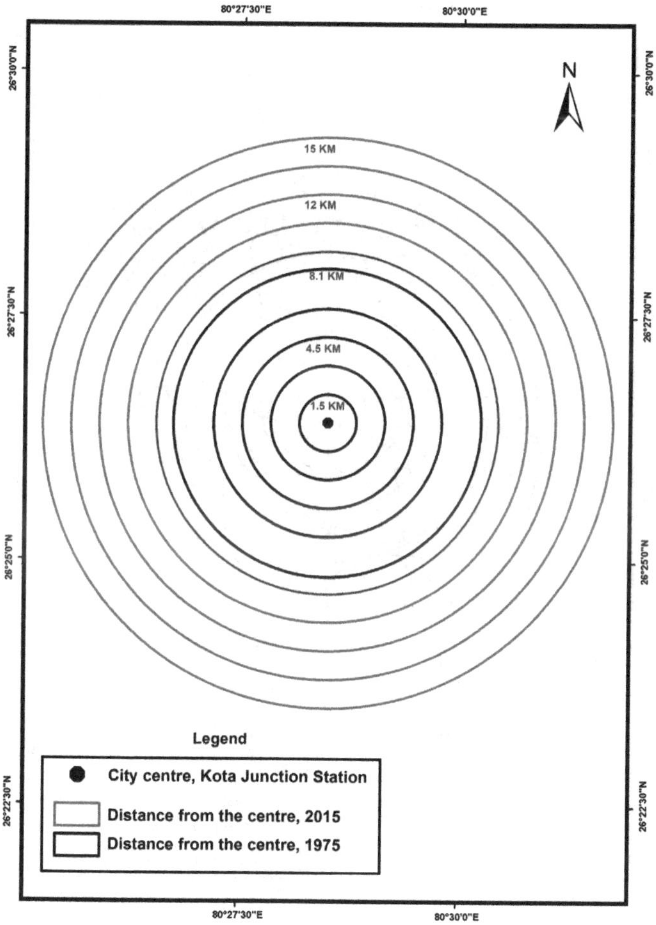

Kota's (Rajasthan) Boundaries with Concentric Circles, 1975 and 2015

Sources: Florczyk et al. (2019) and author's analysis.

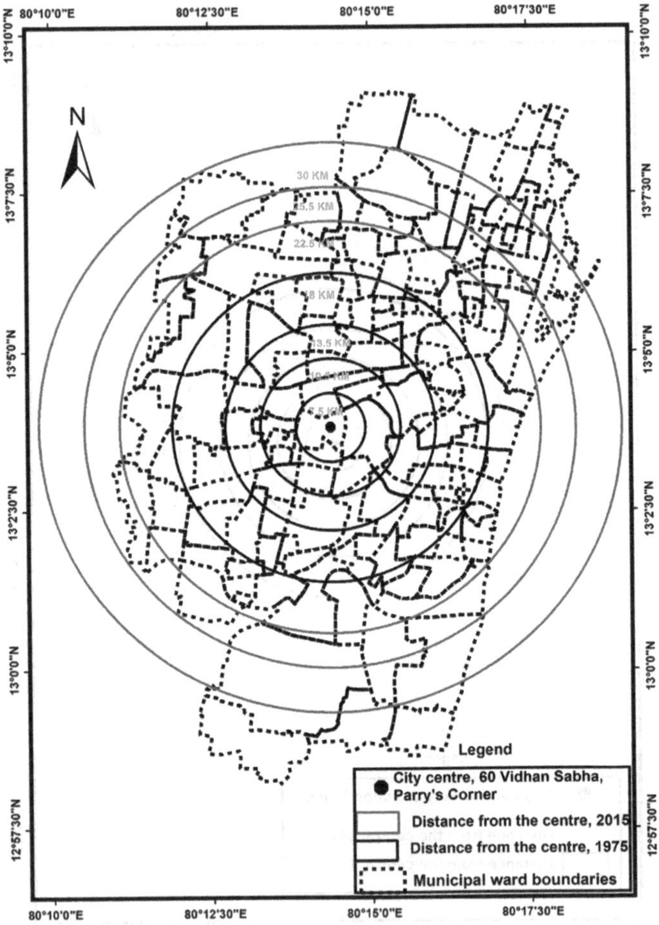

Chennai's (Tamil Nadu) Boundaries with Concentric Circles, 1975 and 2015

Sources: Florczyk et al. (2019) and author's analysis.

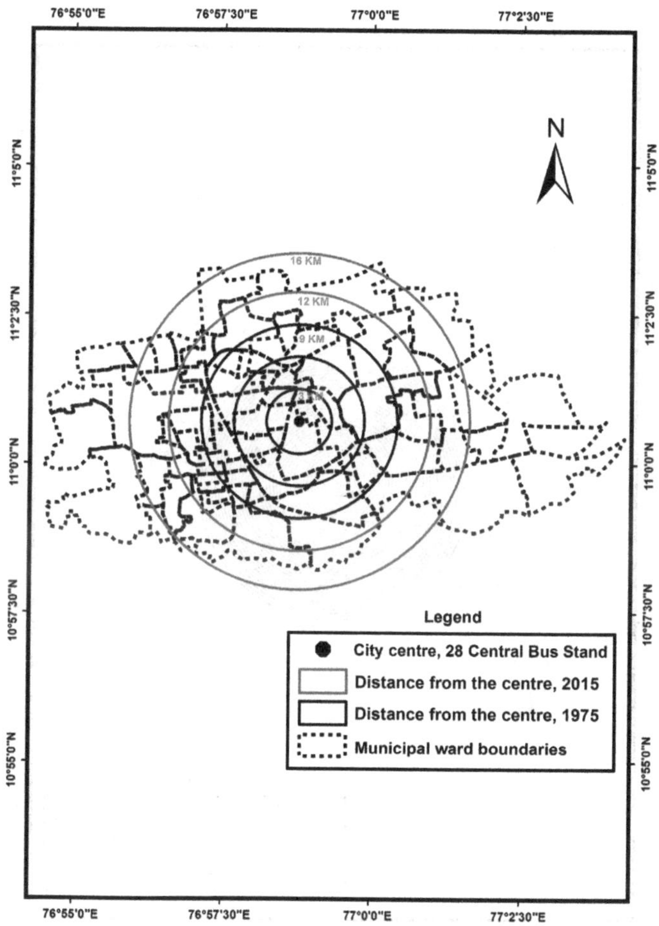

Coimbatore's (Tamil Nadu) Boundaries with Concentric Circles, 1975 and 2015

Sources: Florczyk et al. (2019) and author's analysis.

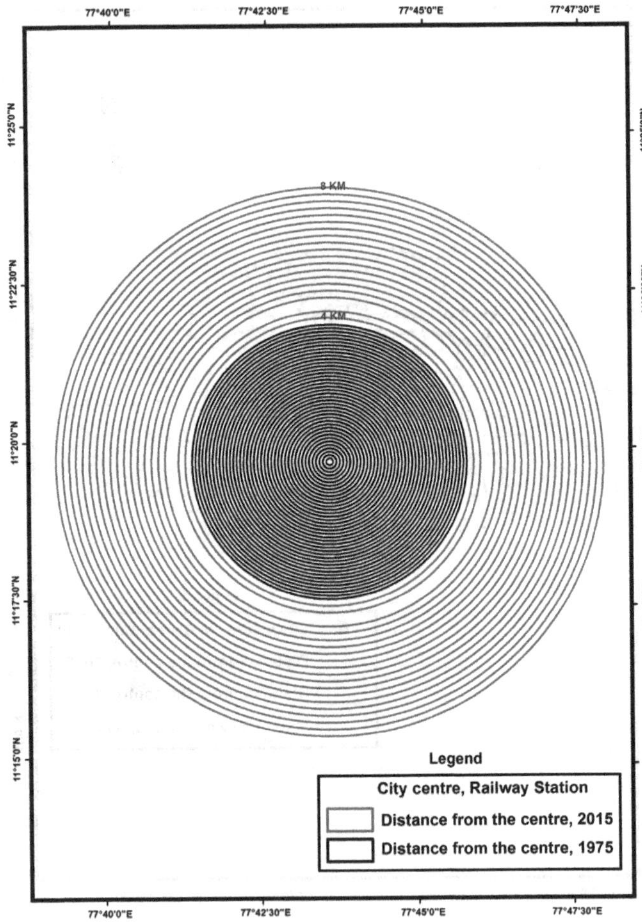

Erode's (Tamil Nadu) Boundaries with Concentric Circles, 1975 and 2015

Sources: Florczyk et al. (2019) and author's analysis.

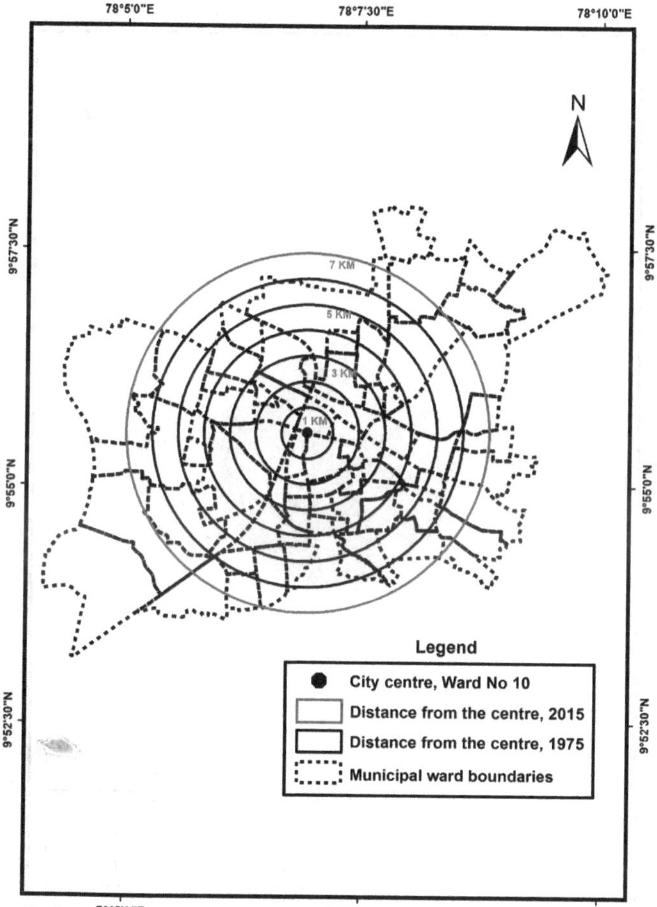

Madurai's (Tamil Nadu) Boundaries with Concentric Circles, 1975 and 2015

Sources: Florczyk et al. (2019) and author's analysis.

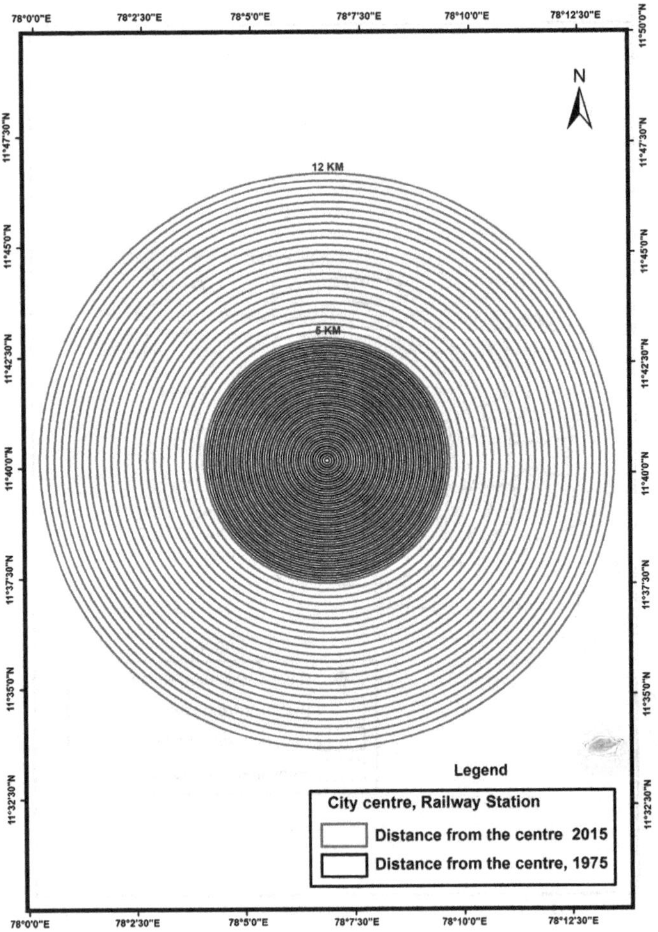

Salem's (Tamil Nadu) Boundaries with Concentric Circles, 1975 and 2015

Sources: Florczyk et al. (2019) and author's analysis.

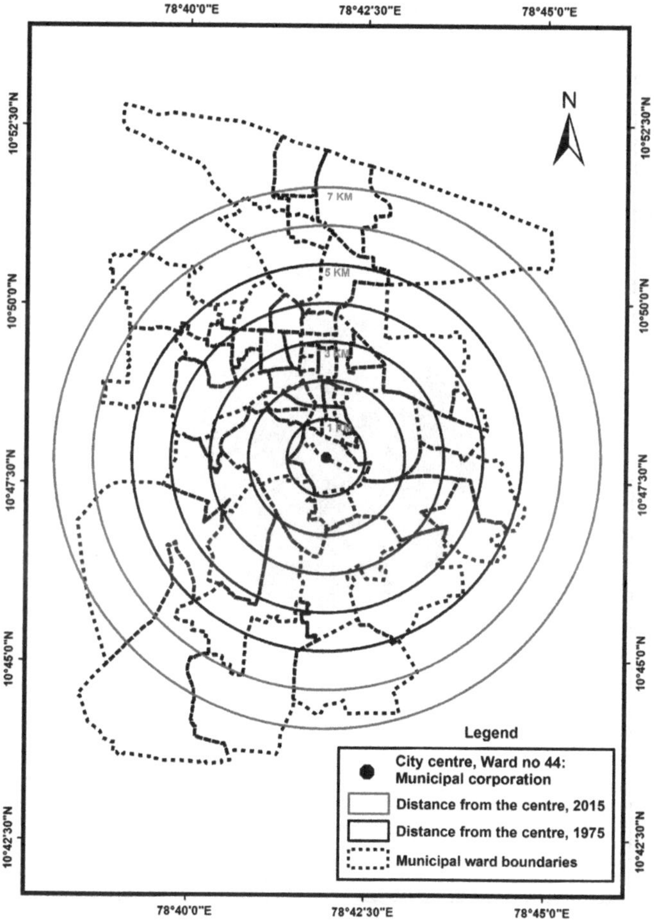

Tiruchirappalli's (Tamil Nadu) Boundaries with Concentric Circles, 1975 and 2015

Sources: Florczyk et al. (2019) and author's analysis.

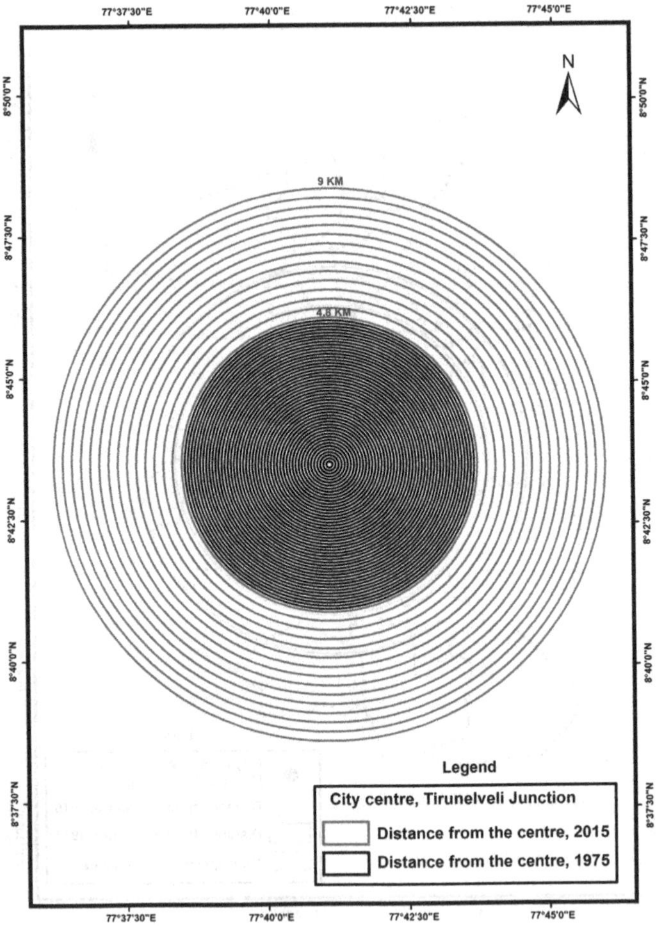

Tirunelveli's (Tamil Nadu) Boundaries with Concentric Circles, 1975 and 2015

Sources: Florczyk et al. (2019) and author's analysis.

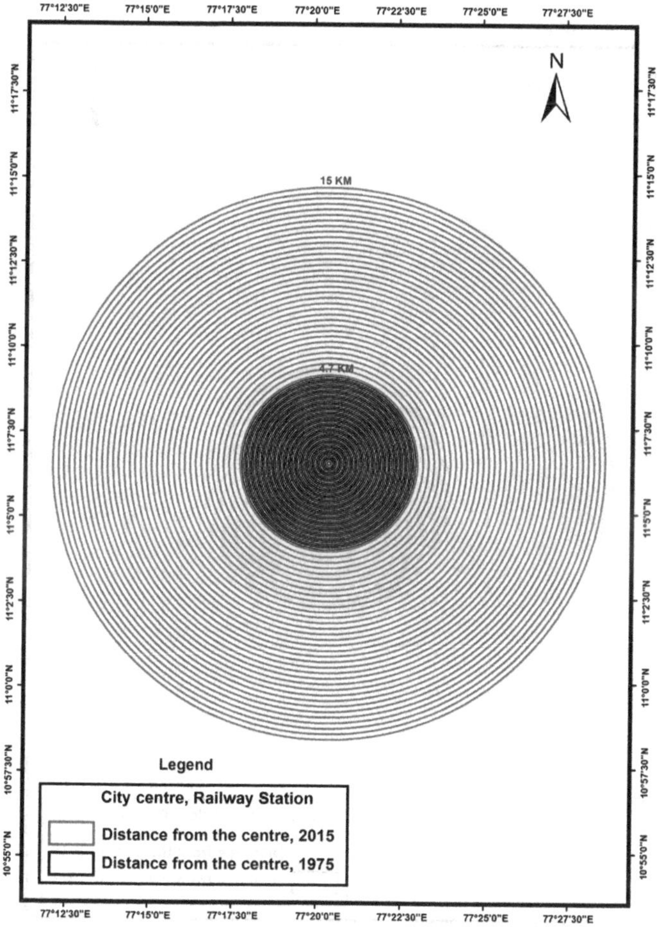

Tiruppur's (Tamil Nadu) Boundaries with Concentric Circles, 1975 and 2015

Sources: Florczyk et al. (2019) and author's analysis.

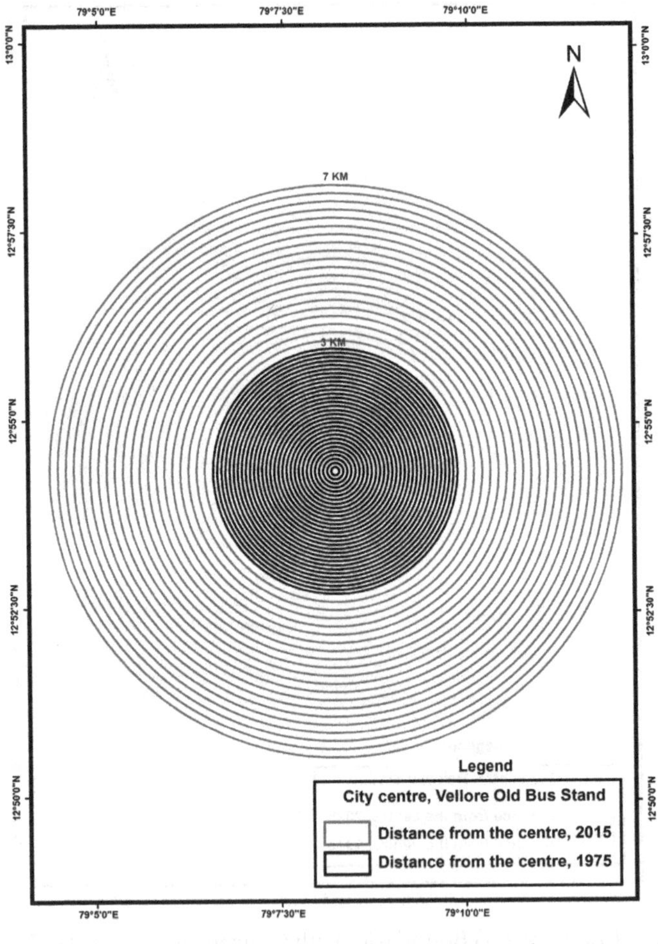

Vellore's (Tamil Nadu) Boundaries with Concentric Circles, 1975 and 2015

Sources: Florczyk et al. (2019) and author's analysis.

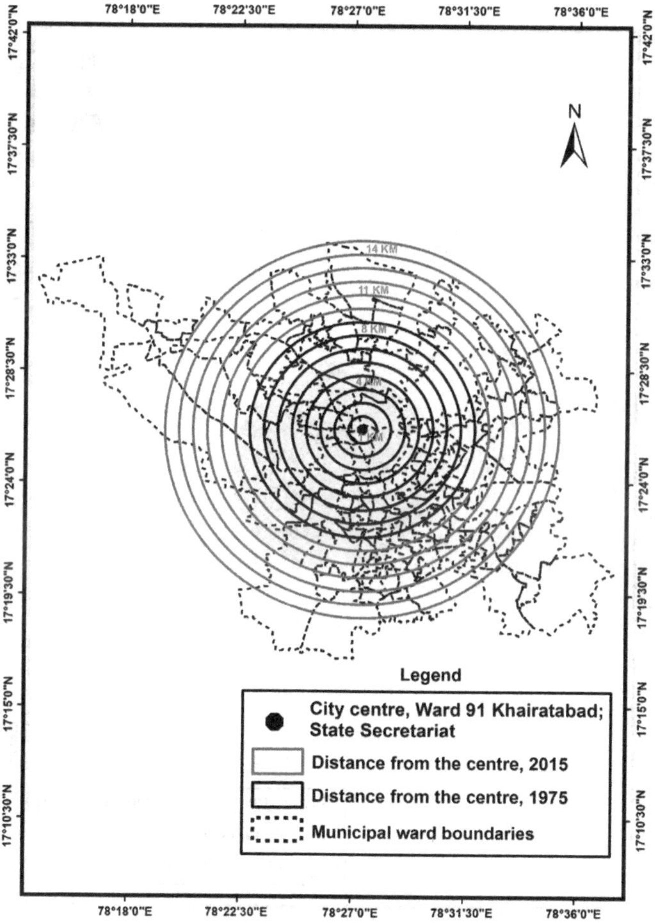

Hyderabad's (Telangana) Boundaries with Concentric Circles, 1975 and 2015

Sources: Florczyk et al. (2019) and author's analysis.

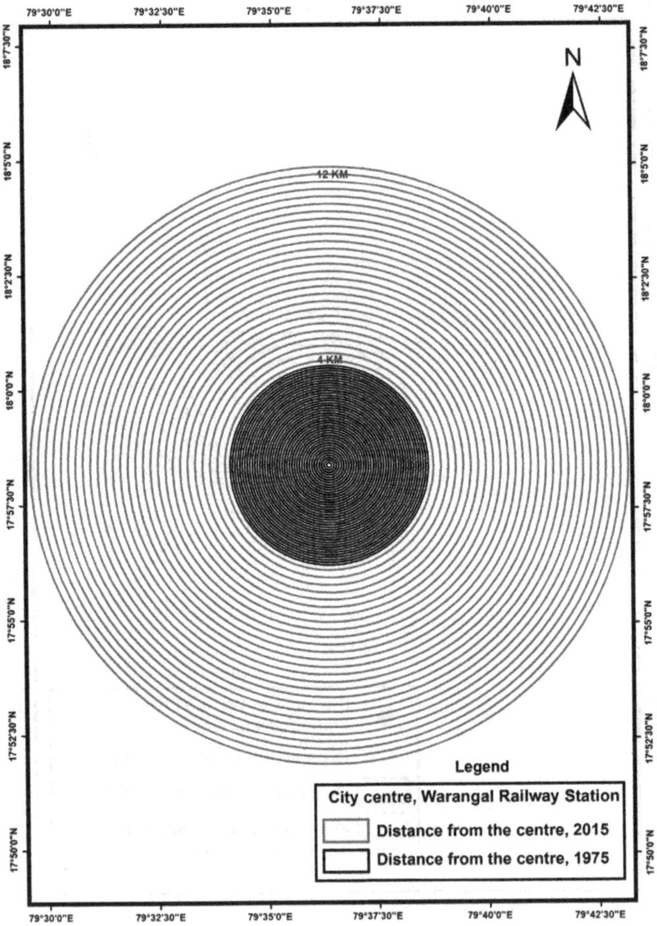

Warangal's (Telangana) Boundaries with Concentric Circles, 1975 and 2015

Sources: Florczyk et al. (2019) and author's analysis.

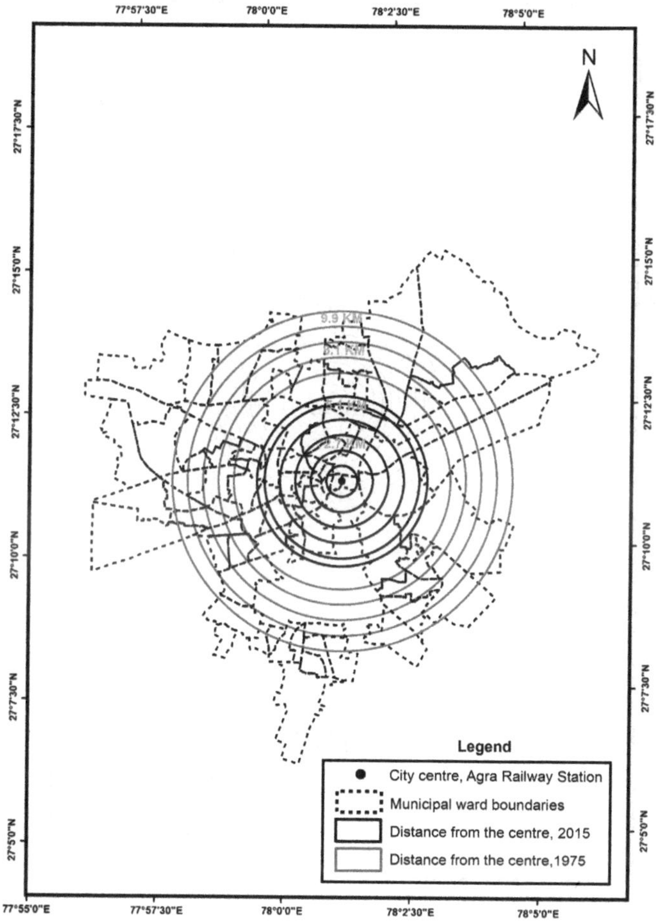

Agra's (Uttar Pradesh) Boundaries with Concentric Circles, 1975 and 2015

Sources: Florczyk et al. (2019) and author's analysis.

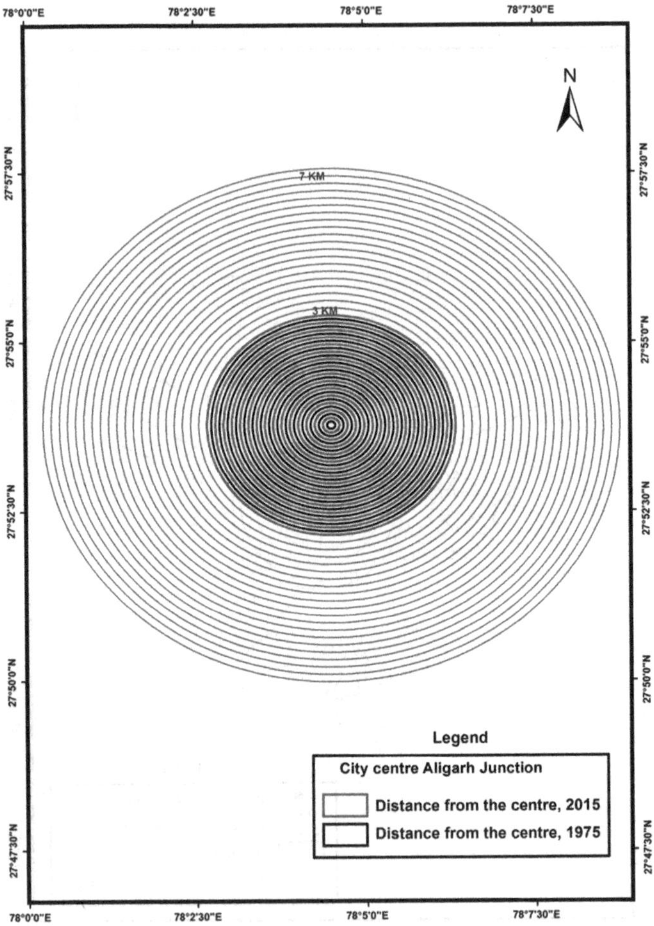

Aligarh's (Uttar Pradesh) Boundaries with Concentric Circles, 1975 and 2015

Sources: Florczyk et al. (2019) and author's analysis.

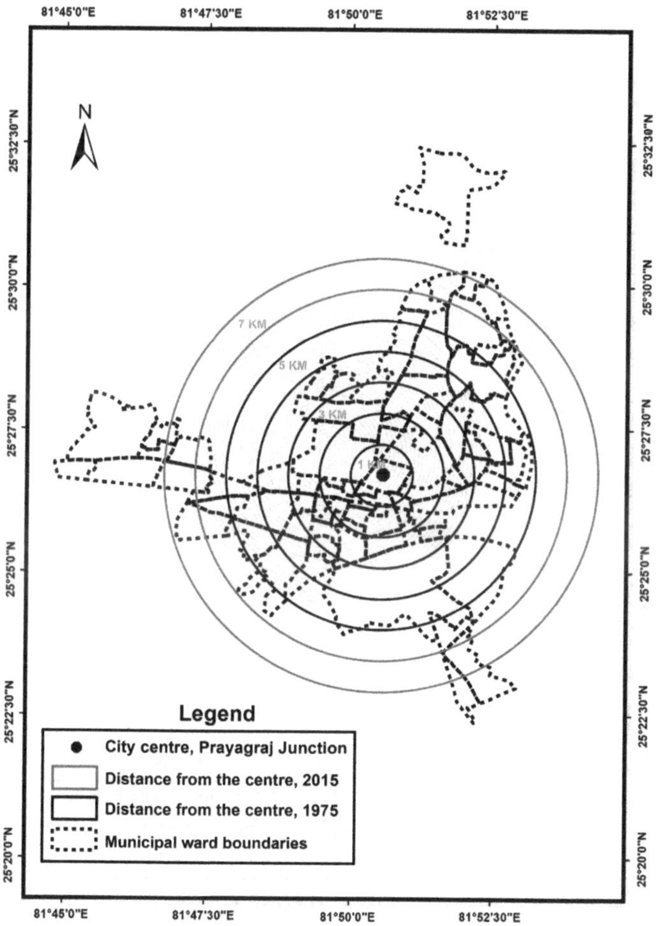

Allahabad's (Prayagraj's) (Uttar Pradesh) Boundaries with Concentric Circles, 1975 and 2015

Sources: Florczyk et al. (2019) and author's analysis.

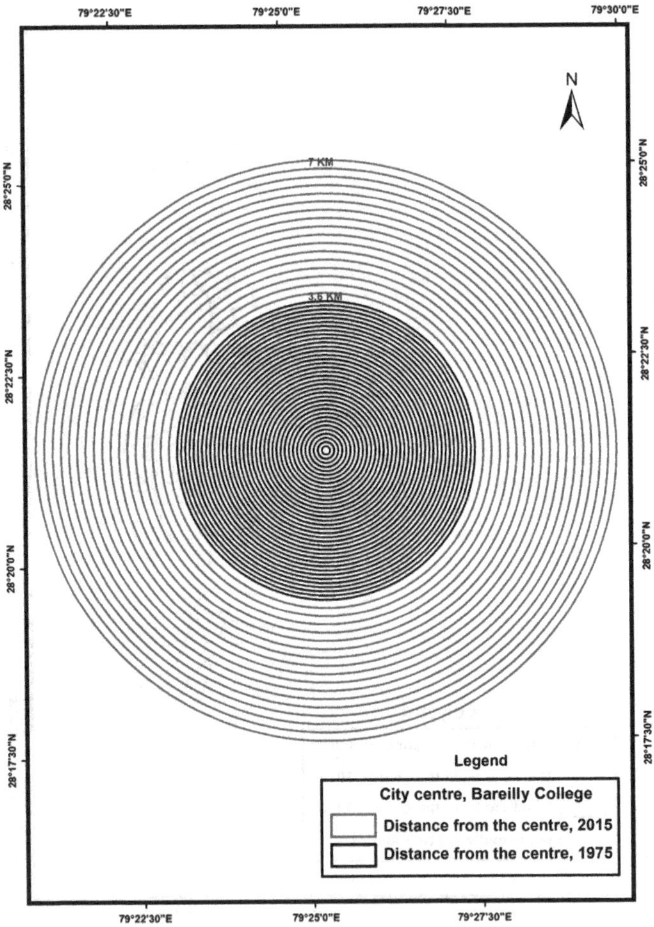

Bareilly's (Uttar Pradesh) Boundaries with Concentric Circles, 1975 and 2015

Sources: Florczyk et al. (2019) and author's analysis.

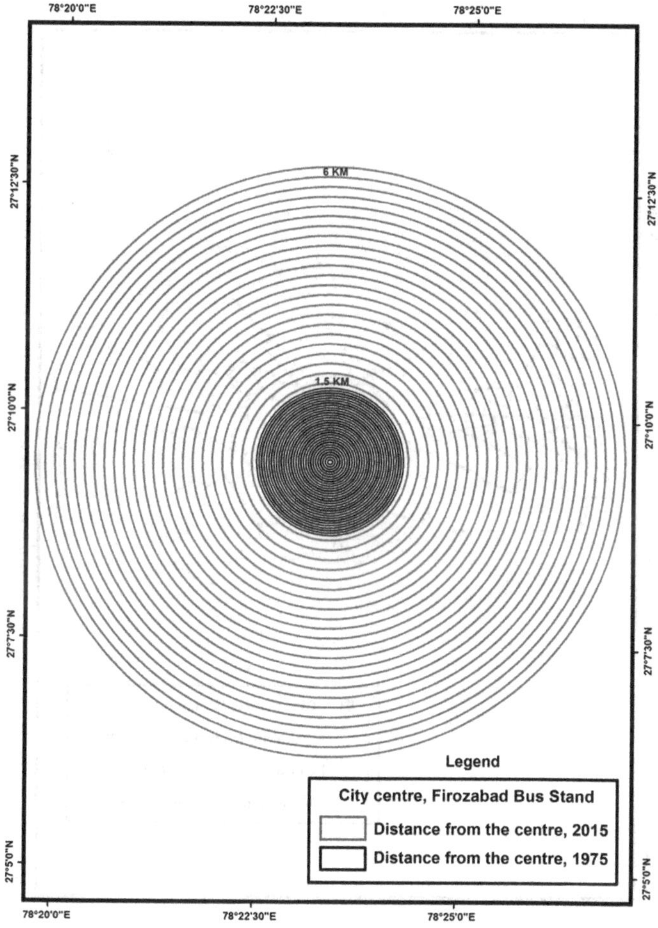

Firozabad's (Uttar Pradesh) Boundaries with Concentric Circles, 1975 and 2015

Sources: Florczyk et al. (2019) and author's analysis.

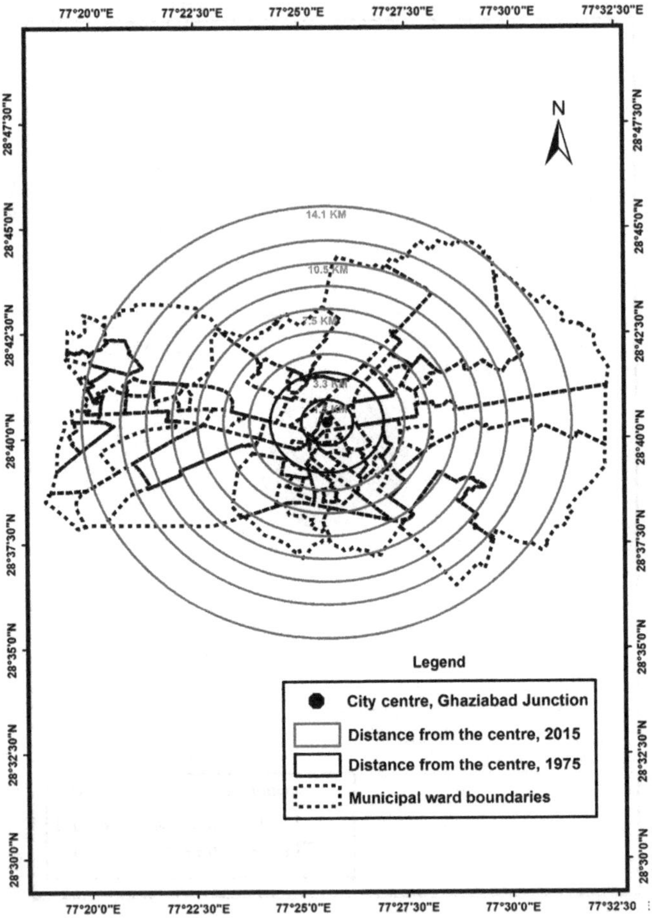

Ghaziabad's (Uttar Pradesh) Boundaries with Concentric Circles, 1975 and 2015

Sources: Florczyk et al. (2019) and author's analysis.

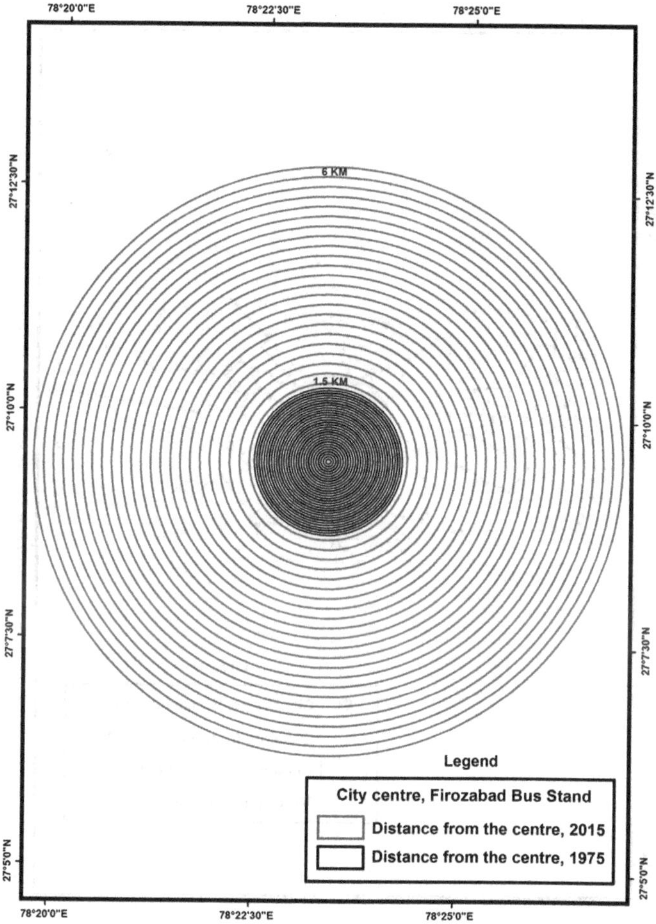

Firozabad's (Uttar Pradesh) Boundaries with Concentric Circles, 1975 and 2015

Sources: Florczyk et al. (2019) and author's analysis.

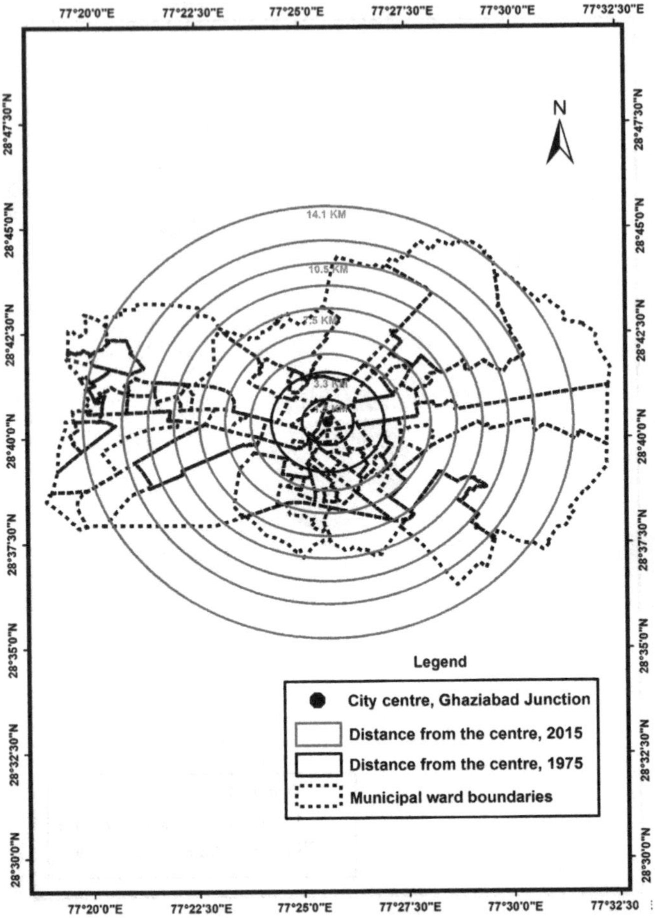

Ghaziabad's (Uttar Pradesh) Boundaries with Concentric Circles, 1975 and 2015

Sources: Florczyk et al. (2019) and author's analysis.

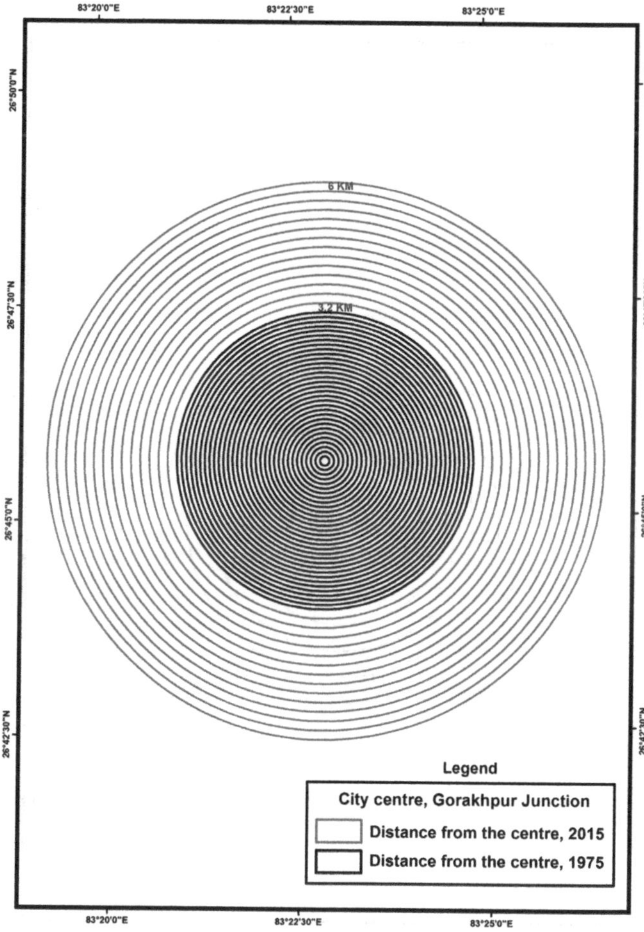

Gorakhpur's (Uttar Pradesh) Boundaries with Concentric Circles, 1975 and 2015

Sources: Florczyk et al. (2019) and author's analysis.

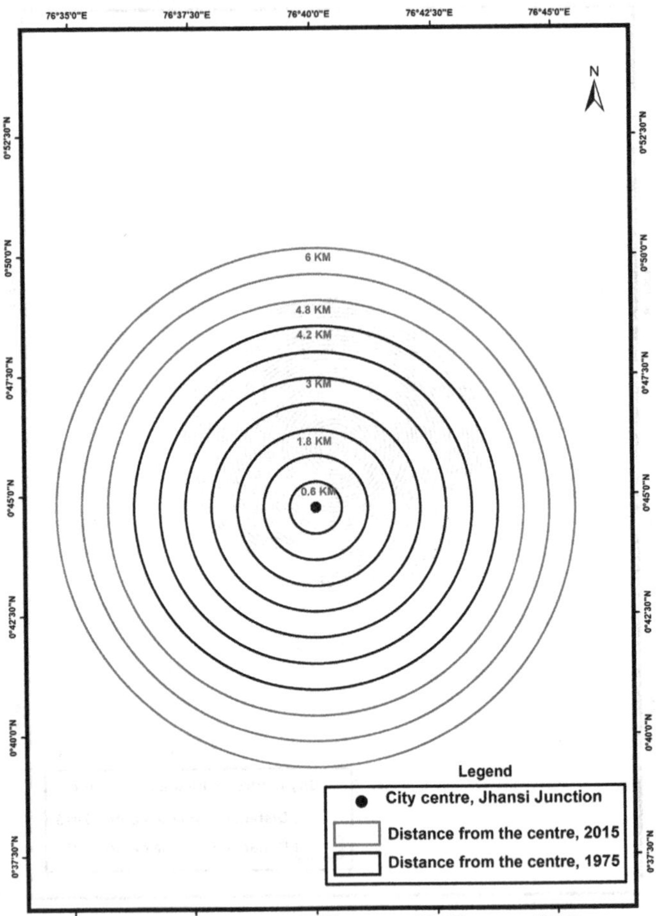

Jhansi's (Uttar Pradesh) Boundaries with Concentric Circles, 1975 and 2015

Sources: Florczyk et al. (2019) and author's analysis.

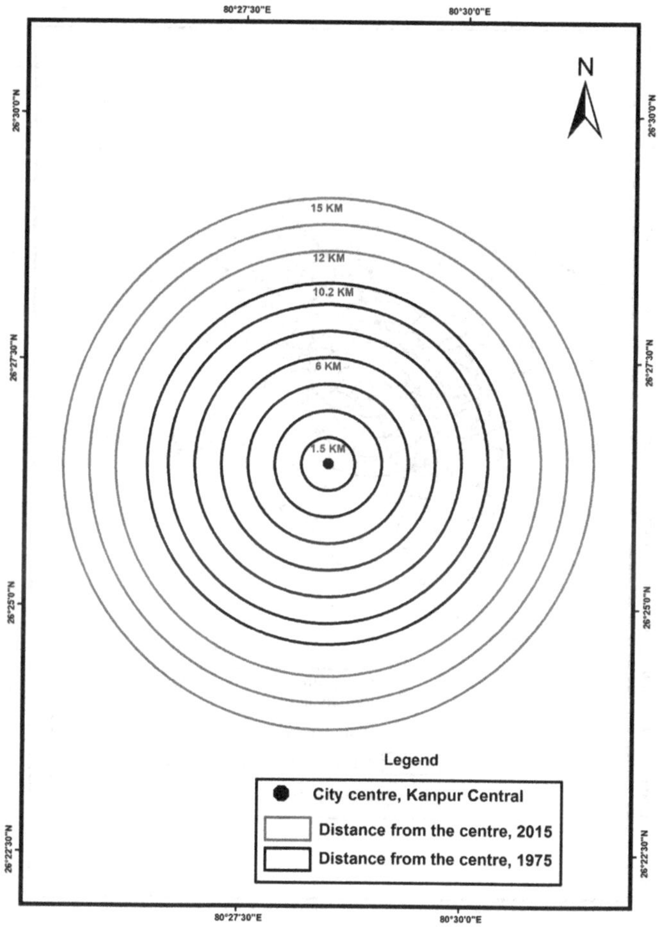

Kanpur's (Uttar Pradesh) Boundaries with Concentric Circles, 1975 and 2015

Sources: Florczyk et al. (2019) and author's analysis.

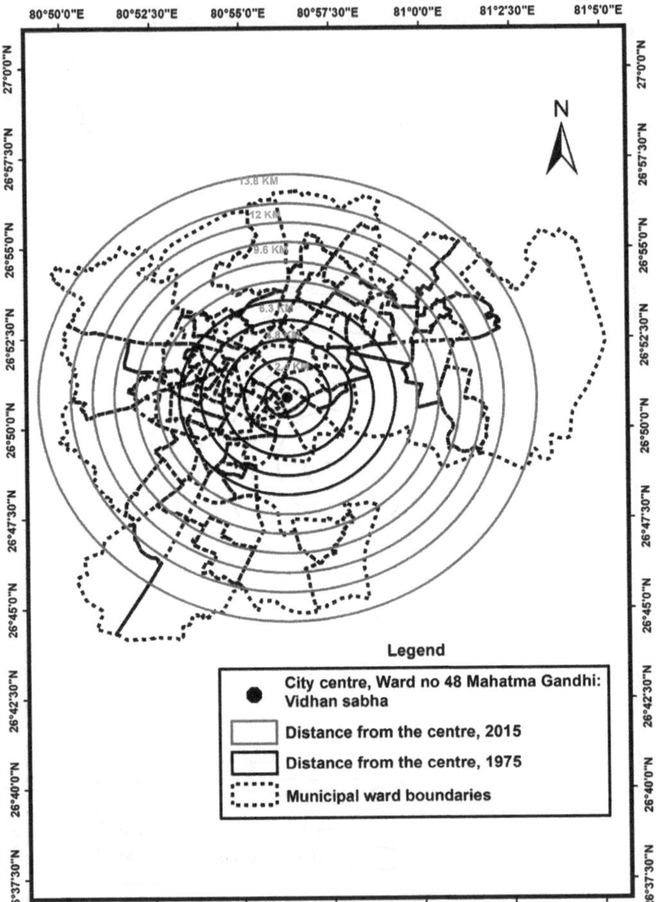

Lucknow's (Uttar Pradesh) Boundaries with Concentric Circles, 1975 and 2015

Sources: Florczyk et al. (2019) and author's analysis.

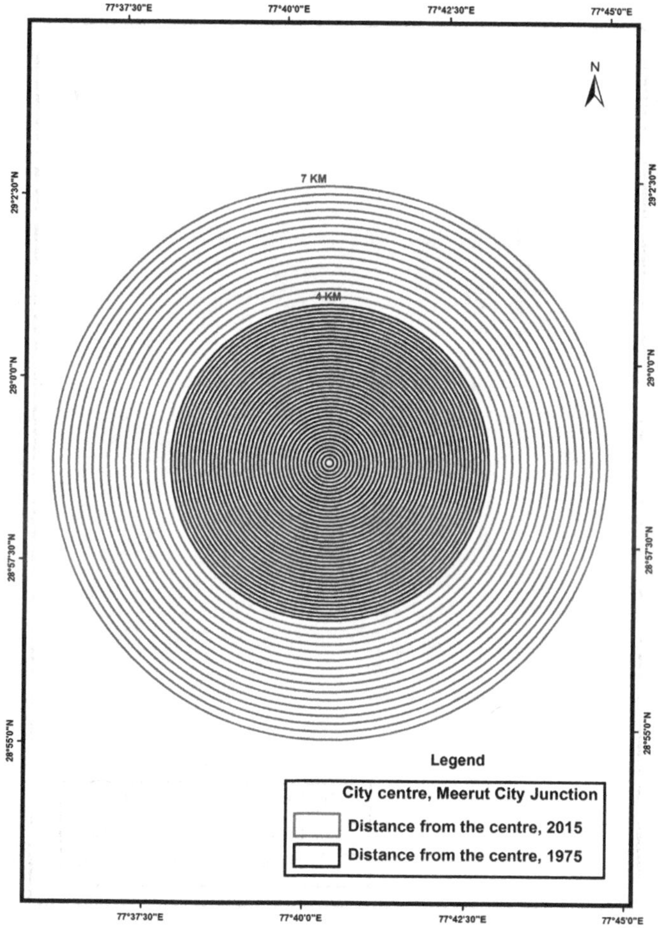

Meerut's (Uttar Pradesh) Boundaries with Concentric Circles, 1975 and 2015

Sources: Florczyk et al. (2019) and author's analysis.

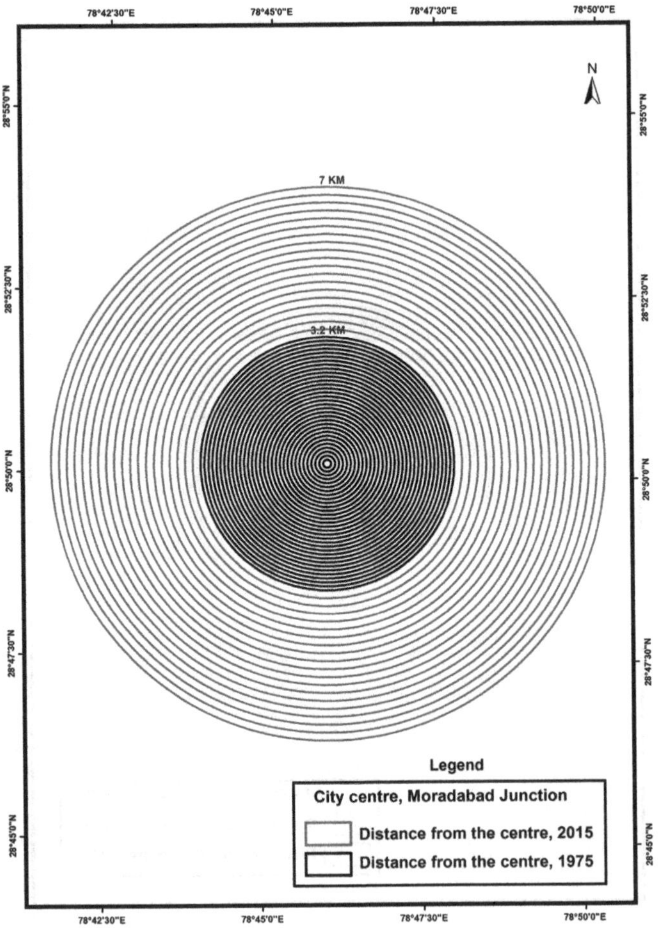

Moradabad's (Uttar Pradesh) Boundaries with Concentric Circles, 1975 and 2015

Sources: Florczyk et al. (2019) and author's analysis.

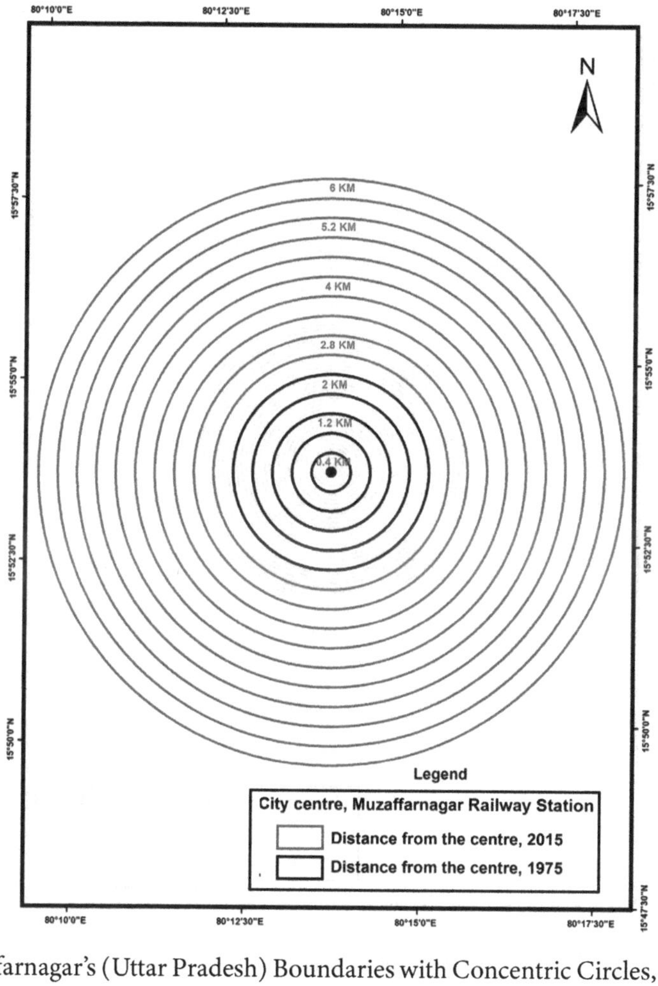

Muzaffarnagar's (Uttar Pradesh) Boundaries with Concentric Circles, 1975 and 2015

Sources: Florczyk et al. (2019) and author's analysis.

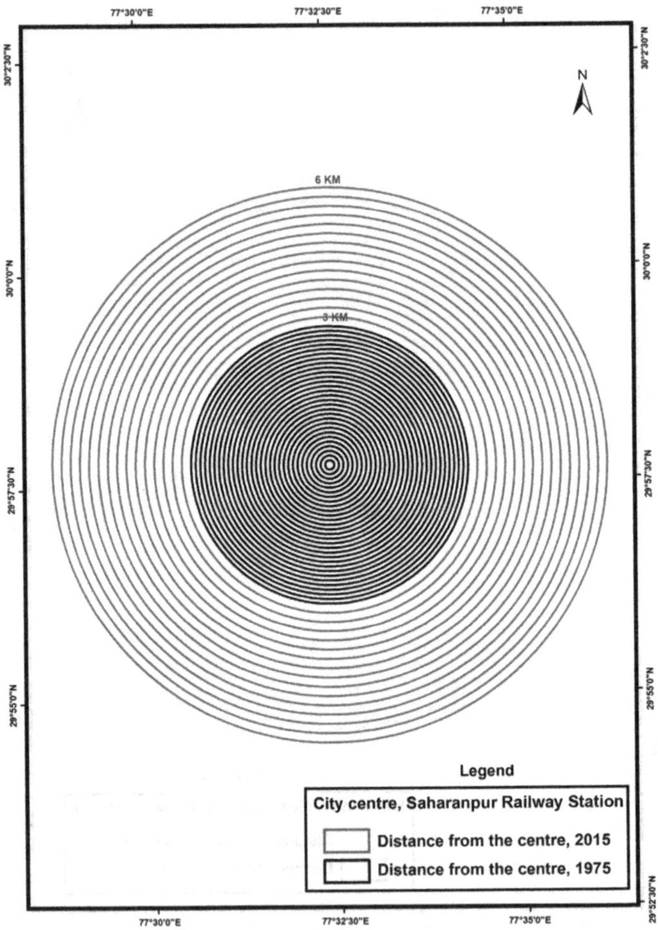

Saharanpur's (Uttar Pradesh) Boundaries with Concentric Circles, 1975 and 2015

Sources: Florczyk et al. (2019) and author's analysis.

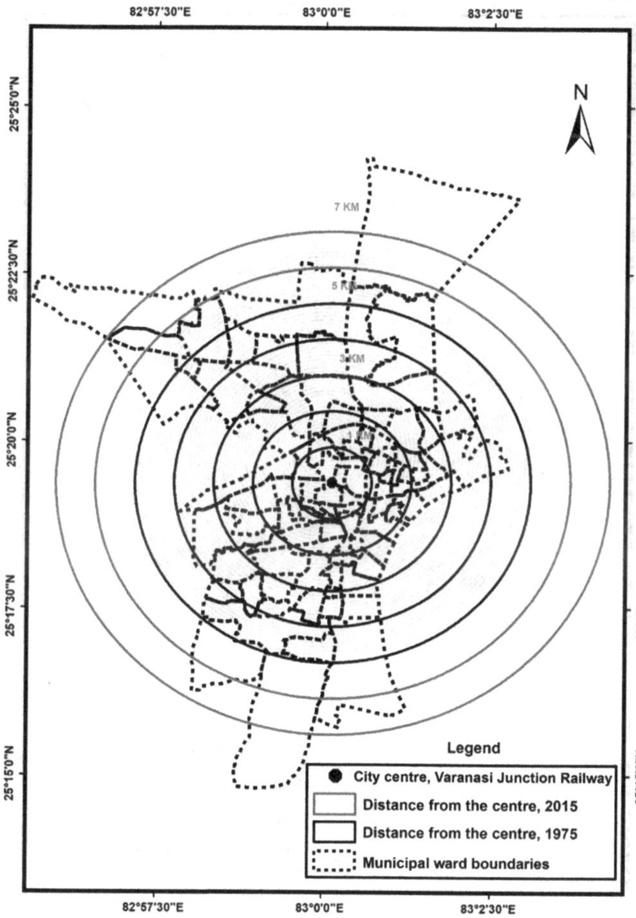

Varanasi's (Uttar Pradesh) Boundaries with Concentric Circles, 1975 and 2015

Sources: Florczyk et al. (2019) and author's analysis.

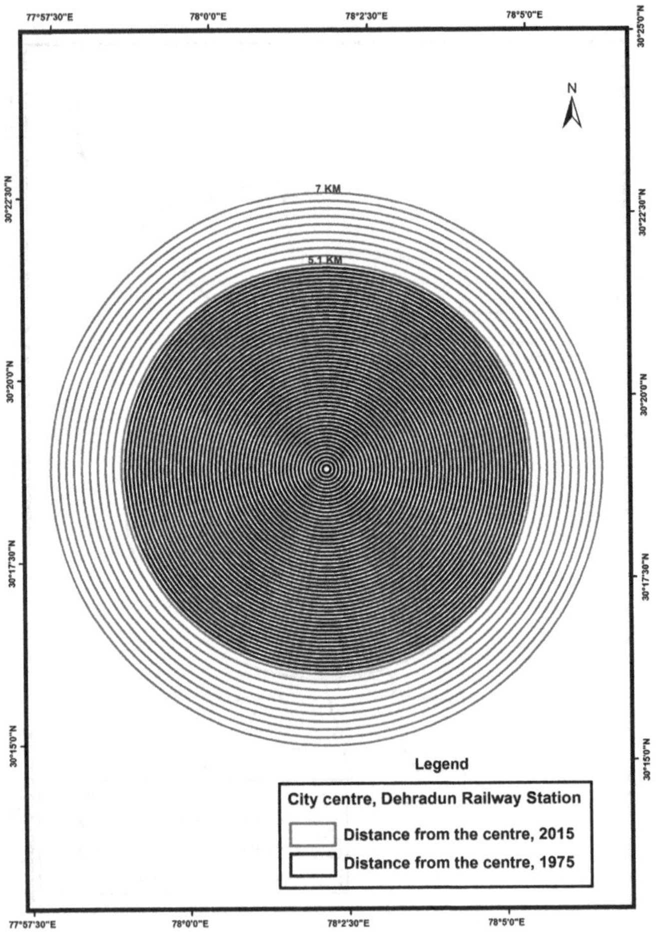

Dehradun's (Uttarakhand) Boundaries with Concentric Circles, 1975 and 2015

Sources: Florczyk et al. (2019) and author's analysis.

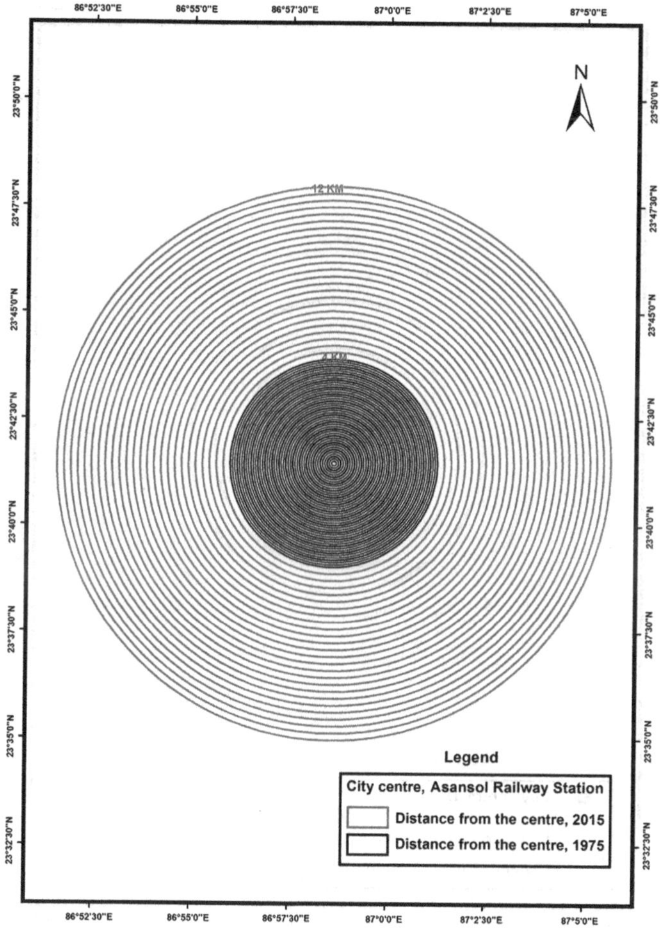

Asansol's (West Bengal) Boundaries with Concentric Circles, 1975 and 2015

Sources: Florczyk et al. (2019) and author's analysis.

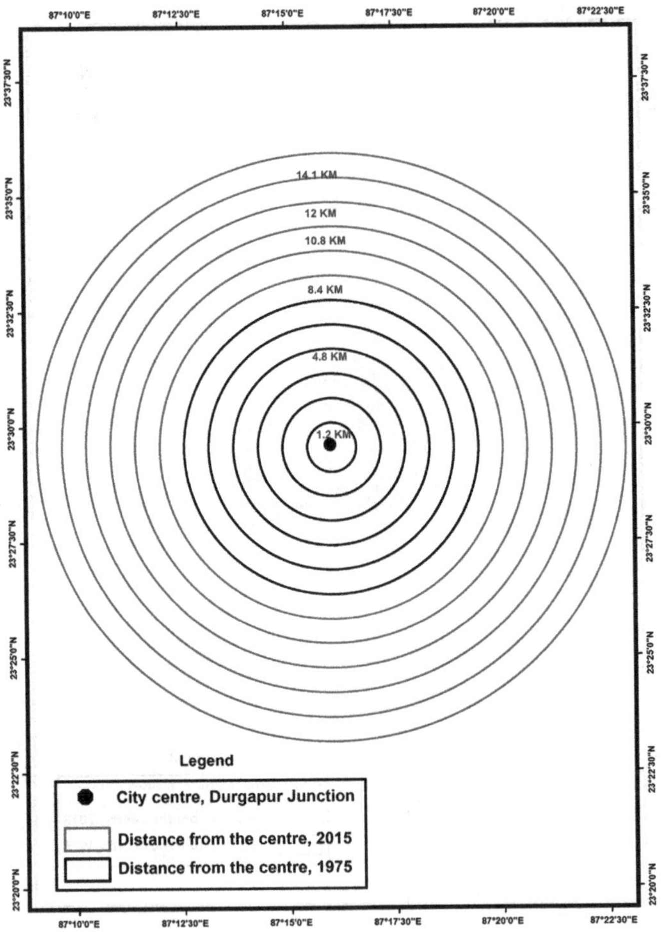

Durgapur's (West Bengal) Boundaries with Concentric Circles, 1975 and 2015

Sources: Florczyk et al. (2019) and author's analysis.

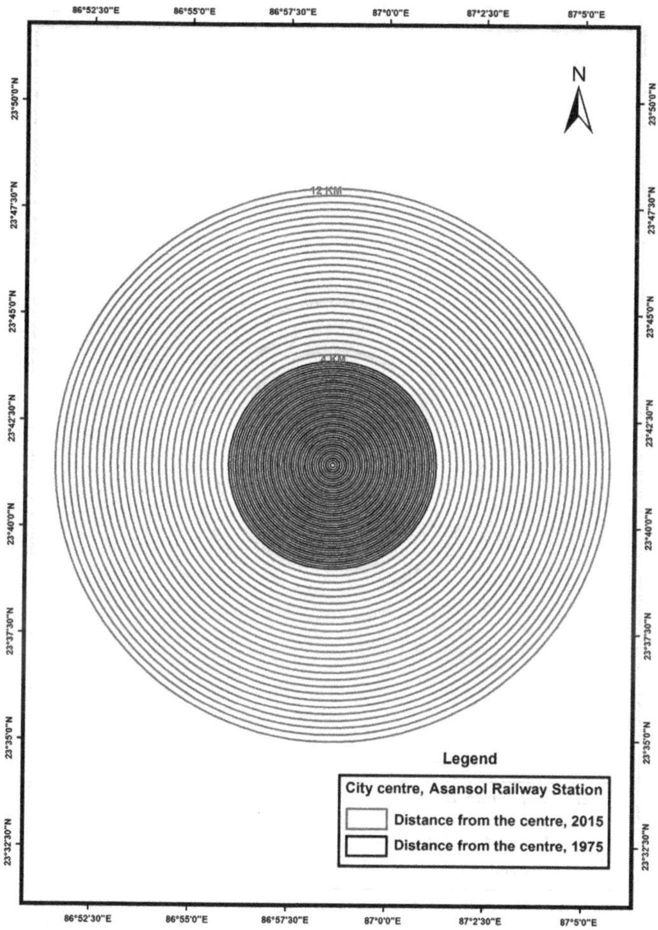

Asansol's (West Bengal) Boundaries with Concentric Circles, 1975 and 2015
Sources: Florczyk et al. (2019) and author's analysis.

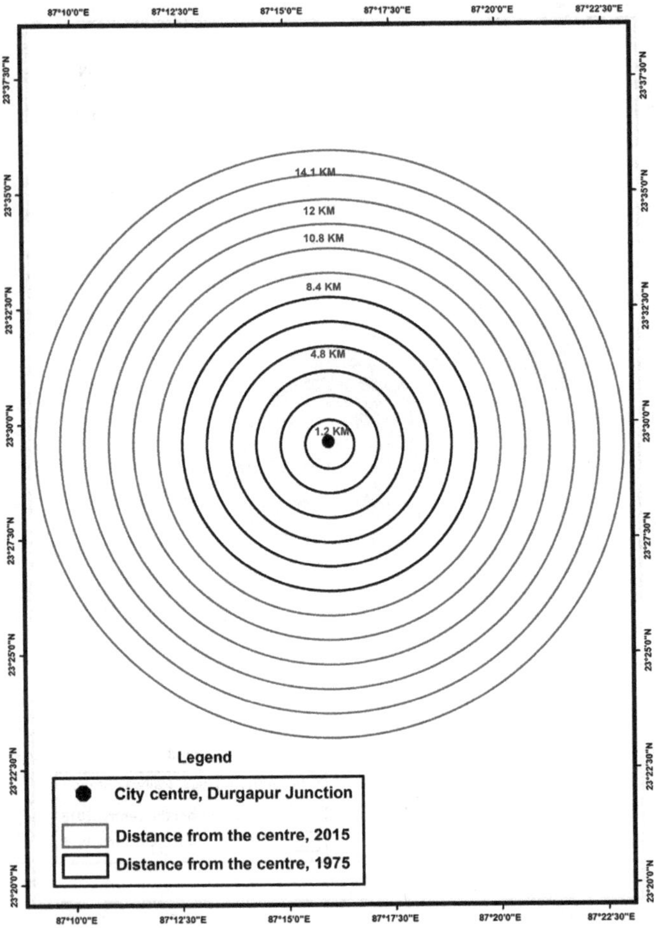

Durgapur's (West Bengal) Boundaries with Concentric Circles, 1975 and 2015

Sources: Florczyk et al. (2019) and author's analysis.

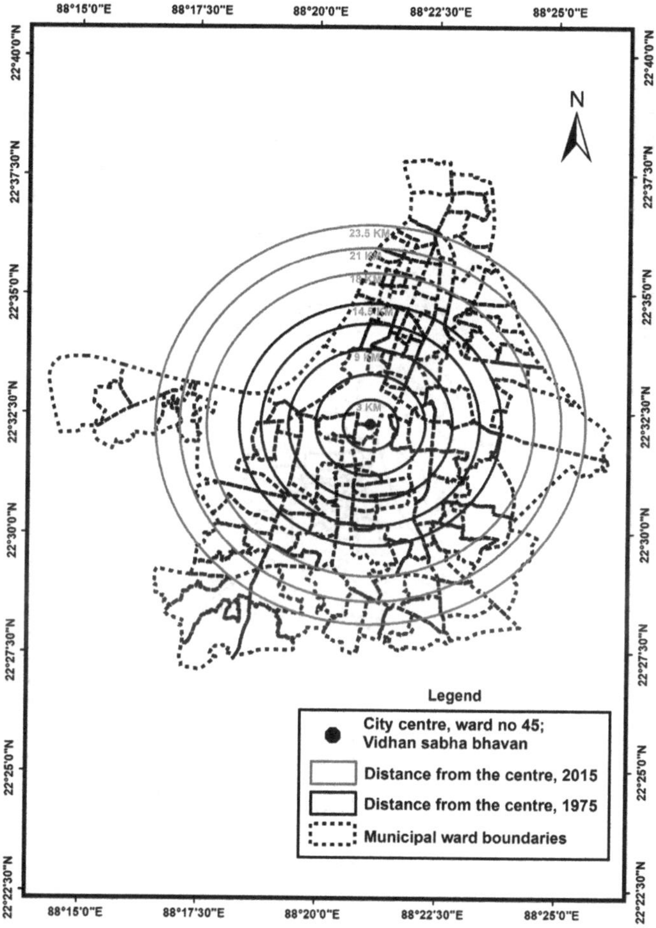

Kolkata's (West Bengal) Boundaries with Concentric Circles, 1975 and 2015

Sources: Florczyk et al. (2019) and author's analysis.

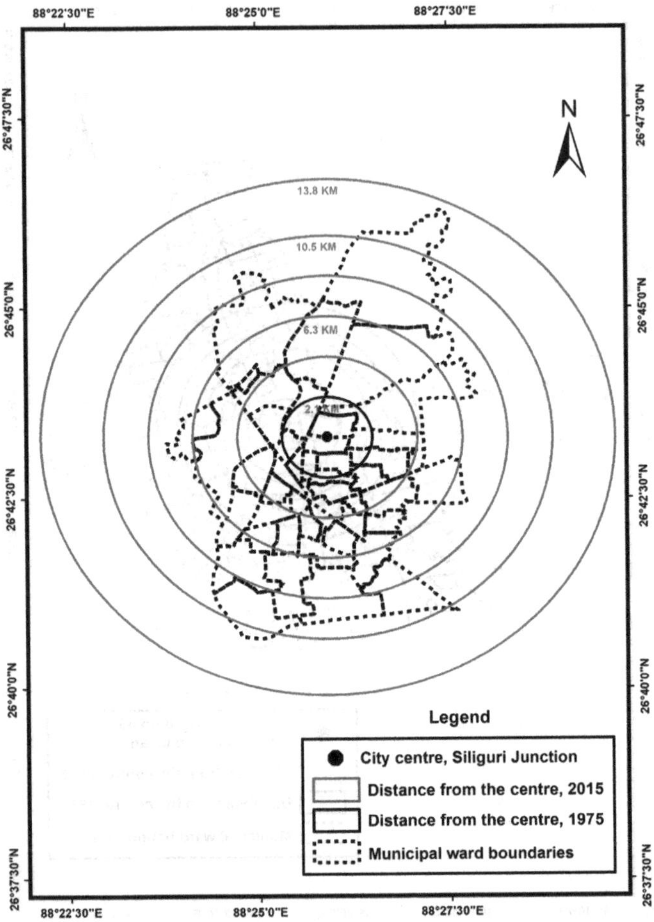

Siliguri's (West Bengal) Boundaries with Concentric Circles, 1975 and 2015

Sources: Florczyk et al. (2019) and author's analysis.

References

Alperovich, G. (1980). Determinants of population density gradient in Tel Aviv metropolitan area. *Urban Studies, 17*(2), 185–192.

Alperovich, G. (1982). Density gradients and the identification of the central business district. *Urban Studies, 19*(3), 313–320.

Alperovich, G., & Deutsch, J. (1992). Population density gradients and urbanisation measurement. *Urban Studies, 29*(8), 1323–1328.

Anas, A., Arnott, R., & Small, K. (1998). Urban spatial structure. *Journal of Economic Literature, 36*(3), 1426–1464.

Annunziata, S., & Cossu, M. (2010). "Urbanity beyond nostalgia: Discovering public life at the edge of the city of Rome." In: Clapson, M., & Hutchison, R. (Eds.), *Suburbanization in global society* (*Research in Urban Sociology, Vol. 10*) (pp. 131–152). Leeds: Emerald Group Publishing Limited. https://doi.org/10.1108/S1047-0042(2010)0000010008

Arifwidodo, S. (2014). "Exploring the relationship between urban form and residential energy use in Bandung, Indonesia." In: Sridhar, K. S., & Wan, G. (Eds.), *Urbanization in Asia: Governance, infrastructure and the environment.* New Delhi: Springer.

Asabere, P. K., & Owusu-Banahene, K. (1983). Population density function for Ghanaian (African) cities: An empirical note. *Journal of Urban Economics, 14*(3), 370–379.

Barrington-Leigh, C., & Millard-Ball, A. (2020). Global trends toward urban street-network sprawl. *Proceedings of the National Academy of Sciences, 117*(4), 1941–1950.

Baum-Snow, N. (2007). Did highways cause suburbanization? *The Quarterly Journal of Economics, 122*(2), 775–805.

Berry, B. J. L., Simmons, J. W., & Tennant, R. J. (1963). Urban population densities: Structure and change. *Geographical Review, 53*(3), 389–405.

Bertaud, A. (2018). *Order without design: How markets shape cities.* Cambridge, MA: MIT Press.

Bertaud, A. (2002). *Bangalore: Note on land use issues.* https://alainbertaud.com/wp-content/uploads/2013/06/AB_-Bangalore_Note_on_-land_Use_issues.pdf, p. 5.

Bertaud, A. (2004). *Mumbai FSI conundrum: The perfect storm: The four factors restricting the construction of new floor space in Mumbai.* Presentation available on www.alain-bertaud.com.

Bertaud, A. (2014). Converting land into affordable housing floor space. *World Bank Policy Research Working Paper*, (6870). Washington, DC: The World Bank.

Bertaud, A., & Brueckner, J. K. (2005). Analyzing building-height restrictions: Predicted impacts and welfare costs. *Regional Science and Urban Economics, 35*(2), 109–125.

Bertaud, A., & Malpezzi, S. (2003). The spatial distribution of population in 48 world cities: Implications for economies in transition. *Center for Urban Land Economics Research, University of Wisconsin, 32*(1), 54–55.

Bontje, M., & Burdack, J. (2011). "Post-suburbia in continental Europe." In: Phelps, N. A., & Wu, F. (Eds.), *International perspectives on suburbanization* (pp. 143–162). London: Palgrave Macmillan. https://doi.org/10.1057/9780230308626_8

Boob, T. N., & Rao, Y. R. M. (2012). Violation of building bye-laws and development control rules: A case study. *IOSR Journal of Mechanical and Civil Engineering, 2*(4), 48–59.

Broitman, D., & Koomen, E. (2020). The attraction of urban cores: Densification in Dutch city centres. *Urban Studies, 57*(9), 1920–1939. https://doi.org/10.1177/0042098019864019

Brueckner, J. K. (2009). "Government land use interventions: An economic analysis." In: Lall, S. V., Freire, M., Yuen, B., Rajack, R., & Helluin, J. J. (Eds.), *Urban land markets: Improving land management for successful urbanization* (pp. 3–23). Dordrecht: Springer Netherlands.

Brueckner, J. K. (2011). Why cities exist. In: *Lectures in Urban Economics* (pp. 1–22). Cambridge, MA: MIT Press.

Brueckner, J. K., & Franco, S. F. (2018). Employer-paid parking, mode choice, and suburbanization. *Journal of Urban Economics, 104*, 35–46.

Brueckner, J. K., & Sridhar, K. S. (2012). Measuring welfare gains from relaxation of land-use restrictions: The case of India's building-height limits. *Regional Science and Urban Economics, 42*(6), 1061–1067.

Chakravorty, S. (2000). "From colonial city to globalizing city? The far-from-complete spatial transformation of Calcutta." In: Marcuse, P., & van Kempen, R. (Eds.), *Globalizing cities: A new spatial order?* (pp. 56–77). Oxford: Blackwell Publishers.

Chimanna, R. R., & Kulkarni, S. S. (2020). Evaluating urban sprawl requirements for local infrastructure facilities of Kolhapur City. *International Journal of Research in Engineering, Science and Management, 3*(8), 8–16.

Ciccone, A., & Hall, R. E. (1993). Productivity and the density of economic activity. NBER Working Paper 4313. Cambridge, MA: National Bureau of Economic Research. https://www.nber.org/papers/w4313

Clapson, M., & Hutchison, R. (Eds.). (2010). *Suburbanization in global society* (*Research in Urban Sociology, Vol. 10*). Leeds: Emerald Group Publishing Limited.

Clark, C. (1951). Urban population densities. *Journal of the Royal Statistical Society. Series A (General), 114*(4), 490–496.

Denis, E., & Marius-Gnanou, K. (2011). Toward a better appraisal of urbanization in India. A fresh look at the landscape of morphological agglomerates. *Cybergeo: European Journal of Geography, 569*, 1–32.

Dowall, D. E., & Monkkonen, P. (2008). Urban development and land markets in Chennai, India. *International Real Estate Review, 11*(2), 142–165.

Drèze, J., & Sen, A. (Eds.). (1997). *Indian development: Selected regional perspectives.* New Delhi: Oxford University Press.

Edmonston, B., & Davies, O. (1976). Population suburbanization in the Western region of the United States, 1900–1970. *Land Economics, 52*(3), 393–403.

Edmonston, B., & Guterbock, T. M. (1984). Is suburbanization slowing down? Recent trends in population deconcentration in US metropolitan areas. *Social Forces*, *62*(4), 905–925.

Firman, T. (2011). "Post-suburban elements in an Asian extended metropolitan region: The case of Jabodetabek (Jakarta Metropolitan Area)." In: Phelps, N. A., & Wu, F. (Eds.), *International perspectives on suburbanization* (pp. 195–209). London: Palgrave Macmillan. https://doi.org/10.1057/9780230308626_11

Florczyk, A. J., Corbane, C., Schiavina, M., Pesaresi, M., Maffenini, L., Melchiorri, M., Politis, P., Sabo, F., Freire, S., Ehrlich, D., Kemper, T., Tommasi, P., Airaghi, D., & Zanchetta, L. (2019). *GHS Urban Centre Database 2015, multitemporal and multidimensional attributes, R2019A*. European Commission, Joint Research Centre (JRC) [Dataset]. PID: https://data.jrc.ec.europa.eu/dataset/53473144-b88c-44bc-b4a3-4583ed1f547e

Franco, S. F. (2020). Parking prices and availability, mode choice and urban form. International Transport Forum Discussion Paper, No. 2020/03. Paris: Organisation for Economic Co-operation and Development (OECD), International Transport Forum. https://doi.org/10.1787/04ae37c3-en

Garcia-Lopez, M.-À. (2012). Urban spatial structure, suburbanization and transportation in Barcelona. *Journal of Urban Economics*, *72*(2–3), 176–190.

Gaspar, J., & Glaeser, E. L. (1998). Information technology and the future of cities. *Journal of Urban Economics*, *43*(1), 136–156.

Giuliano, G. (1998). Information technology, work patterns and intra-metropolitan location: A case study. *Urban Studies*, *35*(7), 1077–1095.

Glaeser, E. L., & Kahn, M. E. (2001). Decentralized employment and the transformation of the American city. *Brookings-Wharton Papers on Urban Affairs*, *2001*, 1–63.

Gnat, S., & Bas, M. (2013). Statistical analysis of chosen aspects of the suburbanization process in Szczecin in 2006-2011. *Real Estate Management and Valuation*, *21*(3), 71–80.

Government of Tamil Nadu Tamil Nadu Urban Development Fund. (2006). *City Corporate Cum Business Plan for Coimbatore Corporation*. Wilbur Smith Associates Private Limited.

Guest, A. M. (1975). Population suburbanization in American metropolitan areas, 1940–1970. *Geographical Analysis*, *7*(3), 267–283.

Hanlon, B., & Vicino, T. J. (Eds.). (2018). *The Routledge companion to the suburbs*. London: Routledge.

Haynes, K. B. (2020). "The Urban Morphology of Hyderabad, India: A Historical Geographic Analysis." *Masters Theses*. Kalamazoo, MI: Western Michigan University, 5155.

Heinrichs, D., Lukas, M., & Henning, N. (2011). "Privatization of the fringes—A Latin American version of post-suburbia? The case of Santiago de Chile." In: Phelps, N. A., & Wu, F. (Eds.), *International perspectives on suburbanization* (pp. 101–121). London: Palgrave Macmillan.

Holian, M. J. (2014). The effect of social and economic development on air pollution in Indian cities. *Environment and Urbanization Asia*, *5*(1), 1–15.

Holian, M. J., & Sridhar, K. S. (2017). The role of road infrastructure and air pollution in the recent suburbanization of India's cities: An exploration. *Environment and Urbanization Asia*, *8*(2), 151–169.

Irani, A., Gothoskar, S., & Sharma, J. C. (2000). Potential and prevalence of teleworking in Mumbai. *Economic and Political Weekly, 35*(26), 2269–2276.

Jain, M., Siedentop, S., Taubenböck, H., & Namperumal, S. (2013). From suburbanization to counterurbanization? Investigating urban dynamics in the National Capital Region Delhi, India. *Environment and Urbanization Asia, 4*(2), 247–266.

Jones, C., & Kammen, D. (2014). Spatial distribution of U.S. household carbon footprints reveals suburbanization undermines greenhouse gas benefits of urban population density. *Environment Science and Technology, 48*(2), 895–902.

Joshi, V., & Little, I. M. D. (1996). *India's economic reforms, 1991-2001*. New Delhi: Oxford University Press.

Jordan, S., Ross, J. P., & Usowski, K. (1998). U.S. suburbanization in the 1980s. *Regional Science and Urban Economics, 28*(5), 611–627.

Kahimbaara, J. A. (1986). The population density gradient and the spatial structure of a third world city: Nairobi, a case study. *Urban Studies, 23*(4), 307–322.

Kahn, M. E. (2000). The environmental impact of suburbanization. *Journal of Policy Analysis and Management, 19*(4), 569–586.

Khatun, H., Falgunee, N., & Kutub, M. J. R. (2015). Analyzing urban population density gradient of Dhaka metropolitan area using geographic information systems (GIS) and census data. *Geografia, Malaysian Journal of Society and Space, 11*(13), 1–13.

Kneebone, E., & Garr, E. (2010). *The suburbanization of poverty*. Washington, DC: Brookings Institute.

Kurland, N. B., & Egan, T. D. (1999). Telecommuting: Justice and control in the virtual organization. *Organization Science, 10*(4), 500–513.

Lee, Y. S., & Shin, H. (2012). Negotiating the polycentric city-region: Developmental state politics of new town development in the Seoul capital region. *Urban Studies, 49*(6), 1333–1355.

Leetmaa, K., Kährik, A., Nuga, M., & Tammaru, T. (2014). "Suburbanization in the Tallinn Metropolitan Area." In: Stanilov, K., & Sýkora, L. (Eds.), *Confronting suburbanization: Urban decentralization in post socialist Central and Eastern Europe* (pp. 192–224). Chichester, UK: John Wiley & Sons, Ltd.

Lin, S. (2014). A comparative study of suburbanization in United States and China. *Journal of Geography and Geology, 6*(4), 132–139.

Macauley, M. K. (1985). Estimation and recent behavior of urban population and employment density gradients. *Journal of Urban Economics, 18*(2), 251–260.

McDonald, J. (1989). Econometric studies of urban population densities: A survey. *Journal of Urban Economics, 26*(3), 361–385.

Margo, R. (1992). Explaining the postwar suburbanization of population in the United States: The role of income. *Journal of Urban Economics, 31*(3), 301–310.

Massey, D. S., & Denton, N. A. (1988). Suburbanization and segregation in US metropolitan areas. *American Journal of Sociology, 94*(3), 592–626.

Mieszkowski, P., & Mills, E. S. (1993). The causes of metropolitan suburbanization. *Journal of Economic Perspectives, 7*(3), 135–147.

Mills, E. S. (1970). Urban density functions. *Urban Studies, 7*(1), 5–20.

Mills, E. S. (1972). *Studies in the structure of the urban economy*. Baltimore, MD: Johns Hopkins University Press.

Mills, E. S. (1992). The measurement and determinants of suburbanization. *Journal of Urban Economics, 32*(3), 377–387.

Mills, E. S., & Price, R. (1984). Metropolitan suburbanization and central city problems. *Journal of Urban Economics, 15*(1), 1–17.

Ministry of Housing and Urban Affairs. (2021). *Draft concept note on smart city scheme*. New Delhi: MoHUA, p. 12.

Mitter, S. (2000). Teleworking and teletrade in India: Combining diverse perspectives and visions. *Economic and Political Weekly, 35*(26), 2241–2252.

Mokhtarian, P., & Henderson, D. (1998). Analyzing the travel behavior of home-based workers in the 1991 CALTRANS Statewide Travel Survey. *Journal of Transportation and Statistics*, (October), 25–40.

Morya, C. P., & Ram, M. (2020). Dynamics of suburbanization and influence of National Capital Territory of Delhi on towns. *GeoJournal, 85*(6), 1725–1743.

Munshi, T., Brussel, M., Zuidgeest, M., & Van Maarseveen, M. (2018). Development of employment sub-centres in the city of Ahmedabad, India. *Environment and Urbanization Asia, 9*(1), 37–51.

Negroponte, N. (1995). *Being digital*. New York: Vintage Books.

Ng, C., & Jin, K. K. (2000). Teleworking in Malaysia: Issues and prospects. *Economic and Political Weekly, 35*(26), 2308–2313.

Padawangi, R. (2010). "The planned suburbanization of a city-state: Singapore's new towns." In: Clapson, M., & Hutchison, R. (Eds.) *Suburbanization in global society* (*Research in Urban Sociology, Vol. 10*) (pp. 293–317). Leeds: Emerald Group Publishing Limited. https://doi.org/10.1108/S1047-0042(2010)0000010015

Patel, S. B. (2013). Life between buildings: The use and abuse of FSI. *Economic and Political Weekly*, 48(6), 68–74.

Paul, S., & Sridhar, K. S. (2015). *The paradox of India's north–south divide: Lessons from the states and regions*. New Delhi: Sage.

Paul, S., Sridhar, K. S., Reddy, A. V., & Srinath, P. (2012). *The state of our cities: Evidence from Karnataka*. New Delhi: Oxford University Press, 2012.xix + 297 pp.

Peiser, R., & Hugel, M. (2022). Is the pandemic causing a return to urban sprawl? *Journal of Comparative Urban Law and Policy, 5*(1), 26–41.

Petersen, E. (2010). "The life cycle of Johannesburg suburbs." In: Clapson, M., & Hutchison, R. (Eds.), *Suburbanization in global society* (*Research in Urban Sociology, Vol. 10*) (pp. 179–204). Leeds: Emerald Group Publishing Limited. https://doi.org/10.1108/S1047-0042(2010)0000010010

Phelps, N. A., & Wu, F. (Eds.). (2011). *International perspectives on suburbanization*. London: Palgrave Macmillan.

Pichler-Milanović, N. (2014). "Confronting suburbanization in Ljubljana: From urbanization of the countryside to urban sprawl." In: Stanilov, K., & Sýkora, L. (Eds.), *Confronting suburbanization: Urban decentralization in post socialist Central and Eastern Europe* (pp. 65–96). Chichester, UK: Wiley-Blackwell.

Pinnegar, S., Freestone, R., & Randolph, B. (2010). "Suburban reinvestment through 'knockdown rebuild' in Sydney." In: Clapson, M., & Hutchison, R. (Eds.), *Suburbanization in global society* (*Research in Urban Sociology, Vol. 10*) (pp. 205–229). Leeds: Emerald Group Publishing Limited. https://doi.org/10.1108/S1047-0042(2010)0000010011

Prakasa Rao, V. L., & Tewari, V. K. (1979). *Structure of an Indian metropolis: A study of Bangalore*. Bengaluru: Institute for Social and Economic Change.

Ramani, A., & Bloom, N. (2021). The donut effect of Covid-19 on cities. NBER Working Paper 28876. Cambridge, MA: National Bureau of Economic Research. https://www.nber.org/papers/w28876

Ramani, E. S., Selvakumar, R., Nasir, N., & Verma, A. K. (2018). Analysis of ward wise urban sprawl changes in Tiruchirapalli Corporation Tamil Nadu, India using remote sensing and GIS. Proceedings of the 5th International Conference on "Computing for Sustainable Global Development", 14–16 March 2018, Delhi. https://www.researchgate.net/publication/341821428_Analysis_of_ward_wise_urban_sprawl_changes_in_Tiruchirapalli_Corporation_Tamil_Nadu_India_using_remote_sensing_and_GIS

Reckien, D., & Luedeke, M. K. B. (2014). The social dynamics of suburbanization: Insights from a qualitative model. *Environment and Planning A: Economy and Space*, *46*(4), 980–1000.

Ren, X. (2010). "Territorial expansion and state rescaling: A critique of suburbanization studies in China." In: Clapson, M., & Hutchison, R. (Eds.), *Suburbanization in global society* (*Research in Urban Sociology, Vol. 10*) (pp. 347–366). Leeds: Emerald Group Publishing Limited. https://doi.org/10.1108/S1047-0042(2010)0000010017

Richardson, H. W. (1976). A note on the dynamics of population density gradients. *The Annals of Regional Science*, *10*(3), 15–18.

Roitman, S. (2010). "The changing image of suburban areas in Latin America and the role of local government." In: Clapson, M., & Hutchison, R. (Eds.), *Suburbanization in global society* (*Research in Urban Sociology, Vol. 10*) (pp. 273–292). Leeds: Emerald Group Publishing Limited. https://doi.org/10.1108/S1047-0042(2010)0000010014

Roitman, S., & Phelps, N. A. (2011). "From country club to edge city? Gated residential communities and the transformation of Pilar, Argentina." In: Phelps, N. A., & Wu, F. (Eds.), *International perspectives on suburbanization* (pp. 122–139). London: Palgrave Macmillan.

Salvati, L. (2014). Urban growth and the spatial structure of a changing region: An integrated assessment. *Journal of Urban and Regional Analysis*, *6*(1), 5–14.

Savage, D., & Dasgupta S. (2006). "Governance framework for delivery of Urban services." In 3i Network (Ed.), *India Infrastructure Report 2006: Urban Infrastructure* (pp. 42–58). New Delhi: Oxford University Press.

Shaw, A. (2018). "Suburbanization in Asia: A focus on India." In: Hanlon, B., & Vicino, T. J. (Eds.), *The Routledge companion to the suburbs* (pp. 100–109). London: Routledge.

Shin, B., Sheng, O., & Higa, K. (2000). Telework: Existing research and future directions. *Journal of Organizational Computing and Electronic Commerce*, *10*(2), 85–101.

Small, K. A., & Song, S. (1994). Population and employment densities: Structure and change. *Journal of Urban Economics*, *36*(3), 292–313.

Sridhar, K. S. (2004). Cities with suburbs: Evidence from India. National Institute of Public Finance and Policy (NIPFP) Working Paper No.23/2004. New Delhi: NIPFP.

Sridhar, K. S. (2007). Density gradients and their determinants: Evidence from India. *Regional Science and Urban Economics*, *37*(3), 314–344. https://doi.org/10.1016/j.regsciurbeco.2006.11.001

Sridhar, K. S. (2010). Impact of land use regulations: Evidence from India's cities. *Urban Studies, 47*(7), 1541–1569.

Sridhar, K. S. (2011). Addendum to determinants of city growth and output in India. *Review of Urban and Regional Development Studies, 23*(2-3) (July/November 2011), 162–165.

Sridhar, K. S. (2018). "The impact of land use regulations on supply of land: The case of India's cities." In: Bhide, S., & Gupta, D. B. (Eds.), *The Land Question in Urban Development* (pp. 101–128). New Delhi: Academic Foundation.

Sridhar, K. S. (2019). "The effect of urban land use regulations on density: The case of selected Indian cities." In: Chakravorty, S., & Palit, A. (Eds.), *Seeking Middle Ground: Land, Markets and Public Policy* (pp. 206–232). New Delhi: Oxford University Press.

Sridhar, K. S. (2020). Is India's urbanization really too low? *Area Development and Policy, 5*(1), 32–49. https://doi.org/10.1080/23792949.2019.1590153

Sridhar, K. S., Manasi, S., & Latha, N. (2021). "Suburbanization and spatial inequality in the distribution of urban services in Indian cities." In: Sridhar, K. S., & Mavrotas, G. (Eds.), *Urbanization in the Global South: Perspectives and challenges.* Abingdon: Routledge.

Sridhar, K. S., Manasi, S., & Smitha, K. C. (2017). *Jobs, Commute, and Public Services in Bengaluru: A Pilot Study from Nagarabhavi.* Institute for Social and Economic Change, Monograph 51, August.

Sridhar, K. S., & Monkkonen, P. (2024). Urban form in India 1975–2015: Have India's cities become flat? *Cities, 145*, 104705. https://doi.org/10.1016/j.cities.2023.104705

Sridhar, K. S., & Narayanan, P. (2016). Suburbanization of India's cities: What is the evidence from Gulbarga? *Environment and Urbanization Asia, 7*(1), 93–112. https://journals.sagepub.com/doi/10.1177/0975425316629836

Sridhar, K. S., & Smitha, K. C. (2018). The geography of economic migrants: Characteristics and location in Bengaluru. In Rajan, S. I. (Ed.), *India Migration Report 2017: Forced migration* (pp. 176–187). London: Routledge.

Sridhar, K. S., Smitha, K. C., & Latha, N. (2018). *The story of an Indian metropolis revisited.* Final report. Bengaluru: Azim Premji University Research Grants Foundation.

Sridhar, K. S., & Sridhar, V. (2003). The effect of telecommuting on suburbanization: Empirical evidence. *Journal of Regional Analysis and Policy, 33*(1), 1–25.

Stanback, T. M. (2019). *The new suburbanization: Challenge to the central city.* London: Routledge.

Stanilov, K., & Sýkora, L. (Eds.). (2014). *Confronting suburbanization: Urban decentralization in post socialist Central and Eastern Europe.* Hoboken, NJ: John Wiley & Sons.

Sun, B., Zhang, T., Li, W., & Song, Y. (2022). Effects of polycentricity on economic performance and its dependence on city size: The case of China. *Land, 11*(9), 1546.

Sun, T., Han, Z., Wang, L., & Li, G. (2012). Suburbanization and subcentering of population in Beijing metropolitan area: A nonparametric analysis. *Chinese Geographical Science, 22*(4), 472–482.

Szabó, B. (2014). Review of Stanilov, K. and Sýkora, L. (eds.): Confronting suburbanization. Urban decentralization in post socialist Central and Eastern Europe. Wiley Blackwell, Chichester, 360 p. *Hungarian Geographical Bulletin, 63*(4), 457–464.

TCPO (Town and Country Planning Organisation). (1999). *A study on planning norms, building bye-laws, tariff structure, land assembly and resource mobilization (of nine metropolitan cities)*. New Delhi: Ministry of Urban Development and Poverty Alleviation.

Teaford, J. C. (2011). "Suburbia and post-suburbia: A brief history." In: Phelps, N. A., & Wu, F. (Eds.), *International perspectives on suburbanization* (pp. 15–34). London: Palgrave Macmillan. https://doi.org/10.1057/9780230308626_2

Thurston, L., & Yezer, A. M. (1994). Causality in the suburbanization of population and employment. *Journal of Urban Economics, 35*(1), 105–118.

Tiebout, C. M. (1956). A pure theory of local expenditures. *Journal of Political Economy, 64*(5), 416–424.

Trân, T. N. Q., Quertamp, F., de Miras, C., Vinh, N. Q., Năm, L. V., & Truong, T. H. (2012). *Trends of urbanization and suburbanization in southeast Asia*. Ho Chi Minh City: General Publishing House.

Tripathi, S. (2019). Do economic reforms promote urbanization in India? *Asia-Pacific Journal of Regional Science, 3*(3), 647–674. https://doi.org/10.1007/s41685-019-00117-8

Uduporuwa, R. J. M., & Manawadu, L. (2015). Evolution of spatial structure of World Heritage City of Kandy, Sri Lanka: An analysis of population density change. *International Journal of Social Science & Human Behavior Study, 2*(1), 41–45.

United States Bureau of the Census. (1984). *1982 Census of Retail Trade: Major retail centers in standard metropolitan statistical areas* (Vol. 3). Washington, DC: US Department of Commerce, Bureau of the Census.

United States Bureau of Labor Statistics. (1997). Internet Usage Data Supplement (IUD). Washington, DC: US Bureau of Labor Statistics. https://www.nber.org/research/data/current-population-survey-cps-supplements-computer-and-internet-use, accessed February 6, 2025.

United States Department of Commerce. (1996). Survey of Income and Program Participation (SIPP), Wave 4, 1996 supplement. Washington, DC: US Department of Commerce. https://www.icpsr.umich.edu/web/ICPSR/studies/2625, accessed February 6, 2025.

Varian, H. R. (2001). The computer-mediated economy. *Communications of the ACM, 44*(3), 93.

Veloso, L. (2010). "Governing heterogeneity in the context of 'compulsory closeness': The 'pacification' of favelas." In: Clapson, M., & Hutchison, R. (Eds.) *Suburbanization in global society* (*Research in Urban Sociology, Vol. 10*) (pp. 253–272). Leeds: Emerald Group Publishing Limited. https://doi.org/10.1108/S1047-0042(2010)0000010013

Voith, R. (1992). City and suburban growth: Substitutes or complements. *Business Review, 31*(Sep/Oct), 21–33.

Walker, R. A. (2018). "A theory of suburbanization: Capitalism and the construction of urban space in the United States." In: Dear, M., & Scott, A. (Eds.), *Urbanization and urban planning in capitalist society* (pp. 383–429). London: Routledge.

Wang, L., Kundu, R., & Chen, X. (2010). "Building for what and whom? New town development as planned suburbanization in China and India." In: Clapson, M., & Hutchison, R. (Eds.), *Suburbanization in global society* (*Research in Urban

Sociology, Vol. 10) (pp. 319–345). Bingley: Emerald Group Publishing Limited. https://doi.org/10.1108/S1047-0042(2010)0000010016

White, M. J. (1976). Firm suburbanization and urban subcentres. *Journal of Urban Economics*, *3*(4), 323–343.

Wu, F., & Phelps, N. A. (2011). "Conclusion: Post-suburban worlds?" In: Phelps, N. A., & Wu, F. (Eds.), *International perspectives on suburbanization* (pp. 245–257). London: Palgrave Macmillan. https://doi.org/10.1057/9780230308626_14

Yudhistira, M. H., Indriyani, W., Pratama, A. P., Sofiyandi, Y., & Kurniawan, Y. R. (2019). Transportation network and changes in urban structure: Evidence from the Jakarta Metropolitan Area. *Research in Transportation Economics*, *74*, 52–63.

Zhou, Y., & Ma, L. J. (2000). Economic restructuring and suburbanization in China. *Urban Geography*, *21*(3), 205–236.

Index

For the benefit of digital users, indexed terms that span two pages (e.g., 52–53) may, on occasion, appear on only one of those pages.

The manufacturer's authorised representative in the EU for product safety is Oxford University Press España S.A. of El Parque Empresarial San Fernando de Henares, Avenida de Castilla, 2 – 28830 Madrid (www.oup.es/en or product.safety@oup.com). OUP España S.A. also acts as importer into Spain of products made by the manufacturer.

Printed in the USA/Agawam, MA
December 8, 2025

897615.022